IMMIGRATION
IN
U.S. HISTORY

MAGILL'S CHOICE

Immigration
in
U.S. History

Volume 2

Indigenous superordination — *Zadvydas v. Davis*
Appendices
Indexes

Edited by
Carl L. Bankston III
Tulane University

Danielle Antoinette Hidalgo
Tulane University

Project Editor
R. Kent Rasmussen

Salem Press, Inc.
Pasadena, California   Hackensack, New Jersey

Cover image: The NARA photograph on the outside cover of these volumes shows an unidenti-fied group of European immigrants at Ellis Island in 1908. The original black-and-white pho-tograph was tinted by R. Kent Rasmussen. Every effort was made to use authentic colors, but the actual colors of hair and clothes may have differed.

Frontispiece: From 1892 through 1954, Ellis Island served as the primary reception center for immigrants reaching the United States from across the Atlantic Ocean. The ornate reception hall is now maintained as a public museum that visitors may tour on their way to the nearby Statue of Liberty.
(Library of Congress)

∞ The paper used in these volumes conforms to the American National Standard for Permanence of Paper for Printed Library Materials, Z39.48-1992 (R1997)

Some essays originally appeared in (in descending order of numbers): *Racial and Ethnic Relations in America* (1999), *Encyclopedia of Family Life* (1999), *Great Events from History: North American Series* (1997), *Great Events from History II: Human Rights* (1992), *Great Events: 1900-2001* (2002), *Women's Issues* (1997), *Magill's Legal Guide* (1999), *Ency-clopedia of the U.S. Supreme Court* (2001), *Identities and Issues in Literature* (1997), *Crimi-nal Justice* (2006), *American Justice* (1996), *The Bill of Rights* (2002), and *Survey of Social Science: Sociology Series* (1994). New material has been added.

Library of Congress Cataloging-in-Publication Data
Immigration in U.S. history / edited by Carl L. Bankston, III, Danielle Antoinette Hidalgo.
    p. cm. — (Magill's choice)
    Includes bibliographical references and indexes.
    ISBN-13: 978-1-58765-266-0 (set : alk. paper)
    ISBN-10: 1-58765-266-8 (set : alk. paper)
    ISBN-13: 978-1-58765-268-4 (v. 2 : alk. paper)
    ISBN-10: 1-58765-268-4 (v. 2 : alk. paper)
    [etc.]
    1. United States—Emigration and immigration—History.   I. Bankston, Carl L. (Carl Leon), 1952 -   II. Hidalgo, Danielle Antoinette.   III. Title.   IV. Series.
JV6450.I565 2006
304.8'7303—dc22
                                                                            2005033560

Second Printing

CONTENTS

COMPLETE LIST OF CONTENTS

Volume 1

Volume 2

IMMIGRATION
IN
U.S. HISTORY

INDIGENOUS SUPERORDINATION

DEFINITION: Intergroup relationship in which members of a "native" dominant group within a geographical area subordinates members of incoming immigrant groups

IMMIGRATION ISSUES: Discrimination; Nativism and racism; Sociological theories

SIGNIFICANCE: The process of indigenous superordination results in a particular form of stratification within the society in which the resident dominant group enjoys a disproportionate share of the resources, prestige, and power.

The differential among groups may be manifest in economic, political, or cultural realms, interactively. The power relationship is then justified by a system of beliefs that rationalizes the superiority of the indigenous group in relation to the incoming groups and that often scapegoats the immigrants by plac-

Immigrants protesting against public perceptions that they are the cause of American social and economic ills. (International Daily News)

ing blame on them as the cause of various societal problems. This type of superordinate-subordinate group relationship is less overtly conflictual than migrant superordination. An example of indigenous superordination is found in the United States, where most voluntary immigrants occupy lower levels of the stratification system.

M. Bahati Kuumba

FURTHER READING

Cook, Terrence E. *Separation, Assimilation, or Accommodation: Contrasting Ethnic Minority Policies.* Westport, Conn.: Praeger, 2003.

Singh, Jaswinder, and Kalyani Gopal. *Americanization of New Immigrants: People Who Come to America and What They Need to Know.* Lanham, Md.: University Press of America, 2002.

Zølner, Mette. *Re-imagining the Nation: Debates on Immigrants, Identities and Memories.* New York: P.I.E.-P. Lang, 2000.

SEE ALSO British as dominant group; Immigrant advantage; Migrant superordination.

IRANIAN IMMIGRANTS

IDENTIFICATION: Immigrants to North America from the Middle Eastern nation of Iran

IMMIGRATION ISSUES: Demographics; Middle Eastern immigrants; Religion

SIGNIFICANCE: Since November, 1979, when Iranian student militants seized the U.S. embassy in Tehran and held sixty-six Americans hostage while demanding the return of Shah Muhammad Reza Pahlavi from his exile in the United States, most Americans have held strongly unfavorable opinions of Iranian Americans. Iranian Americans face a constant struggle to convince other groups in the United States that they personally are not terrorists and do not support the Islamic government in Iran.

The trauma of the 1979 Iranian revolution and subsequent terror and economic deterioration, combined with the long war with Iraq, resulted in widespread dispersions of Iranians outside their homeland. It is estimated that between 1.2 million and 2 million Iranian Americans live in the United States. The majority of Iranian immigrants live in suburban areas such as Los Angeles, Washington, D.C., and Long Island, New York, and hold middle-class jobs.

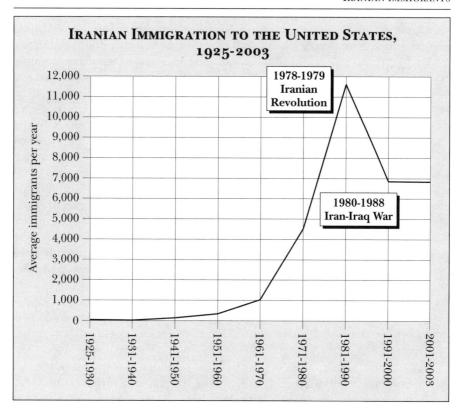

IRANIAN IMMIGRATION TO THE UNITED STATES, 1925-2003

Since the Iranian Revolution and the taking of the U.S. embassy, images of Iranians as unpredictable and wild anti-American fanatics and terrorists have dominated the minds of the American public, according to Ali Akbar Mahdi, an Iranian scholar at Ohio Wesleyan University. For example, when the federal building in Oklahoma City was bombed on April 19, 1995, at first many Americans believed that Middle East terrorists were responsible. Living in such a negative environment is a difficult but conscious choice for most first-generation Iranian immigrants. Second-generation Iranians also suffer from the negative images associated with the national origins of their parents.

Mahdi wrote that the presence of many Iranian immigrants in Western countries is partially due to the religionization of Iranian society. Most of the Iranian immigrants are secular people who do not want to mix religion with politics and education. He said that most of the Iranian immigrants in the United States consist of middle- and upper-class people who are highly educated and have a better-than-average standard of living. Many of those who came from more modest backgrounds have secured middle-class positions for themselves through education, dedication, and hard work.

RELATIONS WITH OTHER GROUPS Iranians who came to the United States before the hostage crisis received a generally positive reception. However, after that crisis and the ensuing rise of Islamic fundamentalism in the Middle East, the American perception of Iran changed from a country of peace to a country of turmoil and unpredictability. The U.S. State Department has labeled the Iranian government as a "rogue state." The unfavorable portrayal of Iranians in the U.S. media helps breed prejudice and discrimination, placing a strain on Iranian Americans. Some researchers accuse the United States of using xenophobia and ungrounded fears to motivate its citizens to follow the views of American political, religious, and cultural leaders. They say that while the United States prides itself in its sociocultural diversity, it simultaneously denounces cultures it cannot understand.

A survey of 157 Iranian Americans conducted by Laleh Khalili, a graduate student at Columbia University and published in *The Iranian Times* in April, 1998, showed that although 37 percent of respondents select mostly other Iranian Americans as friends, 63 percent do not. Khalili found that those who prefer friends who are not Iranian Americans associate with members of other transnational communities rather than typical white Americans. The most frequently mentioned areas of origin are Southeast Asia, the Middle East, and Latin America. According to Khalili, a shared knowledge of what crossing borders entails and similarities in sociopolitical backgrounds provide a context in which Iranians in the United States can operate comfortably.

IMAGE IMPROVEMENT   In an effort to focus on the achievements of Iranian Americans and not dwell on the faults of the Iranian government, some U.S. governors in states such as New York, New Jersey, Delaware, and Florida have officially declared March 21, the Iranian celebration of the new year, as the Day of Iranian Americans. In 1997, Governor Lawton Chiles of Florida said that

> Individuals of people of Iranian heritage have earned an esteemed place in the cultural, economic, and social structure of Florida and have proved themselves an asset to the community, with many of them holding positions in the fields of medicine, research, education, law, business, the arts, and public services.

Chiles went on to call for continued mutual understanding and friendship between established residents and those of Iranian descent. Manucher Shahidi of Long Island, New York, one of the organizers of the movement to make March 21 a special day in the United States, said that the celebration involves being recognized as an official ethnic minority group in the United States.

> This gives us lobbying power in Congress, gives us the right to institute our culture and history into that of America, and most importantly, it guarantees that the United States government will protect our cultural and historical integrity.

Marian Wynne Haber

FURTHER READING   For comprehensive overviews of Iranians in the United States, see Mitra K. Shavarini's *Educating Immigrants: Experiences of Second-Generation Iranians* (New York: LFB Scholarly Publications, 2004), Sandra Donovan's *Iranians in America* (Minneapolis: Lerner, 2006), Firoozeh Dumas's *Funny in Farsi: A Memoir of Growing Up Iranian in America* (New York: Villard, 2003), Azadeh Moaveni's *Lipstick Jihad: A Memoir of Growing Up Iranian in America and American in Iran* (New York: Public Affairs, 2005), and Maboud Ansari's *The Making of the Iranian Community in America* (New York: Pardis Press, 1992). Ellen Alexander Conley's *The Chosen Shore: Stories of Immigrants* (Berkeley: University of California Press, 2004) is a collection of firsthand accounts of modern immigrants from many nations, including Iran. More general works on Middle Eastern immigrants include Aladdin Elaasar's *Silent Victims: The Plight of Arab and Muslim Americans in Post 9/11 America* (Bloomington, Ind.: AuthorHouse, 2004), Yvonne Yazbeck Haddad's *Not Quite American? The Shaping of Arab and Muslim Identity in the United States* (Waco, Tex.: Baylor University Press, 2004), and Amir B. Marvasti and Karyn D. McKinney's *Middle Eastern Lives in America* (Lanham, Md.: Rowman & Littlefield, 2004).

SEE ALSO   Arab American stereotypes; Arab immigrants; Helsinki Watch report on U.S. refugee policy; Middle Eastern immigrant families; Muslims; Refugees and racial/ethnic relations.

IRISH IMMIGRANTS

IDENTIFICATION: Immigrants to North America from Ireland

IMMIGRATION ISSUES: Demographics; European immigrants; Irish immigrants; Religion; Stereotypes

SIGNIFICANCE: Irish Americans have been in the United States since the early colonial period and have played an active role in the development of industry, in labor and social reform, and in politics at all levels. They also profoundly influenced the development of many large cities and have had a lasting influence on educational practices.

The Irish have been a vital component of American life since the days of colonialism. The early Irish immigrants were mainly Presbyterian Protestants from Ulster. Although some belonged to the Church of Ireland, most came in search of financial gains. The majority of the Ulster-born Irish were tenant farmers or skilled artisans of modest means. The Irish who would follow in the famine years would be vastly different in their beliefs, their financial sta-

Irish American children waiting for New York City's St. Patrick's Day parade in 1951. An annual event, the parade has long been an important expression of Irish pride. (Library of Congress)

tus, and their social standing. Each new wave of Irish immigrants would add something to the fabric of American life.

THE "FAMINE IRISH"   Whereas the earliest Irish immigrants had come to the United States to better themselves, the "famine Irish" sought simple survival in an often hostile land. The Penal Laws in Ireland had long put native Irish Catholics at a serious disadvantage in their homeland. Irish farmers were uneducated, poor, and dependent upon their rocky plots of land for subsistence. Families were large. The lifestyle was one of intense social interaction. They had little, but they shared what they had and celebrated their beliefs with tradition, song, dance, and religious ritual. They were dependent upon the potato crop as their sole food source.

When blight struck the potato crop between the years 1845 and 1854, the poor had nowhere to turn. Some had compassionate landlords. However, when Parliament passed the Poor Law Extension Act of 1847, landlords became responsible for the cost of care of their tenantry. Even well-meaning landowners could not cover such expense. Evictions became the rule. The poor then had the option of going to disease-infested workhouses or starving on the road in search of food and shelter. They fled their native land strictly for survival.

Between 1840 and 1860, more than 1.5 million Irish came to the shores of the United States. They settled in cities, concentrating in certain neighborhoods. A large contingent settled in New Orleans. Most of those who fled the famine stayed in eastern cities such as New York or Boston simply because they had no money and no marketable skills to move on. Some would move toward Chicago or join the movement westward in search of employment. Most of the famine Irish were poor and Catholic. They represented the first large wave of non-Anglo-Saxon immigrants in the history of the nation.

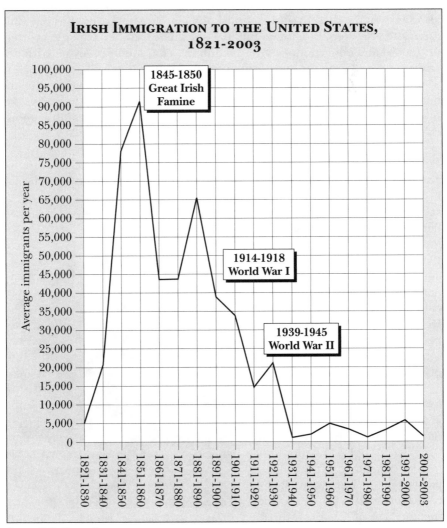

IRISH IMMIGRATION TO THE UNITED STATES, 1821-2003

1845-1850
Great Irish Famine

1914-1918
World War I

1939-1945
World War II

Source: U.S. Census Bureau.

The Irish immigrants were uneducated, Catholic, and considered uncultured by the social elite in the United States. Many were unaccompanied women, a fact that set the Irish apart from previous immigrant groups. The young Irish girls took positions as domestic servants in the homes of the wealthy. They worked to save enough to rescue more relations in Ireland from starvation. These women and the unskilled Irish men who sought to make a living digging ditches or building canals or bridges were scorned by the nativists. However, from the lowest levels of society, these Irish Americans began to build their version of the American Dream.

RELIGION The Irish Catholic poor, social by nature and custom and isolated by their religious beliefs, built their own comfortable enclaves within the cities where they settled. Irish neighborhoods in New York City, Boston, Chicago, and elsewhere developed into parishes. The Catholic parishes evolved into social and educational centers within the communities. As the Irish developed a reputation for hard drinking and fighting, it was the parish priest who often served as counselor and role model. The church cared for the immigrants' spiritual, social, educational, medical, and emotional needs. As the number of immigrants increased, parishes and religious orders built schools, hospitals, and orphanages to meet the needs of the communities.

POLITICS AND SOCIAL REFORMS As the growing numbers of Irish immigrants began to frighten the white Anglo-Saxon Protestants already established in the cities and to threaten the status quo, the children of the famine generation began to see the possibilities that existed for them by virtue of their numbers and their ambition. Politics was a natural extension of the parish culture. Precinct by precinct, the Irish began to embrace the U.S. political system as a tool for personal advancement and a mechanism for social change.

One individual who came up from the streets of New York was young Alfred E. "Al" Smith. Raised on the streets of Brooklyn as the Brooklyn Bridge was being built, he took advantage of the political patronage in Tammany Hall to gain a foothold in politics. Under the tutelage of Charles Murphy and Jimmy Walker, Smith rose up

Alfred E. Smith (right) with future president Franklin D. Roosevelt in 1930. (Franklin D. Roosevelt Library)

through the political ranks in New York and eventually became the governor of New York State. Similar political machines evolved in Kansas City and Chicago, as politicians sought to serve their constituencies. Smith initiated social reforms, including child labor laws, and improved safety requirements to protect workers. Elsewhere in the nation, labor unions were gaining support.

With many successes to his credit in New York, Smith ran unsuccessfully for president in 1928. Many people still distrusted the Irish, and the nativists and many non-Catholics feared papal interference in U.S. politics should Smith be elected. The first Irish Catholic to claim the office of the president of the United States would be another descendant from Irish peasant stock, John F. Kennedy, in 1960. Kennedy would stand as a symbol of the Irish American Dream brought to fruition.

APPRECIATION OF TRADITIONS   During the 1980's and 1990's, Irish Americans no longer bore the stigma of most negative stereotypes. The Irish generally assimilated into U.S. society, often intermarrying with other ethnic groups, yet there continued to be a lingering appreciation of Irish history and traditions, with a renewed interested in traditional Irish music and dance that became a part of American popular culture, transcending ethnic origins and religious beliefs.

Kathleen Schongar

FURTHER READING

Almeida, Linda Dowling. *Irish Immigrants in New York City, 1945-1995*. Bloomington: Indiana University Press, 2001. Study of late twentieth century Irish immigrants in America's largest city, which remains the first stop for many new immigrants.

Fallows, Marjorie. *Irish Americans: Identity and Assimilation*. Englewood Cliffs, N.J.: Prentice-Hall, 1979. Introduction to Irish American history, cultural experiences, and expectations. Religion, labor, politics, and family dynamics are considered within the context of American life.

Golway, Terry. *The Irish in America*. Edited by Michael Coffey. New York: Disney Enterprises, 1997. Enlightened look at the development of Irish Americans, including personal essays by those who lived through the cultural assimilation process during the late eighteenth century and the nineteenth century.

Greene, Victor R. *A Singing Ambivalence: American Immigrants Between Old World and New, 1830-1930*. Kent, Ohio: Kent State University Press, 2004. Comparative study of the different challenges faced by members of eight major immigrant groups including the Irish.

Griffin, William D. *A Portrait of the Irish in America*. New York: Charles Scribner's Sons, 1981. Comprehensive historical perspective on the struggles and successes of Irish assimilation into American culture. Many photographs complement the text.

McCaffrey, Lawrence J. *The Irish Diaspora in America.* Washington, D.C.: Catholic University of America Press, 1984. Provides an overview of Irish immigration and explores significant religious, political, and economic factors in Ireland and in the United States that influenced ethnic relations among American immigrant groups.

Paulson, Timothy J. *Irish Immigrants.* New York: Facts On File, 2005. Broad survey of Irish immigration written for younger readers.

SEE ALSO Anti-Irish Riots of 1844; Celtic Irish; European immigrants, 1790-1892; German and Irish immigration of the 1840's; Immigration and Nationality Act of 1965; Irish immigrants and African Americans; Irish immigrants and discrimination; Irish stereotypes; Scotch-Irish immigrants.

IRISH IMMIGRANTS AND AFRICAN AMERICANS

IMMIGRATION ISSUES: African Americans; European immigrants; Irish immigrants

SIGNIFICANCE: Conflict has existed between Irish Americans and African Americans since the first great waves of Irish immigration during the 1840's.

Before the Civil War of the 1860's, Irish Catholics were confronted with harsh discrimination by Anglo-Protestant Americans. When dangerous work needed to be done, many employers opted to hire cheap Irish labor instead of using slaves, preferring to risk the life of an Irishman over one of their slaves, the latter being valuable property. Struggling to survive at the bottom of the economic ladder, the Irish feared that if slaves were set free, they would face even more competition for scarce jobs. Many also believed that they should focus their energies on improving their own plight before expending any of their resources helping African Americans. Irish Americans' concern for their own survival and their view of African Americans as competition worked to sour relations between the two struggling groups.

During the Civil War, Irish Americans, who were loyal to the Union generally, had no interest in fighting a war to free the slaves. During the war, when disproportionate numbers of poor Irish were drafted to serve in the Union forces, riots broke out in cities throughout the North. On July 13, 1863, anti-draft rioting broke out in New York City, lasting until July 15. Irish Americans, who viewed the conflict as a rich man's war fought by the poor, took out their anger at abolitionists and African Americans by burning, looting, and beating any African Americans in their path. New York militia were called out to stop the rioting.

After the Civil War, the economic struggle between African Americans and Irish Americans continued. Irish Americans and other white immigrants took jobs in the booming industrial sector, and African Americans found themselves once again relegated to southern fields. Many African Americans, seeing immigrants usurp jobs they felt rightly belonged to them, began to engage in nativist rhetoric. Many African Americans vociferously supported the anti-immigration legislation of the 1920's.

As Irish Americans gained greater political and economic power in the twentieth century, they continued to do so at the expense of African Americans. Although literacy tests and other racist laws denied the majority of African Americans the vote until the Voting Rights Act of 1965, the Irish used their access to the ballot to gain control of local political machines and city halls. As they lost their brogues and became established in the mainstream of white America, the Irish used their political influence to monopolize civil service positions while excluding African Americans and new immigrants.

During the 1990's, Irish Americans exceeded the national average in education, income, and employment levels while African Americans consistently lagged behind in all three areas. Although approximately one-third of African Americans could be considered at least middle class, there were three times more poor African Americans than white Americans.

Kathleen Odell Korgen

FURTHER READING

Almeida, Linda Dowling. *Irish Immigrants in New York City, 1945-1995.* Bloomington: Indiana University Press, 2001.

Bean, Frank D., and Stephanie Bell-Rose, eds. *Immigration and Opportunity: Race, Ethnicity, and Employment in the United States.* New York: Russell Sage Foundation, 1999.

Reitz, Jeffrey G., ed. *Host Societies and the Reception of Immigrants.* La Jolla, Calif.: Center for Comparative Immigration Studies, University of California, San Diego, 2003.

SEE ALSO Anti-Irish Riots of 1844; Celtic Irish; European immigrants, 1790-1892; German and Irish immigration of the 1840's; Immigration and Nationality Act of 1965; Irish immigrants; Irish immigrants and discrimination; Irish stereotypes; Scotch-Irish immigrants.

IRISH IMMIGRANTS AND DISCRIMINATION

IMMIGRATION ISSUES: Discrimination; European immigrants; Irish immigrants

SIGNIFICANCE: Discrimination against Irish immigrants to North America has its roots in earlier British history and Protestant prejudice against Roman Catholics.

In the British Isles, the English used notions of a "savage race" in colonialized Ireland to justify systems that dominated and oppressed the Irish long before the American colonies existed. These systems, which placed Irish Catholics on the bottom of cultural hierarchies, became codified by religion. Labels were given substance by combining religious identity with "race." The English also used immigrant groups of English and Scots for social control, according to scholar Roy Forester, in *Oxford Illustrated History of Ireland* (1989). Successive generations of English who were born in Ireland identified themselves as Irish Protestants rather than as English. Scottish people were brought to northern Ireland to serve as buffer groups against Irish kingdoms. These peoples—the Protestant Irish and Scotch-Irish—began identifying themselves as superior to the Irish Catholic "race."

These hierarchies were transferred to North America along with the waves of immigrants; however, cultural and "race" demarcations lost their sharpness in the new land. The Scotch-Irish, as they had in Ireland, acted as buffers in the American colonies until the American Revolution caused distinctions to largely disappear within southern racial slavery hierarchies. Later immigration by Irish Catholics, especially during the 1850's potato famine, in the end contributed more to the enlargement of the "white race" than to the creation of another ethnicity, according to Noel Ignatiev, in *How the Irish Became White* (1995). In the nineteenth century, Irish Catholics faced heavy discrimination, and through this process, a notion of an Irish Catholic "race" developed among other Americans.

James V. Fenelon

FURTHER READING

Almeida, Linda Dowling. *Irish Immigrants in New York City, 1945-1995*. Bloomington: Indiana University Press, 2001.

Paulson, Timothy J. *Irish Immigrants*. New York: Facts On File, 2005.

SEE ALSO Anti-Irish Riots of 1844; Celtic Irish; European immigrants, 1790-1892; German and Irish immigration of the 1840's; Immigration and Nationality Act of 1965; Irish immigrants; Irish immigrants and African Americans; Irish stereotypes; Scotch-Irish immigrants.

IRISH STEREOTYPES

DEFINITION: North American perceptions and misperceptions about Irish immigrants

IMMIGRATION ISSUES: Discrimination; European immigrants; Irish immigrants; Nativism and racism; Religion; Stereotypes

SIGNIFICANCE: Among the millions of western Europeans who have immigrated to the United States, the Irish have been subjected to an exceptional amount of negative stereotyping and discrimination.

Between 1820 and 1920, approximately five million people emigrated from Ireland to the United States. Most of these immigrants were Irish Catholic farmers who were living in abject poverty in an Ireland dominated politically and economically by England. Until the late nineteenth century, Irish Catholics were not allowed to own farms in Ireland, and during the Potato Famine of 1845-1850, more than five hundred thousand Irish farmers were evicted from their farms. The only real choice for these displaced people was to leave Ireland for the United States; however, they were not well received by white Protestants, who then completely controlled the nation's politics, business, and society.

These Irish Catholic immigrants were viewed as a threat for several reasons. Many first-generation Irish immigrants spoke only Gaelic, and they became manual laborers who worked for low wages, creating competition for jobs. The new immigrants built their own Catholic churches and schools and made it very clear that they would not tolerate in the United States the religious discrimination that they and their ancestors had experienced in Ireland.

As early as the 1840's, extremely offensive representations of Irish immigrants began to appear in American newspapers and magazines. The magazine *Harper's Monthly* published numerous drawings in which Irish Americans were depicted as apelike creatures with whom normal Americans would not want to associate. The same magazine printed in its April 6, 1867, issue a drawing by Thomas Nast entitled "The Day We Celebrate." Nast suggested that Irish Americans celebrated St. Patrick's Day by becoming drunk and then attacking police officers. Such stereotypical images of Irish immigrants as violent drunkards appeared in numerous magazines throughout the last six decades of the nineteenth century. Frequently, racist cartoons would simultaneously criticize Irish and Jewish immigrants. The fact that overt discrimination was directed against Jews and Irish Catholics at the same time may well explain why Jewish American and Irish American immigrants came to realize that they had a great deal in common.

Other cartoons ridiculed Irish Americans because of their religious be-

Editorial cartoon from a late nineteenth century California newspaper expressing the fear that the United States would be overwhelmed by foreign immigrants—particularly the Irish and Chinese immigrants caricatured in the cartoon. (Library of Congress)

liefs. Throughout the nineteenth century, the Bible was taught in many American public schools, but the translation used was the King James version, the official translation of Protestant churches. During the 1840's, many Catholic leaders asked school boards to allow Catholic pupils to receive religious instruction based on the Douay translation, which was the approved Roman Catholic version. Numerous contemporary cartoons during the 1840's and 1850's suggested that Catholics were opposed to the reading of the Bible; however, nothing could be further from the truth.

Although disparaging representations of Irish Americans continued to be published in U.S. magazines, most people came to realize that these stereotypical images distorted the truth and revealed more about the prejudices of those creating the images than about Irish Americans whom they attempted to ridicule.

Edmund J. Campion

FURTHER READING

Almeida, Linda Dowling. *Irish Immigrants in New York City, 1945-1995*. Bloomington: Indiana University Press, 2001.

Gabaccia, Donna R. *Immigration and American Diversity: A Social and Cultural History*. Malden, Mass.: Blackwell, 2002.

Paulson, Timothy J. *Irish Immigrants*. New York: Facts On File, 2005.

SEE ALSO   Anti-Irish Riots of 1844; Celtic Irish; European immigrants, 1790-1892; German and Irish immigration of the 1840's; Immigration and Nationality Act of 1965; Irish immigrants; Irish immigrants and African Americans; Irish immigrants and discrimination; Scotch-Irish immigrants.

ISRAELI IMMIGRANTS

IDENTIFICATION: Immigrants to North America from the modern Middle Eastern state of Israel

IMMIGRATION ISSUES: Demographics; Jewish immigrants; Middle Eastern immigrants; Religion

SIGNIFICANCE: Israelis are an ethnically and religiously diverse group, but the term "Israeli Americans" is most often applied to Israeli Jews, both the Ashkenazim of central and eastern European heritage and the Sephardim of Iberian, Middle Eastern, and North African origins. As Jews, their religious observance ranges from a secular orientation to an orthodox one.

Constituting only about 1 percent of the U.S. immigrant population, Israeli immigrants often perceive themselves to be sojourners, temporary residents of the host country. They maintain social, cultural, and economic ties to their country of origin, even while living abroad. Some retain dual citizenship. With the aid of technology and the global economy, their lifestyles seem to fit the new trend of transnationalism (allegiances and orientations that go beyond the boundaries of a single nation). Rather than forsake their homelands and become completely assimilated, new immigrants actively participate in both social worlds.

RATES OF IMMIGRATION   Israeli immigration rates vary depending on how the term "Israeli" is defined and whether only legal immigrants are counted. At the time of the 1990 U.S. Census, approximately 90,000 Israelis lived in the United States. Most were settled in metropolitan areas, especially Los Angeles and New York City's Queens and Brooklyn boroughs.

Certain immigration trends are evident. First, the number of legal Israeli immigrants entering the United States has gradually increased since 1948.

For example, data from the U.S. Immigration and Naturalization Service indicate that the numbers increased from about 1,000 to 2,000 per year between 1967 and 1976 and from 3,000 to 4,000 per year from 1976 to 1986. During the 1990's, an additional 39,397 immigrants came to the United States from Israel, and they continued to come at a rate of more than 4,000 persons per year during the first three years of the twenty-first century.

Second, Israeli immigration was especially pronounced during the 1970's, especially after 1975, when, as 1990 census figures reveal, rates of Israelis traveling to Los Angeles alone more than doubled from 8 percent (1970-1974) to 17 percent (1975-1979). Some have suggested the growth is due in part to increases following war, in this case, the 1973 Yom Kippur War. Third, in response to changing Israeli policy toward emigrants and economic conditions in Israel, the number of Israelis returning to Israel has risen during the 1990's. According to Israeli government estimates, the average yearly number rose from about 5,500 during 1985-1991 to nearly 10,500 during 1992-1994.

MOTIVES FOR EMIGRATION   In contrast to previous Jewish immigrants, contemporary Israelis are not "pushed" to emigrate to the United States because of persecution or extreme economic hardship. Rather, the decision to emigrate is primarily motivated by "pull" factors. Many Israelis cite personal development, particularly greater educational and economic opportunity, as most important. They seek professional advancement, as well as a higher income and standard of living. Others desire to reunite with family members already in the United States or leave to fulfill a personal need for adventure and escape from the limited confines, both geographically and socially, of Israel. Some engage in chain migration, being assisted by Israelis who have already made the trip. Travel, especially among those completing required military service, often leads to extended stays.

Certain features of Israeli society may be "push" factors: high inflation, bureaucratic red tape, burdensome taxes, housing shortages, the difficulty in developing capitalistic enterprises, and government regulations that intrude into personal life. As part of a country prone to societal violence and war, Israelis may mention the need to escape the siege mentality and the tensions permeating society, as well as reserve army duty. Interethnic tensions motivate some to flee from perceived discrimination waged by upper-class Ashkenazim against those of lower status.

RELATIONS WITH THE AMERICAN JEWISH COMMUNITY   Israelis were not initially welcomed with open arms by the American Jewish community. Relations between the two groups have been strained because of historical and cultural factors. Historically, the creation of the State of Israel in 1948 realized the Zionist dream of a Jewish homeland. To emigrate to Israel, or to make *Aliyah* ("ascent"), was a firm demonstration of loyalty to the Zionist cause. To immigrate from Israel and return to the Jewish diaspora, however, has pejoratively been referred to as *Yerida* ("descent"). Hence, *Olim*, "those who go up" to Israel, are admired, in contrast to *Yordim*, "those who go down," who are disparaged for emigrating. Israeli Americans accept this stigmatized identity, often expressing guilt and shame for leaving.

In classifying Israeli immigrants as *Yordim*, American Jews were following the lead of Israelis. In 1976, Prime Minister Yitzhak Rabin himself referred to *Yordim* as "the left-overs of weaklings." Israeli emigration, coupled with rising Arab birthrates, is perceived as a threat to the future of the Jewish homeland. Israeli Americans, on the other hand, are often alienated from American Jews, who, in their minds, have offered only monetary contributions, rather than real sacrifice, for Israel. American Jews often condemn *Yordim*, yet many would never consider emigrating to Israel themselves.

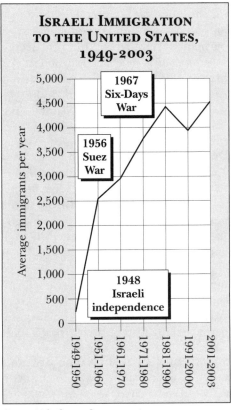

Source: U.S. Census Bureau.

Culturally, a gap exists between Israeli Americans and American Jews. They eat distinct foods and have different lifestyles, political ideologies, and entertainment preferences. Their language also differs; Israelis speak Hebrew as their primary language. Many Israeli Americans also follow the culture of their country of origin, be it Yemenite, Ethiopian, or Russian. An improved relationship between Israeli Americans and American Jews has been prompted by shifts in official Israeli policy toward *Yordim* enacted during the mid-1980's. In an effort to promote the return of Israeli Americans, the Israeli government softened its position regarding emigration and offered enticements such as employment, housing assistance, and travel loans. At the same time, a number of American Jewish organizations initiated outreach programs for Israeli Americans. Previously, such organizations provided little, if any, assistance in an effort to discourage Israelis from staying in America.

THE SOJOURNER MENTALITY AND SELF-IDENTITY Stemming from the negative stereotype of *Yordim*, Israeli Americans label themselves sojourners, insisting, in the face of perhaps contrary evidence, that their stay in the United States is temporary. Lower-status Israelis frequently become settlers, integrating into the host country. Higher-status Israelis often become permanent so-journers; they intend to return to Israel but have no serious plans to do so. As permanent sojourners, they practiced what Natan Uriely, in a 1994 article in *International Sociology*, has termed rhetorical ethnicity. Their identity is rooted in their ethnicity, and they have a strong symbolic commitment to Israel. This is evident in their repeated desires to go home. Israelis resist identifying themselves as Americans or Israeli Americans, preferring an Israeli identity. Many never fully assimilate.

DEMOGRAPHIC PROFILE　S. J. Gold and B. A. Phillips, in the *American Jewish Yearbook* (1996), have provided a demographic profile of Israeli Americans. According to their report (and at the time of their report), Israelis were young, most under age forty-five, and more likely to be male, married, and relatively well educated. They had high rates of employment and earned sub-stantial income that was generally higher than that of the average foreign-born person. Many were employed as managers, administrators, profession-als, or technical specialists. Some were engaged in sales, and a significant number (second only to Koreans in America) were self-employed in indus-tries such as real estate, jewelry and diamonds, retail sales, and construction. Women had less labor force participation in the United States than in Israel, perhaps indicative of their rising social status in the United States.

SOCIAL LIFE IN THE UNITED STATES　Israelis tend to socialize with each other, often in ethnic nightclubs, at communal singing sessions, or at ethnic celebrations such as Israeli Independence Day. A few belong to ethnic organi-zations such as Tzofim, an Israeli group similar to the Boy Scouts. Some form ethnic subgroups based on their country of origin. Friends frequently substi-tute for family and are invited to holiday observances or children's bar/bat mitzvahs. Many Israelis consider themselves to be secular Jews, linking reli-gious observance with being Israeli rather than Jewish. However, many do participate in religious activities in the United States, by joining synagogues at a slightly higher rate than American Jews, providing their children with re-ligious educations, and engaging in religious rituals to a greater extent in the United States than in Israel. Some of the Sephardim have found the ortho-dox Hasidic movement appealing. Perhaps this increased religiosity is a reac-tion to the transition from being a religious majority in Israel to being a reli-gious minority in the United States.

Rosann Bar

FURTHER READING　Sources of information on Israel and emigration in-clude H. Greenberg's *Israel: Social Problems* (Tel Aviv: Dekel, 1979), D. Kass and S. M. Lipset's "Jewish Immigration to the United States from 1967 to the Present: Israelis and Others," in *Understanding American Jewry*, edited by Mar-shall Sklare (New Brunswick, N.J.: Transaction Books, 1982). Books and arti-cles on the Israelis in the United States include D. Elizur's "Israelis in the

U.S.: Motives, Attitudes, and Intentions," in *American Jewish Yearbook* (1979); James Feron's "The Israelis of New York," in *The New York Times* (January 16, 1977); S. J. Gold and B. A. Phillips's "Israelis in the United States," in *American Jewish Yearbook* (1996); P. Ritterbrand's "Israelis in New York," *Contemporary Jewry* (7, 1986); Moshe Shokeid's *Children of Circumstances: Israeli Immigrants in New York* (New York: Cornell University Press, 1988); Zvi Sobel's *Migrants from the Promised Land* (New Brunswick, N.J.: Transaction Books, 1986); and Natan Uriely's "Rhetorical Ethnicity of Permanent Sojourners: The Case of Israeli Immigrants in the Chicago Area," in *International Sociology* (9, 1994).

SEE ALSO   American Jewish Committee; Ashkenazic and German Jewish immigrants; Eastern European Jewish immigrants; Jewish immigrants; Jewish settlement of New York; Jews and Arab Americans; Middle Eastern immigrant families; Soviet Jewish immigrants; Twice migrants.

ITALIAN IMMIGRANTS

IDENTIFICATION: Immigrants to North America from Italy

IMMIGRATION ISSUES: Demographics; European immigrants

SIGNIFICANCE: Italian Americans played an integral role in the development of the United States. Although they have been subjected to ethnic stereotypes—ranging from illiterate peasant organ grinder or shiftless vegetable peddler to unskilled laborer or violent member of an organized crime family—they have achieved distinguished success. Contributions from countless Italian Americans in entertainment, politics, and business have directly shaped and influenced the nation's social landscape.

Italy sent few immigrants to the United States before the Civil War (1861-1865). The 1850 census, the first to record ethnic group populations, listed only 3,645 Italian Americans, and these individuals were primarily skilled artisans, merchants, musicians, actors, and entrepreneurs. However, these numbers do not reflect their overall significance. Sponsored by Spain, England, and France, Italian explorers helped chart the European pathway to the Americas. After Christopher Columbus navigated the Atlantic in 1492, several of his countrymen continued his pursuits. Giovanni Caboto, often referred to as John Cabot in popular history textbooks, obtained financial backing from England's King Henry VII and organized a successful expedition to the New England coast in 1497. Amerigo Vespucci helped popularize interest in America following the publication of two pamphlets highlighting the potential rewards available to new settlers on the eastern seaboard. Giovanni da

THE SOCIETY FOR THE PROTECTION OF ITALIAN IMMIGRANTS

Entrance to the City from the Ellis Island Boat at Battery.

Here "Runners" formerly fleeced the Newcomers.

Courtesy of Leslie's Weekly.

OFFICE,

17 PEARL STREET, NEW YORK.

TELEPHONE, 3641 BROAD.

Flyer from an organization dedicated to protecting Italian immigrants from being exploited upon their arrival in America. (Center for Migration Studies)

Verrazano was the first European to enter New York Harbor during the early sixteenth century.

Although numerous adventurers from other countries also facilitated European migration to America, the efforts of several Italians were crucial for the success of many early colonial enterprises. Roman Catholic missionaries helped carve out the French Empire in the Mississippi Valley. Artisans developed glassware and silk industries in Jamestown, Virginia. Thomas Jefferson recruited Italian masons to help construct his home at Monticello and enlisted the aid of several musicians to form the U.S. Marine Corps Band. Italians also helped design and decorate the interior of the early White House, and Italian opera emerged as one of the most popular forms of entertainment among the upper classes in antebellum America. Although there were few Italian Americans in the nation, they had made a significant cultural impact.

THE GREAT WAVE From 1880 to 1920, more than four million Italians entered the United States. Approximately 80 percent were men, and because 97 percent initially passed through New York City, the bulk of the Italian American community settled in major eastern cities such as Philadelphia, Boston, and New York City; however, a large community also emerged in Chicago.

Following the unification of Italy during the 1860's, southern Italians soon began to feel alienated from and experienced widespread disillusionment with northern leadership. Absentee landlords systematically exploited the peasants, and agricultural policies produced massive hunger among sharecroppers and tenant farmers. Others succumbed to outbreaks of malaria. Northern politicians enacted oppressive conscription laws forcing southerners to serve seven-year terms in the military. As Italy quickly evolved into a two-tiered system in which southerners were excluded from all facets of decision making, a large number of Italians voted with their feet and abandoned their traditional attachment to their villages, emigrating to the United States. Most Italians did not initially intend to remain in the United States. Estimates vary, but between 30 percent and 50 percent returned to the homeland. Strong familial ties and attachments to ancestral villages caused many to return despite the fact that few earned enough to reverse their impoverished status.

The majority of Italian Americans became manual laborers. Ethnic labor contractors, or *padroni*, persuaded many to emigrate from Italy by promising them unlimited economic opportunities upon arrival in North America. The *padroni* secured employment for émigrés and arranged the financing for the transatlantic voyage. Italians helped build railroads and the New York City subway system. Others toiled in dangerous and precarious conditions in factories; several became miners. Some were able to procure opportunities in

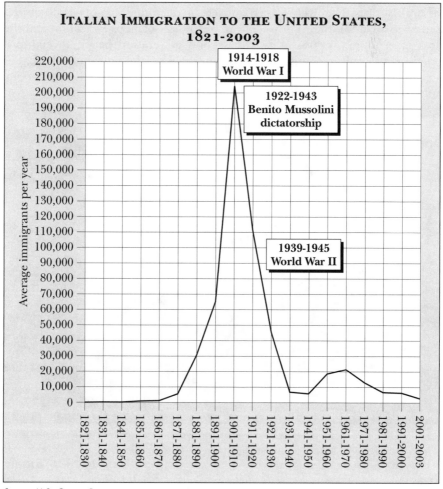

ITALIAN IMMIGRATION TO THE UNITED STATES, 1821-2003

Average immigrants per year

1914-1918 World War I

1922-1943 Benito Mussolini dictatorship

1939-1945 World War II

Source: U.S. Census Bureau.

agricultural communities, but the majority of Italian Americans remained locked in ethnic urban enclaves and were subjected to the outburst of nativist xenophobic practices that accompanied the great wave of migration.

ASSIMILATION AND NATIVISM Racial and ethnic relations in the United States have adhered to a complex hierarchical pecking order. Generally, each wave of immigrants has encountered a number of discriminatory practices designed to eradicate all remnants of ethnic identity. Because the dominant culture reflected a solid Anglo-Saxon bias following the Civil War, new groups from southeastern Europe were expected to embrace assimilationist policies and Americanize. Reformers demonstrated little sympathy for immigrant culture and introduced a variety of measures to diminish and weaken traditional ethnic ways.

Italian American children were extremely susceptible to Anglo-Saxon assimilationists. They were forced into a form of cultural tug-of-war. Required either to abandon their native culture or to face social ostracization and the loss of economic opportunity, the second generation began to embrace Anglo-Saxon culture. This caused considerable psychological problems. For example, Italian American children were expected to find work and contribute to the household economy. This, however, resulted in a premature depar-

Confined to substandard tenement housing in major eastern cities and severely restricted in employment opportunities, many Italian immigrant families took garment work into their homes and employed their children. The mother and her three eldest children in this picture earned a total of about two dollars a week—when work was available—around 1913, while the father sought day work on the street. (Library of Congress)

ture from school. If a child decided to stay in school and pursue a profession, that child risked the wrath of his or her family. Because most Italian Americans considered the family to be sacred, young Italian Americans faced a classic dilemma. As a result, rates of socioeconomic mobility were quite low among the first few generations.

Other forms of nativism also surfaced. Public schools insisted that children speak only English, and officials often shortened and Americanized Italian family names. Some families experienced violence when they attempted to move outside the ethnic enclave. Many people were subjected to racial remarks such as *dago*, *wop*, and *guinea*. Although studies have shown that the rates of alcoholism and mental illness were lower compared with those of other groups, the suicide rate among Italian Americans tripled during the great wave of migration.

Perhaps the greatest example of nativist xenophobic pressure occurred during the 1920's during the trial of two Italian anarchists, Nicola Sacco and Bartolomeo Vanzetti. Nativist sentiment, spurred by fears of communism, had been growing in the United States when Sacco and Vanzetti were arrested under questionable circumstances for murder and robbery in Massachusetts. Both men were judged as violent revolutionaries and subversive ethnic agents rather than on the merits of their case. Although their guilt remains debatable, both men were executed in 1927.

ORGANIZED CRIME   The average Italian American suffered from the negative impression created by a select minority of Italians who attempted to construct vast empires in organized crime. As congressional committees cracked down on criminals, some Americans concluded that all Italian Americans were associated with a nationwide crime syndicate commonly referred to as La Cosa Nostra or the Mafia. These rumors received considerable credibility in 1963 when career criminal Joseph Valachi broke a code of silence and exposed his associates. As a result, the nation became obsessed with the Mafia. References to the Mafia in *The New York Times* increased from 2 in 1962 to 359 in 1969. Mario Puzo's novel *The Godfather* (1969) was made into an Academy Award-winning film, but his violent portrayal of Italian criminals negatively affected many law-abiding Italian Americans. Other gangsters such as John Gotti acquired national fame during the 1980's, and once again Italian Americans were found guilty by association. Numerous popular authors flooded the market with books detailing how murder was used to settle disputes between Italians. Despite the fact that only a select few were involved in criminal activity, all Italian Americans were described as being sympathetic toward the Mafia.

FAMOUS ITALIANS   Not all Italian Americans were unskilled workers or common criminals. Many achieved considerable success in their fields. Joe DiMaggio established a major league baseball record for hitting in fifty-six consecutive games. Heavyweight boxer Rocky Marciano defeated several notable champions, including Joe Louis, Ezzard Charles, and Jersey Joe Wolcott, and retired as an undefeated champion. Frank Capra emerged as one of the nation's finest filmmakers, and his 1946 film, *It's a Wonderful Life*, is considered one of the country's classic movies. Singer Frank Sinatra, who was often unjustly accused of being in the Mafia, entertained generations of Americans with his swagger and ballads. Politician Fiorello La Guardia served as a congressman, New York City mayor, and United Nations relief official. Poet and publisher Lawrence Ferlinghetti provided much-needed support for and helped solidify the Beat generation's place in American literature. Geraldine Ferraro was the first woman to become a vice presidential candidate in 1984. Pop singer Madonna (Ciccone) evolved into a cultural icon during the 1980's. Countless others also achieved prominent status in American life, thus proving that despite being victimized by ethnic stereotyping, Italian Americans have risen to the highest pinnacles of success in the United States.

Robert D. Ubriaco, Jr.

FURTHER READING

Burgan, Michael. *Italian Immigrants.* New York: Facts On File, 2005. General survey of Italian immigration to the United States; part of a series of books on immigration written for younger readers.

Daniels, Roger. *Coming to America.* New York: HarperCollins, 1990. Places the Italian American experience in its proper comparative framework with other ethnic groups.

Greene, Victor R. *A Singing Ambivalence: American Immigrants Between Old World and New, 1830-1930.* Kent, Ohio: Kent State University Press, 2004. Comparative study of the different challenges faced by members of eight major immigrant groups, including Italians.

Mangione, Jerre, and Ben Morreale. *La Storia: Five Centuries of the Italian American Experience.* New York: HarperCollins, 1992. Comprehensive source on the role of Italian Americans in the United States since the colonial era.

Mormino, Gary Ross. *Immigrants on the Hill: Italian Americans in St. Louis, 1882-1982.* Urbana: University of Illinois Press, 1986. Examines why the Italian immigrant community has been able to withstand the process of assimilation that typically undermines the solidarity of ethnic urban enclaves.

Rolle, Andrew F. *Westward the Immigrants: Italian Adventurers and Colonists in an Expanding America.* Ninot: University Press of Colorado, 1999. Study of the role of Italian immigrants in America's westward expansion.

Sterba, Christopher M. *The Melting Pot Goes to War: Italian and Jewish Immigrants in America's Great Crusade, 1917-1919.* Ann Arbor, Mich.: UMI, 1999. Scholarly study of the role of Jewish and Italian immigrants in World War I.

Wepman, Dennis. *Immigration: From the Founding of Virginia to the Closing of Ellis Island.* New York: Facts On File, 2002. History of immigration to the United States from the earliest European settlements of the colonial era through the mid-1950's, with liberal extracts from contemporary documents.

Yans-McLaughlin, Virginia. *Family and Community—Italian Immigrants in Buffalo, 1880-1930*. Ithaca, N.Y.: Cornell University Press, 1971. Revealing study of the early Italian immigrant ordeal in an eastern American city.

SEE ALSO European immigrant literature; European immigrants, 1892-1943; Garment industry; Immigration Act of 1924; Little Italies; Sacco and Vanzetti trial.

JAMAICAN IMMIGRANTS

IDENTIFICATION: Immigrants to North America from the West Indian island of Jamaica

IMMIGRATION ISSUES: African Americans; Demographics; Slavery; West Indian immigrants

SIGNIFICANCE: Jamaican immigrants come from a small, mostly black nation with different patterns of race relations and have had to adjust their expectations as they have dealt with native-born black and white Americans. As a

Jamaican banana plantation around 1900. (Library of Congress)

consequence, they have often had to struggle with an uncertain racial and ethnic identity.

The movement of Jamaicans to the United States began during the early twentieth century and increased greatly after the 1965 relaxation of immigration restrictions. Jamaican immigrants clustered in metropolitan areas along the eastern seaboard and in California, where many attained success as leaders in politics, religion, education, and business.

The Caribbean island of Jamaica was colonized by Spaniards in the sixteenth century. After most of the Arawak Indians died, the Spanish brought African slaves to work their sugar plantations. The British acquired Jamaica in 1670 and continued the practice of slavery. West Indian slavery did not encourage passivity, nor did it damage slaves' self-confidence to the extent that United States slavery did. Jamaican slavery ended in 1838, a generation before slavery's demise in the southern United States. Jamaica gained national independence in 1962.

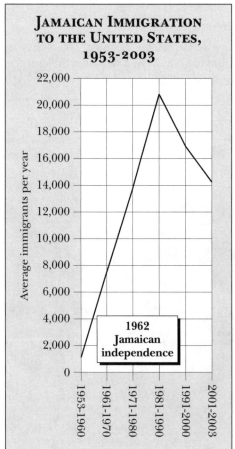

Centuries of slavery left the island with a majority black population (many of whom were very poor), a smaller mixed-race segment, and a small, prosperous white population. Jamaica, unlike the United States, never developed Jim Crow laws, rigid color castes, or a tradition of lynching. Race is not a pressing issue in Jamaica, where blacks occupy positions at all levels of society. Jamaican immigrants to the United States, most of whom are of African ancestry, often experience shock upon entering a society with a powerful white majority and a long history of blatant and rigid color prejudice and discrimination. They develop various strategies to deal with racism, such as confrontation, resignation, and development of heightened race consciousness.

TWENTIETH CENTURY IMMIGRATION Immigration from Jamaica to the United States occurred throughout the twentieth century. Many propertied and educated Ja-

Source: U.S. Census Bureau.

maicans had established themselves in New York City by the 1920's. Other Jamaicans entered the country as temporary migrant farmworkers under special visas. During the World War II labor shortage, Jamaicans were encouraged to work on farms and in factories in the United States. The 1952 Immigration and Nationality Act reduced West Indian immigration; however Jamaican immigration surged following passage of the Immigration and Nationality Act of 1965, which opened admission to nonwhite immigrants from Asia, Latin America, and the Caribbean. Jamaican newcomers settled mostly in the metropolitan areas of New York City and Miami. By 1990, 435,024 Jamaicans lived in the United States, about 80 percent of whom were foreign-born. The leading states of residence were New York, Florida, California, New Jersey, and Connecticut, according to 1990 U.S. Census figures. During the 1990's, Jamaican immigration averaged about 17,000 people per year, and that figure dropped to about 14,000 immigrants per year during the first several years of the twenty-first century.

EDUCATION, BUSINESS, AND LEADERSHIP Jamaicans arriving in the first decades of the twentieth century became black community leaders in the areas of business, politics, and the arts. In New York City, many were business owners and professionals. Some, such as Marcus Garvey, became government, civil rights, or labor union leaders. Others, including Claude McKay, a prominent writer who helped found the Harlem Renaissance of the 1920's, became cultural leaders.

The 1965 Immigration Act established a preference for skilled migrants. Accordingly, Jamaican immigrants in the latter part of the twentieth century tended to be well educated. The departure of many technical, managerial, and professional workers badly needed for the island's economic development has produced a "brain drain" in Jamaica. The value Jamaican immigrants place on education is reflected in the school performance of Jamaican American youth. Rubén Rumbaut's 1992 survey found that the children of Jamaican immigrants tended to have high grade-point averages and to score high on standardized reading and math tests. The children reported spending a large amount of time doing homework (versus watching television) and had very high educational aspirations.

COMPARISONS WITH AFRICAN AMERICANS Economic motivation underlies much Jamaican migration, and some transplanted islanders become business owners. Social scientists vary in their interpretations of West Indian entrepreneurship. Some, such as Thomas Sowell and Daniel Patrick Moynihan, credit West Indians with habits of thrift and hard work that cause them to be more successful economically than U.S.-born African Americans. The implication is that African Americans should not blame race discrimination for their poverty. Others, including Reynolds Farley and Stephen Steinberg, argue that Jamaican immigrants constitute a select group, skilled and highly motivated before they leave the island.

Farley and Steinberg also argue that the differences in economic success between immigrant and U.S.-born African Americans have been exaggerated. Farley cites statistics showing that while West Indians are more often self-employed than U.S.-born African Americans, the self-employment rate for whites is much larger than for either nonwhite group. Statistics for unemployment and income also place Jamaican Americans well below whites. Most Jamaican Americans are not self-employed. Many obtain advanced education and become lawyers, doctors, and teachers; others work in construction. Women have high labor force participation and many work in domestic service and nursing.

QUESTIONS OF IDENTITY As Jamaican Americans attempt to arrive at a sense of racial or ethnic identity, they encounter opposing forces. On one hand, they tend to retain their ethnic identity, thinking of themselves as Jamaican Americans, because of the constant influx of new immigrants who revitalize distinct cultural elements of folklore, food preferences, religion, and speech. This separateness is enforced by the attitudes of African Americans, who sometimes resent the islanders because of their foreignness, their entrepreneurial success, and because some white employers apparently prefer foreign-born workers. On the other hand, Jamaican Americans may adopt an assimilated label, calling themselves black or African American, prompted by daily experiences with racism. Because of the conflicting pressures of living in the United States, second-generation islanders sometimes vacillate, at times identifying with African Americans and other times attempting to distance themselves from them.

Nancy Conn Terjesen

FURTHER READING

Farley, Reynolds, and Walter R. Allen. *The Color Line and the Quality of Life in America.* New York: Russell Sage Foundation, 1987. Includes a chapter on the economic status of West Indians.

Heron, Melonie P. *The Occupational Attainment of Caribbean Immigrants in the United States, Canada, and England.* New York: LFB Scholarly Publications, 2001. Economic study of West Indian immigrants.

Parrillo, Vincent. *Strangers to These Shores.* 5th ed. Boston: Allyn & Bacon, 1997. General treatment of race and ethnic relations with sections on both Jamaicans and Rastafarians.

Rumbaut, Rubén G., and Alejandro Portes, eds. *Ethnicities: Children of Immigrants in America.* Berkeley: University of California Press, 2001. Collection of papers on demographic and family issues relating to immigrants that includes chapters on West Indians.

Vickerman, Milton. *Crosscurrents: West Indian Immigrants and Race.* New York: Oxford University Press, 1999. Study of the West Indian immigrant experience that contains interviews with Jamaicans in New York City who tell of contending forces of racism and equal treatment in the United States.

Waters, Mary C. *Black Identities: West Indian Immigrant Dreams and American Realities.* Cambridge, Mass.: Harvard University Press, 1999. Examines the Jamaican immigrant experience in the United States.

SEE ALSO Afro-Caribbean immigrants; Dominican immigrants; Haitian immigrants; Santería; Universal Negro Improvement Association; West Indian immigrants.

JAMESTOWN COLONY

THE EVENT: Foundation of the earliest British settlement in North America
DATE: Founded on May 14, 1607
PLACE: Jamestown, Virginia

IMMIGRATION ISSUES: European immigrants; Native Americans

SIGNIFICANCE: The first successful British settlement in North America and the beginning of the Virginia Colony, Jamestown has become a historical symbol of British immigration to North America.

In the year 1605, England and Spain had finally made peace, and in England capital was accumulating and commerce flourishing. Captain George Waymouth had returned from a voyage to Nantucket and Maine to explore a possible refuge for Roman Catholics. Five Abenaki Indians whom Waymouth had brought with him and a glowing account of the expedition by Catholic scholar James Rosier had attracted much attention.

ORIGINS After their interest was aroused, Sir John Popham, Lord Chief Justice of England, and Sir Ferdinando Gorges, both powerful members of the mercantile community, petitioned the Crown in the name of a group of adventurers for a charter incorporating two companies, one based in London and the other based in Plymouth. The patent issued on April 10, 1606, granted them the territory known as Virginia, located between latitudes 34 degrees and 41 degrees north. The London Company was authorized to settle between latitudes 34 degrees and 41 degrees north, and the Plymouth Company, between latitudes 45 degrees and 38 degrees north, but neither was to settle within one hundred miles of the other. Because of Sir Walter Raleigh's explorations in the Chesapeake Bay area and Waymouth's investigations in Maine, the adventurers knew exactly what to request.

The absence, before 1618, of the official minutes of the Virginia Company, as the two companies were jointly called, has forced historians to turn to fragmentary and often biased sources, including the sometimes conflicting accounts of Captain John Smith in his memoirs and some settlers' incomplete journal entries. However, enough facts have been ascertained that a basic chronology can be reconstructed.

On December 20, 1606, the Virginia Company of London dispatched for America three ships, the *Godspeed*, the *Discovery*, and the *Susan Constant*, carrying 144 men and boys. Captain Christopher Newport was to be in charge until the expedition reached land. After making landfall on the southern shore of Chesapeake Bay on April 26, 1607, and following a brief skirmish with local members of the Powhatan Confederacy, the 105 survivors turned up the Powhatan (renamed the James) River to search for a favorable site to settle. On May 14, they disembarked on a peninsula extending from the north shore, where they would begin to build James Fort, later called "James Towne." Although the area was low and marshy, it was beautiful, seemed defensible, and provided anchorage for deepwater vessels. The great James River offered the possibility of penetration into the interior for exploring and trading with native communities.

SETTLEMENT Only after the settlers had landed and opened the sealed box containing their instructions did they learn the names of their council, the governing body that had been appointed by the Virginia Company. This council would prove an inferior mode of governance: Its seven members quickly disagreed with one another (there had been contention, for example, over their settlement site), and a considerable number of the other settlers were headstrong adventurers. This lack of concentrated authority in Virginia resulted in bickering and the formation of factions. The strong if near-dictatorial leadership of Smith, the second president of the council, held the settlement together after fear and suspicion led to the ousting of the council's weaker first president, Edward Maria Wingfield.

More pressing than matters of government was the necessity of providing for the settlers' physical needs. Upon their arrival in America, they had divided themselves into three groups: the first was to concentrate on construction and fortifications; the second was to plant crops and keep watch downriver; and the third was to explore the surrounding area. Although the company hoped to find a water route through the continent to the South Sea and encouraged search for minerals, there was little time for such activity. Establishment of a settlement and development of trade were more urgent.

RELATIONS WITH NATIVE AMERICANS The accomplishment of both these aims depended on the amicable relations with local native peoples, members of the great Powhatan Confederacy of about thirty tribes. The Powhatans occupied most of Tidewater Virginia south of the Potomac River. The naïve settlers, rather than meeting the simple-minded "lovable savages" touted by the London promoters, soon realized that these people were both sophisticated and highly wary of the English intrusion into their domain.

Late nineteenth century painting providing a romantic depiction of Pocahontas's alleged rescue of Captain John Smith. (Library of Congress)

James Towne (not yet even a half-moon bunker) lay in the middle of Paspehege hunting grounds. On May 26 approximately two hundred Powhatans attacked the infant settlement, killing one or two and wounding more than a dozen—the first of many such skirmishes that would occur over the next several years. In mid-June, the confederacy's leader Wahunsonacock (known as Powhatan) sent envoys from upriver to make peace and provide food for the now-starving travelers. In the fall, Smith undertook a reconnaissance trip and was detained by Powhatan's half brother Opechancanough, who delivered Smith to Powhatan.

The famous story of Powhatan's mercy at the behest of his young daughter Pocahontas was Smith's fabrication some two decades after this episode; Powhatan more likely expected to bargain with the Europeans, knowing well that he had the upper hand in being able to supply them with food and hoping to strike a deal for weapons in return. Smith agreed but tricked the Indians who escorted him back to Jamestown into accepting trinkets in exchange for valuable corn. It was also during this time that the Indians had their first taste of aqua vitae, or 100-proof alcohol. Powhatan would continue to supply food (at times by force), punctuated by minor attacks on the settlers, during the settlement's early years until, in 1622, after repeated abuse at the hands of the English, he would mount a major uprising.

REBUILDING   After returning to the settlement, Smith found disease, death, and dissension. The settlers had made little headway in building the storehouse and adequate shelter, and although the river was full of sturgeon and they knew that they must boil the water to make it potable, they were eating barley soaked in slimy, brackish water and dying of influenza, typhoid, and starvation. Although the strict discipline of Smith's council presidency and the addition of more immigrants improved conditions at the settlement, the first two years must be judged as disappointing. Not only had the settlers failed in the basics of healthy survival; they had also failed to return commercially valuable resources to England.

The backers in London therefore embarked upon a more ambitious program to be financed on a joint-stock basis. Having negotiated a new charter, the Virginia Company, under the leadership of Sir Thomas Smythe, launched a campaign for financial support. Sixteen hundred persons were to emigrate to Virginia on two great expeditions in the summer of 1609. The joint-stock arrangement would allow a pooling of labor with common stock, since each person's migration to America was counted as equal to one share of stock. By this means a community of interest was developed between the adventurer in England and the colonist. The new charter of 1609 abolished the royal council and placed control in the hands of the council of the company. A governor with absolute authority was to replace the local council in the colony.

The first great contingent of settlers set out on May 15, 1609, with Sir George Somers in command. Ironically, the ship carrying the leaders was blown away from the others in a hurricane and foundered in Bermuda, its passengers not arriving in Jamestown until nearly a year after they had set out. When the other ships arrived in Virginia, Smith refused to give up his post as council president, though he yielded leadership after a famous accident (some have speculated conspiracy) in which he was injured when his gunpowder pouch ignited and exploded.

The departure of Smith for England and the arrival of almost four hundred new settlers in weakened condition placed considerable strain on the economy of the colony. When the leaders of the expedition arrived the following summer, they found only sixty settlers still living, with the settlement in ruins about them. Famine, disease, and attacks by Indians had left even the few survivors on the brink of death or reduced to a subhuman existence that sometimes involved cannibalism. Since the new arrivals were without sufficient provisions, the settlers abandoned hope of maintaining the colony and prepared to leave for England by way of Newfoundland.

As the disheartened colonists were sailing down the James River, miraculously they met Thomas West (Lord De La Warr), their new governor, coming upriver with a year's provisions. Lord De La Warr ordered the colonists to return and reestablish the settlement. The new leadership, with additional supplies and manpower, gave the colonists courage to continue.

In 1612, John Rolfe, who would eventually marry Pocahontas, discovered Virginia's "gold" when he planted the first West Indies tobacco in its soil.

Used initially for medicinal purposes, the new American commodity was soon being smoked "for fun" by Europeans—an "aqua vitae" made of smoke.

Warren M. Billings
Christina J. Moose

FURTHER READING

Bridenbaugh, Carl. *Jamestown, 1544-1699.* New York: Oxford University Press, 1980. Brief history that emphasizes the "people—red, white, and black—who lived on or near Jamestown Island."

Hume, Ivor Noël. *The Virginia Adventure: Roanoke to James Towne.* New York: Alfred A. Knopf, 1994. Historical archaeologist Hume provides an extremely detailed account of the settling of Virginia, comparing primary documents as well as physical evidence and deftly teasing out fact from legend.

Josephy, Alvin M., Jr. *Five Hundred Nations: An Illustrated History of the North American Indians.* New York: Alfred A. Knopf, 1994. Powhatan and Smith are covered in chapter 4 of this lavishly illustrated history of North America from its original occupants' viewpoint.

Morgan, Edmund S. *American Slavery, American Freedom: The Ordeal of Colonial Virginia.* New York: W. W. Norton, 1975. Early chapters include an excellent description of the difficulties faced by Smith and the other settlers.

Morgan, Kenneth. *Slavery and Servitude in Colonial North America: A Short History.* Washington Square, N.Y.: New York University Press, 2001. Brief survey of labor in Britain's North American colonies.

Rountree, Helen C. *Pocahontas's People: The Powhatan Indians of Virginia Through Four Centuries.* Norman: University of Oklahoma Press, 1990. Written by an ethnohistorian and anthropologist, this is one of the best studies of Jamestown and the settlement's relationship to the Powhatan Confederacy.

Vaughan, Alden T. *American Genesis: Captain John Smith and the Founding of Virginia.* Boston: Little, Brown, 1975. A short, balanced biography of Smith combined with a detailed history of Virginia from Smith's departure in 1609 until his death in 1631.

Wepman, Dennis. *Immigration: From the Founding of Virginia to the Closing of Ellis Island.* New York: Facts On File, 2002. History of immigration to the United States from the earliest European settlements of the colonial era through the mid-1950's, with liberal extracts from contemporary documents.

SEE ALSO Anglo-conformity; British as dominant group; History of U.S. immigration; Jewish settlement of New York.

JAPANESE AMERICAN CITIZENS LEAGUE

IDENTIFICATION: Japanese American advocacy organization
DATE: Founded on August 29, 1930

IMMIGRATION ISSUES: Asian immigrants; Citizenship and naturalization; Civil rights and liberties; Japanese immigrants

SIGNIFICANCE: The largest and most influential Japanese American political organization, the Japanese American Citizens League promotes assimilation as the most effective response to racism.

The Japanese American Citizens League (JACL) was founded in 1930 in respose to widespread anti-Asian sentiment in the United States. The JACL promoted assimilation and Americanization as the most effective way for the nisei (second-generation Japanese Americans) to gain the approval of the general public. Initially a loose federation of loyalty leagues, the JACL's influence was minimal until 1941, when it cooperated with the federal government in carrying out President Franklin Delano Roosevelt's Executive Order 9066, which ordered the internment of Japanese Americans in restricted camps during World War II. Because of that cooperation, it lost the respect of many Japanese Americans. After World War II, the JACL achieved a positive public profile as it lobbied for civil rights legislation. However, it has remained controversial for its insistence on accommodation rather than confrontation in the political arena. Now the largest and most influential Japanese American political organization, the JACL must deal with conflicts within its own ranks regarding its basic goals.

FORMATION OF THE JACL   The roots of the JACL can be traced to 1918 in San Francisco, when Thomas Y. Yatabe and a small group of his college-educated friends met to discuss the future of the nisei in America. Calling themselves the American Loyalty League, they were well aware of the racism blocking the economic progress of Asian immigrants and their families at that time. The issei (first-generation Japanese Americans) hoped their children, the nisei, would have opportunities for economic and social advancement. However, as Ronald Takaki has documented in *Strangers from a Different Shore* (1989), widespread discrimination made it difficult for them to find employment other than manual or menial labor. Yatabe and his friends were among the fortunate few who had achieved professional success; a recent dental school graduate, Yatabe drew into his circle another dentist, a doctor, and an attorney. They realized that nisei in general still faced an uncertain future. In their view, the best way to gain acceptance by the general public was to define themselves first and foremost as loyal Americans dedicated to advancement of democratic ideals. Individual enterprise, fair play, and respect for law and order were cornerstones of this philosophy.

In 1922, James "Jimmie" Yoshinori Sakamoto founded a similar group, the Seattle Progressive Citizens League. In 1923, Yatabe established the Fresno American Loyalty League, the first statewide league. In 1928, he and Saburo Kido founded the San Francisco New American Citizens League. All of these groups shared a commitment to being "100 percent American" in their outlook. Realizing how much more effective they would be if they joined together, Clarence Takeya Arai, who was elected president of the Seattle group in 1928, proposed a national meeting of delegates. He envisioned the formation of a national council of Japanese American citizens leagues which would present a positive public profile. This four-day meeting, called to order by Arai on August 29, 1930, in Seattle, Washington, became the founding convention of the JACL: the first national political organization of Japanese Americans.

The nisei leadership at the convention represented a special group of college-educated professionals with economically secure, middle-class, urban backgrounds. Mostly in their late twenties and early thirties, they were strikingly unlike the majority of nisei in America at that time, who were younger (with an average age of seventeen) and from rural, working-class backgrounds. Moreover, they were distinctly different from the issei, who still held political, economic, and social power in local Japanese American communities through the Japanese Associations, which provided legal aid and other services for immigrants. The issei usually chose (or were forced by racism) to remain within their own communities; their English skills often were minimal, and their direct interactions with outsiders were limited. Through Japanese Associations and other local organizations—such as prefectural associations, merchants' and farmers' mutual aid societies, vernacular newspapers, and Japanese language schools—the issei maintained their communities as best they could within the larger American society. The nisei leadership of the JACL, however, insisted on a completely different approach to finding a secure place for Japanese Americans in the United States. Above all, they stressed assimilation, not ethnicity, underscoring their American aspirations rather than their Japanese heritage.

Therefore, one of the first items of business at the founding convention was to remove the hyphen in "Japanese-Americans," on the basis that any Japanese aspect of nisei identity had to be subordinated to their American destiny. More than one hundred delegates from five states (Washington, Oregon, California, Illinois, and New York) and the territory of Hawaii approved resolutions asking that Congress address two timely issues: the constitutionality of the 1922 Cable Act and the eligibility of issei World War I veterans for citizenship. Suma Sugi became their lobbyist for amendment of the Cable Act, which stripped citizenship from any American woman who married an "alien ineligible to citizenship"; through Sugi's efforts and those of the League of

Women Voters, Congress changed the law in 1931, so that citizenship could not be revoked by marriage. Tokutaro "Tokie" Nishimura Slocum became their lobbyist for veteran citizenship, which finally was secured by the Nye-Lea Bill in 1935.

JACL's WORK During its first decade of existence, however, the JACL had little direct effect on the Japanese American community. This situation changed dramatically in 1941, when President Roosevelt issued Executive Order 9066, authorizing the internment of Japanese Americans during World War II. The federal government imprisoned virtually all issei leaders of businesses, schools, and churches on the West Coast. The JACL then took over, directing Japanese Americans not to resist relocation. In fact, the JACL cooperated with the War Relocation Authority (WRA) in identifying community members who might be subversives. Dillon S. Myer, WRA director, worked closely with Mike Masaoka, a JACL official, in administering the camps—a relationship intensely resented by the majority of Japanese Americans. Attorney Wayne Mortimer Collins, who stood against popular opinion to defend Japanese American civil rights during and after World War II, went so far as to blame the JACL for much of the suffering that internees endured.

The JACL succeeded in building a positive public profile after the war by lobbying for civil rights legislation such as amendment of the Immigration and Nationality Act of 1952, thereby guaranteeing the right of all issei to naturalized citizenship. To this day, however, it has remained a controversial organization, especially because of its conservative political stance. The JACL must deal with interfactional conflicts between its "old guard" and younger members who question its basic goals.

Mary Louise Buley-Meissner

FURTHER READING

Chan, Sucheng. *Asian Americans: An Interpretive History.* Boston: Twayne, 1991. Carefully researched investigation of Asian American socioeconomic, political, educational, and cultural realities. Provides contexts for assessing JACL achievements.

Chi, Tsung. *East Asian Americans and Political Participation: A Reference Handbook.* Santa Barbara, Calif.: ABC-Clio, 2005. Useful reference work on Asian American political activism.

Drinnon, Richard. *Keeper of Concentration Camps: Dillon S. Myer and American Racism.* Berkeley: University of California Press, 1987. Painstakingly researched revisionist history of Myer's administration of the War Relocation Authority, including his collaboration with Mike Masaoka and the JACL.

Hosokawa, Bill. *JACL in Quest of Justice.* New York: William Morrow, 1982. History book commissioned by the JACL to record its accomplishments. Mainly covers the 1930's and 1940's, emphasizing the organization's patriotic nature.

Ng, Wendy L. *Japanese American Internment During World War II: A History and Reference Guide.* Westport, Conn.: Greenwood Press, 2002. Comprehensive reference source on all aspects of the internment of Japanese people during World War II.

Niiya, Brian, ed. *Japanese American History: An A-to-Z Reference from 1868 to the Present.* New York: Japanese American National Museum and Facts On File, 1993. Invaluable resource including a narrative historical overview, a chronology of Japanese American history, and dictionary entries for that history. Scholarly research accessible to a general audience.

Segal, Uma Anand. *A Framework for Immigration: Asians in the United States.* New York: Columbia University Press, 2002. Survey of the history and economic and social conditions of Asian immigrants to the United States, both before and after the federal immigration reforms of 1965.

Takaki, Ronald. *Strangers from a Different Shore: A History of Asian Americans.* New York: Penguin Books, 1989. Groundbreaking investigation of Asian American contributions to U.S. socioeconomic and political development. Provides contexts for assessing JACL achievements.

SEE ALSO Alien land laws; Gentlemen's Agreement; Japanese American internment; Japanese immigrants; Japanese segregation in California schools; "Yellow peril" campaign.

JAPANESE AMERICAN INTERNMENT

THE EVENT: Forcible removal of Japanese and Japanese American residents of Western states to isolated internment camps during World War II
DATE: 1942-1945

IMMIGRATION ISSUES: Asian immigrants; Civil rights and liberties; Discrimination; Families and marriage; Japanese immigrants

SIGNIFICANCE: During World War II, the U.S. government's war powers were used to deny due process of the law for aliens and U.S. citizens of Japanese ancestry, to the disapproval of the postwar generation.

Historically in the continental United States there were severe restrictions on Japanese immigration and naturalization, and in 1941 there were only about 40,000 foreign-born Japanese people (issei) plus about 87,000 American-born citizens (nisei). Many were tenant farmers who lived under West Coast state and local restrictions on land ownership, housing, employment, and education; Japanese Americans were a semisegregated community.

EVACUATION   Following the December, 1941, Japanese attack on Pearl Harbor, the Federal Bureau of Investigation arrested 2,192 Japanese security risks, followed by German and Italian counterparts. False reports of Japanese American espionage at Pearl Harbor, Japanese victories in the Pacific, and radio and press rumors combined to create unfounded fears that traitors and saboteurs might assist a Japanese invasion of the West Coast. On February 14, 1942, Lieutenant General John DeWitt, with War Department encouragement, and misrepresenting rumors as security threats, recommended removing persons of the Japanese "enemy race," including American citizens, from his West Coast command area. The Justice Department acquiesced, and on February 19, 1942, President Franklin D. Roosevelt signed Executive Order 9066, authorizing the army to create restricted zones excluding "any or all persons." On March 21, 1942, Congressional Law 503 provided criminal penalties for noncompliance.

INTERNMENT   DeWitt put more than 100,000 West Coast Japanese Americans under curfew, exclusion, removal, collection, and evacuation orders, which resulted in permanent job and property losses. Their ten relocation

Japanese Americans reporting at the assembly center at Santa Anita race track in Arcadia, California, in April, 1942. Given less than two months to prepare for relocation after President Roosevelt signed Executive Order 9066, tens of thousands of loyal American citizens, as well as recent immigrants, had to abandon their homes and businesses before entering the uncertainties of internment. (National Archives)

Internees eating a meal at the Manzanar Relocation Center in California's eastern Sierras.
(NARA)

camps in the Western United States were isolated, barren, crowded, and crude, with barbed-wire fences and armed guards. Liberals and conservatives alike generally seemed to approve this mass imprisonment, conspicuously limited to the Japanese race. Internees who hoped that compliance would demonstrate their loyalty to the United States became demoralized by camp conditions and popular hostility.

In 1943, Japanese American soldiers changed the situation. Aside from their Pacific theater intelligence service, nisei already in uniform plus volunteers from the internment camps formed the 100th Infantry Battalion and the 442d Regimental Combat Team. Their European combat and casualty records earned public respect for the nisei soldiers and a more positive policy for the internees. By early 1944, 15,000 nisei civilians were on restricted camp leave; finally, on December 17, 1944, the West Coast exclusion order was lifted.

Following Japan's surrender on September 2, 1945, detention and exclusion were phased out; the last camp closed March 20, 1946. The 1948 Evacuation Claims Act offered meager compensations—about $340 per case—for those renouncing all other claims against the government.

COURT CASES   Four significant wartime appeals by nisei reached the U.S. Supreme Court. On June 21, 1943, in *Hirabayashi v. United States* and *Yasui v.*

United States, the Court upheld convictions for curfew violations, ruling the curfews constitutional and the emergency real, and found that Japanese Americans "may be a greater source of danger than those of a different ancestry." The Court held that winning the war must prevail over judicial review, implicitly reversing *Ex parte Milligan* (1866). On December 18, 1944, the Court granted *habeas corpus* in *Ex parte Endo*, ruling that Congress had not authorized long-term detention for a "concededly loyal" American citizen; the Court avoided broader questions of internment. On the same day, however, in *Korematsu v. United States*, the Court upheld Korematsu's conviction, on the *Hirabayashi* precedent. Although three dissenting justices argued that the exclusion order was part of a detention process, that Korematsu's offense of being in his own home was not normally a criminal act, and that only his race made it a crime under the exclusion orders, the Court majority upheld the government's wartime powers.

REDRESS America's postwar generation developed different priorities. The Civil Rights movement and Vietnam War protests emphasized racial justice and deemphasized "national security." In 1980 Congress established the Commission on Wartime Relocation and Internment of Civilians to review facts and recommend remedies. Their 1982 report, *Personal Justice Denied*, exposed General DeWitt's misrepresentations, finding that "not a single documented act of espionage, sabotage or fifth column activity was committed by an American citizen of Japanese ancestry," that Executive Order 9066 resulted from "race prejudice, war hysteria and a failure of political leadership," and that "a grave injustice was done," deserving compensation. Of the Supreme Court, the report contended that "the decision in *Korematsu* lies overruled in the court of history."

The commission's work enabled Yasui, Hirabayashi, and Korematsu to file motions to vacate their convictions in the original courts on writ of *coram nobis*, alleging prosecutorial misrepresentation and impropriety. Yasui died while his case was in progress. On April 19, 1984, U.S. district court judge Marilyn Patel granted Korematsu's petition, acknowledging the 1944 Supreme Court decision as "the law of this case" but terming it an anachronism, "now recognized as having very limited application." On this precedent, Hirabayashi's convictions were overturned in 1987.

In 1988, a congressional act signed by President Ronald Reagan accepted the findings of the 1980 commission, provided $1.2 billion in redress for 60,000 internees, and added, "for these fundamental violations of the basic civil liberties and constitutional rights of these citizens of Japanese ancestry, the Congress apologizes on behalf of the Nation." The history of Japanese American internment illustrates both the difficulty of limiting emergency powers during a popular war and the abuses caused by failing to do so.

K. Fred Gillum

FURTHER READING

Broek, Jacobus Ten, Edward Barnhart, and Floyd Matson. *Prejudice, War, and the Constitution.* Berkeley: University of California Press, 1968. Examination of the federal government's decision to intern Japanese people from a legal and constitutional perspective.

Commission on Wartime Relocation and Internment of Civilians. *Personal Justice Denied.* Washington, D.C.: U.S. Government Printing Office, 1982. Federal government report on the internment years.

Irons, Peter. *Justice Delayed.* Middletown, Conn.: Wesleyan University Press, 1989. Study of the postwar legal struggle leading up to reparations during the 1980's.

Ng, Wendy L. *Japanese American Internment During World War II: A History and Reference Guide.* Westport, Conn.: Greenwood Press, 2002. Comprehensive reference source on the internment years.

SEE ALSO   Alien land laws; Asian American literature; Asian American stereotypes; Gentlemen's Agreement; Japanese American Citizens League; Japanese immigrants; Japanese Peruvians; Japanese segregation in California schools; Little Tokyos; Model minorities; *Ozawa v. United States*; "Yellow peril" campaign.

JAPANESE IMMIGRANTS

IDENTIFICATION: Immigrants to North America from the East Asia nation of Japan

IMMIGRATION ISSUES: Asian immigrants; Demographics; Japanese immigrants

SIGNIFICANCE: Although people of Japanese descent have been one of the most discriminated against groups in U.S. history, they have also become some of the highest-achieving and most successful immigrant groups in the United States.

During the 1890's, a few of the Japanese who had moved to Hawaii during the 1880's migrated to California, but large-scale Japanese immigration did not take place until 1900. From 1900 to 1910, more than 100,000 Japanese moved to the West Coast, first and primarily to California but eventually as far north as Vancouver, British Columbia. By 1930, about 275,000 people living in the United States were of Japanese origin or descent. By the end of the twentieth century, this number had reached about 1.8 million.

Before World War II, Japanese immigrants were barred from becoming U.S. citizens and owning land on the West Coast. During World War II, more than 100,000 Japanese Americans were placed in internment camps in the Western United States and in Canada. However, the fighting spirit of the nisei (second-generation Japanese American) army unit during World War II contributed to a greater acceptance of Japanese Americans by other racial and ethnic groups in the postwar period. By the end of the twentieth century, Japanese Americans had received an official apology and reparations for the internment.

EARLY REACTION TO JAPANESE IMMIGRATION   In 1882, Congress passed the Chinese Exclusion Act, primarily at the insistence of Californians who claimed that the Chinese could not be assimilated into American culture. Many Californians, therefore, were outraged when after Chinese immigration was virtually stopped by the 1882 act, Japanese immigration began. These citizens simply could see no difference between Chinese and Japanese immigrants, although, in fact, the Japanese, who had been carefully screened by the Japanese government, were generally better educated than the earlier Chinese immigrants.

Soon after 1900, politicians and journalists agitated to stop Japanese immigration, speaking of the "yellow peril." They maintained that the Japanese could not be assimilated into American culture and represented an outside group that would attempt to control the United States. In 1905, the public

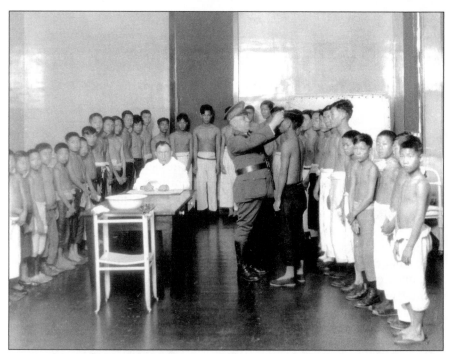

Japanese laborers undergoing health inspection at the Angel Island reception center in San Francisco Bay during the 1920's. (National Archives)

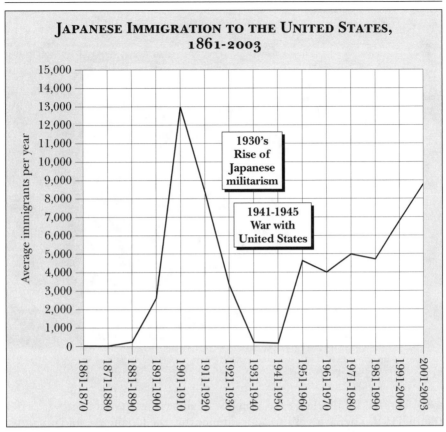

JAPANESE IMMIGRATION TO THE UNITED STATES, 1861-2003

1930's
Rise of
Japanese
militarism

1941-1945
War with
United States

Source: U.S. Census Bureau.

schools of San Francisco banned Japanese children from attending school with white children, causing the Japanese government to become very angry. The issue of San Francisco's school segregation was resolved in 1907 when President Theodore Roosevelt signed a Gentlemen's Agreement with the Japanese government, requiring that it not issue any more visas for workers to come to the United States. The San Francisco school board then allowed Japanese children to attend school with whites.

California and other states continued to harass Japanese immigrants. In 1913, California passed the Alien Land Law, which stipulated that Asians who were ineligible for citizenship could not own land. This meant that the Japanese immigrants, who were mostly agricultural workers, could work only as tenant farmers and could not own the land on which they worked.

Miscegenation laws, making marriages between people of different races illegal, were also enforced against the early Japanese immigrants, most of whom were men. Unable to find wives in the United States, these men turned to matchmakers in Japan. Often the immigrants would marry brides whom they had seen, before the wedding, only in a photograph. White Californians

433

Japanese immigrants awaiting a government health inspection off Angel Island in San Francisco Bay in 1931. (National Archives)

were angered by the Japanese practice of marrying "picture brides." They pointed to this behavior as further evidence that the Japanese could not be assimilated into American culture.

JAPANESE AMERICANS DURING WORLD WAR II   By the start of World War II, two generations of Japanese Americans (issei, or first-generation Japanese Americans, and nisei, second-generation Japanese Americans) lived in the United States and Canada. In 1942, members of the American and Canadian governments felt that the Japanese Americans posed a threat to security. Therefore, on February 19, 1942, President Franklin D. Roosevelt issued Executive Order 9066, requiring people of Japanese origin or descent living in the western part of the United States (California, Oregon, Washington, and the southern part of Arizona) to be placed in internment camps; this order affected more than 100,000 people. The Japanese Americans were given very little time to gather their property or to take care of businesses before they were interned. Property that actually belonged to nisei (who were American citizens) was seized. Areas such as Japantown (Nihonmachi) in the Fillmore district of San Francisco and Little Tokyo in Los Angeles became nearly deserted. What is more, within twenty-four hours of the bombing of Pearl Harbor, the United States government detained one thousand Japanese American community leaders and teachers.

In Canada, the 1942 War Measures Act placed Japanese aliens and Japanese Canadians in camps and required them to pay for their housing. Those who objected to having to live in these camps were placed in prisoner-of-war camps along with captured German soldiers in northern Ontario. In the United States, various court cases were brought to challenge the government's treatment of Japanese Americans, but this treatment was deemed to be legal in decisions such as *Korematsu v. United States* (1944) and *Hirabayashi v. United States* (1943). In the decision handed down in *Hirabayashi*, the Court suggested that because Japanese Americans had chosen to live together as a group and had not assimilated well into the mainstream culture, the U.S. government was justified in being suspicious of them.

In January, 1945, Japanese aliens and Japanese Americans were allowed to leave the camps. Unable to live in the Western United States, these people and their families settled in the East. Soon after the United States released the detainees from camps, the Canadians followed suit.

AFTER WORLD WAR II   For a variety of reasons, life for Japanese Americans improved after World War II. The bravery of the nisei soldiers during World War II had impressed upon many other Americans how loyal Japanese Americans actually were. Having seen firsthand the racial hatred practiced by the Nazis, Americans and Canadians did not want this sort of prejudice practiced in their home countries. Finally, much of the original prejudice and hatred against the Japanese and Asians as a whole stemmed from white Americans' fears of economic competition. The strength of the postwar U.S. economy lessened these fears and created advancement possibilities for many racial and ethnic groups.

In 1952, with the passage of the Immigration and Nationality Act (also known as the McCarran-Walter Act), it became possible for Japanese immigrants to become naturalized citizens. Although many Japanese citizens had entered the United States as wives of U.S. servicemen under the 1945 War Brides Act, many more entered under the 1952 act. From 1947 through 1975, 67,000 Japanese women entered as wives of U.S. servicemen, thus, becoming Japanese Americans. These new Japanese Americans encountered a very different United States from the one experienced by earlier immigrants. After 1952, it was much less likely that Japanese Americans would isolate themselves in areas where only people of Japanese heritage lived. In 1956, California, by popular vote, largely through a campaign orchestrated by Japanese American Sei Fujii, repealed its Alien Land Law, making it possible for people born in Japan to own land in California.

THE MID- TO LATE TWENTIETH CENTURY   In the latter part of the twentieth century, Americans became interested in all things Japanese. Japanese influences could be found in American music, fashion, architecture, philosophy, and religion. Japanese Americans were able to lead the way in introducing other ethnic and racial groups to Japanese culture and philosophy. During the 1960's, recognizing that expressions of cultural heritage were becoming popular, the Japanese Americans in the Fillmore district of San Francisco organized the first annual San Francisco Cherry Blossom Festival to share Japanese philosophy and culture associated with the cherry blossom with other Americans. Other cities such as Seattle, Washington, also organized cherry blossom festivals. One of the better-known festivals is the National Cherry Blossom Festival, held in Washington, D.C., each spring to celebrate the donation of more than three thousand Japanese cherry trees to the American people by the mayor of Tokyo in 1912.

Led by Japanese American citizens' groups, Japanese Americans for many decades attempted to obtain justice from the U.S. government for its treatment of them during World War II. Finally, in 1988, Congress passed the Civil Liberties Act. The American government acknowledged that an injustice had been done, apologized for that injustice, and agreed to pay reparations of twenty thousand dollars to each eligible Japanese American. In 1990, President George Bush began the reparations process.

Annita Marie Ward

FURTHER READING

Chalfen, Richard. *Turning Leaves: The Photograph Collection of Two Japanese Families.* Albuquerque: University of New Mexico Press, 1991.

Chi, Tsung. *East Asian Americans and Political Participation: A Reference Handbook.* Santa Barbara, Calif.: ABC-Clio, 2005.

Hirobe, Izumi. *Japanese Pride, American Prejudice: Modifying the Exclusion Clause of the 1924 Immigration Act.* Stanford, Calif.: Stanford University Press, 2001.

Hoobler, Dorothy, Thomas Hoobler, and George Takei. *The Japanese American Family Album.* New York: Oxford University Press, 1996.

Iida, Deborah. *Middle Son.* Chapel Hill, N.C.: Algonquin Books, 1996.

Kitano, Harry. *The Japanese Americans.* New York: Chelsea House, 1987.

Ng, Franklin, ed. *Asian American Encyclopedia.* 6 vols. New York: Marshall Cavendish, 1995.

Segal, Uma Anand. *A Framework for Immigration: Asians in the United States.* New York: Columbia University Press, 2002.

Yanogisako, Sylvia Junko. *Transforming the Past: Tradition and Kinship Among Japanese Americans.* Palo Alto, Calif.: Stanford University Press, 1985.

SEE ALSO Alien land laws; Asian American Legal Defense Fund; Asian American literature; Asian American stereotypes; Gentlemen's Agreement; Japanese American Citizens League; Japanese American internment; Japanese Peruvians; Japanese segregation in California schools; Little Tokyos; Model minorities; *Ozawa v. United States*; "Yellow peril" campaign.

JAPANESE PERUVIANS

IDENTIFICATION: Japanese immigrants to the United States by way of Peru

IMMIGRATION ISSUES: Asian immigrants; Demographics; Japanese immigrants; Refugees

SIGNIFICANCE: Victims of prejudice and distrust in both their Peruvian homeland and the United States, a small number of Japanese Peruvians became unwilling pawns in World War II rivalries.

In 1940, about thirty thousand people of Japanese descent lived in Peru. It was a time when an already existing anti-Japanese movement was expanding, and about 650 Japanese houses were targeted for assault in Lima. The following year, after Japan brought World War II to the Americas, the Peruvian government seized the property of all Japanese immigrants.

An official at the U.S. embassy in Lima, John K. Emmerson, reported to the U.S. State Department that the Japanese community in Peru was led by well-organized nationalists who constituted a threat to U.S. national security. He suggested that the leaders of the Japanese Peruvian community be brought to the United States to be exchanged for American prisoners of war held in Japan. As a result, this proposal—as well as strong anti-Japanese sentiment from the Peruvian government—caused more than seventeen hundred Japanese Peruvians to be deported at gunpoint and transported to internment camps in the United States between 1942 and 1945.

After World War II ended, the Japanese Peruvians who were detained in the United States were not allowed to return to Peru or to have their belongings returned to them by the Peruvian government. More than three decades later, in 1988, the 112,000 Japanese Americans who were placed in internment camps during the war received an official apology from the U.S. government and $20,000 per person for being incarcerated. However, those Japanese Peruvians who were also interned were denied the apology and compensation. This was because when they were deported from Peru, their passports were taken away by the Peruvian government and they were considered technically to be "illegal aliens" upon their arrival in the United States. Because they were neither U.S. citizens nor permanent residents at that time, they failed to qualify for the reparations even though a majority eventually became American citizens after the war.

Finally in June, 1998, American-interned Latin Americans received an official apology from the U.S. government; however, their compensation was only $5,000 per person. Moreover, they were allowed only two months to make their applications for the payments. Ironically, by that time, Peruvian attitudes toward the Japanese had changed so much that Peruvians had elected a Japanese Peruvian, Albert Fujimori, the president of their country.

Nobuko Adachi

FURTHER READING

Kitano, Harry. *The Japanese Americans.* New York: Chelsea House, 1987.

Ng, Franklin, ed. *Asian American Encyclopedia.* 6 vols. New York: Marshall Cavendish, 1995.

Ng, Wendy L. *Japanese American Internment During World War II: A History and Reference Guide.* Westport, Conn.: Greenwood Press, 2002.

SEE ALSO   Japanese American internment; Japanese immigrants; Japanese segregation in California schools; Latinos; Twice migrants.

JAPANESE SEGREGATION IN CALIFORNIA SCHOOLS

THE EVENT: Government-ordered segregation of Japanese students in San Francisco's public schools

DATE: 1906

PLACE: San Francisco, California

IMMIGRATION ISSUES: Asian immigrants; Civil rights and liberties; Discrimination; Education; Japanese immigrants

SIGNIFICANCE: San Francisco's decision to segregate the small number of Japanese students in its public schools provoked a major international dispute between Japan and the United States that led to the so-called Gentlemen's Agreement of 1907, which limited Japanese immigration to the United States.

On October 11, 1906, scarcely six months after Japan had magnanimously donated more than $246,000 in aid (exceeding the combined donations of the rest of the world) to help alleviate the suffering caused by the San Francisco earthquake, the San Francisco Board of Education repaid Japan's kindness by voting to segregate Japanese children from "white" children in its public schools.

The Japanese government was at first stunned by this blatant expression of racial bigotry. The Japanese hoped that cooler and wiser heads would prevail in California and that the order would be quickly rescinded. After waiting for two weeks, Japanese prime minister Kinmochi Saionji instructed his ambassador, Shuzo Aoki, to deliver a note of protest into the hands of U.S. secretary of state Elihu Root on October 25, in which the government of the United States was reminded that Japanese citizens were guaranteed equal rights by treaty and that the "equal right of education is one of the highest and most valuable rights. . . ." Saionji went on to say that even if the "oriental schools" provided for Asian children were to be equal to other schools, the segregation of Japanese children "constitutes an act of discrimination carrying with it a stigma and odium which it is impossible to overlook."

The Japanese government cautioned its citizens against any anti-American retribution in Japan and counseled the Japanese in San Francisco to bear the insults and discrimination "with equanimity and dignity." Japanese newspapers, although outraged at this blatant racial insult, generally suggested that the wisest course for Japan to take was to appeal to the American sense of honor and fair play.

President Theodore Roosevelt was both embarrassed and outraged at the San Francisco action and promised Aoki and the Japanese government that the matter soon would be resolved. As was his wont, Roosevelt began a propaganda campaign in the press to try to marshal national pressure against San Francisco and to give the Japanese the impression that he was actively engaged in resolving the issue. Much to his horror, several southern congressmen sprang to the defense of their fellow racists in California. They interpreted the issue as being one of states' rights and reminded Roosevelt that the recent *Plessy v. Ferguson* (1896) Supreme Court ruling allowed the individual states to maintain "separate but equal" public education facilities.

For its part, the San Francisco School Board failed to understand the extent and importance of the international crisis that it had caused. For nearly thirty years Chinese people had been excluded as immigrants to the United States and those Chinese who happened to be residents of California had been denied virtually all political and civil rights as a matter of course. Native American, African American, Mexican, Chinese, Korean, "Hindoo," and other children routinely had been segregated from "white" children. Why now this sudden uproar?

BACKGROUND TO BIGOTRY The anti-Japanese bigotry was the result of a series of unfortunate coincidences. First, Japanese immigration to California previously had been but a minor irritant compared to the problems posed by the influx of Chinese laborers during the 1870's and 1880's. Fewer than ten thousand Japanese had come to California before 1900, and perhaps only half of them remained as residents. California labor contractors, however, discovered the industrious Japanese laboring in Hawaiian cane fields after the Hawaiian Revolution of 1894. Thousands were lured to California by these contractors and found ready employment in the developing agricultural sector. As their numbers increased, so did their economic influence at nearly every level. By 1905, organized labor in California had mounted a campaign against Japanese immigration based on the fact that Japanese undercut American workers by working longer hours for less money.

The 1906 earthquake had contributed to the general malaise and sense of anomie in San Francisco in much the same irrational way that citizens of Tokyo would turn against helpless innocent Koreans in the earthquake of 1923.

"White" San Franciscans who lost their homes in the earthquake quite irrationally were outraged that a handful of Japanese had survived with their homes and businesses intact. Even worse, a few enterprising Japanese set up thriving cheap restaurants that catered to the workers involved in the urban recovery. In the eyes of the bigots, then, the Japanese seemed to be prospering at the expense of the suffering "whites."

Third, the *San Francisco Chronicle,* perhaps in an attempt to out-sensationalize William Randolph Hearst's *San Francisco Herald,* chose that time to mount a provocative campaign against Japanese immigration. It published unsubstantiated and patently absurd charges that Japanese were spying on American coastal defenses for Japan and that they were acquiring huge tracts of land in the Central Valley, not only for its rich farmland but also for strategic military purposes. Without question the worst fear that they dredged up was the horror of racial miscegenation. They claimed that hundreds, perhaps thousands, of adult Japanese men were routinely placed side-by-side with young, innocent "white maidens" in the city's schools. Actually, some twenty-three Japanese boys, none older than sixteen years of age, were dispersed throughout the city schools, placed temporarily in lower grades until their English language skills improved.

In response, during the late summer of 1906, a Japanese Exclusion League blossomed, ironically led by four recent European immigrants to the city. Pickets in front of Japanese restaurants handed out printed boxes of matches that read, "White people, patronize your own race." Gangs of thugs assaulted lone Japanese in the streets and threw stones at the windows of Japanese residents. Petitions were circulated urging the exclusion of Japanese immigrants.

A final factor in the bigotry directed against the Japanese was the rabidly racist campaign of the mayor of the city. Eugene Schmitz was facing an imminent indictment for bribery and corruption by a reformist movement and hoped to use the growing anti-Japanese hysteria to gain political support. Schmitz joined the Japanese Exclusion League in a series of outdoor public meetings. Before long, this unprincipled political opportunist had further inflamed the already irrational bigots. The result was that the school board yielded to the demands of the rabble and voted to establish a separate school for all "orientals," including the Japanese. After a few months, the more responsible citizens of the city managed to bolster enough support to force another vote in the school board, but not before many Japanese children were denied the right to an education in their neighborhood schools and not before many Japanese adults were assaulted, threatened, and coerced to pay "protection money" by the local police.

EFFORTS TO NEGOTIATE A SETTLEMENT   Roosevelt met several times with city and state leaders and reached a tacit agreement that the school segregation crisis could be resolved if some agreement could be reached to further restrict the immigration of Japanese laborers. Ambassador Aoki was receptive to Roosevelt's invitation to discuss the issue but reminded him that Japan already restricted the number of passports granted to persons wishing to immigrate to the United States. He suggested that it would be better if the United States would restrict immigration from Hawaii and Mexico, since apparently most Japanese who came to California arrived from those countries. After months of discussion, Roosevelt and the Japanese arrived at what has been called the Gentlemen's Agreement, which severely limited the number of Japanese immigrants.

For the time being, ninety-three Japanese children returned to their neighborhood schools and San Francisco and California settled down to await nervously the next wave of xenophobic hysteria. However, they did not have long to wait.

IMPACT OF EVENT The effect of the San Francisco school segregation incident was most directly felt by the ninety-three children who had their education interrupted for a year. To have required them to travel, in some cases, across the whole city to the "oriental school" was at least inconvenient and in some cases dangerous. The greatest impact was the denial of their human and civil rights. To be singled out for discrimination on the basis of race was, and always will be, a demeaning insult. The only thing that ameliorated and stopped the discrimination was the fact that Japan, by 1906, had become a powerful military world power. Japan could not be insulted with impunity. However, the children of Chinese, Korean, Filipino, Mexican, Native American, African American, and other "nonwhite" origins did not have a strong and proud nation to enforce their rights. Those unfortunate students were forced to endure the insult and degradation of "separate but equal" schools.

The Japanese Exclusion League did not simply evaporate with the hysteria. Like the irrational xenophobia that fed the crisis, the League continued on, nurtured by the fear and hatred of ignorant and bigoted people. It was to surface again in 1913, when the California legislature passed an Alien Land Act which denied landowning to people (such as the Japanese) who could not become citizens. It would flourish again in 1921 and 1924, when the U.S. Congress passed immigration acts favoring immigrants from northern and western Europe and restricting the number of Japanese immigrants to less than one hundred per year. One might argue that the racial bigotry evident in the San Francisco school segregation crisis of 1906 was precisely the same virulent strain of xenophobia that would sanction the incarceration of loyal Americans of Japanese ancestry in 1942.

Curiously, within the so-called Gentlemen's Agreement that resolved the school segregation crisis was the basis for a somewhat different but perhaps more dangerous problem. That agreement allowed for those Japanese already resident in the United States to bring their families to join them. The citizens of California were startled to discover that Japanese residents in California used this rule to bring their parents and sometimes women whom they had married "by proxy" to live with them. The children born to Japanese in the United States were natural-born citizens. The state of California could deny the political and civil rights of aliens but could not do so to their citizen children with the same impunity. Therefore, the Gentlemen's Agreement was but a puny bandage over the cancer of racial bigotry. It covered an unsightly wound, but the problem continued to eat at the American body politic.

It can be argued also that the San Francisco school segregation crisis of 1906 helped to breed a resentment and self-fulfilling paranoia in Japan. Japan bitterly resented the insult perpetrated against its citizens. This anger and resentment, along with the latent American suspicions bred by racial bigotry, would contribute to much of the malice that would lead the two nations into a senseless and horrible war a generation later.

Louis G. Perez

FURTHER READING

Bailey, Thomas A. *Theodore Roosevelt and the Japanese-American Crisis: An Account of the International Complications Arising from the Race Problem on the Pacific Coast.* Stanford, Calif.: Stanford University Press, 1934. Solid but somewhat dated. Integrates the crisis into the greater history of Japanese American foreign relations. Places Roosevelt squarely in the imbroglio. Indexed, but the bibliography is dated.

Boddy, E. Manchester. *Japanese in America.* Los Angeles: E. M. Boddy, 1921. A curious short monograph written to counter the arguments of the Japanese Exclusion League. It examines and refutes each argument with California and federal census and immigration statistics. Still valuable for its glimpse of the visceral quality of the debate. No index or bibliography, but contains a list (with addresses) of the California Japanese residents' associations.

Daniels, Roger. *The Politics of Prejudice: The Anti-Japanese Movement in California and the Struggle for Japanese Exclusion.* Berkeley: University of California Press, 1974. Masterful treatment of the politics of racial bigotry. Together with Penrose, depicts the leaders of the "nativist" movement in California with chilling clarity. Valuable bibliography of primary sources.

Gulick, Sidney L. *The American-Japanese Problem: A Study of the Racial Relations of the East and West.* New York: Charles Scribner's Sons, 1914. Despite being dated, it is an interesting attempt by Christian ministers to refute the arguments of the Japanese Exclusion League. Forms the basis of the work by Boddy. Gulick had been a missionary to Asia.

Iriye, Akira. *Pacific Estrangement: Japanese and American Expansion, 1897-1911.* Cambridge, Mass.: Harvard University Press, 1972. A brilliantly written examination of the mutual animosities between two imperialist states. Masterful incorporation of recent scholarship in both languages. Chapters 5 and 6, "Confrontation: The Japanese View" and "Confrontation: The American View," are excellent. Source notation and bibliography in both Japanese and English languages is impressive.

Neu, Charles E. *An Uncertain Friendship: Theodore Roosevelt and Japan, 1906-1909.* Cambridge, Mass.: Harvard University Press, 1967. A solid revisionist interpretation. Uses Roosevelt's extensive personal correspondence to portray him as a shrewd politician whose own racial prejudices made him more sympathetic to the Japanese Exclusion League bigots than to the Japanese. Good use of primary documents.

Penrose, Eldon R. *California Nativism: Organized Opposition to the Japanese, 1890-1913.* San Francisco: R and E Research Associates, 1973. Despite an annoying lack of organization, this is a surprisingly sophisticated examination of the exclusionist movement. Uses newspapers and correspondence of the principal participants to examine the politics of the movement and the background of its leaders. No index, but appendices include the various anti-Asian exclusion acts.

Ruiz de Velasco, Jorge, and Michael Fix. *Overlooked and Underserved: Immigrant Students in U.S. Secondary Schools.* Washington, D.C.: Urban Institute, 2000. Broad study of the treatment of immigrants in American public schools.

SEE ALSO Alien land laws; Asian American education; Asian American literature; Asian American stereotypes; Gentlemen's Agreement; Japanese American Citizens League; Japanese American internment; Japanese immigrants; Japanese Peruvians; Little Tokyos; Model minorities; *Ozawa v. United States*; "Yellow peril" campaign.

JEWISH IMMIGRANTS

IDENTIFICATION: Jewish immigrants to North America from Europe

IMMIGRATION ISSUES: Civil rights and liberties; Demographics; European immigrants; Jewish immigrants; Middle Eastern immigrants; Religion

SIGNIFICANCE: From their arrival in New Amsterdam in 1654, Jews were the most important non-Christian group in an overwhelmingly Christian America. Their experiences tested and helped define the meaning of religious freedom and the nature of ethnic relations in the United States.

In 1654, twenty-three Jewish refugees, who had fled Brazil when it was retaken by the Portuguese from the Dutch, arrived in New Amsterdam seeking asylum. They were not welcomed by Governor Peter Stuyvesant, who put them in jail and requested permission from the Dutch West India Company to ban all Jews from the colony. The company, which had several substantial Jewish shareholders, refused, and Stuyvesant had to permit the newcomers to remain. Despite facing prejudice, the Jews were able to worship undisturbed. The congregation grew slowly after the British conquered the colony in 1664 and renamed it New York. Other small Jewish settlements emerged in the port cities of Newport, Philadelphia, Charleston, and Savannah. Most new-comers were descendants of Spanish and Portuguese Jews who used Sephar-dic rituals in their synagogues and spoke a dialect of Spanish in their homes.

By 1776, the Jewish population in the British mainland colonies reached between 1,500 and 2,500. The Jews were accepted by their neighbors and could practice their religion unmolested, but they occasionally faced overt prejudice and legal disabilities. Jews could be, but were not always, barred from voting in colonial elections or holding political office because they were unable to take required oaths as a Christian. Jewish merchants and crafts-people participated fully in the commercial life of Newport, Rhode Island. However, even after the London Parliament passed a naturalization act pro-viding special oaths for Jews in the American colonies, Rhode Island courts refused to naturalize Jews, claiming this would violate the purpose for which the colony was founded.

The state and federal constitutions established after the American Revo-lution shifted Jewish-Gentile relations from sometimes uneasy toleration toward civil and political equality. The U.S. Constitution and Bill of Rights provided federal protection for freedom of conscience, and the new state constitutions began to remove test oaths and disestablish religion. The move-ment was steady if uneven. Rhode Island did not grant Jews the right to vote or hold office until 1842; North Carolina did not do so until 1868.

GERMAN JEWS   Until significant numbers of Jews from German-speaking ar-eas of Europe arrived in the United States during the 1840's, the Jewish popu-lation remained small. In 1840, probably fewer than 15,000 Jews were in the United States; when Jewish immigration from Slavic lands began to increase in 1880, there were an estimated 250,000. Unlike their Sephardic predeces-sors, these Jews used Ashkenazic rituals and many spoke Yiddish. The vast ma-jority of migrants were young men and women reacting to economic and po-litical changes that worsened the position of Jews in their home countries.

The German Jewish immigrants flourished in the New World and greatly valued the political and economic freedoms they enjoyed in the United States. As the nation expanded, the young men moved west, some beginning as peddlers serving the scattered farmsteads, then opening mercantile estab-lishments in the towns; a few very successful merchants established major de-partment stores in the new cities. Their services were appreciated by their fel-low townspeople; the first settlers in a town often became respected political and social leaders. During the early years of this migration, a small, thinly scattered Jewish population made finding Jewish marriage partners difficult, and a significant percentage married Gentiles. As they became economically successful, they founded families and brought young relatives to join them. Increased population meant Jews could create their own communal organi-zations, first a synagogue and a cemetery, then clubs that eased social iso-lation, and also philanthropic organizations to care for the poor and the el-derly. Often unable to observe the Sabbath as commanded by orthodox

Jewish law, they were particularly receptive to the relaxed requirements of the Reform movement, designed to modernize Judaism, that had already begun in Germany.

During the nineteenth century, a number of anti-Semitic incidents occurred in the United States. Civil War general Ulysses S. Grant issued an order calling for the expulsion of all Jews from his army department on December 17, 1862, after hearing that some were trading with the enemy. President Abraham Lincoln reversed the order shortly thereafter. When financially successful German Jews began to arrive in resorts that had been the preserve of the highest-ranking social groups of the United States, they experienced prejudice and discrimination. Famous resorts near New York such as Saratoga, Newport, and Long Branch began to turn away Jews, even wealthy New York City investment bankers. Lesser hotels began to use code words such as "restricted clientele" or "discriminating families only" in their advertisements.

EASTERN EUROPEAN JEWS Between 1881 and 1924, approximately 2.5 million Jews, about one-third of the Jewish population of eastern Europe, left their homelands; nearly 2 million came to the United States. The modernization of agriculture in eastern Europe had eliminated many of the petty merchant and artisan occupations on which Jews depended. The major reason for the timing and scale of the migration, however, was the impact of government-sponsored anti-Semitism, especially the pogroms (anti-Jewish massacres) encouraged by the Russian government after the assassination of Czar Alexan-

Early twentieth century scene in a section of New York City that was so predominantly Jewish that it was known as "Little Jerusalem." (Library of Congress)

445

der II in 1881. Unlike the German Jews who had preceded them, these Jews concentrated in major cities, especially on the East Coast. Unlike other European groups of the period, few would return to their countries of origin. Theirs was a migration of families, with an almost even sex ratio. Lacking financial resources, they crowded into the poorest sections of the cities.

The German Jews did not welcome them. Class and cultural arrogance, anxiety that they would be burdened by masses of poor, and fear that the huge influx would exacerbate the already increasing anti-Semitism in the United States led to negative reactions toward the newcomers. Only slowly did the prosperous German Jews overcome their dislike and provide philanthropic support for those needing help. Not until the lynching of murder defendant Leo Frank in Georgia in 1913, amid violent anti-Jewish attacks, did they organize the Anti-Defamation League to combat anti-Semitism.

The reaction of the non-Jewish community was even more negative. Old-line Yankees viewed the Jewish areas of cities as a foreign intrusion corrupting the fabric of American society. Psychologists, using intelligence tests to rank ethnic groups, placed these Jews at the bottom, calling them genetically defective and ineducable. Immigration restrictionists claimed the eastern European Jews proved the need to close the United States to new immigrants.

ANTI-JEWISH PREJUDICE AND DISCRIMINATION Dislike and fear of the newly arriving Jews helped spur the drive to restrict immigration, which took the form of legislation in 1924. It also provoked an outburst of overt prejudice and discrimination in the years from 1920 to 1940. As the children of the massive eastern European Jewish immigration began to enter colleges and professional schools, they faced direct discrimination. Columbia College established quotas limiting admission of Jewish candidates, and other prestigious colleges and medical schools followed its example during the 1920's. Economic opportunities narrowed as few manufacturing companies, corporate law firms, major banks and insurance companies, or government bureaucracies such as the State Department were willing to employ Jews. Restrictive covenants, which barred homeowners from selling their houses to Jewish Americans or members of other "undesirable" groups, proliferated.

In 1922, Henry Ford began to publish a seven-year-long series of anti-Jewish articles in his newspaper, *The Dearborn Independent,* propagating older European stereotypes of Jews as both international bankers conspiring to control the country and communist conspirators determined to undermine capitalism. During the 1930's, the rise of Adolf Hitler inspired right-wing orators to preach ideological anti-Semitism. They defended Hitler, blaming Jews for the Great Depression and the international crises in Europe. More than one hundred anti-Semitic organizations appeared across the nation. In New York City, the Christian Front held street-corner rallies that often ended in fistfights between adherents of the movement and Jewish passersby.

The reluctance to respond effectively to the plight of German Jews during the 1930's reflected the impact of prejudice against Jews. No agency enforced

MILESTONES IN JEWISH IMMIGRATION HISTORY

Year	Event
1654	Arrival of twenty-three Jews, the first in North America, in New Amsterdam
1820-1880	Major years of German Jewish immigration
1880-1924	Major years of Eastern European Jewish immigration
1881-1883	Anti-Jewish pogroms in Russia after the assassination of Alexander II
1892	Foundation of American Jewish Historical Society
1906	American Jewish Committee founded to aid Jews abroad
1913	Leo Frank is lynched; raises fears of persecution in Jewish community
1913	Anti-Defamation League of B'nai B'rith founded to combat prejudice
1922	Henry Ford begins publishing anti-Semitic propaganda in his newspaper
1924	Restrictive immigration law passes, ending large-scale immigration
1933	Adolf Hitler elected chancellor of Germany
1939	United Jewish Appeal organized to coordinate relief for Hitler's victims
1939-1945	Holocaust kills about six million Jews
1948	Israel proclaims independence
1984	Anti-Semitic slurs made during Jesse Jackson's presidential campaign worry Jews
1991	Conflict erupts between Jews and blacks in Crown Heights in Brooklyn

immigration restriction rules more rigidly than the United States consular service in Germany, which insisted on absolute proof of the ability of prospective immigrants to be self-supporting. As a result, despite the desperate need of German Jews to escape, between 1933 to 1940 some 30 percent of the visas available for Germans were never issued.

POST-WORLD WAR II American revulsion at the sight of photographs of Hitler's death camps changed attitudes toward Jews. Overt anti-Semitism was no longer acceptable, and relations of Jews with other ethnic groups eased.

When the courts refused to enforce restrictive covenants, the movement of Jews out of cities and into suburbs increased. Restrictions on college entry and job opportunities began to disappear. New York City home offices of major insurance companies, embarrassed by the revelation that they did not employ any Jewish stenographers in a city with a huge Jewish population, hastened to change their practices. The founding of the state of Israel and its survival under attack increased Jewish pride and improved American perceptions of Jews; they now appeared a normal ethnic group, not greatly different in its support of Old World nationalism from American Poles or Irish Americans.

Although pre-World War II anti-Semitism had surfaced predominantly among members of the Right, during the radical upheaval of the 1960's, Jews began to experience overt expressions of prejudice from members of the Left. Support of Israel when it was attacked by its Arab neighbors was a rallying point for all branches of the Jewish community. To Jewish ears, advocacy of Palestinian rights by radicals too often sounded like attacks on Jews, rather than simply criticisms of Israeli policy.

Even more disturbing was the open expression of anti-Jewish prejudices by African Americans. The long-term alliance of the two groups in the fight for civil rights seemed a thing of the past. Verbal attacks by Louis Farrakhan and his Nation of Islam followers and the slur against New York Jews uttered by Jesse Jackson in his 1984 presidential campaign were particularly worrisome because African Americans seemed the only major group believing it acceptable to express such prejudices publicly. Verbal and physical violence against Jewish shopkeepers in Harlem and the riots in Brooklyn's Crown Heights neighborhood intensified the feelings of antagonism between African Americans and Jews.

Greater acceptance by other Americans helped raise the rate of outmarriage by Jews to more than 30 percent, which, combined with a birthrate that dropped below replacement level, led to fears that the American Jewish population would decline and ultimately disappear. Others were more optimistic, believing that many of the children of outmarriages would remain Jews. Immigration from Israel and the Soviet Union increased the Jewish community. Estimates in 1996 indicated that the Jewish population was stable at almost 6 million people who made up just more than 2 percent of the total American population.

Milton Berman

FURTHER READING

Agosin, Marjorie. *Uncertain Travelers: Conversations with Jewish Women Immigrants to America.* Edited by Mary G. Berg. Hanover, N.H.: University Press of New England, 1999. Fascinating collection of firsthand stories related by Jewish immigrants.

Cohen, Naomi Werner. *Encounter with Emancipation: The German Jews in the United States, 1830-1914.* Philadelphia: Jewish Publication Society of America, 1984. Scholarly study of the reaction of this group to legal equality and citizenship.

Gerber, David, ed. *Anti-Semitism in American History.* Urbana: University of Illinois Press, 1986. Collection of thirteen scholarly articles exploring American attitudes toward Jews.

Greene, Victor R. *A Singing Ambivalence: American Immigrants Between Old World and New, 1830-1930.* Kent, Ohio: Kent State University Press, 2004. Comparative study of the different challenges faced by members of eight major immigrant groups, including eastern European Jews.

Howe, Irving. *World of Our Fathers.* New York: Harcourt Brace Jovanovich, 1976. Well-written description of the life of eastern European Jews in New York City.

Lohuis, Elisabeth ten. *Towards a Winning of the West: Novels by East European Jewish Immigrants to America and Their American Offspring.* [Leiden: s.n., 2003]. Insightful examination of the literature of immigrant Jews.

Marcus, Jacob R. *The Colonial American Jew, 1492-1776.* 3 vols. Detroit, Mich.: Wayne State University Press, 1970. Definitive study of Jewish immigrants during America's long colonial era.

Sola Pool, David de, and Tamara de Sola Pool. *An Old Faith in the New World: Portrait of Shearith Israel, 1654-1954.* New York: Columbia University Press, 1955. Describes the experience of the Sephardic Jewish community through the history of the oldest synagogue in the United States.

Sterba, Christopher M. *The Melting Pot Goes to War: Italian and Jewish Immigrants in America's Great Crusade, 1917-1919.* Ann Arbor, Mich.: UMI, 1999. Scholarly study of the role of immigrants in American fighting forces during World War I.

SEE ALSO American Jewish Committee; Ashkenazic and German Jewish immigrants; Eastern European Jewish immigrants; Israeli immigrants; Jewish settlement of New York; Jews and Arab Americans; Sephardic Jews; Soviet Jewish immigrants.

JEWISH SETTLEMENT OF NEW YORK

THE EVENT: Settlement of the first Jewish immigrants in North America
DATE: August-September, 1654
PLACE: Manhattan Island

IMMIGRATION ISSUES: European immigrants; Jewish immigrants; Refugees; Religion

Significance: The right of Jewish immigrants to live and work in New Netherland, despite intense opposition, laid the groundwork for greater religious toleration.

The first Jewish settlers of record in New Amsterdam were Jacob Barsimon and Solomon Pieterson, both of whom came from Holland in the summer of 1654. The next month, twenty-three other Jews arrived, both old and young, refugees from the Portuguese conquest of Dutch Brazil (New Holland), which had been the richest property of the Dutch West India Company in America. After leaving Recife, Brazil, their ship had been captured by Spanish pirates, from whom they were saved by a French privateer, the *St. Charles*, captained by Jacques de La Motthe. Having little more than the clothes on their backs, the Jewish migrants convinced La Motthe to carry them to New Amsterdam for twenty-five hundred guilders, which they hoped to borrow in that Dutch port. They shortly discovered, however, what Barsimon and Pieterson were already learning: There was much opposition to Jews settling in New Netherland.

Their poverty made the Dutch Jews from Brazil especially vulnerable. Unable to borrow the money, they asked La Motthe for extra time to contact friends and receive money from Amsterdam. Rather than waiting, La Motthe brought suit in the City Court of New Amsterdam, which ordered that their meager belongings should be sold at public auction. Even after all that was

Modern depiction of Dutch colonial governor Peter Stuyvesant (with wooden leg) at the time of the British occupation of New Amsterdam in 1664. (Library of Congress)

worth selling had been sold, the unfortunate exiles still owed almost five hundred guilders. The City Court then ordered that two of the Jews—David Israel and Moses Ambroisius—should be held under civil arrest until the total debt was paid. In October, the matter finally was resolved after the crew of the *St. Charles*, holding title to the remainder of the Jewish debt, agreed to wait until additional funds could be sent from Amsterdam.

The ordeal of the Jewish refugees was far from over. They wanted to remain in New Amsterdam, Director General Peter Stuyvesant complained to the Amsterdam Chamber of the Dutch West India Company. Stuyvesant was against their staying, as were the city magistrates, who resented "their customary usury and deceitful trading with the Christians," and the deacons of the Reformed Church, who feared that in "their present indigence they might become a charge in the coming winter." Indicating that the colonists generally shared his anti-Semitic views, Stuyvesant informed the Amsterdam directors that "we have for the benefit of this weak and newly developing place and the land in general, deemed it useful to require them in a friendly way to depart." As for the future, he urged

> that the deceitful race—such hateful enemies and blasphemers of the name of Christ—be not allowed further to infect and trouble this new colony, to the detraction of your Worships and the dissatisfaction of your Worships' most affectionate subjects.

Despite his vehemence against the Jews, Stuyvesant delayed his expulsion order, waiting instead for guidance from the Amsterdam Chamber of the Dutch West India Company, to whom the unwanted refugees were also appealing. The Jewish community in Amsterdam took up their cause. During the early sixteenth century, the embattled United Provinces—and especially the city of Amsterdam—had become a haven for persecuted European Jews, whose many contributions to Dutch economic and cultural life had brought them considerable religious freedom, political and legal rights, and economic privileges. Not only did Jewish investors own approximately 4 percent of the Dutch West India Company's stock, but also, more than six hundred Dutch Jews had participated in colonizing Dutch Brazil. Virtually all of them left Pernambuco in 1654 with other Dutch nationals, losing practically everything, although the conquering Portuguese had urged them to remain and promised to protect their property. Their loyalty to the Dutch republic could hardly be questioned. Moreover, thinly populated New Netherland desperately needed settlers.

On the other hand, Dominie Johannes Megapolensis, one of the leading Dutch Reformed preachers in New Netherland, was especially disturbed because a few additional Jewish families recently had migrated from Amsterdam. He called upon the Amsterdam Classis of the Reformed Church to use its influence to have the Jews expelled from the American colony. "These people have no other God than the Mammon of unrighteousness," warned

Megapolensis, "and no other aim than to get possession of Christian property, and to overcome all other merchants by drawing all trade toward themselves." Surely, Megapolensis pleaded, these "godless rascals" should be expelled.

Expressing some sympathy for Stuyvesant's anti-Jewish prejudice, the Amsterdam Chamber nevertheless announced in early 1655 that Jews could travel, trade, and live in New Netherland, provided they cared for their own poor. Over the next few years, while not directly defying the company's directive, Stuyvesant and other civil officials delayed, obstructed, and otherwise made life more difficult for the Jews of New Amsterdam. In March, 1655, for example, Abraham de Lucena was arrested for selling goods on Sunday. In July, de Lucena and others petitioned to purchase land for a Jewish cemetery, but were denied. Indeed, Jews were not allowed to purchase land in New Amsterdam. They also were exempted from the city militia, on grounds that other colonists would not serve with them, but were required to pay a heavy tax each month in lieu of service.

The Jews of New Amsterdam resented and resisted such treatment. In November, when Asser Levy and Jacob Barsimon, two young Jews with little money, protested the tax and asked to do service with the militia instead, the town council dismissed their protest and noted that the petitioners could choose to go elsewhere. The same message was conveyed by the heavy rates imposed upon Jews in the general levy to raise funds for rebuilding the city's defense wall. Most discouraging were the restrictions placed on Jews who wished to trade to Albany and Delaware Bay.

In 1656, the Amsterdam Chamber chastised Stuyvesant and insisted that Jews in New Netherland were to have the same rights and privileges as Jews in old Amsterdam. They could trade wholesale, rent and buy property, and enjoy the protection of the law as other Dutch citizens did. However, their religious freedom did not extend to public worship, and they were not allowed to sell retail, work as mechanics, or live and work outside a designated area of town. Despite the opposition of the Burgomasters and Schepens, Stuyvesant, ever the faithful servant of the Dutch West India Company, insisted that Levy be admitted to the burgher right, which allowed him to run a business, vote in town elections, and even hold office. New Amsterdam Jews were not ghettoized, and they could work as mechanics and tradesmen as well as shopkeepers and merchants. Levy became the first Jewish landowner and was one of two Jews licensed as butchers in 1660.

Prejudice remained, but social and economic acceptance came to the Jewish community in New Amsterdam. They were allowed their separate burial ground, and their right to observe the Sabbath on Saturday was respected. They never established a synagogue and may not have had enough people to maintain a congregation, but regular religious services apparently were held. Levy owned a Torah, and others had prayer books and shawls. Most of the Jews in New Amsterdam were Sephardim, descended from Portuguese Jews, although a few were Ashkenazim Jews from Germany, France, and eastern Europe. Their numbers remained quite small, never more than a handful of families, and there seems to have been a good deal of migration in and out. However, the Jews of New Amsterdam were pioneers who prepared the way for the more extensive Jewish community that would emerge in early New York.

Ronald W. Howard

FURTHER READING

Hershkowitz, Leo. "Judaism." In *The Encyclopedia of the North American Colonies*, edited by Jacob Ernest Cook. Vol. 3. New York: Charles Scribner's Sons, 1993. Brief but incisive summary of colonial Judaism.

Kessler, Henry H., and Eugene Rachlis. *Peter Stuyvesant and His New York*. New York: Random House, 1959. Gives insight into the anti-Semitism of Dutch Calvinism and the cooperative efforts of Stuyvesant and the Dutch Reformed preachers against the Jews.

Marcus, Jacob R. *The Colonial American Jew, 1492-1776*. 3 vols. Detroit, Mich.: Wayne State University Press, 1970. Presents a detailed survey of the Jewish experience in early America, relating connections between the various Jewish communities.

Oppenheim, Samuel. *The Early History of the Jews in New York, 1654-1664*. New York: American Jewish Historical Society, 1909. Basic source for details on early Jewish settlers and their trials, tribulations, and successes.

Rink, Oliver A. *Holland on the Hudson: An Economic and Social History of Dutch New York*. Ithaca, N.Y.: Cornell University Press, 1986. An account that relates the Jewish migration to larger economic and social developments in New Netherland.

Smith, George L. *Religion and Trade in New Netherland: Dutch Origins and American Development*. Ithaca, N.Y.: Cornell University Press, 1973. An analysis of religious toleration that emerged in the northern Netherlands and its transference to New Netherland.

Wepman, Dennis. *Immigration: From the Founding of Virginia to the Closing of Ellis Island*. New York: Facts On File, 2002. History of immigration to the United States from the earliest European settlements of the colonial era through the mid-1950's, with liberal extracts from contemporary documents.

SEE ALSO American Jewish Committee; Ashkenazic and German Jewish immigrants; Eastern European Jewish immigrants; Israeli immigrants; Jamestown colony; Jewish immigrants; Jews and Arab Americans; Sephardic Jews; Soviet Jewish immigrants.

JEWS AND ARAB AMERICANS

IMMIGRATION ISSUES: Demographics; European immigrants; Jewish immigrants; Middle Eastern immigrants; Religion; Stereotypes

SIGNIFICANCE: Jewish Americans and Arab Americans conflict in their views of Israel, Palestinians, and the Middle East. Although some members of both groups take inflexible stances in their opposition to each other, other members are trying to bridge the gaps between the cultures.

Some scholars estimate that as many as three million Arabs and Arab Americans live in the United States, a significantly larger number than the 1.2 million Arab Americans counted in the 2000 U.S. Census. An accurate count is difficult to obtain because many Arab Americans are reluctant to reveal their origin for fear of discrimination or even violence from those Americans who, perhaps influenced by negative press coverage of Arabs and events in the Middle East, stereotype Arab Americans as terrorists or as anti-American.

U.S. government figures in 1994 place the number of Jewish Americans at 6 million—4 million religious and 2 million secular Jews. However, because some Jews, like Arab Americans, are reluctant to reveal their religious and ethnic identity for fear of discrimination, their actual numbers must be assumed to be greater. Of the 6 million American Jews, about 250,000 are Sephardic Jews. Of those Sephardic Jews, about 85,000 are Arab Jews, that is, Jews from Arab nations. Arab Jews in the United States are largely from Syria, Egypt, Yemen, Iraq, Saudi Arabia, Tunisia, and Morocco. If Arab Jewish Americans are included in the Arab American population, the total number of Arab Americans is significantly increased. The largest population of Arab Jews in the United States is in Brooklyn, New York. This community of Syrian Jews is stable and affluent.

ORIGINS AND DEMOGRAPHICS   Arab Americans and Jewish Americans come from very diverse backgrounds and subcultures that sometimes seriously conflict. However, they are very much alike in terms of being better educated and more affluent than the average American.

Arab Americans trace their origins to the twenty-one countries of the Arab League (established on March 22, 1945): Algeria, Bahrain, Djibouti, Egypt, Iraq, Jordan, Kuwait, Lebanon, Libya, Mauritania, Morocco, Oman, Palestine, Qatar, Saudi Arabia, Somalia, Sudan, Syria, Tunisia, United Arab Emirates, and Yemen. The earliest Arab immigrants, who arrived between 1900 and World War II, were predominantly Christians from Syria and Lebanon. Most had little formal education and were predominantly illiterate. Their success in running small family businesses, mostly in poor neighborhoods, made it possible for their children to become well educated and enter the professions or obtain high-level, white-collar jobs. Following World War II and especially after 1965, when quota restrictions were lifted, Arab immigration increased significantly. These newer immigrants were more affluent, better educated, largely Muslim professionals and businesspeople.

Arab Americans, affluent and well educated, are one of the most successful ethnic groups in the United States. About half of all Arab Americans live in large metropolitan areas, and around 20 percent in three urban areas: Detroit, Michigan, New York, and Los Angeles-Long Beach. Detroit has the largest Arab American population, which is divided roughly equally between Christians and Muslims. The 1990 U.S. Census obtained the national origins of Arab Americans in the state of Michigan. Of the 77,070 people reporting Arab ancestry, 39,673 had Lebanese roots, 7,656 Syrian, 6,668 Iraqi, 2,695 Palestinian, 1,785 Egyptian, 1,441 Jordanian, 14,842 unspecified Arab or Arabic, and 2,310 other Arab. The census also counted 14,724 persons of Assyrian (Chaldean) ancestry. Assyrians were not included with other Arabs because most members of this group do not consider themselves Arabs.

Jews have been in North America for almost four hundred years. The earliest immigrants were Sephardic Jews in the seventeenth century in New York. The nineteenth century saw the arrival of Ashkenazic Jews from Germany and the surrounding areas. They often worked as merchants and soon became prosperous. During the late nineteenth century, eastern European Jews, many of them lacking resources, migrated in great numbers to the United States, often settling in cities. These late arrivals faced prejudice from both non-Jewish Americans and the earlier German Jews. After World War II and the Holocaust, anti-Semitism diminished greatly, and all Jewish groups found greater acceptance in the United States. Most Jews came to the United States from Europe to escape religious persecution and poverty and, like Arab Americans, have prospered in their adopted country. Both groups are predominantly urban dwellers.

ARAB AND JEWISH AMERICAN RELATIONS   Ironically, the conflicts in the Middle East have brought Arab Americans and Jewish Americans closer. Most of the efforts to improve intergroup relations have centered on events not in the United States but in the Middle East, where Israel and many members of the Arab League have been at war or in conflict since the establishment of the Arab League in 1945 and of the state of Israel in 1948.

The Arab Americans and Jewish Americans most opposed to a just and equitable settlement of the plight of the Palestinians have been the religiously orthodox and fundamentalistic members of the two groups. Those most willing to talk about peace and justice have been the more liberal Jews (Reform and secular Jews) and progressive Arabs. Most of the initiatives toward bringing Arabs and Jews together have generally originated with Jewish Americans and been supported enthusiastically by Arab Americans. A big impediment to improving Arab-Jewish relations has been the conservative and orthodox newspapers published exclusively for Arabs and Jews. Their biases and preju-

CITIES WITH THE LARGEST ARAB AND JEWISH POPULATIONS

Arab Americans	Jewish Americans
1. Detroit, Mich. (metropolitan area)	1. New York (metropolitan area)
2. New York (metropolitan area)	2. Los Angeles, Calif.
3. Los Angeles, Calif.	3. Miami, Fla.
4. Washington, D.C.	4. Philadelphia, Pa.
5. Chicago, Ill.	5. Chicago, Ill.
6. Boston, Mass.	6. Boston, Mass.
7. Anaheim-Santa Ana, Calif.	7. San Francisco, Calif.
8. Bergen-Passaic, N.J.	8. Washington, D.C.
9. Houston, Texas	9. W. Palm Beach-Boca Raton, Fla.
10. Cleveland, Ohio	10. Baltimore, Md.

Sources: Samia El-Badry, "The Arab-American Market," American Demographics, Vol. 16, January, 1994, pages 22-30; David Singer, ed., American Jewish Year Book, 1997. New York: American Jewish Committee, 1997.

dices—and sometimes blatant hatred— often stand in the way of improving intergroup relations. The politics of the Middle East and their effect on American Arabs and Jews have been the focus of social-action organizations in both communities.

ORGANIZATIONS WORKING FOR TOGETHERNESS   On the national level, few organizations have been as active and effective in bringing Arabs and Jews together as the New Jewish Agenda (NJA). Founded during the late 1970's, at its height it had twenty-eight chapters, most of which were in the large urban areas where Jewish Americans and Arab Americans live and work. NJA was started by Jews who felt that conservatives had dominated Jewish life in the United States and who yearned to create a strong progressive voice in the Jewish community. One of its major goals has been to have ongoing Jewish-Arab dialogues on crucial matters of mutual concern to Jews and Arabs in the United States and the Middle East, especially resolution of the Israeli-Palestinian question. Los Angeles, which has one of the largest concentrations of Jews and Arabs in the United States, has a dialogue group organized much like an NJA group. However, the Los Angeles group concentrates on Arab-Jewish issues and does not discuss issues such as racism, anti-Semitism, and nuclear disarmament, which are covered by NJA groups.

American Arab and Jewish Friends (AAJF) was founded in 1981 by George Bashara (an Arab American) and Arnold Michlin (a Jewish American) in metropolitan Detroit. It is a program of the Greater Detroit Interfaith Round Table of the National Conference for Community and Justice (formerly known as the National Conference of Christians and Jews). The AAJF's purpose is to improve mutual understanding and friendship between the Arab and Jewish communities by coming together informally through luncheons, dinners, forums, and its sponsorship of an annual essay scholarship contest for graduating seniors in area high schools. The essays, which describe innovative and meaningful approaches toward the realization of the AAJF goal, are the joint effort of two students, one Jewish and one Arab American.

In large cities such as Washington, D.C., where there are sizable Arab American and Jewish American populations, the two groups often meet at friendly gatherings held by organizations such as the Washington Area Jews for Israeli-Palestinian Peace-Friendship. For several decades, this organization has regularly held dinners where Arabs and Jews can become friends, discuss the issues that divide them, and make efforts to influence policymakers who may be in a position to initiate positive changes in the bitter conflicts that separate Israelis and Palestinians.

The Seeds of Peace summer camp was started by former newspaper editor John Wallach during the early 1990's. The Otisfield, Maine, camp brings together more than 160 teenagers from the Middle East—Palestinian Arabs and Jewish Israelis as well as American Jewish and Arab youngsters—for a month of good, healthy fun as well as serious discussions. Participants are selected by their governments after writing essays on making peace. To run the camp costs about $1.2 million per year, which Wallach receives in private donations. All the campers come on scholarships, each worth around $2,000. The camp has been so successful that other such camps are being organized elsewhere in the United States.

The Middle East Friendship League was established by Professor Robert Frumkin and his colleagues at Kent State University in Kent, Ohio, following the killing of Israeli wrestlers by Arabs at the Olympic Games in Munich, Germany, in 1972. Kent State had a large number of students and faculty from Arab League nations and Israel as well as a sizable number of American Arab and Jewish students and faculty, making it an ideal setting for an experiment in improving Arab and Jewish relations. Although the main purpose of the organization was to promote friendships between Arabs and Jews, its members discussed Middle East issues and engaged in social activism aimed at enhancing the peace process and addressing issues such as Palestinian rights and terrorism. The league met monthly for several years, during which real friendships developed and remained strong even after it disbanded.

RIGHT-WING ORGANIZATIONS No discussion of Arab-Jewish relations in the United States is complete without a mention of the Jewish Defense League (JDL) and Jewish Defense Organization (JDO), two right-wing organizations that are the antithesis of all the previously discussed organizations. The JDL and the JDO are pathologically anti-Arab. The JDL, founded by the late Meir Kahane, was not only involved in defamation of Arab Americans but also the destruction of Arab American property and even murder, including the Arab American leader Alex Odeh. Although, according to the *Encyclopedia of Associations* (published by Gale Research), the JDL is no longer functioning in the

United States, its sister organization, the JDO, is. The JDO has almost four thousand members in ten states. Like the JDL, the JDO states that it will defend Jews by any means necessary and advocates the use of violence. Although the JDL frequently took credit for violent and destructive acts against Arab Americans and their property, the JDO, thus far, has not.

R. M. Frumkin

FURTHER READING

Ashabranner, Brent. *An Ancient Heritage: The Arab-American Minority.* New York: HarperCollins, 1991. Well-balanced book that deals fairly with American Arab and Jewish relations.

Haddad, Yvonne Yazbeck. *Not Quite American? The Shaping of Arab and Muslim Identity in the United States.* Waco, Tex.: Baylor University Press, 2004. Study of the special problems faced by Arab and other Muslim Americans in the aftermath of the September 11, 2001, terrorist attacks that turned many Americans against Arab immigrants.

Levy, Mordecai. *By Any Means Necessary.* New York: Jewish Defense Organization, 1998. Publication of the Jewish Defense Organization that provides insights into the organization's philosophy.

McCarus, Ernest, ed. *The Development of Arab-American Identity.* Ann Arbor: University of Michigan Press, 1994. Excellent anthology that covers every important aspect of the Arab American experience.

Murphy, Caryle. "There's Mideast Peace in the Wilds of Maine." *Washington Post,* August 16, 1997. Discussion of the Seeds of Peace program.

Stroberg, Gerald S. *American Jews.* Garden City, N.Y.: Doubleday, 1974. Study of Jewish Americans' struggle with identity issues.

SEE ALSO   American Jewish Committee; Arab American intergroup relations; Arab immigrants; Ashkenazic and German Jewish immigrants; Eastern European Jewish immigrants; Israeli immigrants; Jewish immigrants; Jewish settlement of New York; Middle Eastern immigrant families; Muslims; Sephardic Jews; Soviet Jewish immigrants.

JUSTICE AND IMMIGRATION

DEFINITION: Issues of fairness, legality, and justice relating to immigration

IMMIGRATION ISSUES: Border control; Illegal immigration; Laws and treaties; Mexican immigrants

SIGNIFICANCE: Immigration constitutes a major source of population growth in the United States; it affects national and regional economic health, ethnic and cultural diversity, utilization of governmental services, and other domestic conditions and raises many issues that pose questions of justice and fair play.

For much of the twentieth century, the United States has absorbed more legal immigrants than the other countries of the world combined. In addition to legal immigration, each year several hundred thousand persons enter the country to reside illegally. During the 1990's, about one in four foreigners settling in the United States did so in violation of immigration laws. Immigration affects American society in fundamental ways, but the costs, benefits, and moral obligations surrounding immigration are matters of dispute. The debate over immigration is fraught with conflicting statistics and conflicting values and centers on three primary topics: humanitarianism, economics, and nationhood.

HUMANITARIANISM A large part of the rationale for accepting immigrants into the United States stems from humanitarian concerns. In theory, U.S. policies seek to assist people of other nations who experience political oppression, discrimination, famine, civil war, or any number of other tribulations. In this context, allowing individuals to try to escape the worst of their problems by immigrating to the United States can be seen as a form of international aid.

The United States, like most Western democratic countries, offers asylum to refugees of political repression. The United States distinguishes between political refugees fleeing persecution and economic refugees seeking a better standard of living. The system, however, is subject to inefficiency and abuse. Ascertaining whether a person is a political or economic refugee is a difficult and time-consuming task. Typically, there is a large backlog of asylum cases awaiting official action, and while the government is processing a case, the applicant may become "lost" within the general population. Such cases constitute one source of illegal immigration. Government efforts to locate and repatriate these illegal refugees are often ineffective. Moreover, many such enforcement actions raise justice issues of their own. Some groups in the United States have dedicated themselves to shielding illegal immigrants from immigration authorities and laws. Such efforts reached a peak during the 1980's, when a number of churches and even cities declared themselves "sanctuaries" for aliens who did not have official refugee status.

American public sentiment for political refugees has fluctuated widely over time. The anticommunist and anti-Soviet feelings prevalent during the Cold War made dissidents and defectors from Eastern Europe and the Soviet Union especially welcome. Unusually brutal governmental crackdowns, such as those by the Chinese government at Tiananmen Square in 1989, raise public sympathy for political refugees, particularly for activists fighting for democracy.

Poignant examples of human tragedy, such as ethnic cleansing in Bosnia and the warehousing of orphans in postcommunist Romania, can spur Americans to adopt foreign children and to sponsor the immigration of adults and families. Some international crises, such as the fall of South Vietnam during the mid-1970's, dramatically increase the number of political refugees coming to the United States. These large waves of refugees can fatigue American public support for immigration. Further, incidents of international terrorism inflicted upon Americans can reduce public acceptance of foreign immigrants (particularly when they belong to groups associated with terrorism, rightly or wrongly, in the public consciousness).

ECONOMICS   Persons without any claim of experiencing political repression can also apply to immigrate to the United States. Many are motivated by economic and societal opportunities. Traditionally, immigration of this sort has contributed significantly to the growth of the U.S. population and economy. A rapid influx of immigrants, however, may overwhelm the country's ability to assimilate them, burdening social services and housing stocks, absorbing employment opportunities, and heightening racial and ethnic tensions. The net economic effects of the presence of immigrants is a matter of debate. Proponents claim that immigrants tend to pay more in taxes than they receive in social services, that they perform jobs American citizens prefer not to take, and that they tend to have a strong work ethic. Yet to the extent that immigrants have lower levels of education and lower wage demands—both are particularly true of illegal immigrants—their presence may skew the economy toward more service-oriented, labor-intensive jobs. The presence of a surplus of cheap labor may reduce incentives to invest in greater mechanization. Some critics charge that large numbers of immigrants make finding employment more difficult for poor Americans, particularly for poor members of minority groups.

To regulate those effects, the federal government controls immigration through eligibility requirements and numerical limits. Deciding who will and will not be permitted to immigrate raises obvious justice issues. Until the mid-1960's, government established immigration quotas on the basis of nationality, at times excluding some national and racial groups entirely. Since the mid-1960's, permission to immigrate to the United States has been awarded largely by lottery.

Persons who are unable to secure legal resident status may resort to illegal means for entering the country. In response, the U.S. government has taken steps to block illegal border crossings. In 1924, the U.S. Border Patrol was established to police the country's borders. The Mexican border is more heavily policed than the Canadian and has been fortified with surveillance devices and metal fencing. These measures have led some critics to identify the U.S.-Mexico border with the infamous Berlin Wall, although others argue that the imprisonment of people within a country and the exclusion of people from a country concern different questions of morality.

U.S. efforts to limit immigration involve economic and market forces in a number of ways. The perceived promise of economic opportunity in the

United States, coupled with immigration restrictions, has given rise to human smuggling operations, particularly in Mexico. During the early 1990's, about half the aliens illegally entering the United States were assisted in some way by smugglers. In addition to taking police measures, the U.S. government has tried to stem illegal immigration by reducing the incentives for it.

The 1994 North American Free Trade Agreement (NAFTA) was touted in part for its projected role in improving economic opportunities in Mexico, thus reducing the incentive to emigrate. At the same time, governmental benefits to illegal aliens were restricted, partly in the hope that such limitations will make the prospect of living illegally in the United States less attractive. Federal welfare payments, food stamps, unemployment compensation, and other federal benefits are available to legal, but not to illegal, immigrants; however, primary education and medical services cannot be withheld from illegal aliens. In ruling on such issues, the U.S. Supreme Court has held that the equal protection clause of the Fourteenth Amendment does not depend on citizenship status.

THE BORDER STATES Border states have been especially sensitive to the economic and social costs of illegal immigration. These states often bear the brunt of service provision, infrastructure maintenance, law enforcement, and other social costs of illegal immigration. In 1994, California voters passed Proposition 187, a referendum that sought to deny state benefits, including health care, welfare, and education, to illegal aliens. (The referendum was immediately challenged as unconstitutional.) Some states have sued the federal government for the costs of supporting illegal aliens, asserting that the federal government was negligent in not stopping such aliens at the country's borders. Border states have also challenged federal census figures, arguing that the allocation of federal benefits (including apportionment of congressional seats) should account for illegal aliens.

RACE, ETHNICITY, AND NATIONHOOD Although the humanitarian motives that ostensibly underlie many U.S. immigration laws seldom are defined in terms of race and ethnicity, the federal government frequently has controlled immigration on the basis of national origin. Beginning during the 1920's, the United States established immigration quotas defined by national origin. Immigrants from European countries historically have been favored.

Immigration patterns have shifted dramatically over time, however, and not always as a result of changes to U.S. immigration policy. During the 1950's, most immigrants came from Europe and Canada. By the 1970's, partly as a result of international events, the majority of immigrants were coming from Asia, Central America, and the Caribbean. The effects of different immigration patterns are compounded by higher birthrates among some immigrant groups; such effects are further accentuated by the disproportionate number of young adults among persons immigrating to the United States.

Consideration of immigration in terms of race and nationality raises the

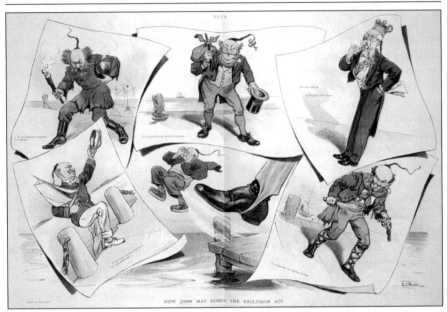

One of the most discriminatory pieces of immigration legislation in U.S. history was the aptly named Chinese Exclusion Act of 1882. This early twentieth century illustration from Puck *suggests five ways in which a Chinese immigrant ("John") might enter the United States in violation of the act: as an anarchist, as an Irishman, as an English wife-hunter, as a yacht racer, or as a Sicilian. A joke underlying this cartoon was the fact that all five alternative immigrant types that it depicts were also unpopular in the United States. (Library of Congress)*

question of how the American people should be defined as a nation. The sense of American nationhood stems more from shared morals, values, and norms than from ethnic, racial, or even cultural characteristics. Yet the traditional conception of the United States as a "melting pot" of various ethnic and racial groups was challenged during the 1980's and 1990's by critics who claimed that such a concept unfairly pressures immigrants and racial minorities to conform to a largely white, middle-class culture. In its place, such critics offered a "salad bowl" metaphor of the United States, envisioning the various cultures of America's citizens as retained in a diverse mosaic. In this view, assimilation, including perhaps even the mastery of English language, is unnecessary and perhaps undesirable. Nevertheless, immigrant groups themselves overwhelmingly desire to adopt American mores and culture, believe that people who come to the United States should learn to speak English, and sense that the country suffers from excessive immigration.

Immigration policies thus cut to the heart of the U.S. sense of nationhood. By defining who can live in the country, who can receive services, and what is required to become a citizen, the government defines what it means to be an American. These policies also describe the nation's sense of its moral obligations to foreign persons in need, and the enforcement of these policies helps to direct the future makeup of the American population.

GOVERNMENT POLICIES American immigration policy has shifted widely over time. Although much of the country's early growth was fed by immigration, the United States has periodically restricted immigration in general or the entry of certain groups in particular. An example of the latter is the Chinese Exclusion Act of 1882, which was repealed in 1943. The first broad immigration control laws were established during the 1920's with the National Origins Act, which attempted to limit the inflow of immigrants and to fix the ethnic proportions of the U.S. population via national quotas.

World War II, the Holocaust, and the political dislocations that followed the war prompted the United States to revise its immigration laws. After a series of ad hoc alterations, in 1952 the Immigration and Nationality Act codified the disparate immigration laws and ended immigration and naturalization prohibitions by race. The Hart-Celler Act of 1965 expanded the 1952 law, ending national origin quotas entirely. In addition, this act established the reuniting of families as a goal of U.S. immigration policy. In a further move away from group- and nationality-based admissions policies, the Refugee Act of 1980 required that decisions to admit refugees be made on a case-by-case basis.

By the 1980's, the growing number of illegal immigrants had once again pushed immigration reform into the public spotlight. The Immigration Reform and Control Act (IRCA) of 1986, an attempt to balance the interests of anti-immigrant and immigrant-rights groups, took two approaches to the problem. To reduce illegal immigration, the act imposed sanctions on employers hiring illegal aliens and strengthened the country's border enforcement. At the same time, the IRCA granted amnesty to illegal aliens who had resided in the country since at least 1982. Further modifications to immigration and refugee laws and policies continued throughout the 1980's and early 1990's, prompted partly by the end of the Cold War and the increase in civil wars around the world. In 1990, for example, the Immigration Act raised immigration quotas by 40 percent, their highest level since 1914.

Steve D. Boilard

FURTHER READING

Bischoff, Henry. *Immigration Issues.* Westport, Conn.: Greenwood Press, 2002. Collection of balanced discussions about the most important and most controversial issues relating to immigration. Among the specific subjects covered are government obligations to address humanitarian problems, the impact of cultural diversity on American society, and enforcement of laws regulating undocumented workers.

Cole, David. *Enemy Aliens: Double Standards and Constitutional Freedoms in the War on Terrorism.* New York: New Press/W. W. Norton, 2003. Critical analysis of the erosion of civil liberties in the United States since September 11, 2001, with attention to the impact of federal policies on immigrants and visiting aliens.

Deveaux, Monique. *Cultural Pluralism and Dilemmas of Justice*. Ithaca, N.Y.: Cornell University Press, 2000. Thoughtful study of the ethical and legal problems arising in a pluralistic society such as that of the United States.

Houle, Michelle E., ed. *Immigration*. San Diego: Greenhaven Press, 2004. Collection of speeches on U.S. immigration policies by such historical figures as Presidents Woodrow Wilson, Franklin D. Roosevelt, John F. Kennedy, and Bill Clinton.

Jacobs, Nancy R. *Immigration: Looking for a New Home*. Detroit: Gale Group, 2000. Broad discussion of modern federal government immigration policies that considers all sides of the debates about the rights of illegal aliens.

Kondo, Atsushi, ed. *Citizenship in a Global World: Comparing Citizenship Rights for Aliens*. New York: Palgrave, 2001. Collection of essays on citizenship and immigrants in ten different nations, including the United States and Canada.

Legomsky, Stephen H. *Immigration and Refugee Law and Policy*. 3d ed. New York: Foundation Press, 2002. Legal textbook on immigration and refugee law.

LeMay, Michael C., and Elliott Robert Barkan, eds. *U.S. Immigration and Naturalization Laws and Issues: A Documentary History*. Westport, Conn.: Greenwood Press, 1999. History of U.S. immigration laws supported by extensive extracts from documents.

Lynch, James P., and Rita J. Simon. *Immigration the World Over: Statutes, Policies, and Practices*. Lanham, Md.: Rowman & Littlefield, 2002. International perspectives on immigration, with particular attention to the immigration policies of the United States, Canada, Australia, Great Britain, France, Germany, and Japan.

Shanks, Cheryl. *Immigration and the Politics of American Sovereignty, 1890-1990*. Ann Arbor: University of Michigan Press, 2001. Scholarly study of changing federal immigration laws from the late nineteenth through the late twentieth centuries, with particular attention to changing quota systems and exclusionary policies.

Williams, Mary E., ed. *Immigration: Opposing Viewpoints*. San Diego: Greenhaven Press, 2004. Presents a variety of social, political, and legal viewpoints of experts and observers familiar with immigration into the United States.

SEE ALSO Demographics of immigration; European immigrants, 1790-1892; European immigrants, 1892-1943; History of U.S. immigration; Illegal aliens; Immigration and Naturalization Service; Immigration "crisis"; Immigration law; Migration; Undocumented workers.

KNOW-NOTHING PARTY

IDENTIFICATION: Nativist political party
DATE: 1852-1856

IMMIGRATION ISSUES: Government and politics; Nativism and racism

SIGNIFICANCE: During its brief ascendancy in the decade before the Civil War, the Know-Nothing Party appealed to voters by campaigning for the interests of native-born Americans over those of immigrants.

The Know-Nothing Party was a political organization that prospered in the United States between 1852 and 1856. During that period, the antiforeign and anti-Catholic feelings of Americans concerned about the large numbers of immigrants arriving in the United States, especially from Ireland, led to the creation of political organizations grounded in prejudice. The secret Order of the Star-Spangled Banner, informally known as the Know-Nothings because the phrase "I know nothing" was the response of members queried regarding the organization, emerged as the most prominent of the nativist organizations.

The Know-Nothings eventually dropped their secrecy to become a force in U.S. politics. Under a new name, the American Party, the Know-Nothings surprised the nation with electoral victories in 1854 and 1855. The new party successfully shifted attention away from the issue of slavery in many parts of the country by playing on unrealistic fears of foreign and papal plots to control the United States. The American Party platform called for reforming immigration laws by limiting the number of immigrants and extending the time requirement for naturalization. Former president Millard Fillmore, the American Party candidate for president in 1856, received 21 percent of the popular vote but carried only the state of Maryland. Unable to emerge as a dominant force in national politics, the American Party split into factions over the issue of slavery.

Donald C. Simmons, Jr.

FURTHER READING

Gabaccia, Donna R. *Immigration and American Diversity: A Social and Cultural History*. Malden, Mass.: Blackwell, 2002.
Holt, Michael. *The Political Crisis of the 1850's*. New York: John Wiley & Sons, 1978.

SEE ALSO Anti-Irish Riots of 1844; German and Irish immigration of the 1840's; History of U.S. immigration; Nativism; Xenophobia.

KOREAN IMMIGRANTS

IDENTIFICATION: Immigrants to North America from the East Asia Korean peninsula

IMMIGRATION ISSUES: Asian immigrants; Demographics

SIGNIFICANCE: Korean Americans are one of the fastest-growing ethnic groups in the United States. Korean American businesses and churches have become increasingly common, and members of other American ethnic groups frequently come into contact with Koreans.

Koreans first began settling in the United States during the 1950's, when American servicemen serving in Korea returned home with brides and war orphans. Korean migration to the United States continued at very low levels, however, until the U.S. Congress changed immigration laws in 1965, giving Asians the same opportunity as Europeans to settle in the United States. This triggered an almost immediate increase in Korean migration: Although only 10,179 Koreans immigrated from 1961 to 1965, the number jumped to 25,618 in the next half-decade, from 1966 to 1970. As more Koreans made their homes in the United States, more followed. During the period from 1986

Residents of Los Angeles's Koreatown watching a parade with floats supporting political candidates in South Korea's presidential elections during the late 1980's. (Korea Society/Los Angeles)

to 1990, 172,851 Koreans immigrated. By 1990, according to the U.S. Census of Population and Housing, the Korean American population had reached 750,000. Between 1991 and 2003, Koreans entered the United States at a rate of about 16,600 immigrants per year.

After the 1965 change in immigration law, Korean immigrants were not only more numerous but also more likely to come as entire family groups. With large numbers of Koreans in the United States, they began to form Korean American communities instead of settling as isolated individuals. Korean businesses and Korean churches began to appear in American cities and suburbs.

California, with a 1990 Korean American population of 259,941, is home to the largest portion of Koreans in the United States. California is followed by New York, which had a Korean American population of 95,648 in 1990. Illinois, New Jersey, Texas, Maryland, Virginia, and Washington also had large Korean populations.

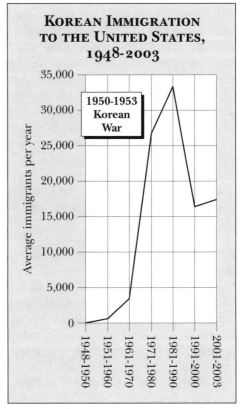

KOREAN IMMIGRATION TO THE UNITED STATES, 1948-2003

Source: U.S. Census Bureau.

KOREAN BUSINESSES As new immigrants, Koreans often have few job opportunities in the United States. However, Koreans do have a strong tradition of helping one another, and this has contributed to the growth of Korean-owned businesses in the United States. In the rotating credit system known as the *kye*, groups of Koreans pool money to make interest-free loans to group members.

Changes in the U.S. economy also encouraged the development of Korean businesses. During the 1970's and 1980's, as poverty became increasingly concentrated in American inner-city areas, many small business owners began closing or selling stores in these areas. New Korean immigrants, who had limited English-language abilities and few contacts to find jobs in established U.S. corporations, moved into ownership of small businesses. By the 1990's, Korean Americans had the highest rate of business ownership of any ethnic or racial group, and more than half of all first-generation Korean immigrants were self-employed.

Korean businesses have become the basis for many local and national Korean organizations. The Korean American Grocers' Association is one of the most important of the national business-based organizations, with local groups in most areas that have substantial Korean populations. The Korean Dry Cleaning and Laundry Association is another national Korean American organization based on small-business ownership.

The Korean pattern of employment has had consequences for the relations between Korean Americans and members of other groups. Koreans are often highly dependent on one another for financial and social support, sometimes creating the impression that they isolate themselves from the rest of American society. They tend not to live in the inner-city neighborhoods where they own their businesses, leading to cultural misunderstandings and conflicts between Korean business owners and their customers, many of whom are African American.

KOREAN CHURCHES Although Korean culture is traditionally Confucian and Buddhist, numerous Christian congregations, mostly Protestant, exist in South Korea. It is estimated that about 70 percent of Korean Americans are Christians and that the overwhelming majority of them are members of Korean churches. By the 1990's, there were more than two thousand Korean churches in the United States. Churches have become social centers for many Korean Americans, places where they can come together with others who speak their language and share their culture.

Korean American churches are places of worship, but they fulfill many other needs as well. Church members provide one another with information on available employment and housing. Language classes at churches teach English to new immigrants and Korean to U.S.-born children. The churches help to pass Korean culture on to children who may never have visited the home country of their parents.

KOREANS AND AMERICAN SOCIETY Korean businesses and churches both help to maintain Korean Americans as a separate group in American society. However, when U.S.-born Korean Americans become a larger proportion of the population, the separateness of Korean Americans is likely to diminish.

Many Korean American business owners do not pass on their businesses to their U.S.-born children. Instead, these children are typically encouraged to achieve high educational levels and obtain professional jobs in U.S. corporations. Over time, then, the distinctive employment patterns of Korean Americans are likely to disappear. Korean Americans have also shown increasing rates of marriage with members of other racial and ethnic groups, suggesting that members of this Asian ethnic group will gradually assimilate or blend into the larger American society.

Carl L. Bankston III

FURTHER READING   Comprehensive overviews of Korean immigration include *Korean-Americans: Past, Present, and Future* (Elizabeth, N.J.: Hollym International, 2004), edited by Ilpyong J. Kim; Sheila Smith Noonan's *Korean Immigration* (Philadelphia: Mason Crest, 2004); and Stacy Taus-Bolstad's *Koreans in America* (Minneapolis: Lerner, 2005). *From the Land of Morning Calm: The Koreans in America* (New York: Chelsea House, 1994), by Ronald Takaki, uses documents on Korean immigration and oral histories of individual Korean Americans to help readers understand the background of this group. It is illustrated with photographs and contains a chronology of Koreans in the United States. *Caught in the Middle: Korean Merchants in America's Multiethnic Cities* (Berkeley: University of California Press, 1996), by Pyong Gap Min, looks at the situation of Korean businessmen in urban neighborhoods and how they are affected by racial and ethnic inequality in the United States. *Blue Dreams: Korean Americans and the Los Angeles Riots* (Cambridge, Mass.: Harvard University Press, 1995), by Nancy Abelmann and John Lie, is a detailed examination of the impact of the 1992 riots on Korean Americans. Other useful studies include Moon H. Jo's *Korean Immigrants and the Challenge of Adjustment* (Westport, Conn.: Greenwood Press, 1999), Nazli Kibria's *Becoming Asian American: Second-Generation Chinese and Korean American Identities* (Baltimore: Johns Hopkins University Press, 2002), and Wayne Patterson's *The Ilsei: First-Generation Korean Immigrants in Hawai'i, 1903-1973* (Honolulu: University of Hawai'i Press, 2000). Ellen Alexander Conley's *The Chosen Shore: Stories of Immigrants* (Berkeley: University of California Press, 2004) is a collection of first-hand accounts of modern immigrants from many nations, including two from Korea.

SEE ALSO   Amerasians; Asian American education; Asian American stereotypes; Korean immigrants and African Americans; Korean immigrants and family customs; War brides; "Yellow peril" campaign.

KOREAN IMMIGRANTS AND AFRICAN AMERICANS

IMMIGRATION ISSUES: African Americans; Asian immigrants; Economics

SIGNIFICANCE: Korean immigrants to the United States have tended to open small businesses, such as groceries, in central areas of American cities, where many of their customers have been African Americans. As a consequence, sometimes culture clashes and conflicts occur between members of these two minority groups.

During the widespread rioting that followed the acquittal of the police officers who beat black motorist Rodney King, some Korean business owners used firearms to protect their establishments against looters. (AP/Wide World Photos)

Ownership of a small business is the most common job for people of Korean ancestry in the United States. Assisted by rotating credit associations (organizations that Koreans form to grant each other interest-free business loans requiring little collateral), Korean Americans have specialized in self-employment in small stores. The majority of Korean businesses in the United States are located in California and New York. In 1990, according to the U.S. Bureau of the Census, 44 percent of all Korean business owners lived in California and 12 percent of Korean business owners lived in New York. Within these states, they were concentrated in the Los Angeles-Long Beach area and in New York City.

Korean businesses are most often located in central areas of cities. During the 1970's and 1980's, owners of inner-city businesses began to leave, and Koreans, having access to business loans from their rotating loan associations but few job opportunities in established American businesses, began buying small urban shops. Although their businesses were in the city, the Koreans tended to settle in the suburbs. The people who do live in central urban areas and make up the majority of the customers in Korean businesses are African Americans. Korean shop owners are often looked upon by their inner-city customers as exploiters who come into neighborhoods to make a profit on the people and then take the money elsewhere. These customers complain about high prices, poor merchandise, and discourteous treatment. As new arrivals to the United States, Korean merchants sometimes have trouble with English and do not communicate well with those who come into their shops.

Korean businesspeople tend to hire other Koreans to work in their shops. Most of these shops are family enterprises, so family members frequently provide labor. As a result, Koreans not only live outside the communities where their stores are located but also hire few people who live in those communities. African Americans complain that Korean merchants do not hire black employees, do not buy from black suppliers of goods, and do not invest in the black neighborhoods in which they have located their businesses.

Although African American shoppers frequently view Koreans as outsiders and exploiters, the Koreans sometimes look with suspicion on those living in the neighborhoods where their businesses are located. Having little understanding of the history of U.S. racial inequality, Korean business owners may see low-income urban residents as irresponsible and untrustworthy. The high crime rates in these neighborhoods can lead them to see all members of the communities, even the most honest, as potential shoplifters or robbers.

MISTRUST AND CULTURE CLASH   The cultural gap between African Americans and the Korean Americans who often own stores in black neighborhoods has resulted in a number of well-publicized clashes. In the spring of 1990, African Americans in Brooklyn began a nine-month boycott of Korean stores after a Korean greengrocer allegedly harassed an African American shopper. In 1992, trouble flared up again in the same neighborhood when an African American customer in a Korean grocery was allegedly harassed and struck by the owner and an employee. During 1995, an African American man was arrested while attempting to burn down a Korean-owned store, and both white and Korean store owners in Harlem received racial threats.

California, home to the nation's greatest number of Korean businesses, has seen some of the most serious conflicts between Koreans and African Americans. In April of 1992, a judge gave a sentence of probation to a Korean shopkeeper convicted in the shooting death of a fifteen-year-old African American girl, Latasha Harlins. Two weeks after that, on April 29, riots broke out in South Central Los Angeles after the acquittal of police officers who had been videotaped beating an African American motorist, Rodney King. Although none of the police officers was Korean, Korean groceries and liquor stores in South Central Los Angeles became targets of the riots. The riots destroyed more than one thousand Korean businesses and an estimated twenty-three hundred Korean-owned businesses were looted.

Korean shop owners began leaving South Central Los Angeles in the years after the riots. Those who remained became even more wary of the local population than they were previously.

EFFORTS AT IMPROVING RELATIONS   Korean and African American leaders have made efforts to improve relations between the two groups. In the days following the riots in Los Angeles, some African American and Korean leaders formed the Black-Korean Alliance to improve communication and find common ground. In New York, the Korean-American Grocer's Association has tried to find ways of bringing African Americans and Koreans together. These have included sending African American community leaders on tours of South Korea and providing African American students with scholarships to Korean universities.

It may be difficult to resolve the problems between Korean merchants and their African American customers as long as American central cities continue to be places of concentrated unemployment and poverty. Investment in low-income communities and the creation of economic opportunities for their residents are probably necessary in order to overcome the suspicion and resentment between members of these two minority groups.

Carl L. Bankston III

FURTHER READING Up-to-date discussions of a variety of aspects of Korean-African American relations can be found in *Blacks and Asians in America: Crossings, Conflict and Commonality* (Durham, N.C.: Carolina Academic Press, 2004), edited by Hazel M. McFerson. Claire Jean Kim's *Bitter Fruit: The Politics of Black-Korean Conflict in New York City* (New Haven, Conn.: Yale University Press, 2000) examines the boycott of Korean stores in New York. In Patrick D. Joyce's *No Fire Next Time: Black-Korean Conflicts and the Future of America's Cities* (Ithaca, N.Y.: Cornell University Press, 2003), *Koreans in the Hood: Conflict with African Americans* (Baltimore: Johns Hopkins University Press, 1999), edited by Kwang Chung Kim and *Caught in the Middle: Korean Merchants in America's Multiethnic Cities* (Berkeley: University of California Press, 1996), by sociologist Pyong Gap Min the situation of Korean businesspeople in U.S. cities is examined. Nancy Abelmann and John Lie discuss the consequences for Koreans of the 1992 Los Angeles riots in *Blue Dreams: Korean Americans and the Los Angeles Riots* (Cambridge, Mass.: Harvard University Press, 1995). Ivan Light and Edna Bonacich give a history of Korean American business in *Immigrant Entrepreneurs: Koreans in Los Angeles, 1965-1982* (Berkeley: University of California Press, 1988). Lauren Lee's *Korean Americans* (New York: Marshall Cavendish, 1995) provides a readable, in-depth description of this ethnic group.

SEE ALSO African immigrants; Asian American education; Asian American stereotypes; Ethnic enclaves; Indigenous superordination; Korean immigrants; Korean immigrants and family customs; War brides; "Yellow peril" campaign.

KOREAN IMMIGRANTS AND FAMILY CUSTOMS

IMMIGRATION ISSUES: Asian immigrants; Families and marriage

SIGNIFICANCE: Korean American families have faced the challenges of balancing the conservative, traditional principles of their ancestral homeland, Korea, with the more liberal, egalitarian beliefs of the American family.

Most Korean Americans have strong family ties to South Korea. Confucian principles influence social and familial behavior. A patrilineal system dominates the traditional Korean family, which means that husbands are the commanders of their wives and families. Wives are expected to obey their husband and serve their husbands' parents and families. Wives' must bear children to perpetuate their husband's family lineage.

According to Confucian philosophy and centuries of tradition, Korean women obey their fathers until their marriage, at which time they must obey their husbands. After their husbands die, they must obey their sons. These strong patrilineal beliefs have posed difficulties when Koreans emigrate to the United States and attempt to adapt to mainstream American culture, which often tends to encourage gender equality. However, such unique traditional values as found among Korean immigrants in the United States help Korean Americans maintain their cultural identity and focus on the rich traditions of their native country.

HISTORICAL OVERVIEW Koreans traveled to America after 1882, when the Korean American trade and travel treaty was signed. American missionaries traveled to Korea to convert Korean Buddhists to Christianity. Sheltered and submissive Korean women found that church work offered them some freedom and was socially rewarding. From 1903 to 1905 seven thousand Koreans emigrated to the United States for political and financial reasons. Some of the first Korean immigrants were men working on Hawaiian sugar plantations. Emigrating to the mainland, they searched for better conditions in agricultural areas and for opportunities in the professions they learned in their native Korea. Some Americans resented the fact that Korean immigrants took jobs in the United States and excluded them from participating in the professions. As a result, Koreans often started their own businesses in city districts where Korean families clustered.

The influx of Koreans to America slowly grew. By 1940 there were 8,568 Korean Americans. The Korean War, which ended in 1953, increased Korean immigration. Many U.S. servicemen returned home from the Korean War with Korean brides, while Korean students enrolled in U.S. colleges and American families adopted Korean infants. The 1965 Immigration and Nationality Act also contributed to the increase in Korean Americans by easing immigration restrictions. The 1990 U.S. Census Bureau reported that there were almost 800,000 Koreans in the United States.

The Canadian Employment Equity Act of 1986 classified Korean Canadians as a "visible minority." This act allowed the Canadian government to collect data on Korean Canadians as well as on other minorities and ethnic immigrants in Canada during the 1980's. About one third of Korean Canadians emigrated to Canada during the 1980's.

DEMOGRAPHICS   Korean Americans and Canadians live primarily in urban areas. In the United States, Honolulu, Los Angeles, Chicago, and New York are important cities with substantial Korean populations. In some cities geographic areas have developed which have come to be known as Koreatowns. Approximately 50 percent of Korean Canadians lived in the Toronto vicinity in 1991.

Education of men, which is valued in Korean culture, stems from historical Confucian beliefs. Koreans believe that success, power, and respect are attainable with education.

Members of a Los Angeles Korean church on Easter Sunday in 1950. Christian churches play an important role in promoting fellowship among Korean immigrants and their families. (University of Southern California, East Asian Library)

Some 57 percent of Korean Canadians had university degrees during the late 1990's, more than any other visible minority group. The high educational levels that Koreans have attained are evidenced by the large percentages of Korean professionals, managers, and entrepreneurs. In the United States, 40 percent of Korean men own businesses, such as grocery stores or dry cleaners. Many Korean medical professionals are forced to work in high-crime, inner-city areas because of the difficulties they face in finding jobs. In spite of such problems, unemployment rates among Koreans are low. They accept difficult working conditions and set themselves the goal of acquiring enough capital to improve their situation. The success of Korean-owned businesses has been attributed to the fact that Koreans work long hours, have strong work ethics, and make sacrifices for their families.

FAMILY INTERACTION WITH MAINSTREAM SOCIETY   The business success of Korean immigrants has caused resentment among other ethnic groups. In some cities African American and Korean relations have suffered because of cultural differences. The 1992 Los Angeles upheaval seriously affected local Korean businesses. Many were vandalized, looted, or burned. Korean Americans have better relations with Latinos. Both are entrepreneurial ethnic groups, and many Korean Americans speak Spanish as a second language.

Some Korean youth feel that they play dual roles as immigrants. They believe that being Korean American is a high-maintenance ethnic status. Even Korean children born in the United States are often expected to speak Korean and English, know Korean geography, and marry other Koreans. The majority of Korean Americans speak the Korean language at home. Korean American teenagers face some difficulties at school because of the language barrier that isolates their parents. The limited English proficiency of many parents is a cause for concern among both parents and children.

Traditional Korean culture is significantly different from American culture. Traditional Koreans place high value on filial piety. This devotion to older family members and particularly to husbands' families is lacking in American culture. Aging Korean parents expect that their children will respect them, and parents are frustrated when their children do not.

Korean American wives are burdened by double roles, while husbands are frustrated by the Americanization of their wives. Women must balance the role of traditional Korean wives, whose goal is to serve their husbands' families, with the role of employed American wives, whose goals are gender equality, personal satisfaction, and independence. Korean American husbands, influenced by filial piety, may fear their wives' challenge to male dominance at home. They feel that the gradual lessening of their wives' obedience is a problem that stems from American culture.

MAINTAINING CULTURAL IDENTITY   In fulfilling social and religious roles, Korean churches adhere closely to traditional Korean beliefs. They encourage fellowship among Korean immigrants; provide social services for their congregations and the community, such as helping immigrants adjust to the new culture; and provide their members opportunities for leadership and status among Korean Americans. Sundays are often filled with activities sponsored by Korean churches. After Sunday services, congregations may have Love Feasts, at which traditional Korean foods are served. Churches teach children Korean culture in Sunday afternoon workshops or summer camps.

Korean American churches preserve and promote traditional customs and festivals, as well as adapt customs to American ways. The Korean Lunar New Year's Day festival, called Sol-Nal, occurs in January or February. Like New Year's Day in the West, Lunar New Year's Day is a time to celebrate and make resolutions. Korean families gather for memorial services honoring ancestors or visit living elders. New clothes, special foods, candles, and incense are important to this festival.

The Harvest Moon Festival is celebrated in September or October on the fifteenth day of the eighth lunar month. Its purpose is to give thanks for successful harvests and is thus similar to Thanksgiving in the United States. Ancestors are honored during the Harvest Moon Festival. Festive foods, such as fruits, vegetables, zucchini pancakes, meat, rice, and wine are served. Crescent-shaped rice cakes filled with sweet sesame seeds or bean paste are the highlight of the Harvest Moon Festival. Moon-viewing is important to the festival and has inspired Korean poetry.

In Korea, traditional weddings were arranged by brides' and groom's parents. Often, brides and grooms met for the first time at their wedding. During the late twentieth century, western traditions of dating, love, engagements, and white wedding gowns have become the cultural norm among Korean Americans. Some Korean Americans have two wedding ceremonies, a Christian and a Buddhist one. Wedding feasts may be held in honor of brides and grooms, because food is an important part of such ceremonies. Tables are laden with traditional Korean foods such as Kimchi, or spicy preserved cabbage; pulgolgi, or spicy beef; fish; rice; noodles; and vegetables.

Korean American families have managed to retain some of the cultural norms of traditional Korea while adapting to their current life conditions in the United States and Canada. They have found ways to synthesize Korean and American values by adapting both. Unique values will eventually emerge, allowing Korean Americans to balance change with continuity.

Celia Stall-Meadows

FURTHER READING

Conley, Ellen Alexander. *The Chosen Shore: Stories of Immigrants.* Berkeley: University of California Press, 2004.

Jo, Moon H. *Korean Immigrants and the Challenge of Adjustment.* Westport, Conn.: Greenwood Press, 1999.

Kibria, Nazli. *Becoming Asian American: Second-Generation Chinese and Korean American Identities.* Baltimore: Johns Hopkins University Press, 2002.

Koh, Frances. *Korean Holidays and Festivals.* Minneapolis: EastWest Press, 1990.

Kwon, Okyun. *Buddhist and Protestant Korean Immigrants: Religious Beliefs and Socioeconomic Aspects of Life.* New York: LFB Scholarly Publications, 2003.

Patterson, Wayne. *The Ilse: First-Generation Korean Immigrants in Hawai'i, 1903-1973.* Honolulu: University of Hawai'i Press, 2000.

SEE ALSO Amerasians; Asian American education; Asian American stereotypes; Chinese immigrants and family customs; Filipino immigrants and family customs; Korean immigrants; Korean immigrants and African Americans; Southeast Asian immigrants; Vietnamese immigrants; War brides; "Yellow peril" campaign.

Ku Klux Klan

IDENTIFICATION: White supremacist organization
DATE: Founded in 1866
PLACE: Pulaski, Tennessee

IMMIGRATION ISSUES: African Americans; Civil rights and liberties; Discrimination

SIGNIFICANCE: After the Civil War, a group of white supremacists, disaffected by the war's outcome, grew into an organization of institutionalized race hatred and anti-immigrant sentiment that has survived into the twenty-first century.

With the end of the Civil War and the emancipation of African American slaves in the South, tension arose between old-order Southern whites and Radical Republicans devoted to a strict plan of Reconstruction that required southern states to repeal their black codes and guarantee voting and other civil rights to African Americans. Federal instruments for ensuring African American rights included the Freedmen's Bureau and the Union Leagues. In reaction to the activities of these organizations, white supremacist organizations sprouted in the years immediately following the Civil War: the Knights of the White Camelia, the White League, the Invisible Circle, the Pale Faces, and the Ku Klux Klan (KKK).

BEGINNINGS The last of these would eventually lend its name to a confederation of such organizations, but in 1866 it was born in Pulaski, Tennessee, as a fraternal order for white, male, Anglo-Saxon Protestants joined by their opposition to Radical Reconstructionism and an agenda to promote white, Southern dominance. This incarnation of the Klan established many of the

Hooded Klansmen marching in Virginia in early 1922. Much of the power of the Klan to intimidate immigrants and members of minority groups was based on its secretiveness and the spookiness of its members hooded outfits. (Library of Congress)

weird rituals and violent activities for which the KKK became known throughout its history. They named the South the "invisible empire," with "realms" consisting of the southern states. A "grand dragon" headed each realm, and the entire "empire" was led by Grand Wizard General Nathan B. Forrest. Positions of leadership were dubbed "giant," "cyclops," "geni," "hydra," and "goblin." The white robes and pointed cowls stem from this era; these were donned in the belief that African Americans were superstitious and would be intimidated by the menacing, ghostlike appearance of their oppressors, who thus also maintained anonymity while conducting their activities.

Soon the Klan was perpetrating acts of violence, including whippings, house-burnings, kidnappings, and lynchings. As the violence escalated, Forrest disbanded the Klan in 1869, and on May 31, 1870, and April 20, 1871, Congress passed the Ku Klux Klan Acts, or Force Acts, designed to break up the white supremacist groups.

SECOND RISE OF THE KLAN   The next rise of the Klan presaged the period of the Red Scare (1919-1920) and the Immigration Act of 1921, the first such legislation in the United States to establish immigration quotas on the basis of national origin. In November, 1915, in Stone Mountain, Georgia, a second Ku Klux Klan was founded by preacher William J. Simmons, proclaiming it a "high-class, mystic, social, patriotic" society devoted to defending womanhood, white Protestant values, and "native-born, white, gentile Americans." Such an image of the Klan was perpetrated by the popular 1915 film *Birth of a Nation*, in which a lustful African American is shown attempting to attack a white woman, and the Klan, in robes and cowls, rides to the rescue.

The new Klan cloaked itself as a patriotic organization devoted to preserving traditional American values against enemies in the nation's midst. An upsurge of nationalist fervor swelled the ranks of the Klan, this time far beyond the borders of the South. This second Klan adopted the rituals and regalia of its predecessor as well as the same anti-black ideology, to which it added anti-Roman Catholic, anti-Semitic, anti-immigrant, anti-birth-control, anti-Darwinist, and anti-Prohibition stances. Promoted by ad-man Edward Y. Clarke, its membership reached approximately 100,000 by 1921 and over the next five years, by some estimates, grew to 5 million, including even members of Congress.

The second Klan perpetrated more than five hundred hangings and burnings of African Americans. In 1924, forty thousand Klansmen marched down Pennsylvania Avenue in Washington, D.C., sending a message to the federal government that there should be a white, Protestant United States. Finally, the Klan's growing wave of violence alienated many of its members, whose numbers dropped to about 30,000 by 1930.

Klan activities increased again prior to World War II, and membership rose toward the 100,000 mark, but in 1944 Congress assessed the organization more than a half million dollars in back taxes, and the Klan dissolved itself to escape. Two years later, however, Atlanta physician Samuel Green united smaller Klan groups into the Association of Georgia Klans and was soon joined by other reincarnations, such as the Federated Ku Klux Klans, the Original Southern Klans, and the Knights of the Ku Klux Klan. These groups revived the agenda of previous Klans and were responsible for hundreds of criminal acts. Of equal concern was the Klan's political influence: A governor of Texas was elected with the support of the Klan, as was a senator from Maine. Even a Supreme Court justice, Hugo L. Black, revealed in 1937 that he had been a member of the Ku Klux Klan.

CHALLENGES During the 1940's, many states passed laws that revoked Klan charters, and many southern communities issued regulations against masks. The U.S. Justice Department placed the Klan on its list of subversive elements, and in 1952 the Federal Bureau of Investigation used the Lindbergh law (one of the 1934 Crime Control Acts) against the Klan. Another direct challenge to the principles of the KKK came during the 1960's with the advent of the Civil Rights movement and civil rights legislation. Martin Luther King, Jr., prophesied early in the decade that it would be a "season of suffering."

On September 15, 1963, a Klan bomb tore apart the Sixteenth Street Baptist Church in Birmingham, Alabama, killing four young children. Despite the outrage of much of the nation, the violence continued, led by members of the Klan who made a mockery of the courts and the laws that they had broken. Less than a year after the bombing, three civil rights workers were killed in Mississippi, including one African American and two whites from the North involved in voter registration. This infamous event was later documented in the motion picture *Mississippi Burning.* Viola Lee Liuzzo was killed for driving freedom marchers from site to site. Such acts prompted President Lyndon B. Johnson, in a televised speech in March, 1965, to denounce the Klan as he announced the arrest of four Klansmen for murder.

After the conviction of many of its members during the 1960's, the organization became somewhat dormant, and its roster of members reflected low numbers. Nevertheless, as it had in previous periods of dormancy, the Klan refused to die. Busing for integration of public schools during the 1970's engendered Klan opposition in the South and the North. In 1979, in Greensboro, North Carolina, Klan members killed several members of the Communist Party in a daylight battle on an open street. Klan members have patrolled the Mexican border, armed with weapons and citizen-band radios, trying to send illegal aliens back to Mexico.

The Klan has been active in suburban California, at times driving out African Americans who attempted to move there. On the Gulf Coast, many boats fly the infamous AKIA flag, an acronym for "A Klansman I Am," a motto that dates back to the 1920's. Klan members have tried to discourage or run out Vietnamese fishers. Klan leaders active since 1970 include James Venable, for whom the Klan became little more than a hobby, and Bill Wilkinson, a former disciple of David Duke. Robert Shelton, long a grand dragon, helped elect two Alabama governors. Duke, a Klan leader until the late 1980's, decided to run for political office and was elected a congressman from Louisiana despite his well-publicized past associations; in 1991, he ran for governor, almost winning. During the 1980's the Klan stepped up its anti-Semitic activities, planning multiple bombings in Nashville, Tennessee. Klan leaders during the 1990's have trained their members and their children for what they believe is an imminent race war, learning survival skills and weaponry at remote camps throughout the country.

A major blow was struck against the Klan by the Klanwatch Project of the Southern Poverty Law Center, in Montgomery, Alabama, when, in 1984, attorney Morris Dees began pressing civil suits against several Klan members, effectively removing their personal assets, funds received from members, and even buildings owned by the Klan.

FURTHER READING

Chalmers, David. *Backfire: How the Ku Klux Klan Helped the Civil Rights Movement.* Lanham, Md.: Rowman & Littlefield, 2003. Study of the Klan's contributions to focusing public attention on the justness of the aims of the Civil Rights movement.

_____. *Hooded Americanism: The History of the Ku Klux Klan.* New York: F. Watts, 1981. Considered the bible of books about the Klan, this study has seen numerous editions and updatings.

Ezekiel, Raphael. *The Racist Mind: Portraits of American Neo-Nazis and Klansmen.* New York: Viking Press, 1995. Explores conditions of childhood, education, and other factors in an attempt to explain racist behavior.

Quarles, Chester L. *The Ku Klux Klan and Related American Racialist and Anti-semitic Organizations: A History and Analysis.* Jefferson, N.C.: McFarland, 1999. General overview of the history of white racist organizations.

Randel, William. *The Ku Klux Klan: A Century of Infamy.* Philadelphia: Chilton Books, 1965. Excellent history of origins and events that also uses a moral perspective.

Stanton, Bill. *Klanwatch: Bringing the Ku Klux Klan to Justice.* New York: Weidenfeld, 1991. A former Klanwatch director explains new initiatives to disable the Klan, most of which have been effective.

Wade, Wyn Craig. *The Fiery Cross: The Ku Klux Klan in America.* New York: Simon & Schuster, 1987. Wade recounts the Klan's history and episodes of violence, revealing its legacy of race hatred.

SEE ALSO African immigrants; Ashkenazic and German Jewish immigrants; Discrimination; History of U.S. immigration.

LATINOS

IDENTIFICATION: Immigrants to the United States and their descendants of Latin American origin

IMMIGRATION ISSUES: Border control; Cuban immigrants; Demographics; Labor; Latino immigrants; West Indian immigrants

SIGNIFICANCE: According to the 2000 U.S. Census, more than 16 million residents of the United States were born in Latin American nations; this number represented 52 percent of all foreign-born residents of the country. The large and growing Latino minority has had a significant impact on the United States, both culturally and economically. Although linked by language, Latinos are a diverse group, consisting of many different races and nations of origin.

The Latino minority, also often referred to as the Hispanic American sector of United States society, continues to increase proportionately to the total population with each succeeding decade. In 1996, some 25 million (9.7 percent) of residents of the United States traced their cultural, racial, or ethnic origins to some Spanish or Portuguese antecedents. Included in this group are recent immigrants, those who have arrived from Latin American nations both legally and illegally, and U.S. citizens whose families have been residents of the United States for many generations. The combination of this group's high birthrate coupled with the constant influx of immigrants into the United States has led to the prediction that by the year 2020 the total Latino population of the United States will exceed 51 million, representing 15.7 percent of an estimated total U.S. population of 326 million.

Although Latinos share a common cultural heritage, and most of them share a common linguistic heritage, the Latino population of the United States is far from a homogeneous cultural group. Its members can be characterized better by their diversity than by their similarity. Strong nationalistic identification with their countries or regions of origin serves to divide Mexican Americans from Cuban Americans from Puerto Ricans—and a host of other nationals—and to mitigate against their acting in concert politically, economically, or socially. For example, the large Cuban American colony in greater Miami, Florida, tends to be highly conservative politically, while the Puerto Ricans of New York state and the Mexican Americans of California generally are Democratic or liberal in political affiliation.

LATIN AMERICAN MIGRATION TO THE UNITED STATES

Year	Event	Impact
1910-1920	Mexican Revolution	Ten years of political and economic chaos force a quarter million Mexicans to resettle north of the U.S.-Mexico border.
1942-1964	Bracero program	Wartime labor shortages create a need for farmworkers that is filled by a Mexican and U.S. program that brings Mexicans to the United States to work the fields. The program establishes a pattern of migration of farmworkers.
1945-1950	Puerto Rican immigration	Following World War II, seventy-five-dollar economy air flights permit thousands of Puerto Ricans to resettle in the New York area. Since Puerto Ricans are U.S. citizens, no official entry papers are required.
1957-1960	Cuban Revolution	The takeover by the leftist Fidel Castro sends more than one million Cuban businesspeople and professionals to Miami.
1980-1990	Central American conflicts	Civil wars in El Salvador, Nicaragua, and Guatemala send more than one million political and economic refugees north, mostly to California and the East Coast.
1981-1990's	Mexican economic crises	The continuing erratic behavior of the Mexican economy, in addition to the inability of the country to provide employment for those entering the workforce each year, sends a constant wave of Mexican immigrants north to find work.

RACE AND ETHNICITY   Members of the Latino community run the gamut of virtually every racial and ethnic group found in the world. The initial voyages of exploration and discovery of the Western Hemisphere by Europeans from Spain, England, Portugal, France, and the Netherlands led quickly to a racial amalgamation of these primarily light-skinned European immigrants with the bronze-skinned indigenous peoples mistakenly called "Indians" (under the false belief that they occupied the Asian continent). This admixture of races resulted in what has been referred to as the mestizo, soon to become the predominant racial entity throughout much of Central and South America, as well as what would ultimately become the U.S. Southwest.

When the European settlers in Mexico, Central America, and South America found that they could not successfully exploit the indigenous peoples in mining and agriculture, they turned to the importation of Africans, initially as indentured servants but ultimately as slaves. England, France, Portugal, Spain, and the Netherlands entered into an extensive and lucrative tranship-ment of Africans to the Western Hemisphere, where they were sold as labor for the mining of precious metals and the manufacture of sugar, cotton, rice, and a wide variety of other marketable crops.

Owners of black slaves bred their human chattels with other slaves as part of the existing economic system, and soon African Americans—now typed as mulattos, quadroons, octoroons, and other racial mixtures—became part of a gene pool already containing a mixture of European and American Indian strains. In the course of the centuries that followed, Asians joined the hetero-geneous racial population that spread throughout the Western Hemisphere. Chinese settled in substantial numbers along the borders of Mexico's north-ernmost states. Faced with persecution by warring factions during the Mexi-can Revolution of 1910, they migrated to the United States in large numbers.

RELIGION   When Europeans landed in what became Mexico in the six-teenth century, they encountered a highly civilized society that was in many ways more advanced than that of Europe at the time. Spaniards, however, did not perceive or value the cultural sophistication of the newly discovered civili-zation—considering it their responsibility, on the contrary, to replace what they perceived as a heretic religion (in which the Aztec emperor was revered as a demigod) with Roman Catholicism. The Europeans therefore adopted a program of ruthless destruction of what they considered idolatry.

Similarly, in other parts of the continent, Portuguese, French, and English forced their own brands of Christianity on the native peoples whom they con-quered and exploited. In the initial four centuries following the opening of the hemisphere, Catholicism and Protestantism became the dominant reli-gions throughout North, South, and Central America.

Nevertheless, some indigenous peoples attempted to retain their identifi-cation with their old gods. Often this took the form of hiding their ancient sa-cred images behind the altars of European places of worship. Today, in more tolerant times, native and European religions are often practiced side by side, venerating gods and saints together, although by different names, as can be seen in modern Guatemala.

African slaves, seized and transported from their native lands to the Western Hemisphere, often brought their native religions with them, a source of comfort and hope under truly trying conditions. These African religions, sometimes modified by exposure to Christian sects, have open, active communicants in countries such as Haiti, Cuba, the Dominican Republic, and Brazil. Immigrants to the United States from these nations often bring these ancestral religious practices with them. These religious societies play an active role in the daily lives of their followers in the United States.

LANGUAGE Most second- and third-generation Latinos in the United States have a good command of English. Newcomers, however—like most immigrants from non-English-speaking nations—often lack basic English-language skills, severely limiting their ability to progress economically, politically, and socially. In a few areas, there are neighborhoods large and insular enough in their organization, where Spanish is so widely spoken among commercial establishments that English is unnecessary to carry on daily activities. Opportunities exist in most areas for newcomers to acquire basic English skills necessary to move into the mainstream of U.S. culture. Nevertheless, immigrants from isolated communities to the south, often still committed to tribal mores and language, find it difficult to blend into the larger culture. Some do not even speak Spanish but depend on their native languages, such as Mayan, Quechua, and Nahuatl, for communication. Lacking either English or Spanish, quite often these small, essentially tribal, groups are subject to exploitation by unscrupulous business interests and often are forced to work for miserably low wages and threatened with being turned into U.S. immigration authorities if they seek redress under the law.

MEXICO Mexico leads all other nations both in the number of foreign-born living in the United States and in the quantity of new arrivals each year. With a population approaching 100 million, Mexico cannot provide enough jobs for those entering its workforce every year. This pool of surplus labor, combined with the availability of unskilled or entry-level jobs in the United States, has accounted for Mexico's primary position in terms of immigrant influx.

Included in this wave of new arrivals are members of Mexico's Indian communities, who speak a variety of tribal tongues as their first language. Primarily from rural areas and with a minimum of education, they are subject to economic exploitation to a greater degree than are other immigrants.

Mexicans have lived in areas in what is now the United States before they were incorporated into the union. Texas, New Mexico, Arizona, and California were under the Mexican flag until the Mexican War of 1846-1848. The Treaty of Guadalupe Hidalgo signed in 1848 between the two countries ceded this territory to the United States for $15 million—a cheap price for the Americans.

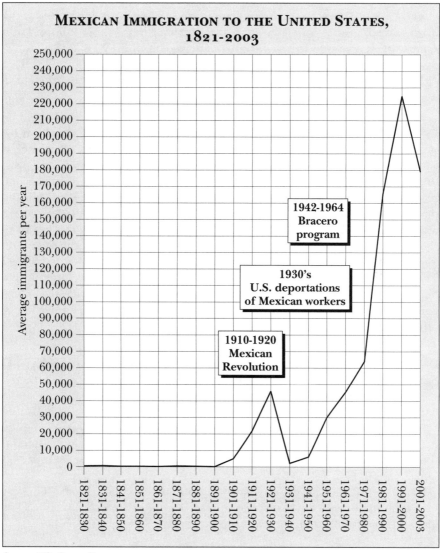

MEXICAN IMMIGRATION TO THE UNITED STATES, 1821-2003

Average immigrants per year

1942-1964
Bracero
program

1930's
U.S. deportations
of Mexican workers

1910-1920
Mexican
Revolution

Source: U.S. Census Bureau.

PUERTO RICO The United States defeated Spain in the brief Spanish-American War in 1898. In the ensuing Treaty of Paris, Spain gave up Puerto Rico, the Philippine Islands, and Guam to the victorious Americans. The United States also reluctantly agreed to the island of Cuba's independence under that treaty. However, the Americans retained sovereignty over Puerto Rico, viewing it as critical to U.S. defenses in the event of an attack from the Caribbean. In 1953, Puerto Rico achieved Commonwealth status, becoming a self-governing territory.

Following World War II, thousands of Puerto Ricans moved to the continental United States. In the immediate postwar period, airplane fares to the mainland sold for as little as seventy-five dollars. Almost three million Latin American citizens now live in the Northeast, mostly in the New York area. Because they are by law U.S. citizens, immigrants from the island are required only to demonstrate proof of birth in Puerto Rico before entering the continental United States.

CUBA The takeover in 1959 of the island of Cuba by Fidel Castro and his supporters resulted in a mass exodus of much of the country's upper-class and middle-class professional and business interests, who did not agree with the imposition of what eventually became a socialist, communist-supported, regime. Numbering close to one million, most of these refugees established themselves initially in the greater Miami area. In the spring of 1980, a second wave of refugees, called Marielitos and numbering perhaps one hundred thousand, managed to immigrate, with the permission of both the Castro regime and the administration of President Jimmy Carter, to the United States. The Cuban community, still centered in southern Florida, developed into a powerful economic and political force. During the 1990's, desperate Cubans continued to attempt to escape to the United States utilizing primitive boats, rafts, and even inner tubes.

CENTRAL AMERICA Throughout the 1970's and 1980's, the countries of El Salvador, Guatemala, and Nicaragua were plagued by civil wars. As a consequence of those unsettled political times, between one million and one and a half million Central American refugees had easy access, since the United States compared the leftist government of Daniel Ortega to Castro's regime in Cuba. U.S. supporters of Salvadoran and Guatemalan refugees insisted on the same opportunity for victims of political oppression in those countries as well.

Most of these three groups have continued to remain in this country through one form of amnesty or another, concentrating in California, Florida, and communities on the eastern seaboard.

DOMINICAN REPUBLIC As has been the case with so many of the small Caribbean island nations, the Dominican Republic cannot furnish enough job opportunities for all its citizens. Depending primarily on the export of sugar, some mining, and the attraction of cruise ships to its ports, this country, which shares the island of Hispaniola with Haiti, exports a substantial number of its working-class citizenry as well.

Many Dominican immigrants seeking illegal entry into the United States have used Puerto Rico as a staging area. False documents are obtained to establish a Puerto Rican identity. Most Dominicans have gravitated to the New York area after arriving in the United States. The little island nation ranked fourteenth in recent figures on immigration to the United States.

OTHER LATIN AMERICANS   The balance of the Western Hemisphere's Latin American countries have contributed immigrants as well, although generally as smaller percentages of their total populations. For example, the drug trade and the resulting political unrest has caused Bolivians, Peruvians, and Colombians to seek asylum in the United States, which continues to represent a beacon of hope to citizens of those countries where political disorder or economic deprivation threaten the lives of their citizens.

DIVERSITY VS. UNITY   Despite the formidable growth of the Latino element in U.S. society, its diversity has prevented this group from reaching its potential as a unitary political force. Instead, the members of each particular ethnic entity have shown a preference to confine their organizational efforts to members of their own particular community—to establish themselves as Mexican American, Cuban American, or Puerto Rican political associations, with membership confined to their own ethnic group. Nevertheless, should there come a time when diverse organizations such as these come to realize the potential strength that their combined numbers represent, the fast-growing Latino contingent could become a major factor in determining the course of the future of the United States. In the interim, the Latino sons of immigrants have followed the paths of other racial and ethnic minorities in U.S. society in past decades. Many, showing a high degree of individual initiative, have worked their way into positions of greater responsibility in business and the professions.

Carl Henry Marcoux

FURTHER READING

Bohon, Stephanie. *Latinos in Ethnic Enclaves: Immigrant Workers and the Competition for Jobs.* New York: Garland, 2000. Examination of Latino employment in major urban centers.

Conley, Ellen Alexander. *The Chosen Shore: Stories of Immigrants.* Berkeley: University of California Press, 2004. Collection of firsthand accounts of modern immigrants from many nations, including Bolivia, Cuba, and Mexico.

Crosthwaite, Luis Humberto, John William Byrd, and Bobby Byrd, eds. *Puro Border: Dispatches, Snapshots and Graffiti from La Frontera.* El Paso, Tex.: Cinco Puntos Press, 2003. Collage of illustrations and writings that attempts to portray the various cultural and geographical considerations of those people who live on the line.

Cull, Nicholas J., and David Carrasco, eds. *Alambrista and the U.S.-Mexico Border: Film, Music, and Stories of Undocumented Immigrants.* Albuquerque: University of New Mexico Press, 2004. Collection of essays on dramatic works, films, and music about Mexicans who cross the border illegally into the United States.

Fox, Geoffrey. *Hispanic Nation.* Secaucus, N.J.: Carol Publishing Group, 1996. Argues that the old political and cultural differences that divided various Latino groups have already begun to diminish and that Latinos in the twenty-first century will become the largest and most influential minority in the United States.

Gonzalez, Gilbert G. *Guest Workers or Colonized Labor? Mexican Labor Migration to the United States.* Boulder, Colo.: Paradigm, 2005. Reexamination of the history of Mexican immigration to the United States that looks at the subject in the context of American dominance over Mexico.

Greene, Victor R. *A Singing Ambivalence: American Immigrants Between Old World and New, 1830-1930.* Kent, Ohio: Kent State University Press, 2004. Comparative study of the different challenges faced by members of eight major immigrant groups, including Mexicans, through the early twentieth century.

López, David, and Andrés Jiménez, eds. *Latinos and Public Policy in California: An Agenda for Opportunity.* Berkeley, Calif.: Berkeley Public Policy Press, 2003. Collection of essays on the condition and government treatment of Latinos in California.

Nevin, Joseph. *Operation Gatekeeper: The Rise of the "Illegal Alien" and the Making of the U.S.-Mexico Boundary.* New York: Routledge, 2002. Details the federal government's *Operation Gatekeeper,* which in the 1990's targeted the San Diego-Tijuana border in efforts to stop illegal immigration. The author argues that this assault on immigration did not effectively reduce unauthorized immigration and served to inflame anti-Hispanic racism in the United States.

Rodriguez, Clara E. *Changing Race: Latinos, the Census, and the History of Ethnicity.* New York: New York University Press, 2000. Study of the demographics of the Latino population of the United States.

SEE ALSO Censuses, U.S.; Chicano movement; Cuban immigrants; Cuban immigrants and African Americans; Dominican immigrants; Immigration "crisis"; Japanese Peruvians; Latinos and employment; Latinos and family customs; League of United Latin American Citizens; Mexican American Legal Defense and Education Fund; Proposition 227; Undocumented workers.

LATINOS AND EMPLOYMENT

IMMIGRATION ISSUES: Cuban immigrants; Economics; Labor; Latino immigrants

SIGNIFICANCE: Latinos occupied a comparatively disadvantaged position in the U.S. labor market relative to the white population and to other minorities throughout the twentieth century. This overall trend, however, varied over time in response to changes in the economy.

Latinos were the fastest-growing minority group in the United States during the last quarter of the twentieth century. In 1980, they made up 6.5 percent of the civilian population, and by 1996, they had increased to 10.6 percent. The Bureau of the Census projected that this group would reach 14 percent of the total U.S. population by the year 2010. Empirical research on their employment situation has lagged behind such rapid changes, and it is difficult to discern patterns and trends when the available statistical information is not broken down into national-origin subgroups.

HISTORICAL BACKGROUND　During the late nineteenth century and early twentieth century, Mexican laborers (mainly displaced peasants) began to cross the border into the American Southwest to find work. Throughout the twentieth century, U.S. immigration policy alternatively encouraged and restricted the entry of Mexicans, but the net result has been essentially a steady stream of immigrants. Their numbers, along with the descendants of earlier Mexican immigrants, have made Mexicans the largest subgroup of Latinos in the United States.

During World War I, Puerto Ricans were granted citizenship to ease U.S. labor shortages. By 1920, nearly 12,000 Puerto Ricans had left their home for the United States, settling mostly in New York City and finding employment mainly in manufacturing and services. Their numbers have grown, making them the second largest Latino subgroup.

Cubans constitute the third most numerous subgroup. From 1959, the year when Fidel Castro assumed power following the Cuban Revolution, to 1990, the Cuban population in the United States—which had previously numbered only about 30,000—grew to 1,044,000 people.

THE LATINO LABOR FORCE　The Latino share in the civilian labor force was 5.7 percent of the total in 1980, but it had almost doubled by 1996, to 9.6 percent. The Bureau of Labor Statistics projected further growth to 11 percent by the year 2005.

During the 1980's and 1990's, the labor force participation rates (that is, the percentage of persons who are employed) for the Latino population age sixteen and older approximated those of the non-Latino white population in the same age group (66.5 percent for Latinos and 67.2 percent for non-Latino whites in 1996). However, the rate for Latino men (79.6 percent) was higher than that for non-Latino white men (75.8 percent) in the same year, while Latinas had a lower rate (53.4 percent) than non-Latino white women (59.1 percent).

The occupational distribution of the Latino population reflects both the traditional background of the subgroups and the economic changes of later decades. According to the *Statistical Abstract*, in 1996, Mexicans were mostly operators, fabricators, and laborers (24.5 percent); they also had the highest percentage of workers in farming, forestry, and fishing among all the other subgroups (8.4 percent). Cubans had the highest proportion in managerial and professional occupations (21.7 percent) as well as in technical, sales, and administrative support positions (32.7 percent). The advances made by Puerto Ricans were evidenced by the fact that their concentration in the latter positions (32.1 percent) and in managerial and professional occupations (19 percent) closely approximated those of the Cubans. However, this advance may be more apparent than real because of changes in the occupational structure that have reduced the availability of lower-level, high-paying blue-collar occupations in favor of low-paying white-collar occupations.

COMPARISON WITH NON-LATINO WHITES A comparison of the occupational distribution of Latinos with that of non-Latino whites reveals that the former are concentrated in lower-level occupations and that white men are concentrated in managerial and professional occupations. During the late 1980's, Mexican American men were concentrated in skilled and semiskilled blue-collar jobs, although they were advancing to better jobs; Puerto Rican men were in service and lower-level white-collar jobs. Latinas were more likely than white or black women to be semiskilled manual workers.

Regarding the evolution of Latino earnings and incomes, Gregory DeFreitas reports that in 1949, U.S.-born men of Mexican and Puerto Rican ancestry had incomes that were 55 percent and 76 percent, respectively, of the white non-Latino level. During the 1960's, both groups improved relative to whites; but during the 1970's, the Puerto Ricans experienced a decline and the Mexicans remained at the same level. Latinos generally suffered de-

A Cuban architect working in Miami during the mid-1960's. Among Latino immigrants, Cubans have had a disproportionately strong representation in the professions. (Library of Congress)

creases in income during the 1970's. Median Latino incomes declined in absolute and relative terms after the 1970's. By 1987, Latino income was still almost 9 percent lower in real terms than it had been in 1973 and, when compared with the income of non-Latino whites, even lower than it had been fifteen years earlier.

According to U.S. government statistics, the median income of Latino households, at constant 1995 dollars, was $25,278 in 1980; it rose later to $26,037 in 1990 but fell to $22,860 in 1995. It was 64 percent of the white non-Latino median income, which in 1995 was $35,766, and practically equal to that of African Americans, which stood that year at $22,393.

Since the 1950's, Latinos have made progress in occupational mobility and earning levels, especially during periods of economic expansion. Cuban Americans are nearly equal with non-Latino whites in educational and economic achievement; Mexican Americans and Puerto Ricans, however, are still the most disadvantaged.

UNEMPLOYMENT   Unemployment has been a long-term problem for Latinos. Their actual unemployment rates reflect structural factors such as business-cycle fluctuations, industrial restructuring, and changes in demand as well as individual characteristics such as educational level and previous work experience. As indicated in the *Statistical Abstract of the United States* (1997), in 1980, the total unemployment rate was 7.1 percent, while it was 10.1 percent for Latinos. By 1992, these rates had risen to 7.5 and 11.6 percent, respectively. In 1996, both had decreased; the total rate stood at 5.4 percent and the Latino rate at 8.9 percent.

The rates, however, vary among the national-origin subgroups. Cuban Americans' unemployment rates have been almost as low as those of non-Latino whites, largely because of their above-average educational levels and accumulated work experience. By contrast, Mexican Americans and Puerto Ricans have generally experienced above-average unemployment. Puerto Ricans' unemployment rates are usually twice as high as those of Cuban Americans. Some scholars claim that Puerto Ricans' history of "circular migration" (their frequent returns to the island) tends to destabilize their employment.

FACTORS THAT INFLUENCE THE LATINO LABOR MARKET   Education is one of the main factors that affect the labor market situation for Latinos. De-Freitas, after analyzing the trends in earnings of Latinos and non-Latinos from 1949 to 1979, found that those Latinos who were better educated were able to approximate the earnings of non-Latino whites during the 1960's.

Limited English ability is another relevant factor. Several empirical studies carried out during the 1980's found that language limitations could account for up to one-third of wage differentials between Latino and non-Latino white men. Other research has established that Puerto Rican and Cuban American men, who are concentrated in urban areas, tend to have lower participation rates in the labor force than men from the same national-origin

Mexican migrant worker harvesting sugar beets. (Library of Congress)

subgroups with better English language skills. Mexican Americans, who are mainly operators, fabricators, laborers, and agricultural workers, have higher participation rates because those occupations do not require a good command of English.

Empirical studies have tried to establish the extent of discrimination suffered by Latinos in the labor market. According to the findings of a major study undertaken by the General Accounting Office (1990) to evaluate the effects of the Immigration Reform and Control Act of 1986, discrimination in hiring is practiced against "foreign-looking" or "foreign-sounding" applicants. In particular, an audit carried out as part of the study found that Hispanic job seekers were more likely than similarly qualified Anglos to be unfavorably treated and less likely to receive interviews and job offers. Consequently, discrimination could partially account for the higher Latino unemployment rates.

Self-employment may be a way to escape unemployment, low wages, and obstacles to promotion. However, capital is required to start a business, and many poorer Latinos find it difficult to accumulate savings and are not likely to receive loans from credit institutions. Cuban Americans, who have a higher status background, have opened many small businesses, creating an "ethnic enclave" of Latino businesses in Miami. The benefits of this type of social and economic arrangement have been highly debated. Some contend that it is an avenue of economic mobility for new immigrants; others argue that it may hinder their assimilation into the larger society. However, given the small proportion of self-employed Latinos and the level of their earnings, it is not likely that this type of employment will soon become a prevalent means to reduce inequality for Latinos in the labor market.

Graciela Bardallo-Vivero

FURTHER READING

Bean, Frank D., and Stephanie Bell-Rose, eds. *Immigration and Opportunity: Race, Ethnicity, and Employment in the United States.* New York: Russell Sage Foundation, 1999. Collection of essays on economic and labor issues relating to race and immigration in the United States, with particular attention to the competition for jobs between African Americans and immigrants.

Bohon, Stephanie. *Latinos in Ethnic Enclaves: Immigrant Workers and the Competition for Jobs.* New York: Garland, 2000. Examination of Latino employment in major urban centers.

Briggs, Vernon M. *Immigration and American Unionism.* Ithaca, N.Y.: Cornell University Press, 2001. Scholarly survey of the dynamic interaction between unionism and immigration. Covers the entire sweep of U.S. national history, with an emphasis on the nineteenth century.

Gonzalez, Gilbert G. *Guest Workers or Colonized Labor? Mexican Labor Migration to the United States.* Boulder, Colo.: Paradigm, 2005. Reexamination of the history of Mexican immigration to the United States that looks at the subject in the context of American dominance over Mexico.

Karas, Jennifer. *Bridges and Barriers: Earnings and Occupational Attainment Among Immigrants.* New York: LFB Scholarly Publishing, 2002.

Knouse, Stephen B., P. Rosenfeld, and A. L. Culbertson, eds. *Hispanics in the Workplace.* Newbury Park, Calif.: Sage Publications, 1992. Collection of scholarly studies of Latino employment issues.

Kretsedemas, Philip, and Ana Aparicio, eds. *Immigrants, Welfare Reform, and the Poverty of Policy.* Westport, Conn.: Praeger, 2004. Collection of articles on topics relating to the economic problems of new immigrants in the United States, with particular attention to Haitian, Hispanic, and Southeast Asian immigrants.

Sarmiento, Socorro Torres. *Making Ends Meet: Income-Generating Strategies Among Mexican Immigrants.* New York: LFB Scholarly Publications, 2002. Study of Latino employment issues.

Waldinger, Roger, ed. *Strangers at the Gates: New Immigrants in Urban America.* Berkeley: University of California Press, 2001. Collection of essays on urban aspects of immigration in the United States, particularly race relations and employment.

SEE ALSO Bracero program; Chicano movement; Latinos; Latinos and family customs; Mexican deportations during the Depression; Operation Wetback; Undocumented workers.

LATINOS AND FAMILY CUSTOMS

IMMIGRATION ISSUES: Cuban immigrants; Families and marriage; Labor; Latino immigrants

SIGNIFICANCE: Although new roles and traditions are emerging within Latino families, many Latinos continue to find satisfaction in following traditional practices, viewing the family as a source of stability, protection, and support throughout persons' lifetimes.

Because the historical and cultural experiences of the various groups known collectively as "Latinos" differ widely, it is impossible to discuss a monolithic tradition. There are no universal customs or lifestyles that can fully reflect Latino family life. Nevertheless, there is a strong tradition among Latinos of emphasizing the importance of family, kin, and neighborhood ties.

As with other ethnic and cultural groups, the Latino family functions as a conduit for transmitting social skills and cultural values from one generation to the next. It is important to remember that cultural traditions based on ancestral customs and national origins exert long-lasting influence on Latino family structure and behavior. Family life among Mexican Americans is not identical to that found among Puerto Ricans, Cuban Americans, or Dominican Americans, in part because of such factors as variations in economic and social status; persons' urban versus rural origins; distinctions between professionals, skilled laborers, and unskilled laborers; and differences between persons with high literacy skills and levels of education and those with limited literacy and education. Although members within a particular Latino extended family may share the same cultural origins, the length of time each member has lived in the United States is often very different. Individual family members may not share the same beliefs about what is important in life. Latino families often find themselves forging delicate compromises when their traditional values clash with mainstream American attitudes.

LA FAMILIA There are probably more similarities than differences between the various Latino groups when it comes to basic family characteristics and values. The concept of *la familia* is central to Latino identity, since individuals are considered to be representatives or symbols of the families who raise them. The actions of family members are commonly viewed as bringing honor or shame to the entire family, not solely to individual members.

The extended Latino family includes all the members of the nuclear family plus aunts, uncles, cousins, grandparents, and even godparents. Whether extended family members are related by blood, marriage, or close friendship, they play an important role in improving the economic status of the family. The ability to call upon extended family members for assistance allows for greater flexibility in sharing caregiving responsibilities, giving mothers and younger women the opportunity to add to their families' economic resources by working outside the home.

Eating together is an activity that gives family members an opportunity to strengthen their ties to one another, to share news, and to discuss important family decisions. In preparing family meals, many Latinos include traditional foods and use recipes that have been handed down from generation to generation. Extended family members often participate in these family meals.

FAMILY LOYALTY AND SIZE   Because Latinos have traditionally defined themselves in terms of their obligations to their families, they are willing to set aside other demands in order to fulfill such obligations. If a close family member or relative needs assistance of some kind—whether financial, physical, or emotional—most Latinos consider that such needs outweigh their own personal desires and plans. It is not uncommon for Latinos to take time off from work or school if another family member needs help when visiting a doctor, registering a car, or consulting a lawyer. Especially among immigrant families, Latino children are expected to serve as translators for their Spanish-speaking elders and facilitate families' contact with the broader English-speaking society.

Although large Latino families are not as common as they once were, Latinos continue to outpace other American ethnic groups in terms of birth rates and family size. Although changing attitudes toward divorce and family planning methods have had some effect on family size, Latinos have historically

Latino family on the porch of their Los Angeles home during the early 1970's. The father in this family had to work two jobs to support his large family. (Library of Congress)

495

placed great value on having large families. Their reverence for traditional ways has made many Latinos reluctant to have smaller families with fewer children. Many Latinos face a conflict of cultural values when making the decision to have children, since their cultural tradition of placing family responsibilities first contradicts the tradition of individualism that is encouraged by mainstream American society. Even the most enduring reasons given for having children, such as a desire to carry on the family name or to ensure that family members will be cared for in old age, reflect a mixture of selflessness and self-interest.

According to the 1990 U.S. Census, nearly 70 percent of all Hispanic families were headed by married couples. While 76 percent of Cuban American and 73 percent of Mexican American and South American families were headed by married couples, this was the case for only 56 percent of Puerto Rican and 50 percent of Dominican American families. Central American families had the highest percentage of families headed by fathers whose wives were absent (14 percent), while families headed by women were highest among Dominican Americans (41 percent) and Puerto Ricans (36 percent). Figures from 1990 show that 65 percent of Hispanic families had children under the age of eighteen as compared to 48 percent for all American families.

The Bureau of the Census has estimated that the Hispanic population will increase to 88 million (a fourfold increase over the 1990 population) and will represent 60 percent of the U.S. population by the middle of the twenty-first century. Such growth is expected to occur because of a natural increase within Hispanic families already living in the United States rather than because of a rise in immigration. This projected growth will widen the median age gap between the Hispanic and non-Hispanic white populations. According to the 1990 census, the median age of Hispanics was 25.4 years, whereas non-Hispanic whites' median age was 34.8 years. By the middle of the twenty-first century the median ages are projected to reach 32.1 years and 54.2 years, respectively.

TRADITIONAL FAMILY ROLES   Certain cultural expectations persist among Latinos regarding appropriate roles for family members. It is expected that Latino parents will make whatever personal sacrifices are necessary to improve the welfare of and opportunities available to their children. Such demands are intergenerational, since young adults are expected to make similar sacrifices to assist their elderly relatives and parents, as well as younger siblings. The demand for self-sacrifice is accompanied by an expectation that family members will maintain their pride and dignity. Among Latinos, persons' self-worth and self-respect are defined in terms of how their behavior reflects their upbringing and reinforces the community's regard for their family. It is often considered disrespectful and ungrateful to place individual needs above the welfare of the family as a whole, and betraying the family's esteem and public image is considered more shameful than to bring shame upon oneself.

Historically, Latinos have vested men with ultimate authority to make family decisions. The patriarchal structure that resulted was based on the assumed superiority of men, producing a cultural tradition known as *machismo*. While defining desired traits and behaviors for Latino men as providing leadership, protection, and economic security for the family, *machismo* also dictated reciprocal traits and behaviors for Latina women. Women were expected to respect male authority, to take responsibility for domestic duties, and to honor the family reputation by seeking social relationships and recreation among friends and extended family members.

Despite the negative characteristics often associated with the concept of *machismo*, it arose from the expectation that men earned respect within the Latino community by exercising their authority in the family in a just and fair manner. As traditional stereotypes have given way to a more accurate view of family structure and relationships, Latinos have acknowledged the equally important role that women have played in shaping family life and making important decisions.

Latino families encourage children to have respect for authority. Children are expected to express reverence toward their elders, including grandparents and other aging relatives. Obedience is valued, yet discipline within the family is increasingly affected by parental absence. Although they can call upon members of their extended family, many Latino parents who work multiple jobs to earn enough money to support their children find it difficult to ensure that their children are always under adult supervision.

FAMILY NAMING CUSTOMS AND CELEBRATIONS Many Latino families maintain the custom of recognizing persons' heritage by using the surnames of both parents. In Spanish, this combination of surnames is called *el nombre completo*, or "full name." Persons' first and middle names are followed by their father's and mother's first surnames. Although most Latino families have assimilated the mainstream American custom of adopting one surname for legal purposes, many Latinos identify themselves to each other by their full names as a sign of respect for their kinship ties and cultural origins.

Baptism is an important event in many Latino families. Among Roman Catholic Latinos, this ceremony celebrates the birth of infants and welcomes them as part of the church family. Godparents, or *padrinos*, are chosen from among parents' close relatives or family friends to help care for children and serve as role models in guiding them to adulthood. Other family events with religious dimensions include childrens' first Communion and young girls' quinceañera (part of the fifteenth birthday celebration marking the end of childhood and the beginning of womanhood). Special family traditions mark the observance of saints' and holy days, including *Semana Santa* (Holy Week before Easter) and *Navidad* (Christmas). The Christmas procession known as *Las Posadas* revolves around the family theme of Joseph and Mary's search for lodging in Bethlehem before the birth of Jesus.

Some Latinos observe other family-related holidays or celebrations. Mexican Americans observe *Día de los Muertos* (Day of the Dead) to honor deceased relatives. There are also family traditions associated with patriotic holidays celebrated in Latinos' countries of origin—particularly *Dieciseis* for Mexican Americans, *Día de la Raza* for Puerto Ricans and Dominican Americans, and Independence Day for Cuban Americans.

BLENDING THE OLD AND THE NEW   Although the child-centered focus of *la familia* persists, many Latino parents share family responsibilities instead of holding tightly to their traditional family roles. Latino men and Latina women take advantage of educational and career opportunities, choosing to postpone marriage until later in life. When they marry, many husbands and wives find it easier to share family responsibilities that were formerly defined either as male or female. While families acknowledge that their members have individual goals, many Latinos find comfort in honoring their attachment to their families as a positive cultural attribute and reaffirm the tradition of pulling together to provide mutual assistance in times of need. While such values are hardly unique to Latino families, they do serve to reaffirm cultural roots and ties within the Latino community.

Wendy Sacket

FURTHER READING

Acosta-Belén, Edna, and Barbara R. Sjostrom, eds. *The Hispanic Experience in the United States: Contemporary Issues and Perspectives.* New York: Praeger, 1988. Collection of essays reflecting the research interests of sociologists and cultural anthropologists who have explored issues relating to Latino family life.

Carrasquillo, Angela L. *Hispanic Children and Youth in the United States: A Resource Guide.* New York: Garland, 1991. In addition to directing readers to resource material on family life, language, education, health care, justice, and other social issues, Carrasquillo offers a useful introduction to the history, culture, and diversity of Latino children.

Conley, Ellen Alexander. *The Chosen Shore: Stories of Immigrants.* Berkeley: University of California Press, 2004. Collection of firsthand accounts of modern immigrants from many nations, including Bolivia, Cuba, and Mexico who relate poignant tales of adjusting to life in the United States.

Hoobler, Dorothy, and Thomas Hoobler. *The Mexican American Family Album.* New York: Oxford University Press, 1994. Focusing on the experiences of Mexican Americans, the Hooblers have gathered a broad range of first-person accounts—including personal recollections, diary entries, and letters—to accompany the photographs that comprise this chronicle of family life.

Rumbaut, Rubén G., and Alejandro Portes, eds. *Ethnicities: Children of Immigrants in America.* Berkeley: University of California Press, 2001. Collection of papers on demographic and family issues relating to immigrants. Includes chapters on Mexicans, Cubans, and Central Americans.

Shorris, Earl. *Latinos: A Biography of the People*. New York: W. W. Norton, 1992. Drawing on extensive primary research as well as life portraits of his own family and friends, Shorris offers a lively social history of various Latino groups and their experiences in the United States.

Zambrana, Ruth E., ed. *Understanding Latino Families: Scholarship, Policy and Practice*. Thousand Oaks, Calif.: Sage Publications, 1995. Among the most useful essays in this collection are "Variations, Combinations, and Evolutions: Latino Families in the United States," by Aida Hurtado; "The Study of Latino Families," by William A. Vega; and "Contemporary Issues in Latino Families," by Douglas S. Massey, Ruth E. Zambrana, and Sally Alonzo Bell.

SEE ALSO Chicano movement; Latinos; Latinos and employment; Mexican deportations during the Depression.

LAU V. NICHOLS

THE CASE: U.S. Supreme Court decision on bilingual education
DATE: January 21, 1974

IMMIGRATION ISSUES: Asian immigrants; Chinese immigrants; Civil rights and liberties; Court cases; Education

SIGNIFICANCE: In this decision, the Supreme Court ruled that public school systems must provide bilingual education to limited-English-speaking students.

In 1954, the Supreme Court ruled in *Brown v. Board of Education* that the Fourteenth Amendment to the U.S. Constitution forbade school systems from segregating students into separate schools for only whites or African Americans. The decision effectively overturned a previous Court ruling, in *Plessy v. Ferguson* (1896), that such facilities could be "separate but equal." Instead of desegregating, however, Southern school systems engaged in massive resistance to the Court's order during the next decade. Congress then passed the Civil Rights Act of 1964, which prohibited many types of discrimination. Title VI of the law banned discrimination by recipients of federal financial assistance, including school systems.

CHINESE-SPEAKING STUDENTS In 1965, Congress adopted the Immigration and Nationality Act, under which larger numbers of Asian immigrants arrived in the United States than ever before. Their non-English-speaking children were enrolled in public schools. In the San Francisco Unified School District, students were required to attend school until sixteen years of age, but in 1967, 2,856 students could not adequately comprehend instruction in English. Although 433 students were given supplemental courses in English on a full-time basis and 633 on a part-time basis, the remaining 1,790 students received no additional language instruction. Nevertheless, the state of California required all students to graduate with proficiency in English and permitted school districts to provide bilingual education, if needed. Except for the 433 students in the full-time bilingual education program, Chinese-speaking students were integrated in the same classrooms with English-speaking students but lacked sufficient language ability to derive benefit from the instruction. Of the 1,066 students taking bilingual courses, only 260 had bilingual teachers.

Some parents of the Chinese-speaking children, concerned that their children would drop out of school and experience pressure to join criminal youth gangs, launched protests. Various organizations formed in the Chinese American community, which in turn conducted studies, issued proposals, circulated leaflets, and tried to negotiate with the San Francisco Board of Education. When the board refused to respond adequately, a suit was filed in federal district court in San Francisco on March 25, 1970. The plaintiffs were Kinney Kinmon Lau and eleven other non-English-speaking students, mostly U.S. citizens born of Chinese parents. The defendants were Alan H. Nichols, president of the San Francisco Board of Education, the rest of the Board of Education, and the San Francisco Board of Supervisors.

FINDINGS AND RULINGS   On May 25, 1970, the Office for Civil Rights (OCR) of the U.S. Department of Health, Education, and Welfare issued the following regulation pursuant to its responsibility to monitor Title VI compliance:

> Where inability to speak and understand the English language excludes national-origin minority group children from effective participation in the educational program offered by a school district, the district must take affirmative steps to rectify the language deficiency in order to open its instructional program to these students.

OCR had sided with the Chinese-speaking students. One day later, the court ruled that the school system was violating neither Title VI nor the Fourteenth Amendment; instead, the plaintiffs were characterized as asking for "special rights above those granted other children." Lawyers representing the Chinese Americans then appealed, this time supported by a friend-of-the-court brief filed by the U.S. Department of Justice. On January 8, 1973, the Court of Appeals also ruled adversely, stating that there was no duty "to rectify appellants' special deficiencies, as long as they provided these students with access to the same educational system made available to all other students." The appeals court claimed that the children's problems were "not the result of law enacted by the state . . . but the result of deficiency created by themselves in failing to learn the English language."

On June 12, 1973, the Supreme Court agreed to hear the case. Oral argument was heard on December 10, 1973. On January 21, 1974, the Supreme Court unanimously overturned the lower courts. Justice William O. Douglas delivered the majority opinion, which included the memorable statement that

> There is no equality of treatment merely by providing students with the same facilities, textbooks, teachers, and curriculum; for students who do not understand English are effectively foreclosed from any meaningful education.

The Supreme Court returned the case to the district court so that the school system could design a plan of language-needs assessments and programs for addressing those needs. In a concurring opinion, Chief Justice Warren E. Burger and Justice Harry A. Blackmun observed that the number of underserved non-English-speaking, particularly Chinese-speaking, students was substantial in this case, but they would not order bilingual education for "just a single child who speaks only German or Polish or Spanish or any language other than English."

The Supreme Court's decision in *Lau* ultimately resulted in changes to enable Chinese-speaking students to obtain equal educational opportunity in San Francisco's public schools, although it was more than a year before such changes began to be implemented. The greatest impact, however, has been among Spanish-speaking students, members of the largest language minority group in the United States.

RECOGNITION OF BILINGUALISM   Subsequently, Congress passed the Equal Educational Opportunities Act in 1974, a provision of which superseded *Lau* by requiring "appropriate action to overcome language barriers that impede equal participation," which a federal district court later applied to the need for new methods to deal with speakers of "Black English" in *Martin Luther King, Jr., Elementary School Children v. Michigan Board of Education* (1979). Also in 1974, the Bilingual Education Act of 1968 was amended to provide more federal funds for second-language instruction so that school districts could be brought into compliance with *Lau.* Bilingualism was further recognized when Congress passed the Voting Rights Act of 1975, which established guidelines for providing ballots in the languages of certain minority groups.

In 1975, OCR established informal guidelines for four bilingual programs that would enable school districts to come into compliance with the Supreme Court ruling. The main requirement was first to test students to determine language proficiency. Students with no English proficiency at all were to be exposed to bilingual/bicultural programs or transitional bilingual education programs; secondary schools also had the option of providing "English as a second language" or "high intensive language training" programs. If a student had some familiarity with English, these four programs would be required only if testing revealed that the student had low achievement test scores.

Because the OCR guidelines were not published in the *Federal Register* for public comment and later modification, they were challenged on September 29, 1978, in the federal district court of Alaska (*Northwest Arctic School District v. Califano*). The case was settled by a consent decree in 1980, when the federal agency agreed to publish a "Notice of Proposed Rulemaking"; however, soon after Ronald Reagan took office as president, that notice was withdrawn. By 1985, a manual to identify types of language discrimination was compiled to supersede the 1975 guidelines, but it also was not published in the *Federal Register* for public comment. Meanwhile, methods for educating limited-English-speaking students evolved beyond the OCR's original conceptions, and further litigation followed. In 1981, a U.S. circuit court ruled in *Castañeda v. Pickard* that bilingual educational programs are lawful when they satisfy three tests: (1) the program is recognized by professionals as sound in educational theory; (2) the program is designed to implement that theory; and (3) the program actually results in overcoming language barriers.

During the presidency of Ronald Reagan, civil rights monitoring focused more on "reverse discrimination" than on violations of equal educational opportunities. Congressional hearings were held to goad OCR into action. Although in 1991 OCR's top priority was equal educational opportunities for national-origin minority and Native American students with limited-English proficiency (LEP) or non-English proficiency (NEP), results were difficult to discern, and a movement to make English the official language of the United States (the "English-only" movement) threatened to overturn *Lau* and related legislation. Moreover, by the late 1990's the controversy over bilingual education had revived, as many teachers, parents, policymakers, and legislators—including a significant number of Latinos—acknowledged the disappointing results of bilingual programs and sought solutions through legislation. In 1998, for example, California voted to curtail bilingual education by passing Proposition 227. Such measures were perceived as appropriate means of forcing quick English-language acquisition by some, but as simplistic and counterproductive by others.

Michael Haas

FURTHER READING

Biegel, Stuart. "The Parameters of the Bilingual Education Debate in California Twenty Years After *Lau v. Nichols*." *Chicano-Latino Law Review* 14 (Winter, 1994): 48-60. The status of *Lau* in light of the 1990's English-only movement.

Brittain, Carmina. *Transnational Messages: Experiences of Chinese and Mexican Immigrants in American Schools*. New York: LFB Scholarly Publications, 2002. Broad study of the special problems faced by immigrants in American public schools.

Bull, Barry L., Royal T. Fruehling, and Virgie Chattergy. *The Ethics of Multicultural and Bilingual Education.* New York: Teachers College Press, 1992. Contrasts how liberal, democratic, and communitarian approaches to education relate to bilingual and multicultural education.

Lee, Stacey J. *Up Against Whiteness: Race, School, and Immigrant Youth.* New York: Teachers College Press, 2005. Study of cultural biases in education that focuses on the special problems of immigrant schoolchildren.

Newman, Terri Lunn. "Proposal: Bilingual Education Guidelines for the Courts and the Schools." *Emory Law Journal* 33 (Spring, 1984): 577-629. Legal requirements of *Lau* presented as guidelines for school systems in establishing bilingual programs.

Orlando, Carlos J., and Virginia P. Collier. *Bilingual and ESL Classrooms: Teaching in Multicultural Contexts.* New York: McGraw-Hill, 1985. Discusses the need for bilingual education, alternative approaches available, and resources required.

United States Commission on Civil Rights. *A Better Chance to Learn: Bilingual-Bicultural Education.* Washington, D.C.: Author, 1975. Assesses the national impact of *Lau*; contains the text of the Supreme Court decision and related documents.

Wang, L. Ling-chi. "*Lau v. Nichols*: History of Struggle for Equal and Quality Education." In *Asian-Americans: Social and Psychological Perspectives*, edited by Russell Endo, Stanley Sue, and Nathaniel N. Wagner. Palo Alto, Calif.: Science & Behavior Books, 1980. Describes how the *Lau* case was pursued, especially the resistance to implementation.

See also Bilingual education; Bilingual Education Act of 1968; English-only and official English movements; Proposition 227.

League of United Latin American Citizens

IDENTIFICATION: Latino advocacy organization
DATE: Founded in 1929
PLACE: Corpus Christi, Texas

IMMIGRATION ISSUES: Civil rights and liberties; Latino immigrants; Mexican immigrants

SIGNIFICANCE: One of the oldest Hispanic advocacy organizations in the United States, the League of United Latin American Citizens has always concerned itself with the rights of Mexican immigrants.

The League of United Latin American Citizens (LULAC) was formed in order to unite all Latin American organizations under one title. In 1927, the main Latin American groups were the Sons of America, the Knights of America, and the League of Latin American Citizens, and there were other less well-known groups. The Sons of America had councils in Sommerset, Pearsall, Corpus Christi, and San Antonio, Texas; the Knights of America had a council in San Antonio; the League of Latin American Citizens had councils in Harlingen, Brownsville, Laredo, Peñitas, La Grulla, McAllen, and Gulf, Texas.

As more Anglo-Americans moved into Texas during the early nineteenth century, persons of Spanish or Mexican descent experienced open discrimination and segregation that placed them in the position of second-class citizens. They had been under the rule of six different countries before Texas entered the union in 1845. Most continued to live and work as they always had, without being assertive about their rights. As time progressed, many Hispanics found that prejudice and discrimination were becoming less tolerable. Groups began to form to give more impact to requests that these practices cease. The Sons of America Council No. 4 in Corpus Christi, led by Ben Garza, originated a unification plan, believing that if all Hispanic organizations would regroup into one strong, unified, and vocal organization, more attention would be brought to the plight of those who were being discriminated against.

On August 14, 1927, delegates from the Sons of America, the Knights of America, and smaller groups met in Harlingen, Texas, to form LULAC. The resolution that was presented was adopted by those in the meeting. It was expected that the leaders of the major groups—Alonso Perales, Luz Saenz, José Canales, and Juan Lozano of the Rio Grande Valley of south Texas— would be invited by the president general of the Sons of America to begin the unification process. In response to concerns about the merger expressed by some members, Council No. 4 of the Sons of America drafted an agreement between itself and the Knights of America to unite. These two groups waited a year for the merger to be completed. Perales, president general of the Latin American League, stayed in close contact with Garza to maintain interest in the merger among the three main groups. However, the president general of the Sons of America never called the convention. After the long wait, Council No. 4 withdrew from the Sons of America on February 7, 1929. Participants at this meeting again voted to have a general convention for the purpose of unification. On February 17, 1929, invitations were sent to all the groups to meet in Corpus Christi, Texas, to vote on the merger.

Along with interested members of the Hispanic groups, Douglas Weeks, a professor at the University of Texas, attended not only to study the merger but also to open the convention as a nonaligned attendee. Garza was elected chairman pro tem. His popularity as an energetic and fair civic leader made him a good spokesperson for the new group. The assembly had to choose a chairman, plan a single constitution, and select a name that would encompass the goals of the previously separate groups. The committee chosen to select a name included Juan Solis and Mauro Machado of the Knights of America, Perales and Canales of the Latin American League, E. N. Marin and A. de Luna of Corpus Christi, and Fortunio Treviño of Alice, Texas. Machado, of the Knights of America, proposed "United Latin American Citizens." This was amended to read "League of United Latin American Citizens," which was seconded by Canales. On February 17, 1929, LULAC formally came into being at Corpus Christi, Texas.

The naming committee undertook other proposals before coming back to the general convention. Canales proposed a motto, "All for One and One for All," as a reminder of their purpose in uniting and as a basis for their future activities. They set some basic rules to guide the league until the constitutional convention could be held. This meeting was called for May 18 and 19, 1929, with an executive committee made up of Garza, M. C. González as secretary, and Canales and Saenz as members at large. On May 18, the first meeting under the new title was called. The constitution proposed by Canales was adopted, and new officers were elected. The officers were Garza, president general; González, vice president general; de Luna, secretary general; and Louis C. Wilmot of Corpus Christi, treasurer general. George Washington's prayer was adopted from the ritual of the Sons of America, and the U.S. flag was adopted as the group's official flag. Now, in union, the new group could work to remove the injustices that had been building for many years. LULAC was chartered in 1931 under the laws of the state of Texas and later in New Mexico, Arizona, California, and Colorado, as other councils were formed. LULAC began issuing *LULAC Notes*, but in August, 1931, the first issue of *LULAC News* was published. During the 1990's, this magazine carried the subtitle *The Magazine for Today's Latino*.

EVOLUTION   In the formative years, auxiliaries were started by women whose husbands were active LULAC members. In August, 1987, LULAC amended its constitution to admit women into the organization. Between 1937 and 1938, junior LULAC councils were formed under the sponsorship of adult councils. In 1940, LULAC councils peaked, but with the beginning of World War II, the councils weakened with the departure of the men to military service. In 1945 and 1946, LULAC began to make great strides as educated, trained men returned from the service. Prestigious positions were filled by Hispanics and discrimination lessened. Non-Hispanics were joining, and LULAC was moving toward its objectives.

When the Civil Rights movement of the 1960's began, other Hispanic groups with a more militant response to discrimination began to form. Leaders such as the charismatic preacher, Reies López Tijerina in New Mexico and Rodolfo Gonzáles in Denver marched in protest of the treatment Hispanics were receiving. César Chávez led farm groups in California on peaceful marches, which frequently erupted into violent confrontations as the number of militant members rose. LULAC did not totally support all these movements. It preferred mediation to resolve serious disagreements and education for all Hispanics as better ways of blending peacefully into the U.S. mainstream.

LULAC has evolved to stress education. Parents are encouraged to prepare their children well to enter school. English is encouraged as the primary language, Spanish as the second language. As students mature, they are encouraged to finish high school and enter college. For those who aspire to higher learning, LULAC sponsors many scholarships; it also offers other forms of financial aid and counseling. LULAC Education Centers are located in sixty cities in seventeen states to provide this help. With corporate and federal aid, these centers have made it possible for disadvantaged Hispanic American youth to become productive members of their American communities.

Among its other pursuits, LULAC has used the courts to advance the rights of Hispanics. In 1987, for example, LULAC filed a class-action suit against the federal Immigration and Naturalization Service (INS) to force the INS to process amnesty applicants of immigrants more expeditiously. When *League of United Latin American Citizens v. Immigration and Naturalization Service* was settled in the organization's favor in 2003, more than 100,000 immigrants were able to become permanent legal residents in the United States.

Norma Crews

FURTHER READING

De la Garza, Rodolfo O., ed. *Ignored Voices: Public Opinion Polls and the Latino Community.* Austin: Center for Mexican American Studies, University of Texas at Austin Press, 1987. Argues that the opinions of Hispanic people were virtually ignored, politically and otherwise, except in heavily Hispanic communities.

Garcia, F. Chris, ed. *Latinos and the Political System.* Notre Dame, Ind.: University of Notre Dame Press, 1988. Discusses some of the political problems that prompted the formation of organizations such as LULAC.

Garcia, Mario T. *Mexican-Americans: Leadership, Ideology, and Identity, 1930-1960.* New Haven, Conn.: Yale University Press, 1989. A thorough treatise on Hispanic assimilation into the mainstream of U.S. business and community.

Jonas, Susanne, and Suzanne Dod Thomas, eds. *Immigration: A Civil Rights Issue for the Americas.* Wilmington, Del.: Scholarly Resources, 1999. General study of civil rights issues arising in immigrant communities.

Mirande, Alfredo. *The Chicano Experience: An Alternative Perspective.* Notre Dame, Ind.: University of Notre Dame Press, 1985. A view into the life of the less accepted Hispanic, the Chicano. Gives information on La Raza, a more militant group representing Hispanics of the 1960's and 1970's.

Shorris, Earl. *Latinos: A Biography of the People.* New York: W. W. Norton, 1992. A collection of information on Hispanics in the United States, and a general overview of those Hispanics who immigrated and settled during the twentieth century.

SEE ALSO   Border Patrol, U.S.; Bracero program; Chicano movement; Latinos; Latinos and employment; Mexican American Legal Defense and Education Fund; Mexican deportations during the Depression; Undocumented workers.

LITERATURE

IMMIGRATION ISSUES: African Americans; European immigrants; Literature

SIGNIFICANCE: Much North American literature has been written by or about immigrants. Additionally, a significant number of North American authors have emigrated to other continents and written about their adopted homes.

Native Americans constitute only a small percentage of the population of North America, so it can be argued that virtually all North American literature has been written by immigrants from other continents. Chroniclers of the founding of the English colonies during the sixteenth and seventeenth centuries were John White, John Smith, and William Bradford. The best collection is that of Richard Hakluyt, titled *Divers Voyages Touching the Discovery of America* (1582). The Puritans Anne Bradstreet and Edward Taylor came in the seventeenth century from England to New England, where both wrote poetry. Another poet, Phillis Wheatley, was taken as a slave to Boston from Africa in the eighteenth century. England was denounced before the Revolutionary War by native son Thomas Paine, an immigrant to Virginia.

There were some voyage narratives written in French also. Jesuit missionaries to North America in the seventeenth century wrote reports in French that have come to be known as the Jesuit relations. These missionaries were great scholars and produced dictionaries and religious literature in various Native American languages. In addition, the seventeenth century produced voyage narratives in Dutch and Swedish.

Michel-Guillaume-Jean de Crèvecœur left Normandy for New York, where as J. Hector St. John he wrote *Letters from an American Farmer* (1782) about the metamorphosis of a Frenchman into an American. Although Crèvecœur contrasted favorably freedom in America with oppression in Europe, his experience of that reality differed greatly from the American Dream. During the Revolutionary War, for refusing to take sides, he lost his farm, was imprisoned, and fled for England. On his return, he found that his farm was ruined, his wife dead, and his children missing. His book, however, recounts the promise of a nation in which such disturbances would not be the norm. The book remains as the tale of what America has always meant to immigrants.

Upton Sinclair wrote *The Jungle* (1906) about Polish immigrants working in Chicago's meatpacking plants. With its depiction of the immigrants'

Upton Sinclair, author of The Jungle. (Library of Congress)

squalid living and working conditions, Sinclair's novel fits squarely into the tradition of naturalism. Willa Cather wrote about Swedish immigrants in Nebraska in *O Pioneers!* (1913) and about Bohemian immigrants to the same prairie in *My Ántonia* (1918). She also wrote about French missionaries in New Mexico in *Death Comes for the Archbishop* (1927). O. E. Rölvaag's *I de dage* (1924) and *Riket grundlægges* (1925, translated together as *Giants in the Earth: A Saga of the Prairie*, 1927) are about Norwegian immigrants to the Dakotas. Kate Chopin wrote about the Creole culture in New Orleans in her novel *The Awakening* (1899) and in her short stories.

INTERNAL MIGRATIONS   Henry Wadsworth Longfellow's long poem *Evangeline* (1847) is about the migration of the French Canadians from Nova Scotia to Louisiana after they were expelled from their homeland, Acadia, by the British in the eighteenth century. The Harlem Renaissance was a literary and musical movement instigated by African Americans who had migrated from the southern United States to New York to find employment during and after World War I. The Harlem Renaissance also attracted many immigrants of African heritage from the West Indies. One such immigrant was the poet Claude McKay, whose British education in his native Jamaica resulted in a formal poetic style that was distinctive from the innovative jazz rhythms of Langston Hughes, an African American poet who migrated to New York during the Harlem Renaissance.

Another Jamaican who went to New York during the Harlem Renaissance was Marcus Garvey, who became leader of a movement that proposed to take all black people in North America and the West Indies back to Africa. Garvey is fictionalized in Ralph Ellison's novel *Invisible Man* (1952).

John Steinbeck's *The Grapes of Wrath* (1939) is about people who are made to feel like immigrants within their own country during the Great Depression. When drought results in agricultural disaster and widespread foreclosure in Oklahoma, the farmers must leave to find work as migrant workers in California. After the Civil Rights movement in the United States during the 1960's, American literature became an amalgam of books by and about immigrants from continents other than Europe. Many of the authors of these books were born in the United States, but their parents' or grandparents' tales of immigration form the basis for much of this literature. Maxine Hong Kingston's *The Woman Warrior* (1976) and Amy Tan's *The Joy Luck Club* (1989) are classics of Asian American literature. Sandra Cisneros and Ana Castillo are notable voices of Latin American culture, as are Rudolfo Anaya and Rolando Hinojosa.

EMIGRANTS FROM NORTH AMERICA   Many North American writers have, for various reasons, felt compelled to venture abroad. Some have traveled to seek adventure and cultures different from that of North America. Many have traveled to Europe in order to experience the culture that has most influenced North American literature. Others have traveled to escape prejudice and lack of opportunity.

During the early nineteenth century, Washington Irving was the first U.S. diplomatic officer stationed in Spain. *The Alhambra* (1832) is a collection of stories inspired by his life in Spain. Irving also wrote *A History of New York from the Beginning of the World to the End of the Dutch Dynasty, by Diedrich Knickerbocker* (1809) about Dutch immigrants in New York. Longfellow traveled in Europe, where his study of languages and literature was preparation for his position as the first professor of Romance languages at Harvard.

John Steinbeck's novel The Grapes of Wrath *was inspired by the large-scale internal migrations of the Great Depression of the 1930's, when Dust Bowl conditions in Oklahoma drove many people west in search of work.* (Library of Congress)

In 1867, Mark Twain toured Europe and the Holy Land and sent back journalistic accounts of his travels to a California newspaper. Later incorporated into *The Innocents Abroad* (1869)—the best-selling travel book of the nineteenth century—these accounts reflect Twain's opinion that Europe's artistic traditions were stifling. In the work, Twain states his preference for the artistic freedom afforded him in North America, where there was no preexisting tradition to which he must conform.

Other North American authors have differed with Twain. During the late nineteenth and early twentieth centuries, Henry James wrote many of his novels and short stories about Great Britain and Europe; James found the tensions of Europe's class system engrossing. Also during the early twentieth century, Ezra Pound, who was born in Idaho, found Europe a necessary aesthetic stimulus for writing poetry. Pound was particularly fond of Italian culture, especially opera, as is evident in his *Cantos* (1970). Pound aligned himself politically with Benito Mussolini, Italy's Fascist dictator, for which he was charged with treason at the end of World War II. T. S. Eliot was another North American poet whose attraction for the Old World was aesthetic and political. Born in St. Louis and educated at Harvard, Eliot became a British subject, as the novelist Henry James had done earlier.

Pound and Eliot were part of the "lost generation," a group of American writers who, in the aftermath of World War I, found themselves emotionally and culturally adrift. The group included F. Scott Fitzgerald, Hart Crane, John Dos Passos, and Ernest Hemingway. Hemingway, for one, set most of his greatest novels in Europe, with American protagonists who find themselves unmoored in events large and small. Fitzgerald was less influenced artistically by his time abroad than the other members of the lost generation, although his novel *Tender Is the Night* (1934) has a French setting. The Canadian writer Morley Callaghan was one of the lost generation. He and Hemingway met while both wrote for the *Toronto Star,* and they were in Paris together.

Many African Americans have emigrated to Europe in order to enjoy greater personal and artistic freedom than they experienced in the United States. James Baldwin and Richard Wright are best known for their works about the oppression suffered by African Americans in the United States, but both lived in France for extended periods. Other African American writers felt thwarted artistically in their own country because, as African Americans, they were expected to write about racial issues and they could not be appreciated on strictly aesthetic grounds. Chester Himes, who had great difficulty getting published in the United States, emigrated to France to write detective novels, and Frank Yerby left for Europe to write historical novels.

Douglas Edward LaPrade

FURTHER READING

Alba, Richard D. *Ethnic Identity: The Transformation of White America.* New Haven, Conn.: Yale University Press, 1990. Cites the decline of national origin as a basis for social division among European Americans and the maintenance of the line between European and non-European Americans in social division.

Benmayor, Rina, and Andor Skotnes, eds. *Migration and Identity*. New Brunswick, N.J.: Transaction, 2005. Collection of essays on identity issues among immigrants.

Boelhower, William Q. *Through a Glass Darkly: Ethnic Semiosis in American Literature*. New York: Oxford University Press, 1987. Adopts the stance that literature by minorities and immigrants should be assimilated into mainstream American literature.

Cheung, King-Kok, and Stan Yogi, comps. *Asian American Literature: An Annotated Bibliography*. New York: Modern Language Association of America, 1988. Focuses mostly on primary sources, which are divided into Chinese American, Japanese American, Filipino American, and so on.

Cull, Nicholas J., and David Carrasco, eds. *Alambrista and the U.S.-Mexico Border: Film, Music, and Stories of Undocumented Immigrants*. Albuquerque: University of New Mexico Press, 2004. Collection of essays on dramatic works, films, and music about Mexicans who cross the border illegally into the United States.

Daniels, Roger. *Coming to America: A History of Immigration and Ethnicity in American Life*. New York: HarperCollins, 1990. Debunks many widely held myths about the immigrant experience.

Fabre, Michel. *From Harlem to Paris: Black American Writers in France, 1840-1980*. Urbana: University of Illinois Press, 1991. Includes discussions of many notable African American writers.

Fender, Stephen. *Sea Changes: British Emigration and American Literature*. Cambridge, England: Cambridge University Press, 1992. Analyzes reasons for British emigration to America from colonial times until World War II.

Kim, Elaine H. *Asian American Literature: An Introduction to the Writings and Their Social Context*. Philadelphia: Temple University Press, 1982. Distinguishes between Asian and Asian American identities, and between first and second generation immigrants.

Lohuis, Elisabeth ten. *Towards a Winning of the West: Novels by East European Jewish Immigrants to America and Their American Offspring*. [Leiden: s.n., 2003]. Difficult to find but potentially useful study of Jewish immigrant literature.

Lowery, Ruth McKoy. *Immigrants in Children's Literature*. New York: P. Lang, 2000. Examination of the depictions of immigrants in children's fiction that focuses on seventeen novels.

Saldívar, Ramón. *Chicano Narrative: The Dialectics of Difference*. Madison: University of Wisconsin Press, 1990. Discusses works by José Antonio Villarreal, Anaya, Hinojosa, and others.

Simone, Roberta. *The Immigrant Experience in American Fiction: An Annotated Bibliography*. Metuchen, N.J.: Scarecrow Press, 1995. Arranges primary and secondary sources alphabetically according to immigrant group, from Armenian to Yugoslavian.

Sollors, Werner, and Maria Diedrich, eds. *The Black Columbiad: Defining Moments in African American Literature and Culture.* Cambridge, Mass.: Harvard University Press, 1994. A collection of essays, most of which focus on the diaspora as the defining moment in African American identity.

Takaki, Ronald. *Strangers from a Different Shore: A History of Asian Americans.* Boston: Little, Brown, 1989. Cites literary sources to describe the Asian immigrant experience.

Wilentz, Gay. *Binding Cultures: Black Women Writers in Africa and the Diaspora.* Bloomington: Indiana University Press, 1992. Discusses three novels by African women and three by African American women.

SEE ALSO Asian American literature; Chinese immigrants; European immigrant literature; Melting pot.

LITTLE HAVANA

IDENTIFICATION: Cuban residential enclave
PLACE: Miami, Florida

IMMIGRATION ISSUES: Cuban immigrants; Ethnic enclaves; Latino immigrants

SIGNIFICANCE: Originally a lightly populated enclave of Miami, Little Havana grew into the largest center of Cuban immigrants in the United States, and its residents became a major force in both Miami and Florida politics. In 2000, the U.S. Census found that nearly 60 percent of the residents of Miami were foreign born, with the overwhelming part of these people of Cuban origin.

The term "Little Havana" was originally coined by the English-speaking community in Miami during the late 1920's and early 1930's to describe the small enclave of Cubans that lived in the Eighth Street and Flagler Avenue area. After the Cuban Revolution of 1959 led by Fidel Castro, a large number of Cuban refugees arrived in Miami. They, and more than a half million Cubans who arrived during the 1960's, settled in the Little Havana area of Miami. Though many Cuban immigrants have dispersed to other U.S. cities, the enclave of Little Havana has remained.

Little Havana encompasses an area of about four square miles. It is located in the southwest portion of Miami, hence the Cuban name for the area, Souwesera. Upon the arrival of the immigrants during the 1960's, the area took on a distinct Cuban flavor. Cuban businesses sprang up everywhere, especially on Eighth Street (also known as Calle Ocho). Most store signs were in Spanish; later signs reading "English spoken here" were placed in many store-

Cuban immigrants playing chess in a public park in Little Havana. (Cuban Archives, Otto G. Richter Library, University of Miami)

fronts in an attempt to avoid alienating other Miami residents. However, anyone living and doing business in Little Havana did not need to speak English.

The first wave of Cubans fleeing the 1959 revolution arrived with nothing except the clothes on their backs and nearly empty suitcases. Because they were often unfamiliar with the language or the culture, they tended to congregate with fellow Cuban Americans, much as the Irish, Swedish, Norwegians, and Italians had done during their mass migrations in the final third of the nineteenth century.

The Cubans accepted almost any employment they could find, which created racial conflict with other economically challenged groups in Miami, especially the African American community. The African American community felt that the Cuban refugees were taking many of the jobs and positions to which they aspired. Tensions ran high and finally boiled over with the Miami riots of 1980. Although these riots were the direct result of a Hispanic police officer being acquitted in the shooting of an African American, the underlying cause was all the years of tension between the two communities.

As time passed, many of the residents of Little Havana, some of whom had become prosperous, moved to suburbs such as Hialeah and Coral Gables and other Florida cities. Though this lessened the tensions between Cuban Americans and other ethnic and racial groups in Miami, it created problems between the Cuban Americans and the white, European American populace. The tensions were largely cultural: The white community resented the Cubans' use of Spanish, even among themselves, and attempted to legislate that they use only English. Though the "English only" proponents failed, they are likely to try again. Unlike other minorities or ethnic groups that migrated to the United States, the Cuban community has sought to preserve its cultural heritage more vigorously and openly. This in itself has created tensions with the U.S. population as a whole.

Peter E. Carr

FURTHER READING

Bardach, Ann Louise. *Cuba Confidential: Love and Vengeance in Miami and Havana.* New York: Random House, 2002.

Bohon, Stephanie. *Latinos in Ethnic Enclaves: Immigrant Workers and the Competition for Jobs.* New York: Garland, 2000.

Levine, Robert M., and Moisés Asís. *Cuban Miami.* New Brunswick, N.J.: Rutgers University Press, 2000.

Zebich-Knos, Michele, and Heather Nicol. *Foreign Policy Toward Cuba: Isolation or Engagement?* Lanham, Md.: Lexington Books, 2005.

SEE ALSO Chinatowns; Cuban immigrants; Cuban immigrants and African Americans; Cuban refugee policy; Ethnic enclaves; Florida illegal-immigrant suit; Generational acculturation; Little Italies; Little Tokyos.

LITTLE ITALIES

DEFINITION: Predominantly Italian ethnic enclaves in major cities

IMMIGRATION ISSUES: Ethnic enclaves; European immigrants

SIGNIFICANCE: The "Little Italies" that arose in major eastern cities during the late nineteenth century tended to separate Italian immigrants from mainstream American society, while allowing them to maintain their ways of life, eating familiar foods, speaking their native language, and maintaining their close-knit family organization and religious practices.

Millions of people from 1880 to 1930 came to the United States with the hope of finding a life better than the one they had left in their country of origin. The U.S. Census indicates that during this fifty-year period more than four million Italians (mostly from poor backgrounds) migrated to U.S. cities such as New York City, Boston, Philadelphia, and Chicago. In these cities, the Italian immigrants moved to areas that contained other Italians, specifically their *paesani*, or people from the same village in Italy. Italian communities known as Little Italies developed as an outcome of this migration.

In *The Italian Americans* (1970), Joseph Lopreato shows how Little Italies shielded Italian immigrants from the ways and demands of American society.

Clam seller in New York City's Little Italy around 1900. (Library of Congress)

He points out that these immigrants, having distanced themselves from the old culture in Italy, needed a certain amount of time to understand and participate in the social organizations of the new society in the United States. The Little Italies acted as bridges between the old life in Italy and the new life in the United States.

Works such as *Italian Americans into the Twilight of Ethnicity* (1985), by Richard Alba, and *The Italians* (1976), by Patricia Snyder Weibust, Gennaro Capobianco, and Sally Innis Gould, describe the growth and decay that Little Italies have undergone in U.S. cities. Between the 1880's and early 1940's, the Little Italies flourished, giving birth to many Italian American-owned businesses (including restaurants, bakeries, groceries, clothing shops, butcher shops, and pasta shops), Italian-language newspapers, and mutual benefit societies (organizations involved in helping Italian immigrants deal with sickness, death, and loneliness). Moreover, these communities were host to celebrations of *festa* (Italian religious festivals) and other religious activities.

Before World War II, Little Italies reached their peak in development and activities. However, after the 1940's, these communities began to shrink, partly because second- and third-generation Italian Americans were becoming wealthier and leaving the Little Italies for the suburbs. In addition, few Italians were immigrating to the United States. Since the 1970's, the bulk of Italian Americans have lived outside the Little Italies, where only a semblance remains of the old order. The number of Italian American-owned businesses,

Italian-language newspapers, and mutual benefit societies in these communities has decreased tremendously. Certain activities, such as the *festas*, have continued to be held in Little Italies, some as simple appearances and others to keep the memories alive of an earlier time.

Louis Gesualdi

FURTHER READING

Burgan, Michael. *Italian Immigrants*. New York: Facts On File, 2005.

Mangione, Jerre, and Ben Morreale. *La Storia: Five Centuries of the Italian American Experience*. New York: HarperCollins, 1992.

Mormino, Gary Ross. *Immigrants on the Hill: Italian Americans in St. Louis, 1882-1982*. Urbana: University of Illinois Press, 1986.

Yans-McLaughlin, Virginia. *Family and Community—Italian Immigrants in Buffalo, 1880-1930*. Ithaca, N.Y.: Cornell University Press, 1971.

SEE ALSO   Chinatowns; Ethnic enclaves; Generational acculturation; Italian immigrants; Little Havana; Little Tokyos.

LITTLE TOKYOS

DEFINITION: Predominantly Japanese enclaves in western U.S. cities

IMMIGRATION ISSUES: Asian immigrants; Ethnic enclaves; Japanese immigrants

SIGNIFICANCE: Slower to develop in American cities than Chinatowns, most of the "Little Tokyos" of western U.S. cities disappeared during World War II and afterward took on much different forms.

The first "Little Tokyo" arose in Southern California during the late nineteenth century. Around 1885, Japanese immigrants in Los Angeles gradually populated a small section of the city that became known as Little Tokyo. By 1910, Japanese shops, restaurants, language schools, and shrines were established, and Little Tokyo became the home of nearly 37,000 Japanese.

Before World War II, Little Tokyos were also established in Seattle (almost 11,700 Japanese immigrants) and in San Francisco, where the Japanese ethnic community was the third largest in the United States, at about 5,000. Other Little Tokyos of more than 1,000 were in Sacramento and Stockton, California, Portland, Oregon, and New York City.

Although Japanese people began immigrating to the United States as early as the mid-1850's, Little Tokyos took much longer to be established than

Chinatowns, probably because of the cultural differences between the two groups. The Japanese traditionally believed that agriculture was the most virtuous occupation and that people who made their living as merchants were less respectable. As a result, the majority of the early Japanese immigrants gravitated to rural areas to be farmers, as opposed to the Chinese immigrants, who were usually merchants in the city.

In Canada, before World War II, more than 97 percent of Japanese immigrants resided in the province of British Columbia. By 1931, nearly one-third of the Japanese population (about 8,300) lived in Vancouver, and more than half of them were in the district known as Little Tokyo. This was the only Japanese ethnic community in Canada in those days. However, no physical structures or symbolic buildings such as shrines were built because of severe anti-Asian sentiment.

During World War II, Little Tokyos practically disappeared from North America following the incarceration of people of Japanese

Sign at the entrance of a Japanese-owned shop in Los Angeles's Little Tokyo in April, 1942. Along with virtually all persons of Japanese ancestry living on the West Coast, the proprietor of the shop was about to be "relocated" to an internment camp for the duration of World War II, and he wished to serve notice that he would not be taking his business with him. (Library of Congress)

descent in internment camps. During the 1970's and 1980's, when the political and economic relationships between the United States and Japan flourished, Japanese Americans began to revitalize Little Tokyos. However, by then, Little Tokyos had become more tourist attractions than residential areas. Today new generations of Japanese Americans tend to live in all parts of the city and suburbs.

In Canada, after World War II, Japanese internees were not allowed to return to their homes in British Columbia. They had to choose between going to Japan or relocating to other provinces east of the Rocky Mountains. In 1949, Japanese Canadians were finally permitted to return to British Columbia. Some people returned and reestablished Little Tokyo in Vancouver. However, new generations of Japanese Canadians, like Japanese Americans, tend to live in the suburbs. Although Vancouver's Little Tokyo still maintains shops and restaurants along with cultural activities, people who work there do not live in that area.

Since the 1970's, Japanese corporations have sent many nationals to work in the United States and Canada. These workers are often encouraged to live among North Americans in order to become more proficient at speaking English and to avoid creating a threatening Japanese "ghetto." Japanese supermarkets, bookstores, and restaurants have sprung up in various cities where many Japanese nationals work, including Seattle, Portland, Chicago, New York City, and Vancouver. These new "Little Tokyos," which are smaller in size than the prewar Little Tokyos and may not be as concentrated, are usually just shopping centers.

Nobuko Adachi

FURTHER READING

Hoobler, Dorothy, Thomas Hoobler, and George Takei. *The Japanese American Family Album.* New York: Oxford University Press, 1996.

Kitano, Harry. *The Japanese Americans.* New York: Chelsea House, 1987.

Laguerre, Michel S. *The Global Ethnopolis: Chinatown, Japantown, and Manilatown in American Society.* New York: St. Martin's Press, 1999.

SEE ALSO Alien land laws; Chinatowns; Ethnic enclaves; Generational acculturation; Japanese immigrants; Little Havana; Little Italies.

MACHINE POLITICS

DEFINITION: Largely nonideological form of politics dominated by a small elite, usually corrupt, based on the exchange of material benefits for political support

IMMIGRATION ISSUE: Government and politics

SIGNIFICANCE: Machine politics was at its peak during the late nineteenth and early twentieth centuries in response to the needs of a growing urban population, which included many immigrants. The excesses of machine politics generated numerous political reform measures that remain part of contemporary politics.

Machine politics is characterized by a tightly organized political structure dominated by an individual "boss" or a small cadre of leaders who stay in power by brokering a variety of benefits such as jobs, contracts, protection, and other privileges in exchange for political support. This exchange frequently takes the form of benefits for money in the form of campaign contributions, kickbacks, and outright bribery.

The prototype of the political machine is as old as the American nation. The New York Society of Tammany was founded in 1785 as a social club named after a Delaware Indian chief. It rapidly evolved into a partisan organization that supported candidates for public office and remained a force in politics through the early twentieth century. Like other such organizations during the early nineteenth century, its strength increased with the expansion of voting during the Jacksonian era. The power of political machines further increased with the growth of immigration. By organizing the newly arrived voters through strict party discipline, Tammany Hall was able to control the political "spoils." It rapidly became a widely copied model of graft-ridden politics.

"Boss" William Marcy Tweed (1823-1878) was one of the most crooked politicians in U.S. history but in his drive to buy and solicit votes, he did much to help immigrants in New York City. (Library of Congress)

When immigration increased after the Civil War, the political machine reached its zenith. In the case of Tammany, this period marked the rise of one of history's most famous bosses, William Marcy Tweed, or "Boss Tweed." Tweed became a Tammany leader or "sachem" in 1857. He was soon elected, with Tammany support, to the New York Board of Supervisors and from there expanded his base by controlling patronage and public contracts. By 1868, he was a state senator and a dominant force in politics. It has been estimated that his corrupt "ring" had stolen nearly two hundred million dollars from public funds and other sources. Tweed was eventually arrested and died in jail, but machine politics continued to prosper through the early twentieth century. Most cities had some degree of machine politics.

Some of the most famous machine bosses include Frank Hague of Jersey City, James Curley of Boston, Ed Crump of Memphis, Tom Pendergast of Kansas City, Huey Long of Louisiana, and Richard J. Daley of Chicago. The growth of machines paralleled the rise of large cities. Though there were "courthouse gangs" or rural versions of the machine, the typical structure was a well-controlled urban population organized by a political party that cared primarily for staying in office for reasons of power and money rather than ideology.

FUNCTIONS OF THE MACHINE Though the corruption of machine politics cannot be minimized, scholars have found that the rise of machines can be explained by the unique set of social and economic conditions associated with immigration. As the United States became more urban, new tasks had to be performed to meet changing conditions. The political machine filled this vacuum. Most important, the machine performed a much-needed welfare function. It helped families and individuals find jobs through political patronage, obtain housing, and deal with personal crises such as fire or illness by providing financial and even emotional support. It also helped to socialize the newly arriving immigrants into both American culture and political life. It facilitated the assimilation of newcomers because it needed balanced tickets in which various ethnic voting blocks were included. This fact provided upward mobility and helped to lower the level of ethnic conflict. Machines also centralized power, which generated a measure of support from business and commercial interests. Centralization had become necessary, because a legacy of the Jacksonian era was the "long ballot" and the multiplying of elected offices. By centralizing decision making, the machine increased the efficiency of a fragmented system and helped to personalize government.

DECLINE OF MACHINES Although machine politics persists in American politics, the classic machine organization had declined by the mid-twentieth century for a number of reasons. Primarily, a large-scale reform movement motivated by the corruption and waste of the machines was successful in passing a number of "good government" measures. Among these were civil service and merit system reforms which undermined the machine's patronage base, the short ballot, nonpartisan elections, city manager forms of government, direct primaries, and at-large elections. These structural reforms contributed greatly to the demise of the machine. Just as important, a growing middle class became far less tolerant of the scandals and corruption associated with the machine. Coupled with the rise of new management theories which aimed at removing politics from government in order to model it on a businesslike paradigm, the culture which supported the traditional machine disappeared. Finally, the growth of welfare programs initiated by the New Deal of President Franklin D. Roosevelt in response to the Great Depression eliminated the functional basis of the machine. New agencies and programs took over the welfare activities of the machine.

Although the classical machine was undermined by reform efforts as well as changing social circumstances, machine politics continues in one form or another. Some would argue that machine politics, stripped of its corruption, represents a form of responsive politics in action. Nevertheless, the ultimate legacy of machine politics is the structural and social reforms that marked the end of the machine era. While some would argue that the reform legacy has weakened political parties too much and that the bureaucratic structures that accompanied reform have created their own set of problems, the positive functions of machines did not outweigh their corruption and the cynicism they caused, which served to undermine public faith in democratic institutions.

Melvin Kulbicki

FURTHER READING Informative views of Tammany Hall include Seymour Mandelbaum's *Boss Tweed's New York* (New York: John Wiley & Sons, 1965) and William Riordon's *Plunkitt of Tammany Hall* (New York: Dutton, 1963). The Daley machine of Chicago is the subject of Milton L. Rakove's *Don't Make No Waves—Don't Back No Losers* (Bloomington: Indiana University Press, 1975). Broader perspectives are taken in Lincoln Steffens's *The Shame of the Cities* (New York: Sagamore Press, 1957), Alfred Steinberg's *The Bosses* (New York: Macmillan, 1972), Susan Welch and Timothy Bledsoe's *Urban Reform and Its Consequences* (Chicago: University of Chicago Press, 1988), and Edward C. Banfield and James Q. Wilson's *City Politics* (Cambridge, Mass.: Harvard University Press, 1963). A classic novel about machine politics is Edwin O'Connor's *The Last Hurrah* (Boston: Little, Brown, 1956).

SEE ALSO Discrimination; Ethnic enclaves; European immigrants, 1790-1892; Hull-House; Irish immigrants; Know-Nothing Party; Nativism.

MAIL-ORDER BRIDES

DEFINITION: Women who immigrate to other countries to marry local citizens whom they meet through supervised introduction services conducted through correspondence

IMMIGRATION ISSUES: Families and marriage; Women

SIGNIFICANCE: Thousands of marriages in the United States and other countries are arranged by mail, typically through international dating and introduction services.

The system of arranging marriages with "mail-order brides" is an old part of the North American social landscape. During the nineteenth century, there were so few women in the Canadian and U.S. frontiers that newspapers in those regions routinely carried advertisements for wives placed by lonely farmers or ranchers. While little is known about how many marriages were formed through the mail or how successful they were, this was apparently a fairly common form of courtship.

MODERN MAIL-ORDER BRIDES   During the twentieth century, finding mates by mail became a comparatively rare occurrence in North America. After mass transportation and the automobile became common, dating became the primary form of courtship. American cultural values placed heavy emphasis on romantic love as a motivation for marrying. The ideal of romantic love required that men and women develop intense emotional intimacy before marriage, and intimacy can rarely be created at a distance.

Despite the cultural emphasis on dating and romantic love, mail-order marriages began to become more common in the period following World War II. Sociologists, psychologists, and anthropologists have often noted that men and women tend to look for different characteristics in mates. Men are more likely to look for youth and physical attractiveness. Women are more likely to look for mates who are financially secure. As worldwide transportation and communications have improved, men in relatively prosperous countries could make contact with younger women in comparatively low-income countries. Between 1968 and 1981, for example, more than seven hundred women emigrated to France from the island of Mauritius as mail-order brides for lonely middle-aged French farmers.

During the 1970's, Asia, and especially the Philippines, became an important source of mail-order brides for men in the United States. Because the Philippines was an American colony from 1898 to 1945, Filipinas are often able to speak English and are typically more familiar with American culture than other Asian women. Filipino and American entrepreneurs set up introduction services to put American men searching for wives in contact with Filipinas searching for financially stable husbands. Most often, international introduction services put potential spouses in contact with one another by marketing catalogs containing the photographs of women with their addresses and personal information. By the late 1990's several of these catalogs were available through the Internet as well as by regular mail.

It has been estimated that by the 1990's approximately nineteen thousand mail-order brides left the Philippines each year to join husbands and fiancés abroad, with the United States as their primary destination. In 1997 the social scientist Concepcion Montoya identified Filipina mail-order brides, who often established social networks among themselves, as a rapidly emerging American community.

With the collapse of the Soviet Union in 1991, Russia and eastern Europe became major sources of mail-order brides for the Americas and Western Europe. The difficulties of the Russian economy during the 1990's caused many young Russian women to seek more prosperous lives abroad. As in the Philippines, catalogs served as the primary way in which men initially made contact with potential brides. One of the best-known of these catalogs was *European Connections*, a quarterly containing photographs of women in Russia and eastern Europe. For $8.00 to $15.00, American men could order the addresses of women in the catalog. European Connections and other introduction services also arranged expeditions to Russia for American and western European men.

STEREOTYPES AND NEGATIVE VIEWS Many Americans hold unfavorable views of men who marry foreign women whom they have met through the mail. Popular opinion often holds that men who seek brides abroad are looking for obedient wives whom they can easily dominate. Many people see husbands of mail-order brides as such undesirable mates that they cannot find mates by more conventional means. Women who become mail-order brides are often seen either as exploited victims or as opportunists selling themselves for comfortable lives.

A number of widely publicized incidents have reinforced the negative views many people hold about introductions and marriages by mail. Some mail-order brides have indeed suffered at the hands of their husbands. According to news reports, for example, sixteen Filipina mail-order brides between 1980 and 1995 were murdered by husbands in Australia. In the United States a similar occurrence received national attention in 1995. A man in Seattle, Washington, had brought a Filipina wife he had met through the mail to the United States. The marriage did not work out and the wife sought a divorce. In response, the husband contacted the Immigration and Naturalization Service, claiming that his estranged wife no longer qualified for residence in the United States and should be deported back to the Philippines. The woman, who had become pregnant with another man's child, was sitting in a Seattle courthouse waiting for a hearing on her residency status when her husband drew a gun and killed her and several of her friends.

There is no doubt that mail-order brides are sometimes exploited by their husbands and that women in a new country can be vulnerable. Cultural conflicts and conflicts of expectations can also trouble international marriages. Women from the Philippines, for example, often expect to have full control over matters pertaining to the household and do not see themselves as imported servants. While there is little information on the success rates of mail-order marriages, available evidence suggests that the horror stories of wife abuse are the exception rather than the rule and that many of these marriages work out to the satisfaction of both parties.

RESEARCH ON MAIL-ORDER MARRIAGES The sociologists William M. Kephart and Davor Jedlicka have conducted extensive research on the mail-order marriage process. Kephart and Jedlicka conducted interviews with agents and clients of international introduction services and studied the advertisements in their catalogs. These researchers found that the process began when men selected photographs of women and sent the women photographs of themselves. Selection on the basis of appearance, however, was only a first step. Next, prospective partners began exchanging letters. Usually these letters were quite long and detailed and contained extensive information on the tastes, interests, values, and plans of both parties. By necessity, the exchange of letters meant that the women had good, if not excellent, English-language skills. Once couples decided to marry, the American men usually went abroad to meet their future wives. This step became a necessity after January

1987, when the marriage-fraud provision of the 1986 Immigration Act prohibited foreigners from coming to the United States to marry people whom they had never met.

Kephart and Jedlicka found that the majority of American men who became involved in mail-order marriages had had some unfortunate experience with courtship and marriage in the United States. Over half of them had been divorced and 75 percent had been through some kind of traumatic experience with women in the United States. Most were at least thirty-seven years old. The men earned above-average incomes and were above average in educational attainment and occupational level.

Most of the women involved in mail-order marriages were twenty-five years old or younger. Contrary to popular stereotypes, fewer than 10 percent came from the countryside or held menial jobs in their home countries. The majority were college students and about 30 percent held professional, managerial, or clerical jobs requiring fairly high levels of education. Marrying foreign men did not seem to be the choice of peasant women, but of middle-class women with aspirations that could not be easily satisfied in their native countries.

Carl L. Bankston III

FURTHER READING

Kephart, William M., and Davor Jedlicka. *The Family, Society, and the Individual.* 7th ed. New York: HarperCollins, 1991.

Larsen, Wanwadee. *Confessions of a Mail Order Bride: American Life Through Thai Eyes.* Far Hills, N.J.: New Horizon Press, 1989.

Montoya, Concepcion. "Mail Order Brides: An Emerging Community." In *Filipino Americans: Transformation and Identity*, edited by Maria P. P. Root. Newbury Park, Calif.: Sage Publications, 1997.

SEE ALSO Filipino immigrants and family customs; Japanese immigrants; Korean immigrants and family customs; Picture brides; Russian immigrants; War brides; Women immigrants.

MARIEL BOATLIFT

THE EVENT: Massive influx of Cuban refugees into the United States
DATE: May-September, 1980
PLACE: Cuba, Florida, and waters between

IMMIGRATION ISSUES: Cuban immigrants; Refugees

SIGNIFICANCE: This sudden increase in Cuban refugees provoked an agonizing reappraisal of U.S. refugee policy.

After Fidel Castro became ruler of Cuba in January, 1959, relations between the United States and Cuba steadily deteriorated, as Castro turned his country into a communist state allied with the Soviet Union, the main U.S. rival during the Cold War. Diplomatic relations with Cuba were broken, and an economic embargo was imposed upon the country.

The communization of Cuba alienated Cubans as well. From 1959 to 1962 (when Castro halted all further airplane flights from the island), about 200,000 Cubans fled their homeland, most of them settling in Miami. In late 1965, special freedom flights of refugees were organized with the cooperation of the Castro government; although registration for these flights was closed off in 1966, the flights themselves continued until 1973. The early refugees were disproportionately from Cuba's professional and white-collar classes; with extensive financial assistance from the U.S. government, and their own hard work, they achieved a remarkable level of prosperity in the United States in a short time.

Hopes for rapprochement with Castro rose in 1977, when Jimmy Carter became president of the United States. A United States Interests section of the Swiss embassy was established in Havana, under a State Department official, Wayne Smith, to handle relations between Cuba and the United States. When Castro persisted in his military intervention in the African nation of Angola, however, plans for lifting the U.S. embargo were shelved indefinitely. In October, 1979, relations with Castro deteriorated when Washington, D.C., welcomed the hijacker of a Cuban boat as a freedom fighter.

Between January and March, 1979, Castro, to polish his image abroad and to gain badly needed foreign currency, allowed more than 115,000 Cuban Americans to visit their relatives in Cuba. The apparent prosperity of the Cuban Americans caused discontent among Cubans on the island because of the austerity and lack of consumer choices in the island's socialist economy.

MARIEL REFUGEES On April 1, 1980, six Cubans commandeered a Havana city bus and drove it through the gate of the Peruvian embassy, demanding asylum; in the ensuing melee, one Cuban guard was killed. Castro responded by removing the police guards from the embassy. By April 9, 1980, about ten thousand more Cubans had crowded into the embassy, demanding the right of political asylum. On April 16, with Castro's permission, airplane flights began to take asylum-seekers to Costa Rica; on April 18, however, Castro, embarrassed by the blow to his image abroad, suddenly canceled these flights. On April 20, he opened the port of Mariel to all those who wished to leave the island and to anyone who wished to ferry discontented Cubans to Florida.

Persons sympathetic to the plight of the would-be emigrants chartered boats to sail to Mariel, pick up those who wanted to leave, and bring them to Key West, Florida. Once in Mariel, the boats' skippers were forced to accept everyone whom Cuban authorities wanted to be rid of, including criminals, the mentally ill, and homosexuals. Because some of the boats were not seaworthy, a tragic accident was always a possibility; and the U.S. Coast Guard sometimes had to rescue refugees from boats in danger of sinking.

President Carter, distracted by the Iranian hostage crisis and the worsening of relations with the Soviet Union after the latter's occupation of Afghanistan, vacillated in regard to the boatlift. In a speech given on May 5, Carter urged the people of the United States to welcome the refugees with open arms. On May 14, however, he threatened criminal penalties for those who used boats to pick up Cubans, and ordered the Coast Guard to stop the boatlift by arresting and fining the skippers and seizing the boats. Without cooperation from Castro, this order was largely ineffective. It was not until September 25, after hard bargaining between Castro and State Department negotiators Smith and Peter Tarnoff, that Castro ended the boatlift; several hundred would-be refugees who had missed the boatlift were allowed to take air flights out of Cuba in November.

Between April and September, 1980, south Florida bore the brunt of the tidal wave of refugees, which is estimated to have reached as many as 125,000. In the Miami area, social services, health services, schools, and law enforcement authorities found their resources strained to the breaking point by the sudden influx. Housing was suddenly in short supply; quite a few Mariel refugees in Florida had to sleep in the Orange Bowl, underneath a highway overpass, or in tent cities. On May 6, Carter, in response to pleas from Florida governor Bob Graham, declared Florida a disaster area and authorized ten million dollars in relief for that state to help defray the cost of the refugee influx; U.S. Marines were sent to Florida to help process the refugees.

CAMPS AND DISCRIMINATION   In June, 1980, President Carter ordered all those refugees who had not found relatives or others willing to sponsor them placed in detention camps in Wisconsin, Pennsylvania, and Arkansas. In Pennsylvania and Arkansas, the refugees, bored and fearful about their future, rioted. By October, the majority of the Marielitos had been released into various communities, and the detention camps were closed.

News of the riots fueled a growing backlash in U.S. public opinion against the Mariel refugees. The much-publicized presence of criminals among the refugees also helped generate a feeling of revulsion against the entire group: Marielitos were blamed for the upsurge in violent crime in Miami in 1981. In 1980, a year of economic downturn, many people in the United States feared that more Cuban refugees would mean higher unemployment.

Once released from custody, Marielitos faced a difficult adjustment. Unlike earlier Cuban refugees, the Marielitos did not arrive in the midst of general prosperity; they came when the twin plagues of inflation and recession were besetting a U.S. economy still struggling to absorb refugees from Vietnam, Laos, and Cambodia. Hence, Marielitos did not receive as much financial assistance from the federal government as earlier Cuban refugees. In addition, more of the Marielitos were poorly educated people from blue-collar backgrounds; more of them were single men without family ties; and a larger percentage of them were black or mulatto. Marielitos of all colors faced prejudice and discrimination, not merely from Euro-Americans but also from longer-settled Cuban Americans, who saw the Marielitos as insufficiently hardworking and feared that popular U.S. resentment of the Marielitos might rub off on them. In 1983, Marielitos in Miami had an unemployment rate of 27 percent; although the rate had been cut to 13 percent by 1986, they still lagged behind longer-settled Cuban Americans in employment and income.

Marielitos who ran afoul of the law quickly discovered that, however minor their offenses, they had fewer rights than native-born U.S. criminals. Marielitos who had criminal records in Cuba or who committed crimes in the United States faced incarceration for an indefinite term in federal prisons. In 1985, President Ronald Reagan secured a promise from Castro to take back Marielito criminals; only a few hundred had been deported when Castro, enraged by U.S. sponsorship of Radio Martí—an anti-Castro radio broadcast—canceled the agreement.

In November, 1987, a new agreement provided for the deportation to Cuba of Marielito criminals in return for the acceptance by the United States of Cuban political prisoners; upon hearing of the agreement, Marielitos held in federal prisons in Oakdale, Louisiana, and Atlanta, Georgia, rioted, taking hostages. The riots ended only when the Reagan administration promised that no prisoner would be sent back to Cuba without individual consideration on his or her case, and that some of those whose offenses were relatively minor would be released into the community. As late as 1995, however, eighteen hundred Marielitos were still incarcerated in federal prisons, and hundreds of them were still being held a decade later.

THE AMERICAN REACTION When the Mariel boatlift began, Islamic militants in Iran had already publicly humiliated the United States government by seizing and holding captive U.S. diplomatic personnel. The seemingly uncontrollable Cuban refugee influx came to be seen as a symbol, not of the bankruptcy of communism, but of Carter's alleged ineptitude in conducting U.S. foreign policy. U.S. voters' anger over the refugee influx, together with widespread frustration over the economic recession and the Iranian hostage crisis, helped doom Carter's bid for reelection in November, 1980.

The Mariel boatlift of 1980 revived xenophobia among people in the United States. Until 1980, much of the U.S. public had seen Cuban refugees as courageous freedom fighters, comparable to Czechs or Hungarians fleeing Soviet tanks rather than to Puerto Ricans or Mexicans fleeing poverty. However, the presence of criminals and misfits among the Marielitos shattered the benign Cuban stereotype. After 1980, sentiment built steadily for reducing the number of immigrants and refugees admitted into the United States. The ultimate consequence of the Mariel boatlift of 1980 was President Bill Clinton's decision in August, 1994, when faced with a new exodus from Cuba, to eliminate the privileged status of Cuban asylum-seekers.

Paul D. Mageli

FURTHER READING

Hamm, Mark S. *The Abandoned Ones: The Imprisonment and Uprising of the Mariel Boat People.* Boston: Northeastern University Press, 1995. One of the best studies to date of the Marielito prison riots of 1987; also contains much information on the 1980 boatlift itself. Argues that federal policy denied the prisoners basic human rights.

Larzelere, Alex. *Castro's Ploy, America's Dilemma: The 1980 Cuban Boat Lift.* Washington, D.C.: National Defense University Press, 1988. Detailed study of the boatlift, especially valuable for its look at the decision-making process within the Carter administration. Relies heavily on interviews conducted in 1986 with Carter-era officials.

Loescher, Gil, and John A. Scanlan. *Calculated Kindness: Refugees and America's Half-Open Door, 1945-Present.* New York: Free Press, 1986. Chapter nine examines the effect of the Mariel boatlift on the shaping of U.S. refugee policy in general. Criticizes Carter's response to the boatlift as indecisive.

Pedraza-Bailey, Silvia. *Political and Economic Migrants in America: Cubans and Mexicans.* Austin: University of Texas Press, 1985. Chapter two compares the demographic portrait of the Marielitos with that of earlier Cuban refugees. Explains why the proportion of Afro-Cubans among the Marielitos was greater than in previous refugee flows.

Portes, Alejandro, and Alex Stepick. *City on the Edge: The Transformation of Miami.* Berkeley: University of California Press, 1993. Chapter two shows that Miami's English-speaking whites and better-established Cuban Americans were both guilty of prejudice and discrimination against Marielitos. One of the few deep studies of the Marielitos' adjustment problems; regional focus, however, limits the book's usefulness for those interested in the Marielito experience throughout the United States.

Smith, Wayne S. *The Closest of Enemies: A Personal and Diplomatic History of the Castro Years.* New York: W. W. Norton, 1987. Chapter eight provides a first-hand account of the intergovernmental talks that ended the boatlift. One must be skeptical, however, of the author's tendency to blame U.S. policy failures on his superiors' refusal to follow his advice.

Zebich-Knos, Michele, and Heather Nicol. *Foreign Policy Toward Cuba: Isolation or Engagement?* Lanham, Md.: Lexington Books, 2005. Broad study of American immigration and refugee policy as it pertains to Cuba.

SEE ALSO Coast Guard, U.S.; Cuban immigrants; Cuban immigrants and African Americans; Cuban refugee policy; González rescue; Haitian boat people; Refugees and racial/ethnic relations.

MELTING POT

DEFINITION: Metaphor equating a cooking vessel in which diverse ingredients are blended to the United States, in which diverse immigrants are assimilated and blended into a single society

IMMIGRATION ISSUES: Language; Native Americans; Religion; Sociological theories

SIGNIFICANCE: This two-century-old metaphor has long been applied to the United States, but by the late twentieth century, as members of ethnic and racial minorities increasingly asserted their distinctiveness and autonomy, the aptness of the metaphor was called into question.

In the melting pot metaphor, the melting together of diverse nationalities and races creates one entity, a new American identity. In 1782, French immigrant Michel-Guillaume-Jean de Crèvecœur, using the more American-sounding pen name J. Hector St. John, published a collection of essays titled *Letters from an American Farmer.* These essays praised the quality of rural life in colonial America. In one essay titled "What Is an American?" he wrote, "Here, individuals of all nations are melted into a new race of men." European immigrants left oppression, hunger, ignorance, and poverty behind to pursue life, liberty, and happiness in North America. From Crèvecœur's perspective, they blended their cultures into a new identity, dedicated to the goals of freedom and equality.

HISTORY   Crèvecœur came to Canada in 1754 during the French and Indian War as a soldier. After the war, he roamed the country and surveyed land around the Great Lakes. In 1765, he became a citizen of New York, married, and became a gentleman farmer. During the Revolution, he refused to take sides against British loyalists, so American patriots arrested and jailed him as a spy. When he was released, he fled, in fear for his life, to France, leaving his wife and children behind. French citizens found his essay collections interesting, and he became a minor celebrity. Benjamin Franklin helped Crèvecœur secure an appointment as French consul to New York. When he returned in 1783, he found his wife dead, his farmhouse burned, and his children living in foster homes.

In later essays, Crèvecœur revised his idealistic theory of a homogenous American society. He observed that the first wave of immigrants on the frontier lived in isolation with weak ties to government, religion, or morality. Their communities and farms symbolized hard work and self-reliance, and they were reluctant to make room for succeeding waves of immigrants. Some were assimilated, but debtors, speculators, traders, and castoffs of society moved on. Many of these people created problems with the Native American population.

English author and playwright Israel Zangwill (1864-1926), who coined the term "melting pot," wrote mostly about Jewish life and culture. (Library of Congress)

In 1908, Israel Zangwill saw his Broadway play *The Melting Pot* performed. The four-act play dramatizes and resolves the conflict of Jewish separatism and Russian anti-Semitism. Walker Whiteside, star of the play, spoke the lines, "America is God's Crucible, the great Melting Pot where all the races are melting and reforming." Although critics gave the play bad reviews, audiences kept it running for 136 performances. The metaphor of the melting pot entered the American vocabulary.

Ironically, Zangwill became an ardent Zionist only eight years after the opening of *The Melting Pot* and repudiated the theme of his play. He declared that a character's statement that there should be neither Jew nor Greek was wrong. According to Zangwill, different races and religions could not mix, or at least not do so easily; a person's natural ethnicity would return.

AT ISSUE The theory that American society is homogenous assumes that people from different ethnic backgrounds will resolve their differences in an environment of freedom and opportunity. The process of "melting" the origins, religions, languages, and traditions of Europeans, Asians, Africans, and Native Americans into a unique American identity is demonstrably incomplete. Whether the melting of various ethnicities into a new whole is a worthy or a possible goal is a source of controversy.

Many immigrants have been unwilling or unable to abandon their past identity for a new one. Strangers in a strange land naturally cling to what is familiar; assimilation has often been slow and difficult. Established groups, in turn, have set up legal, economic, and religious barriers to prevent assimilation of different races. In 1660, eighteen languages were spoken on Manhattan Island. In that heavily populated area during the 1990's, at least that many are spoken, probably many more. Those who criticize the metaphor of the melting pot point out that the United States has always been and continues to be multiethnic, multilingual, and multicultural, and that therefore the melting pot is more of a misguided ideal than an accurate representation of the acculturation process in the United States. The ideal, critics of the melting pot may argue, often covers morally questionable motives that are based on hatred of difference.

On the other hand, the melting pot metaphor still seems apt for Americans whose ancestors represent multiple ethnic groups, for example, someone with a German-Scotch-Cherokee heritage. To many others, however, the term "multicultural" applies to American society more realistically. Many Americans with distinct ethnicity like to use the metaphor of a bowl of tossed salad, in which each culture is represented as a separate entity.

Martha E. Rhynes

FURTHER READING

Barone, Michael. *The New Americans: How the Melting Pot Can Work Again.* Washington, D.C.: Regnery, 2001.

Benmayor, Rina, and Andor Skotnes, eds. *Migration and Identity.* New Brunswick, N.J.: Transaction, 2005.

Bischoff, Henry. *Immigration Issues.* Westport, Conn.: Greenwood Press, 2002.

Crèvecœur, Michel-Guillaume-Jean de. "What Is an American?" In *Letters from an American Farmer.* New York: Fox, Duffield, 1904.

Jacoby, Tamar, ed. *Reinventing the Melting Pot: The New Immigrants and What It Means to Be American.* New York: Basic Books, 2004.

Singh, Jaswinder, and Kalyani Gopal. *Americanization of New Immigrants: People Who Come to America and What They Need to Know.* Lanham, Md.: University Press of America, 2002.

Vought, Hans Peter. *Redefining the "Melting Pot": American Presidents and the Immigrant, 1897-1933.* Ann Arbor, Mich.: UMI, 2001.

Zølner, Mette. *Re-imagining the Nation: Debates on Immigrants, Identities and Memories.* New York: P.I.E.-P. Lang, 2000.

SEE ALSO Assimilation theories; Bilingual Education Act of 1968; Chinese American Citizens Alliance; Cultural pluralism; European immigrant literature; Generational acculturation; History of U.S. immigration; Immigrant advantage; Immigration Act of 1921; Justice and immigration; Migration.

MEXICAN AMERICAN LEGAL DEFENSE AND EDUCATION FUND

IDENTIFICATION: National nonprofit organization whose mission is to protect and to promote the civil rights of Latinos in the United States
DATE: Founded in 1968

IMMIGRATION ISSUES: Civil rights and liberties; Education; Latino immigrants; Mexican immigrants

SIGNIFICANCE: Also known as MALDEF, the Mexican American Legal Defense and Education Fund has been one of the most active and influential rights organizations to look after the interests of immigrants in the United States.

The Mexican American Legal Defense and Education Fund (MALDEF) was founded in San Antonio, Texas, in 1968 as a legal aid society after decades of discrimination and the violation of the civil rights of Mexican Americans. It was established by a group of Hispanic attorneys who wanted to protect by "legal actions and legal education" the constitutional rights of Mexican Americans. Although Mexican Americans are still its most important constituency, MALDEF now represents the broader Hispanic community, including both documented and undocumented aliens.

From its first office in San Antonio, MALDEF established its national headquarters in Los Angeles, four regional offices in San Francisco, Chicago, San Antonio, and Washington, D.C., and a program office in Sacramento, California. The organization is administered by a thirty-six-member board of directors, composed mostly of Hispanics, and its membership includes attorneys, businessmen, educators, judges, law school professors, and public officials.

MALDEF has attorneys in each of its regional offices, but a national network of referral lawyers from private law firms, corporations, and businesses also provides pro bono services. Its activities are funded by foundations, such as Walt Disney, Kaiser, and General Electric; private corporations, such as Allstate Insurance, AT&T, AMOCO, Anheuser-Busch, Coca Cola, and IBM; labor unions; and individual contributions. With these resources MALDEF assists its clients in obtaining employment, education, immigration, political access, and job training. It achieves these goals through litigation, advocacy, educational outreach, law school scholarships, and leadership development.

The organization's most important strategy is litigation, which is used to implement legal action to eliminate discriminatory practices. MALDEF initiates "class action" suits with one or more Mexican Americans representing a larger group, pursues cases that reverse previous discriminatory practices, such as in hiring and promotion practices, and establishes new precedents. It has engaged in various lawsuits involving voting rights violations and discriminatory election systems and utilizes many of its resources on the equitable enforcement of immigration legislation. Its top priority is the elimination of barriers to the political process. Since MALDEF has long been opposed to the Immigration Reform and Control Act of 1986, it fights discrimination by employers against "foreign looking" legal immigrants and Hispanic American citizens.

MALDEF continually monitors and lobbies for policies that directly benefit Hispanics. Most prominent has been its efforts to defeat English-only proposals in Congress and in various states, such as its challenge to the California "Unz initiative" (Proposition 227) in 1997, which called for the virtual abolition of bilingual development programs that served over one million school students with limited English proficiency. In other recent initiatives, MALDEF challenged the Texas high school "graduation" test requirement and supported the extension of a family-based visa program. It offers law school scholarships to qualified students and sponsors efforts for more effective census data that better represent the Hispanic population. It is probably the most important modern Hispanic organization in that it has addressed the problems, needs, and concerns of its clients more than any other Hispanic organization. Its sponsorship of litigation and its lobbying activities have markedly helped the Hispanic community in areas such as education, employment, and political activism, all crucial to the future of Hispanics in U.S. society.

Martin J. Manning

FURTHER READING

Brittain, Carmina. *Transnational Messages: Experiences of Chinese and Mexican Immigrants in American Schools.* New York: LFB Scholarly Publications, 2002.

Gonzalez, Gilbert G. *Culture of Empire: American Writers, Mexico, and Mexican Immigrants, 1880-1930.* Austin: University of Texas Press, 2004.

Jonas, Susanne, and Suzanne Dod Thomas, eds. *Immigration: A Civil Rights Issue for the Americas.* Wilmington, Del.: Scholarly Resources, 1999.

SEE ALSO   Asian American Legal Defense Fund; Bracero program; Chicano movement; Farmworkers' union; Mexican deportations during the Depression; Operation Wetback; Undocumented workers.

MEXICAN DEPORTATIONS DURING THE DEPRESSION

THE EVENT: Federal government initiative to deport Mexican laborers from the United States
DATE: Early 1930's

IMMIGRATION ISSUES: Civil rights and liberties; Discrimination; Government and politics; Illegal immigration; Labor; Latino immigrants; Law enforcement; Mexican immigrants

SIGNIFICANCE: Massive unemployment during the Depression prompted deportation of immigrant workers in order to redistribute their jobs to U.S. citizens.

During the early decades of the twentieth century, the immigration of Mexican nationals into the United States was a growing phenomenon. It was not viewed as a problem because the cheap labor they provided was welcomed, particularly on farms and ranches. U.S. immigration laws generally were enforced selectively with regard to Mexicans. During World War I, at the request of U.S. businesses, the provisions of the Immigration Act of 1917 that required immigrants to pay an eight-dollar "head tax" and prove their literacy were waived for Mexican laborers. This special order legitimized U.S. dependence on cheap Mexican labor and institutionalized Mexico's special status.

At the end of World War I, the order was not rescinded; in fact, U.S. companies intensified their recruitment of Mexican farmworkers. Industrial companies in the Northeast and Midwest, such as steel mills and automobile manufacturers, also began recruiting Mexicans from the Southwest, resulting in an expanding migration in terms of both numbers of immigrants and their geographic spread. The Emergency Quota Act of 1921 and the National Origins

Mexican farm workers harvesting carrots in California's Imperial Valley during the late 1930's. Because of the abundance of cheap labor, these workers were paid only eleven cents for each crate of forty bunches of carrots that they picked, cleaned, tied, and crated. At that rate, each worker was lucky to earn one dollar for a full day's work. (Library of Congress)

Act (Immigration Act of 1924) had each limited immigration from Europe, but no restrictions were imposed on the number of immigrants from countries in the Western Hemisphere. Thus, a large and growing population of Mexican immigrants had established itself in the United States in the first decades of the twentieth century.

A CHANGE IN ATTITUDE   During the 1920's, the U.S. government's attitude toward Mexican immigrants gradually changed from lax enforcement to severe restrictions. As social and economic conditions deteriorated on a global scale, the great pool of cheap Mexican labor was increasingly resented by unemployed U.S. citizens. Despite pressure from businesses, laws restricting entry—that is, the head tax and literacy test—began to be strictly enforced against Mexicans by immigration authorities. Two new laws also were passed that had a further chilling effect on Mexican immigration to the United States: the Deportation Act of March 4, 1929, which made illegally entering the United States a misdemeanor punishable by a year in prison or a fine of as much as one thousand dollars, followed by the May 4, 1929, law making it a felony for a deported alien to reenter the United States illegally. These laws, followed by the October, 1929, stock market crash that marked the onset of the Great Depression in the United States, set the stage for a period of repressive measures against Mexican nationals in the United States.

As the Depression caused more unemployment, the caseloads of social welfare agencies increased. By 1931, as the pool of unemployed immigrants requiring assistance grew, local agencies intensified their efforts to force repatriation; on the federal level, calls to deport immigrants increased also. President Herbert Hoover endorsed the aggressive efforts to expel aliens, restrict legal immigration, and curtail illegal entry. William N. Doak, who took office as Hoover's secretary of labor in December, 1930, proposed that any alien holding a job be deported. The Bureau of Immigration, at that time a part of the Department of Labor, began an aggressive campaign of rooting out illegal aliens, with the objective of reducing unemployment and thus hastening the end of the Great Depression. Many of the aliens deported under this program, however, were already unemployed.

Although Mexicans were not specifically targeted by the immigration authorities, they were numerically the most affected as a group. The response of the Mexican government to the problem varied: At times, land reform programs were established for repatriating Mexican citizens; at other times, Mexico feared the addition of more unemployed citizens to its labor surplus. Opportunities for Mexican Americans to obtain land in Mexico usually required money to be invested, although occasionally there were programs that offered land to destitute repatriates.

CALIFORNIA'S RESPONSE   In the southwestern states, particularly, immigration officials aggressively sought deportable Mexicans, and social service agencies encouraged Mexicans to volunteer for repatriation. The most ambitious of these programs was undertaken in Los Angeles County, California, but cities such as Chicago and Detroit, where Mexicans had been recruited by industry during the early 1920's, also were actively attempting to get even legal Mexican residents to leave during the 1930's.

The Los Angeles Citizens Committee on Coordination of Unemployment Relief, headed by Charles P. Visel, had been charged with assisting the unemployed residents of the city, especially through creation of jobs, for which longtime local residents would be given preference. Inspired by Labor Secretary Doak's earlier pronouncements that some 400,000 deportable aliens were believed to be in the country, Visel set out to identify and deport as many illegal aliens as possible from the city of Los Angeles. Visel contacted Doak and requested that a sufficient number of immigration agents be deployed in Los Angeles to create a hostile environment, from which he hoped aliens would flee voluntarily. Visel planned to open his campaign with press releases and a few well-publicized arrests.

Although the plan was not aimed specifically at Mexicans, some statements made by Visel did mention Mexicans as a group to be targeted. The Spanish-language newspapers in Southern California stirred up the Mexican community, both in Los Angeles and in Mexico, by publishing inaccurate stories that virtually all Mexicans were being targeted for deportation. In the first three weeks of February, 1931, immigration agents had investigated several thousand people, 225 of whom were determined to be subject to deportation. Figures released by Visel's committee in March, 1931, indicated that 70 percent of the persons deported up to that time in the Los Angeles campaign were Mexicans. According to the Mexican Chamber of Commerce, an estimated 10,000 of the more than 200,000 Mexicans thought to be living in Los Angeles prior to 1931 had left; many of these repatriates owned businesses and homes in Southern California. It should be noted, however, that the Chamber of Commerce would be more likely to have contact with the more prosperous members of the population than with the unemployed or laborers.

Concurrent with the federal and local campaigns to deport illegal aliens, Los Angeles County officials began attempting to repatriate destitute Mexicans. Many Mexican nationals had entered the United States at a time when penalties for illegal entry were nonexistent or seldom enforced against Mexicans; thus, their legal status was uncertain. With chances of unemployed Mexicans finding employment in the United States slim, welfare officials were beginning to put pressure on alien relief recipients to return to Mexico, at times leading them to believe that if they did not leave voluntarily, they would be cut off from aid immediately.

Frank Shaw, a member of the Los Angeles County Board of Supervisors, was the first area official to propose paying the cost of transporting families back to Mexico by train. In March, 1931, 350 Mexicans signed up for the first trip. Many more trips were made, but statistics on the numbers who were repatriated under the county program are clouded by the fact that the same trains that carried county-aided Mexicans also carried deportees and Mexicans who had made their own arrangements to leave, and accurate records were not kept. Overall, the various efforts to reduce the number of immigrants in Southern California during the early 1930's caused a noticeable, but temporary, reduction of the Mexican population in the area.

Irene Struthers Rush

FURTHER READING

Byrd, Bobby, and Susannah Mississippi Byrd, eds. *The Late Great Mexican Border: Reports from a Disappearing Line.* El Paso, Tex.: Cinco Puntos Press, 1996. Sixteen essays that chronicle life on the U.S./Mexico border and the issues and influences that are part of this landscape.

Cardoso, Lawrence A. "The Great Depression: Emigration Halts and Repatriation Begins." In *Mexican Emigration to the United States, 1897-1931.* Tucson: University of Arizona Press, 1980. Brief discussion of federal deportation efforts and local repatriation efforts during the early 1930's. Includes ballads (*corridos*) written by returning Mexicans lamenting their plight.

Gonzalez, Gilbert G. *Guest Workers or Colonized Labor? Mexican Labor Migration to the United States.* Boulder, Colo.: Paradigm, 2005. Reexamination of the history of Mexican immigration to the United States that looks at the subject in the context of American dominance over Mexico.

Hoffman, Abraham. *Unwanted Americans in the Great Depression: Repatriation Pressure, 1929-1939.* Tucson: University of Arizona Press, 1974. Well-researched, comprehensive look at the deportation and repatriation of Mexicans, particularly from Los Angeles County, during the 1930's.

LeMay, Michael C., and Elliott Robert Barkan, eds. *U.S. Immigration and Naturalization Laws and Issues: A Documentary History.* Westport, Conn.: Greenwood Press, 1999. History of U.S. immigration laws supported by extensive extracts from documents.

Meier, Matt S., and Feliciano Ribera. *Mexican Americans and American Mexicans: From Conquistadors to Chicanos.* Rev. ed. of *The Chicanos,* 1972. New York: Farrar, Straus & Giroux, 1993. Comprehensive history of the Mexican presence in the United States. Pages 153-157 discuss deportation and repatriation during the 1930's.

Samora, Julian. *"Los Mojados": The Wetback Story.* Notre Dame, Ind.: University of Notre Dame Press, 1971. Discusses illegal immigration from Mexico in the twentieth century, including a chapter by a graduate student assisting the author, who attempted to enter the country illegally.

SEE ALSO Border Patrol, U.S.; Bracero program; Deportation; Immigration law; Latinos and employment; Mexican American Legal Defense and Education Fund; Operation Wetback; Undocumented workers.

MIDDLE EASTERN IMMIGRANT FAMILIES

IDENTIFICATION: Immigrants to North America from the predominantly Muslim nations of the Middle East

IMMIGRATION ISSUES: Families and marriage; Jewish immigrants; Middle Eastern immigrants

SIGNIFICANCE: In a tradition-bound region such as the Middle East, the family, despite the evolving social, economic, and political context, continues to be an important, all-pervasive institution.

Notwithstanding differences between the approximately two dozen Arab and non-Arab countries in the Middle East, the family's impact is still great on classes, income and educational levels, members of different faiths, and among rural and urban inhabitants. Generally, family life is shaped for the younger generation by the older generation, and relations between the sexes are still governed considerably by strict family codes.

Middle Eastern family members place greater value on the integrity, pride, and prestige of the family than is true of family members in the West. Thus, there is more respect for parents by children, and family ties are stronger. Sex roles of family members are more clearly defined, and greater stress is placed on both premarital chastity for girls and postmarital fidelity for women. Premarital sex among girls is seen as dishonoring girls' families, while marital infidelity is seen as dishonoring husbands' as well as wives' families. Traditionally, it has behooved girls' fathers or older brothers to sanction female family members whom they believe to be wayward—in extreme cases, by killing them. Such immutable family tradition is often reinforced by a strict interpretation of Qur'ānic law, as is done by Muslim fundamentalists.

The fact that marriage in Middle Eastern countries is a union of two families rather than of two individuals, as in the West, is demonstrated at every step: in the selection of brides, which is often performed by parents to maintain families' status; in the determination of the bride price; in betrothal and wedding ceremonies; and in the raising of children, sickness, and funerals. Obviously, these traditional family attitudes and rituals have weakened among modernized, often Westernized, well-educated, upper-income, urban families and their emancipated women family members.

KINSHIP AND GENEALOGY As in the West, descent among Middle Eastern families is patrilineal—that is, it is determined through the male line. Middle Eastern societies are both patrimonial and distinctly male dominated. Especially in rural areas, they are also patrilocal—that is, married couples traditionally go to live in husbands' fathers' households. In such an extended family arrangement, households often consist of a man, his wife, his unmarried sons and daughters, and his married sons with their wives and children. In more evolved city environments, the nuclear family, as in the West, has become more commonplace.

While the extended family satisfies some of the economic, security, and emotional needs of its members, it also creates occasions for intergenerational conflict. Despite the fact that Islam tolerates polygamy, cases of polygamy had become rare by the twenty-first century, eliminating this potential additional source of tension. As the outer world impinges increasingly on traditional family values, young people try to elude the stifling patriarchal grip by migrating to a distant, anonymous, and more liberal urban environment and, in many cases, abroad.

The birth of male children is marked by elaborate celebrations, because they are expected to perpetuate family tradition and are considered greater and more secure economic assets than girls. Despite some changes, women are still generally subordinate to men. Family judgment, especially in the villages, is severe, and deeds considered improper often weigh more heavily than meritorious acts.

THE EVOLVING FAMILY Under the impact of some industrialization, urbanization, conscription and army life, improved communications, and the provision of some kind of social security by governments or other organizations—no matter how rudimentary—individuals are no longer as willing to be subordinated to parents, uncles, aunts, and other older family members as they were previously. Moreover, with the centralization of governmental power, persons are beginning to show greater loyalties to the nation and perhaps less to families. Mobility, the demands of revolution and war, and the emergence of the modern interdependent world are increasingly propelling individuals in this direction.

Finally, the changing status of Middle Eastern women, who are now better educated and more likely to work outside the home and participate in economic and even political life than in earlier times, also helps to explain the changes in traditional family values. Thus, more women now have a say in the choice of their spouses, as parents' unilateral early determination of spouses for their children has become less common. Divorce, which has become widespread, is no longer the exclusively male prerogative that it once was. In short, the Middle Eastern family is in a state of transition.

FAMILY VALUES Changes in the Middle Eastern family should not be exaggerated. Generally speaking, the family is still the premier institution in society. Consequently, family values continue to involve the frequently unquestioned authority of male heads of households as well as the lingering practice of endogamous marriage—that is, marriage within the extended family. Even the payment of a bride price by grooms or their families, while less frequent, is still practiced. Most importantly, while fundamental values of North Americans include individualism, freedom, equal rights and equal opportunities, and the chance to realize individual goals, Middle Easterners focus on the importance of the group and hierarchy. Respect for elders, the separateness of sex roles, the complementariness of social roles, and the ethic of sacrifice to the family are still strong. Such cohesive kinship relations have often given Middle Eastern communities a relatively unified view of the outside world.

In this scheme of things, Islam has contributed to the strengthening of family institutions through its detailed guidance of family practice and its legal and moral authority. Islam and the family have, in fact, helped to stabilize Middle Eastern societies, which have witnessed much turmoil since World War II.

In the United States, with over two million immigrant families from the Middle East, and Canada, with over a hundred thousand, family values continue to be strong among the first resettled generation. However, as the second and subsequent generations have become more assimilated as they learn English in the schools and experience other socializing factors, original family values have tended to become diluted among Middle Easterners. Thus, the younger generation, whose members are more "Americanized" than their parents and who are concerned with their individuality and rights, no longer tend to return to the Middle East to marry spouses selected for them by their families. Moreover, they often marry spouses from outside their ethnic groups. Among the younger generation, the nuclear family has become the norm. Young people are also not as wont to send remittances to family members in the Middle East as earlier generations of immigrants have been. Such fund transfers, whether their purpose is to buy land, build a home, purchase appliances, or cover the bride price, have in some cases been a significant source of revenue for recipient local economies.

A somewhat analogous impact of environment on family may be found among the fifty thousand or so Ethiopian Jews (Falashas) who were airlifted to Israel during the 1980's. The changes that have taken place among the Falashas are twofold. The internal structure of the family has been reorganized, as parental authority, age, and gender have all acquired new contexts and meaning, and the family's external borders have been redrawn, as many of its functions have been taken over by other religious and secular institutions.

The predominance of Muslim families among Middle Eastern immigrants in North America is essentially a post-World War II phenomenon. Earlier groups of immigrants, which included large groups of people who belonged to an array of Middle Eastern Christian sects and a few Jews who came to North America during the late nineteenth and first half of the twentieth centuries, tended to be more Westernized than today's emigrants, bilingual from the start, and subject to less stringent family rules. They therefore found it less difficult to assimilate than the later waves of Muslim immigrants.

Peter B. Heller

Further Reading

Afzal-Khan, Fawzia, ed. *Shattering the Stereotypes: Muslim Women Speak Out.* New York: Olive Branch Press, 2005. Collection of interviews with Muslim immigrants to North America.

Dumas, Firoozeh. *Funny in Farsi: A Memoir of Growing Up Iranian in America.* New York: Villard, 2003. Lighthearted reflections of life in the United States by a young Iranian immigrant.

Haddad, Yvonne Yazbeck. *Not Quite American? The Shaping of Arab and Muslim Identity in the United States.* Waco, Tex.: Baylor University Press, 2004. Study of the special problems faced by Arab and other Muslim Americans in the aftermath of the September 11, 2001, terrorist attacks that turned many Americans against Arab immigrants.

Hassoun, Rosina J. *Arab Americans in Michigan.* East Lansing: Michigan State University Press, 2003. Study of one of the largest concentrations of Arab immigrants in North America.

Kaldas, Pauline, and Khaled Mattawa, eds. *Dinarzad's Children: An Anthology of Contemporary Arab American Fiction.* Fayetteville: University of Arkansas Press, 2004. Collection of short stories focusing on themes of great interest to immigrant Arab children.

Marvasti, Amir B., and Karyn D. McKinney. *Middle Eastern Lives in America.* Lanham: Rowman & Littlefield, 2004. Study of Middle Eastern families living in the United States.

Moaveni, Azadeh. *Lipstick Jihad: A Memoir of Growing Up Iranian in America and American in Iran.* New York: Public Affairs, 2005. Autobiography of an Iranian immigrant.

Nordquist, Joan, comp. *Arab and Muslim Americans of Middle Eastern Origin: Social and Political Aspects—A Bibliography.* Santa Cruz, Calif.: Reference and Research Services, 2003. Comprehensive bibliography of diverse aspects of Middle Eastern immigrants.

Orfalea, Gregory. *The Arab Americans: A Quest for Their History and Culture.* Northampton, Mass.: Olive Branch Press, 2005. Study of the special challenges faced by Arab immigrants in the United States.

Westheimer, Ruth, and Steven Kaplan. *Surviving Salvation: The Ethiopian Jewish Family in Transition.* New York: New York University Press, 1992. Study of Falasha Jews.

See also Arab American intergroup relations; Arab American stereotypes; Arab immigrants; Iranian immigrants; Israeli immigrants; Jews and Arab Americans; Muslims.

MIGRANT SUPERORDINATION

DEFINITION: Process whereby immigrant groups of outsiders subdue the native peoples of territories

IMMIGRATION ISSUES: Native Americans; Sociological theories

SIGNIFICANCE: The classical form of migrant superordination is colonization, in which an immigrant group uses force to dispossess the indigenous group of land, resources, or work.

The superordinate/subordinate relationships that result from migrant superordination processes can take economic, political, and cultural forms. Such relationships are characterized by the institutionalization of dominant-minority relations in which the migrants enjoy disproportionate power, resources, and prestige. The power relationship is then justified by a system of beliefs that rationalizes the superiority of the immigrant group in relation to the indigenous people.

Reactions to migrant superordination on the part of the indigenous peoples may range from physical resistance and rebellion to accommodation and assimilation. Historical examples of migrant superordination include the European conquest of Native Americans in the Western Hemisphere and of Africans in South Africa.

M. Bahati Kuumba

FURTHER READING

Cook, Terrence E. *Separation, Assimilation, or Accommodation: Contrasting Ethnic Minority Policies.* Westport, Conn.: Praeger, 2003.

Zølner, Mette. *Re-imagining the Nation: Debates on Immigrants, Identities and Memories.* New York: P.I.E.-P. Lang, 2000.

SEE ALSO British as dominant group; Immigrant advantage; Indigenous superordination.

MIGRATION

DEFINITION: Movement of peoples from one region to another

IMMIGRATION ISSUES: Asian immigrants; Chinese immigrants; European immigrants; Refugees; Sociological theories

SIGNIFICANCE: Immigration—inward migration—and emigration—outward migration—are two of the primary processes (alongside fertility and mortality) that influence a population's ethnic and racial composition and that create shifts in intergroup relations. The reasons why peoples migrate vary from region to region and era to era.

Migration simply consists of the movement of people from one place to another. Migration can be internal (within a country) or international, and both types can have significant impacts. Immigration (the movement into a new country) and emigration (movement from a country) are forms of international migration. Net migration rate is the difference between the rate of immigration and the rate of emigration. It is expressed as the number of people per 1,000 who enter or leave an area during one year. Migration may have a number of important effects, such as relieving population pressure in crowded areas, spreading culture from one area to another, and bringing groups into contact—and possible conflict.

Sociologists also study the experiences of immigrants in relation to prejudice, discrimination, and social stratification and mobility. They explore the differing experiences of immigrants of differing ethnicities and races; such studies have revealed much about the nature of prejudice and about the disparity between the ideology and the reality of American life. A look at various aspects of immigration to the United States allows an examination of these processes at work in the real world.

Since the sixteenth century, most immigrants to North America have come for similar reasons: to escape persecution, to find economic opportunities, and to enjoy the freedoms available in the United States. Yet despite the traditional emphasis on the forces that pushed people out of their countries of origin and the separate forces that pulled them toward the United States, a number of studies, such as David M. Reimers's *Still the Golden Door* (1985), emphasize structural forces—economic and political—that have influenced population movements.

IMMIGRATION PATTERNS Many studies of immigration to the United States identify two massive waves of immigration between 1820 and 1914. The first decades of the nineteenth century brought increasing numbers of immigrants; 151,000 arrived during the 1820's, nearly 600,000 during the 1830's, more than 1 million during the 1840's, and 2.3 million during the 1850's. Many were Irish Catholics escaping political persecution and famine and Germans fleeing political upheavals. These "old immigrants" came to cities on the East Coast; some moved inland to the farmlands of the Great Plains.

"New immigrants" were those from eastern and southern Europe who arrived between the 1880's and World War I. This second period of immigration far surpassed the earlier waves in numbers, rising from 788,000 in 1872 to 1,285,000 in 1907. By 1914 nearly 15 million immigrants had arrived in the United States, many from Austria-Hungary, Italy, Russia, Greece, Romania, and Turkey. The federal Dillingham Commission (1907) regarded this group as poor, unskilled, and mostly male, and its report reinforced prejudices about eastern and southern Europeans. It concluded that these immigrants would be more difficult to assimilate into American society. As the children or grandchildren of immigrants became indistinguishable from other Americans, however, the concept of American society as a "melting pot" into which many nationalities merged into one, took hold.

Often invisible in early immigration studies were the numbers of Africans and Latin Americans who had not come voluntarily to the United States. Africans were forcibly brought to the United States as slaves. Many Mexicans did not technically immigrate but were absorbed into the United States when lands from Texas to California were conquered in the Mexican War (1846-1848). These groups needed to adapt to a new nation and a new culture, as did European immigrants, but they faced both discrimination and a lack of understanding about their circumstances. Asian immigrants formed another group that was long invisible in immigration histories. Chinese men were imported as cheap labor to build the railroads during the mid-nineteenth century, and they were expected to leave when their job was done. Many Japanese, Filipino, and Korean immigrants came first to Hawaii as agricultural laborers, and some moved on to California.

REASONS FOR MIGRATION Some structural reasons for emigration and immigration have not changed greatly over the last three hundred years. Many individuals have come to North America to escape religious or political persecution. Early refugees in this category included the English Pilgrims and French Huguenots. Later religious groups came from Norway, Holland, and

European immigrants arriving at the federal government's immigrant reception center on Ellis Island, in New York Harbor, around 1912. (Library of Congress)

Russia, among them Jews and Mennonites. From the early nineteenth century to the present, immigrants have come because of economic changes in their native lands and opportunities in the United States.

The enclosure movement in England and western Europe, which began in the eighteenth century, forced many peasants off the land. They sought new land in America. Factories brought ruin to skilled artisans, who came to the United States hoping to open workshops. Many Europeans and Asians also came to escape political turmoil. Revolutions in 1830 and 1848 in Europe, and the Taiping Rebellion in China in 1848, led refugees to seek safety in the United States. Twentieth century upheavals such as World War II, the Cuban Revolution, repression in Southeast Asia, and civil wars in Lebanon and El Salvador have continued to bring refugees to the United States.

IMMIGRANTS AND U.S.-BORN AMERICANS Immigrants and refugees have not settled equally in all regions of the United States. Large immigrant communities in California, New York, and Florida have led to the need for government services in many languages. Students in schools speak Vietnamese, Spanish, Korean, Ethiopia's Amharic, Haitian Creole, and a number of Chinese dialects. Many require courses in English as a second language. Courts need to provide translators, and social service agencies struggle to communicate with many immigrant groups.

Some Americans have responded to foreigners with resentment. Some states and localities have passed laws declaring English to be the only official language. Sociologists studying immigration, however, have found that the large number of immigrants has led to a gradual shift in the population of the United States and its culture. Television stations around the country broadcast programs in many languages. Spanish-speaking markets in particular represent many new business opportunities, and large American companies are beginning to offer advertisements in Spanish.

Americans have been proud of their heritage of immigration yet ambivalent about immigrant groups who have come to the United States. Federal legislation has expressed the varying reactions of Americans toward immigrants and immigration over time. Before 1820 there were no laws requiring lists of passengers arriving in the United States. Immigrants brought skills and talents that were needed by the new country, and they were welcomed. Non-British immigrants during the early nineteenth century, however, did experience discrimination. Irish Catholics and German immigrants, whose religion or language was different from that of the majority, faced ridicule and were stereotyped as drunkards or dullards. Asian immigrants faced racial prejudice, and Chinese people were eventually barred from immigrating to the United States.

Despite mixed reaction to foreigners, the first federal immigration law was not passed until 1875. In that year prostitutes and convicts were prohibited from entering as immigrants. Additional exclusions for lunatics and idiots were added later.

Japanese immigrants awaiting processing at the federal government's immigrant reception center on San Francisco Bay's Angel Island during the 1920's. (National Archives)

By the 1880's, increasing immigration from areas outside northern Europe, the closing of the frontier, and increasing urbanization led to attempts to control immigration. Some Americans claimed that southern and eastern Europeans were replacing American stock and that immigration produced a declining birthrate among Americans. Others were more worried about Asian immigrants. The Chinese Exclusion Act of 1882 specifically denied entry to Chinese people, while the Forant Act (1885) made it unlawful for employers to import aliens to perform labor in the United States. This law was aimed at large companies who were importing eastern Europeans to fill low-wage jobs instead of hiring American labor, and it reflected suspicion that immigration caused wages to decline. The Immigration Act of 1917 barred Asians not by nationality, but by excluding geographically any immigrants from East or South Asia.

Immigration to the United States was regulated for most of the twentieth century by the Immigration Act of 1924, which reflected the nation's desire to encourage European immigration and discourage non-Western immigrants. This law established a series of quotas for immigrants from all countries except the Western Hemisphere. Larger quotas were assigned to countries whose citizens were more traditionally identified with the American population. The Immigration and Nationality Act of 1952 tightened the quota system.

IMMIGRATION REFORM A significant change in United States policy toward immigration came with the Immigration and Nationality Act of 1965. This law removed strict quotas and Asian exclusion. Instead, it created preferences for persons with certain skills and gave priority to people with immediate family in the United States. The consequences of this legislation led to greater changes in immigration than were anticipated. By 1974, for example, foreign-born physicians made up 20 percent of all medical doctors in the United States. The "brain drain" from developing countries continued, as scientists, engineers, and scholars sought better conditions and higher salaries in the United States. The law also brought increasing non-European immigration, as family members petitioned to bring relatives from Asia, Africa, and Latin America.

The increasing number of undocumented immigrants in the United States has led to calls for policing the U.S. border with Mexico more efficiently and for penalties for employers of illegal immigrants. Illegal immigrants have been accused of stealing jobs from United States citizens, draining social services, and changing the very nature of American society. In 1986 the Immigration Reform and Control Act attempted to resolve these issues for many illegal immigrants. Those who could show permanent residency in the United States since 1982 could become legal residents. Employers who hired illegal immigrants were to be fined, and additional funds were appropriated for stronger immigration enforcement.

Immigration reforms have continued, showing the changing response of American society over time. The Kennedy-Donnelly Act of 1988 permitted a lottery to provide visas for permanent resident status, and the 1990 Immigration Act raised annual immigration ceilings and ended restrictions on homosexuals, communists, and people with acquired immune deficiency syndrome (AIDS); it also granted safe haven status for Salvadorans. This law was not without opposition from those who feared that disease or undesirable ideas would be spread by immigrants.

REFUGEES Refugees have become an increasingly important part of population movements. Emigration from countries experiencing conflict has increased in the twentieth century, and the United States has traditionally thought of itself as a nation receptive to the oppressed. The need to resettle large numbers of eastern European refugees after World War II was recognized by the Refugee Relief Act of 1953. During the 1980's the church-sponsored sanctuary movement broke immigration laws by providing asylum for Salvadorans who feared deportation by immigration authorities enforcing strict refugee policies.

The impact of immigration on American society has continued to challenge cherished concepts and ideologies and to highlight prejudices. The idea of the United States as an open door, a place where people from all lands can find a haven, is still shared by many. Since the 1980's, however, this ideal has faced considerable challenges. The large numbers of Central Americans, Asians, and Haitians seeking asylum in the United States has led to tighter controls at borders and interdiction on the high seas.

While some scholarship, particularly since the 1980's, has stressed structural rather than personal reasons for population movements and has challenged the concept of the melting pot, American society has continued to mold immigrants from many nations. At the same time, American society has changed as a result of this immigration.

James A. Baer

FURTHER READING

Bischoff, Henry. *Immigration Issues.* Westport, Conn.: Greenwood Press, 2002. Collection of balanced discussions about the most important and most controversial issues relating to immigration. Among the specific subjects covered are the economic contributions of immigrants, government obligations to address humanitarian problems, the impact of cultural diversity on American society, bilingual education, assimilation vs. cultural pluralism, and enforcement of laws regulating undocumented workers.

Daniels, Roger. *Coming to America: A History of Immigration and Ethnicity in American Life.* New York: HarperCollins, 1990. Well-written scholarly account of U.S. immigration from the colonial period through the 1980's.

Foner, Nancy, Rubén G. Rumbaut, and Steven J. Gold, eds. *Immigration Research for a New Century: Multidisciplinary Perspectives.* New York: Russell Sage Foundation, 2000. Collection of papers on immigration from a conference held at Columbia University in June, 1998. Among the many topics covered are race, government policy, sociological theories, naturalization, and undocumented workers.

Greene, Victor R. *A Singing Ambivalence: American Immigrants Between Old World and New, 1830-1930.* Kent, Ohio: Kent State University Press, 2004. Comparative study of the different challenges faced by members of eight major immigrant groups: the Irish, Germans, Scandinavians and Finns, eastern European Jews, Italians, Poles and Hungarians, Chinese, and Mexicans.

Lynch, James P., and Rita J. Simon. *Immigration the World Over: Statutes, Policies, and Practices.* Lanham, Md.: Rowman & Littlefield, 2002. International perspectives on immigration, with particular attention to the immigration policies of the United States, Canada, Australia, Great Britain, France, Germany, and Japan.

Meltzer, Milton. *Bound for America: The Story of the European Immigrants.* New York: Benchmark Books, 2001. Broad history of European immigration to the United States written for young readers.

Roleff, Tamara, ed. *Immigration.* San Diego: Greenhaven Press, 2004. Collection of articles arguing opposing viewpoints on different aspects of immigration, such as quotas and restrictions, revolving around questions of whether immigrants have a positive or negative impact on the United States.

Williams, Mary E., ed. *Immigration: Opposing Viewpoints.* San Diego: Greenhaven Press, 2004. Presents a variety of social, political, and legal viewpoints of experts and observers familiar with immigration into the United States.

Yans-McLaughlin, Virginia, ed. *Immigration Reconsidered.* New York: Oxford University Press, 1990. Collection of essays and theories of immigration, approaches to comparative research, and immigrant networks.

SEE ALSO Demographics of immigration; European immigrants, 1790-1892; European immigrants, 1892-1943; History of U.S. immigration; Illegal aliens; Immigration and Naturalization Service; Immigration "crisis"; Immigration law; Justice and immigration; Undocumented workers.

MODEL MINORITIES

DEFINITION: Members of minority groups that have attained exceptional educational and economic success and have achieved high degrees of assimilation into a dominant society

IMMIGRATION ISSUES: Asian immigrants; Chinese immigrants; Japanese immigrants; Refugees; Stereotypes

SIGNIFICANCE: In the United States, the term "model minority" has most often been applied to Asian Americans, notably Japanese and Chinese Americans.

The concept of the model minority has been studied and debated since the 1960's, when the term first appeared. Its validity has been both defended and attacked, and the possible harmful effects of the concept as an accepted and unquestioned stereotype have been argued. Another particularly contentious issue is that the suggestion that certain minorities are "models" implicitly contains the opposite idea: Other minorities are less than "models" and are perhaps even deficient in some way.

DEFINITION AND HISTORY OF THE TERM   A so-called model minority is any minority group (typically of non-European background) that does well despite having faced discrimination. The criteria by which a minority group is judged as doing well or not doing well vary, but they have included average family income; success in entrepreneurship; children's educational achievement (for recently settled groups); and extent of symptoms of deviance or social pathology. The higher the first three, and the lower the last one, the likelier a group is to be considered a model minority. Since every ethnic or minority group in the United States has produced at least a few high achievers and at least a few failures and criminals, social scientists' judgments of ethnic group success or failure are always statements of averages; they are often based on census data.

The term first appeared in an article in *The New York Times Magazine* of January 9, 1966, entitled "Success Story, Japanese-American Style," by American sociologist William Petersen. Before World War II, Petersen points out, those Japanese Americans born in Japan could neither own land in California nor become naturalized American citizens; their American-born children (the nisei) were barred from many types of employment. During World War II, Japanese Americans living in the Pacific coast states were herded into internment camps. Yet in the two decades after World War II, Japanese Americans achieved a level of education higher than that of white Americans; a level of family income at least equal to that of whites, and a level of social pathology (such as juvenile delinquency) lower than that of whites. Hence, Petersen calls Japanese Americans "our model minority."

In *Japanese Americans: The Evolution of a Subculture* (1969), Harry L. Kitano, a Japanese American sociologist, also uses the term "model minority," acknowledging its origin with Petersen. Kitano expresses ambivalence about the term, which he regards as an ethnocentric white majority's view of a racial minority. Yet, like Petersen, Kitano ascribes the economic success of Japanese Americans after World War II to ethnic Japanese cultural values.

MODEL GROUPS   Japanese Americans are not the only Asian American ethnic group that has been noted by social scientists for its level of achievement since the 1960's. Chinese Americans have also been so identified. The business success of both Chinese and Japanese Americans has been attributed by some sociologists and historians to ethnic cultural values, as exemplified by the rotating credit systems that immigrants established to help provide one another with funds to start businesses. Korean business success has been similarly explained. The academic success of Indochinese refugee schoolchildren has been ascribed to the congruence of the refugees' Confucian ethic with the ethic of the American middle class. Louis Winnick, a scholarly expert on urban neighborhoods, went so far as to lump all Asian Americans together as a model minority.

Some non-Asian groups have been viewed as model minorities as well. During the early 1970's, post-1959 Cuban refugees were praised in the mass media for having overcome adversity quickly. Thomas Sowell, a black conservative intellectual, asserts that British West Indian immigrants (who are mainly black) outperform native-born black Americans economically and educationally. Similarly, Ivan Light argued in 1972 that British West Indian immigrants do better in small business than native-born black Americans; they do so, he said, because of their rotating credit system. Writing in 1993, two journalists (white New Yorker Joe Klein and Haitian émigré Joel Dreyfuss) contended that Haitian immigrants exhibit fewer social pathologies and more signs of economic and educational advance than native-born black Americans. Social scientist Kofi Apraku has described post-1965 African immigrants (such as refugees from Ethiopia) as above average in occupational and entrepreneurial attainment.

Students of a Japanese-language school in Sacramento, California, around 1910. A long tradition of strong family support for education has contributed to the image of Asian Americans as "model minorities." (Sacramento Ethnic Survey, Sacramento Archives and Museum Collection Center)

SOCIOLOGICAL VIEWPOINT Sociologists who employ or support the model minority concept usually adhere to the assimilation model of interethnic relations. According to this theoretical model, the ultimate destiny of any American ethnic or minority group is to climb upward into the broad middle class. Such thinkers tend to see the progress of any ethnic or minority group as a function of its cultural values rather than of the extent of the discrimination it suffers. The relative slowness of any particular group to overcome poverty and win the acceptance of the majority is ascribed, at least in part, to that group's cultural values; hence, one can regard some minorities as "models" and others as less exemplary.

Such structural theorists as sociologist Stephen Steinberg, by contrast, argue that it is not cultural deficiencies that retard minorities' progress but discriminatory barriers erected by the majority. These barriers can be far more widespread and insidious than is first apparent. Such theorists also contend that the seemingly miraculous progress of some model minorities can be explained by the social class background of the immigrants and by the opportunity structure that they found upon arrival rather than by any alleged superiority of those minorities' cultural values.

IMPLICATIONS The model minority concept has most often been applied in discussions of the relative success of certain Asian ethnic immigrant groups in the United States. The term has engendered much debate because of its implicit criticism of other groups—if these "model" groups could succeed, it suggests, then others should be able to as well. This implication then leads to the question: If certain groups cannot succeed as well as others in American society, where does the problem lie—with discrimination, with the attitudes of the dominant culture, or with the cultural attributes and attitudes of the minority groups themselves?

The model minority concept has surfaced repeatedly in debates over the status of African Americans, the minority group that has been in the United States the longest but that has arguably assimilated least effectively. During the late 1950's and the 1960's, many white Americans felt anxieties about the Civil Rights movement; the urban unrest of the late 1960's exacerbated fears and uncertainties about the future of race relations. Then, during the late 1970's and 1980's, white resentment of affirmative action programs, which primarily benefited African Americans, grew. At the same time, there was some bewilderment that inner-city black poverty persisted despite affirmative action. The model minority concept, with its evidence of Asian American success, seemed to suggest that such programs might be, or should be, unnecessary.

Hence, from 1966 onward, the notion of Asian Americans as a model minority found receptive ears among conservative white Americans. By the middle and late 1980's, it was being purveyed in a speech by President Ronald Reagan (in 1984), in magazine articles, and on television news programs (which placed special emphasis on the scholastic achievements of Asian American youth). Although most African Americans during the 1980's resented being compared unfavorably with Asian Americans, some conservative black intellectuals, Sowell, Walter E. Williams, and Shelby Steele among them, defended the concept and pointed to Asian American success as an example for African Americans to follow.

CONTROVERSY AND CHALLENGES Because of its use in arguments over public policy, the model minority thesis is hotly disputed. Thus a laudatory report on Indochinese refugee schoolchildren was criticized by sociologist Rubén Rumbaut for having covered only the Vietnamese, Sino-Vietnamese, and Lao, omitting data on the less successful refugees, the Hmong and the Cambodians. The overall high Asian American average in income and education, Asian American scholars Ronald Takaki, Deborah Woo, Peter Kwong, and Arthur Hu point out, hides a bipolar distribution: Chinese immigrants, for example, include both sweatshop laborers and scientists.

Many of the Asian American youth who excel in school, it is emphasized, are children of well-educated immigrants who either hold professional jobs in the United States or did so in Asia; Asian immigrant teenagers from poorer, less well-educated families are not always high achievers, and they are sometimes members of urban juvenile gangs. Asian American family incomes, it is conceded, may equal or surpass those of whites, but only because of a larger number of earners per family. Per capita income is less than that of whites; moreover, Asian Americans tend to live in areas with a higher than average cost of living, such as Hawaii, New York, and California. Also, Asian Americans statistically must achieve higher education levels than white Americans to equal their incomes.

Sowell's portrait of British West Indian immigrants to the United States as an ethnic success story has also been challenged. These immigrants, economist Thomas Boston argues in *Race, Class, and Conservatism* (1988), exceed both the average British West Indian and the average native-born black American in educational level; hence, the superior West Indian economic performance in the United States is no simple rags-to-riches story. Sociologist Suzanne Model, using census data, asserts that any West Indian socioeconomic lead over American-born African Americans had disappeared by 1990.

If the "model" part of "model minority" has been criticized, so has the "minority" part, at least regarding Asian Americans. Although everyone agrees that certain Asian American groups have been unjustly persecuted, some scholars, such as political scientist Lawrence Fuchs, argue that no Asian American group was ever discriminated against as consistently, or for as long a time, as black Americans were.

Some view the Asian American model minority stereotype as potentially harmful to Asian Americans themselves. Writing during the late 1980's, Takaki and Woo warned that widespread acceptance of the stereotype might lead to governmental indifference to the plight of those Asian Americans who are poor and to neglect of programs that would help Asian immigrants learn English and find jobs. Takaki, worried about the loss of legitimate minority status, points to examples of low-income Asian American university students being denied aid under educational opportunity programs. He also thinks that the envy generated among black and white Americans by the model minority stereotype partially explains the violent anti-Asian incidents of the 1980's.

Paul D. Mageli

FURTHER READING

Barringer, Herbert R., Robert W. Gardner, and Michael J. Levin. *Asians and Pacific Islanders in the United States.* New York: Russell Sage Foundation, 1993. Compares Asian Americans' income, education, and family structure with those of other Americans.

Chua, Lee-Beng. *Psycho-social Adaptation and the Meaning of Achievement for Chinese Immigrants.* New York: LFB Scholarly Publications, 2002. Sociological analysis of the adaptative processes which Chinese immigrants to the United States experience, with a close examination of traditional Chinese belief systems.

Gibson, Margaret A. *Accommodation Without Assimilation: Sikh Immigrants in an American High School.* Ithaca, N.Y.: Cornell University Press, 1988. Examines the excellent academic performance of American-born Sikh youth in the face of majority prejudice.

Kitano, Harry L. *Japanese Americans: The Evolution of a Subculture.* Englewood Cliffs, N.J.: Prentice-Hall, 1969. Classic exposition of the model minority thesis that ascribes the economic success of Japanese Americans after World War II to specific cultural traits inherited from Japan.

Kramer, Eric Mark, ed. *The Emerging Monoculture: Assimilation and the "Model Minority."* Westport, Conn.: Praeger, 2003. Collection of essays on a wide variety of topics relating to cultural assimilation and the notion of "model minorities," with particular attention to immigrant communities in Japan and the United States.

Louie, Vivian S. *Compelled to Excel: Immigration, Education, and Opportunity Among Chinese Americans.* Stanford, Calif.: Stanford University Press, 2004. Close study of the pressures within Chinese American families for children to excel in education.

Petersen, William. *Japanese Americans: Oppression and Success.* New York: Random House, 1971. Elaboration and expansion of the model minority thesis propounded in Petersen's 1966 article in *The New York Times Magazine.*

Takaki, Ronald. *Strangers from a Different Shore: A History of Asian Americans.* Boston: Little, Brown, 1989. Chapter titled "Breaking Silences" is an eloquent and easily accessible critique of the Asian American model minority thesis.

SEE ALSO Asian American education; Asian American women; Assimilation theories; Chinese immigrants and family customs; Generational acculturation.

MONGRELIZATION

DEFINITION: Racialist term for allegedly negative results of race mixing

IMMIGRATION ISSUE: Nativism and racism

SIGNIFICANCE: The term "mongrelization" was adopted by racist proponents of immigration restriction during the early decades of the twentieth century to dramatize their fear of the consequences of permitting unlimited immigration into the United States.

A leading exponent of ideas about "mongrelization" was Madison Grant, a naturalist who was a founder and president of the New York Zoological Society. In his book *The Passing of the Great Race* (1916), Grant classified national and ethnic groups as "races" and arranged them in an evolutionary order, with the "Nordic" peoples of northern and western Europe considered the most highly evolved, and the peoples of eastern and southern Europe, especially Jews, Italians, and Slavs, ranked as markedly inferior.

Grant believed that it had been scientifically established that mental as well as physical traits were genetically determined and could not be significantly altered by the environment. He also believed that in any mixture, inferior genes would triumph and "produce many amazing racial hybrids and some ethnic horrors that will be beyond the powers of future anthropologists to unravel." Grant was sure that

> the surviving traits will be determined by competition between the lowest and most primitive elements and the specialized traits of Nordic man; his stature . . . and his splendid fighting and moral qualities, will have little part in the resultant mixture.

Milton Berman

FURTHER READING

Curran, Thomas J. *Xenophobia and Immigration, 1820-1930*. Boston: Twayne, 1975.
Gabaccia, Donna R. *Immigration and American Diversity: A Social and Cultural History*. Malden, Mass.: Blackwell, 2002.
Perea, Juan F., ed. *Immigrants Out! The New Nativism and the Anti-Immigrant Impulse in the United States*. New York: New York University Press, 1996.

SEE ALSO Asian American stereotypes; Japanese immigrants; Japanese segregation in California schools; Nativism; Xenophobia; "Yellow peril" campaign.

MUSLIMS

IDENTIFICATION: Immigrants to North America who adhere to the Islamic religion

IMMIGRATION ISSUES: Demographics; Middle Eastern immigrants; Religion

SIGNIFICANCE: As early as the late nineteenth century, Muslim American communities of significant size and number were forming in the United States and Canada. However, some people felt threatened by the rise of Islam in North America, and these fears reached unprecedented levels toward the end of the twentieth century.

In March, 1998, *Newsweek* magazine estimated that six million Muslim Americans were living in the United States. It found that 42 percent of these Muslims were African Americans, 24.4 percent were South Asian Americans, 12.4 percent were Arab Americans, and 21.2 percent were of other ancestry. According to that article, although the Muslim community faces many hostile stereotypes, it had enough political clout for First Lady Hillary Rodham Clinton to host a Ramadan party for Muslims, who overwhelmingly supported her husband over Senator Robert Dole during the 1996 presidential election.

Muslim women praying in New York City during the month of Ramadan. (Frances M. Roberts)

Newsweek found that the children of Muslim immigrants were adopting mainstream American ways. Muslim women have active mosque and professional roles, and some young people are dreaming of becoming Muslim American politicians. Muslims actively opposed the U.S. bombing of Iraq, and the American Muslim Council organized a lobbying campaign against this bombing.

In December, 1997, the Muslim crescent and star, the Christian cross, and Jewish Hanukkah lamps were featured in Washington, D.C., holiday displays. However, vandals painted a swastika—the Nazi symbol—on the Muslim display. Like the Muslim symbols in the display, the religion of Islam has gained some level of recognition and influence in the United States but has not yet gained acceptance. Many Americans and Canadians see Islam as a threatening, foreign religion that inspires vicious acts of terrorism. This impression, reinforced by the 1993 bombing by foreign-born Muslims of the World Trade Center in New York, led many Americans to suspect that Muslims were behind the April, 1995, bombing of the federal building in Oklahoma City, Oklahoma. Some committed hate crimes against innocent Muslim Americans. Later it was determined that the Oklahoma bombings had been committed by a non-Muslim American man, Timothy McVeigh.

By the late 1990s, many American Muslims feared that their civil rights might be compromised if further acts of terrorism were committed in the name of Islam. That fear was realized after the terrorist attacks on the Pentagon and New York City's World Trade Center of September 11, 2001. In the tightening of immigration rules and inroads into civil liberties that followed those events, Muslims—and even immigrants, such as Sikhs, whom many Americans thought looked like Muslims—suffered disproportionately.

PRACTICAL PROBLEMS   Being a practicing Muslim is not easy in the United States and Canada. Muslims do not eat pork or pork products or consume alcohol and often find it hard to obtain meat butchered according to Islamic tradition. Required to pray five times per day, Muslims sometimes find it difficult to fit their prayers into schedules designed for non-Muslims. Schools and businesses generally do not recognize Islamic holidays, and not every community has a mosque. The practical problems that are experienced by devout Muslims are in many respects similar to those experienced by Orthodox Jews.

During Ramadan (the ninth month of the Islamic calendar, which falls in the spring), Muslims and their families fast during the day. This makes it difficult for Muslims to entertain non-Muslim business clients and social guests. During their holiest month, observant Muslims suffer from heightened isolation.

FUTURE PROJECTIONS   The Muslim population in North America is increasing. Muslim Americans will almost certainly outnumber Jewish Americans within the first quarter of the twenty-first century, and the Muslim Canadian population is also growing rapidly. Therefore, both Muslims and the larger society have a strong interest in Muslim participation in interfaith relations. In addition, religious scholars are beginning to document New World changes in Islam to illustrate the impact of democracy and multiculturalism on a nearly fourteen-hundred-year-old religious tradition.

Susan A. Stussy

FURTHER READING

Afzal-Khan, Fawzia, ed. *Shattering the Stereotypes: Muslim Women Speak Out.* New York: Olive Branch Press, 2005. Collection of interviews with Muslim immigrants to North America.

Cole, David. *Enemy Aliens: Double Standards and Constitutional Freedoms in the War on Terrorism.* New York: New Press/W. W. Norton, 2003. Critical analysis of the erosion of civil liberties in the United States since September 11, 2001, with attention to the impact of federal policies on immigrants and visiting aliens, particularly Muslims.

Ghanea Bassiri, Kambiz. *Competing Visions of Islam in the United States: A Study of Los Angeles.* Westport, Conn.: Greenwood Press, 1997. Scholarly community study by a Muslim author that covers the African American, Arab, Pakistani, and Iranian elements of the Los Angeles Muslim community and the differences in belief and practice among the groups.

Haddad, Yvonne Yazbeck. *Not Quite American? The Shaping of Arab and Muslim Identity in the United States.* Waco, Tex.: Baylor University Press, 2004. Examination of issues of Arab American identity and challenges to their rights after the terrorist attacks on the United States of September 11, 2001.

Hassoun, Rosina J. *Arab Americans in Michigan.* East Lansing: Michigan State University Press, 2003. Study of one of the largest concentrations of Arab immigrants in North America.

Kaldas, Pauline, and Khaled Mattawa, eds. *Dinarzad's Children: An Anthology of Contemporary Arab American Fiction.* Fayetteville: University of Arkansas Press, 2004. Collection of short stories focusing on themes of great interest to immigrant Arab children.

Koszegi, Michael A., and J. Gordon Melton, eds. *Islam in North America: A Sourcebook.* New York: Garland, 1992. Impressive collection of essays on Islam in the United States and Canada. Chapter 7 includes a useful directory of Islamic organizations.

Leonard, Karen Isaksen. *Muslims in the United States: The State of Research.* New York: Russell Sage Foundation, 2003. Perhaps the most useful starting point for further research, this study contains a historical overview of Muslim immigration to the United States, as well as chapters on various aspects of Muslim immigration and adjustment to living in America.

Marvasti, Amir B., and Karyn D. McKinney. *Middle Eastern Lives in America.* Lanham: Rowman & Littlefield, 2004. Study of Middle Eastern families living in the United States.

Nordquist, Joan, comp. *Arab and Muslim Americans of Middle Eastern Origin: Social and Political Aspects—A Bibliography.* Santa Cruz, Calif.: Reference and Research Services, 2003. Comprehensive bibliography of diverse aspects of Middle Eastern immigrants.

Orfalea, Gregory. *The Arab Americans: A Quest for Their History and Culture.* Northampton, Mass.: Olive Branch Press, 2005. Study of the special challenges faced by Arab immigrants in the United States.

Turner, Richard Brent. *Islam in the African American Experience.* Bloomington: Indiana University Press, 1997. Traces the development of Islam in the United States from colonial days, when Muslim slaves tried to preserve their religion in the African diaspora, to the present Muslim expressions of faith in the African American community.

SEE ALSO Arab American intergroup relations; Arab American stereotypes; Arab immigrants; Asian Indian immigrants and family customs; Iranian immigrants; Israeli immigrants; Jews and Arab Americans; Middle Eastern immigrant families.

NATIVISM

DEFINITION: Negative ethnocentrism, or an intense opposition to an internal minority on the grounds of its alien connections and its apparent threat to the dominant culture

IMMIGRATION ISSUES: Chinese immigrants; Discrimination; European immigrants; Irish immigrants; Nativism and racism

SIGNIFICANCE: In the United States, periodic upsurges of nativism have resulted in immigration restrictions, attempts to force minority groups to assimilate into Anglo-American culture, and vigilante violence against immigrant groups.

As a nation of immigrants, the United States has always exhibited a certain ambivalence toward immigrants. On one hand, immigrants have been welcomed as a necessary addition to the labor force and as a source of economic growth. On the other hand, they have been feared and resented because of their alien ways and their competition for jobs and political power. Nativists, the most outspoken critics of immigration, feared that the American way of life, and even the republic itself, was in danger from the constant stream of newcomers. They developed an ideology of nativism that comprised three identifiable strains: anti-Catholic nativism; racial nativism; and antiradical nativism. These three strains often overlapped in the various nativist organizations that emerged in the nineteenth and twentieth centuries.

ANTI-ROMAN CATHOLIC NATIVISM Anti-Catholic nativism had its roots in the religious views of the earliest English settlers in the American colonies. As products of the Protestant Reformation in Europe, the early colonists viewed the pope as a foreign monarch who exercised dangerous influence through the Roman Catholic Church. The large influx of Irish Catholic immigrants during the early nineteenth century fueled an upsurge of anti-Catholic propaganda, which alleged that Irish Catholics were agents of the pope intent on undermining republican institutions. During the 1830's, inventor Samuel F. B. Morse's tract, *Foreign Conspiracy Against the Liberties of the United States* (1834), which called for the formation of the Anti-Popery Union to resist the papal plot, became required reading in many Protestant Sunday schools. In 1834, an anti-Catholic mob burned the Ursuline Convent in Charlestown, Massachusetts. Ten years later, riots erupted in Philadelphia when Irish Catholics opposed the use of the Protestant King James version of the Bible in public schools.

The American Protective Association (APA), organized in 1887, was the most visible manifestation of anti-Catholic nativism during the late nineteenth century. Its members swore never to vote for Catholic candidates, employ Catholic workers over Protestants, or join with Catholic strikers. The APA drew strong support from workers in the midwestern and Rocky Mountain states who feared competition from cheap Irish labor. By the late 1890's, however, as Irish and German Catholics became an important part of the electorate, the more extreme anti-Catholic sentiment dissipated. The APA itself disappeared during the 1890's.

RACIAL NATIVISM During the late nineteenth century, a racial strain of nativism, cultivated by the self-professed guardians of Anglo-Saxon culture and apparently supported by scientific research, began to be directed against immigrant groups. Ever since colonial times, white settlers had viewed themselves as culturally and physically different from, and superior to, Native Americans and African Americans. Some intellectuals adapted the biological research of Charles Darwin to argue that certain races would inevitably triumph over others because of their inherent superiority. English and American intellectuals confidently trumpeted the superiority of the Anglo-Saxon "race" and its institutions, and researchers set out to "prove" their cultural assumptions by measuring the cranial volumes of skulls from members of various ethnic groups and devising crude intelligence tests. As a new wave of immigrants from Asia and southern and eastern Europe began to arrive, these newcomers were quickly labeled racially inferior.

Racial nativism reached its zenith during the early twentieth century. Influenced by the European eugenics movement, with its emphasis on breeding the right racial groups, American nativists expressed alarm over the impact of the new immigrants. Madison Grant's widely read *The Passing of the Great Race* (1916) summarized many of the racial nativist arguments. He argued that the superior Nordic "race" was being destroyed by the influx of southern and eastern Europeans, and warned that race mixing would result in an inferior hybrid race and the destruction of Anglo-Saxon civilization. Jewish and Italian immigrants, in particular, were often singled out for criticism in nativist publications because of their alleged racial inferiority.

Short-lived nativist newspaper published in Boston in 1852. (Library of Congress)

ANTIRADICAL NATIVISM Immigrants also came under attack for political reasons during the late nineteenth century. Nativist writers worried that most immigrants came from nondemocratic societies, harbored socialist or anarchist sympathies, and would foment revolution in the United States. The participation of some immigrants in the labor agitation of the period seemed to confirm these fears of alien radicalism. Antiradical nativism intensified following the 1917 Bolshevik Revolution in Russia and the onset of an economic crisis in the United States. Although most immigrants were not socialists, immigrants nevertheless constituted a majority of the membership of the American Socialist Party. During the Red Scare of 1919-1920, when many Americans feared that a communist revolution was imminent, immigrants and radicalism became synonymous in the public mind.

IMPACT ON PUBLIC POLICY Nativism had its most significant impact on public policy in the area of immigration restrictions designed to discriminate against Asians and southern and eastern Europeans. In 1882, the Chinese Exclusion Act cut off further immigration by Chinese laborers. During World War I, Congress overrode a presidential veto to enact literacy tests for all immigrants, which discriminated against southern and eastern Europeans who had less access to basic education. During the 1920's, the United States adopted a system of quotas based on national origins for European immigration, imposing a maximum annual limit of 150,000 and allocating most of the slots to northern and western European countries. The national origins quota system formed the basis of immigration law until it was abolished in 1965.

Richard V. Damms

FURTHER READING

Bennett, David H. *The Party of Fear: From Nativist Movements to the New Right in American History.* Chapel Hill: University of North Carolina Press, 1988. Exploration of the evolution of nineteenth century nativism to twentieth century conservatism.

Billington, Ray Allen. *The Protestant Crusade, 1800-1860: A Study of the Origins of American Nativism.* New York: Macmillan, 1938. Classic historical work on early nineteenth century nativism.

Gabaccia, Donna R. *Immigration and American Diversity: A Social and Cultural History.* Malden, Mass.: Blackwell, 2002. Survey of American immigration history, from the mid-eighteenth century to the early twenty-first century, with an emphasis on cultural and social trends, attention to ethnic conflicts, nativism, and racialist theories.

Higham, John. *Strangers in the Land: Patterns of American Nativism, 1860-1925.* New Brunswick, N.J.: Rutgers University Press, 1955. Standard account of American nativism after the Civil War.

Lee, Erika. *At America's Gates: Chinese Immigration During the Exclusion Era, 1882-1943.* Chapel Hill: University of North Carolina Press, 2003. Study of immigration from China to the United States from the time of the Chinese Exclusion Act to the loosening of American immigration laws during the 1960's, with an afterward on U.S. immigration policies after the terrorist attacks of September 11, 2001.

Perea, Juan F., ed. *Immigrants Out! The New Nativism and the Anti-Immigrant Impulse in the United States.* New York: New York University Press, 1996. Collection of essays that identify a resurgence of nativism during the 1980's and 1990's.

SEE ALSO   Asian American stereotypes; Assimilation theories; Cultural pluralism; Japanese immigrants; Japanese segregation in California schools; Know-Nothing Party; Mongrelization; Sacco and Vanzetti trial; Xenophobia; "Yellow peril" campaign.

NATURALIZATION

DEFINITION: Process by which immigrants become citizens

IMMIGRATION ISSUES: Chinese immigrants; Citizenship and naturalization; Civil rights and liberties

SIGNIFICANCE: The U.S. Supreme Court has played a critical role in determining the rights of both resident aliens, noncitizens legally living in the United States, and undocumented aliens, noncitizens in the country illegally. The Court has also influenced the rights of aliens to become citizens and to maintain citizenship.

The U.S. Constitution touches on the definition of citizenship only indirectly and makes no provisions for how aliens, or noncitizens, may become citizens. Moreover, although the amendments to the Constitution enumerate rights, it is not clear to what extent these rights apply to people who live in the United States but are not U.S. citizens. Because the Supreme Court is entrusted with interpreting the Constitution and establishing whether laws are consistent with this document, it has played a critical role in determining the rights of aliens.

EXCLUSION AND DEPORTATION   Congress has the constitutional power to decide which noncitizens may enter the United States and who may be excluded. During the first century of the nation's existence, Congress made little use of its power to restrict immigration. One of the earliest pieces of immigration legislation was the Chinese Exclusion Act of 1882, which barred the entry of Chinese laborers for a period of ten years. The Supreme Court upheld the right of Congress to exclude an entire national group from entering the country in *Chae Chan Ping v. United States* (1889) and in *Fong Yue Ting v. United States* (1893).

In theory, Congress could exclude all aliens from entering the United States because there is no constitutional right to immigration. Prior to entry, aliens have no constitutional rights. In *Chew v. Colding* (1953), the Court ruled that those who have successfully entered the country are protected by First Amendment rights to free speech, Fourth Amendment protections against unreasonable searches and seizures, and Fourteenth Amendment guarantees of equal protection of the law. Outside of the United States, however, these protections do not apply. The lack of constitutional rights by aliens seeking entry became clear in *Shaughnessy v. United States ex rel. Mezei* (1953).

Ignatz Mezei was a Romanian citizen who was a resident of the United States for twenty-five years. He returned to Romania to visit his mother in 1948. When he attempted to reenter the United States, first an immigration inspector and then the U.S. attorney general ordered him excluded. He was held on Ellis Island, which the Court ruled was "on the threshold" of U.S. territory. His confinement there could not be considered a violation of the Fourth Amendment because he was not in U.S. territory. The Court affirmed this principle in *United States ex rel. Knauff v. Shaughnessy* (1950), in which the German wife of an U.S. citizen was denied entry into the United States and held for months on Ellis Island.

The Knauff-Mezei doctrine, that aliens outside the United States do not have constitutional protection, continued to be in effect, but the Court moderated it somewhat in the following years. In *Landon v. Plasencia* (1982), the Court ruled that an alien who has established legal resident status in the United States does not lose that status merely by traveling overseas and may be deported but not excluded.

Congress has consistently excluded individuals on political grounds, such as association with a government opposed to the United States or membership in a political organization thought to be opposed to U.S. interests. Writers, artists, and intellectuals have often been among those excluded on these grounds. In 1969 the Justice Department refused to grant a visa to the Belgian journalist Ernest Mandel, who had been invited to speak at universities in the United States. Citing the Chinese Exclusion Act, the Court upheld the right of Congress to determine on political grounds who can be admitted to the country.

In deportation, a noncitizen who has already entered the United States, either legally or illegally, is denied the right to remain and sent back to the country of origin. The Court officially recognized the right of Congress to enact deportation laws in the 1892 case *Nishimura Ekiu v. United States*. Aliens facing deportation enjoy more rights than those who are excluded because the former are actually in U.S. territory. Undocumented aliens, those in the United States illegally, make up the bulk of the deportations from U.S. soil. Deportation proceedings are not considered trials but civil procedures, so those being deported do not have all the safeguards given to defendants in criminal trials.

Being an undocumented alien is in itself a reason for deportation. However, resident aliens are also subject to deportation. In *Marcello v. Bonds* (1952), the Court upheld the government's right to deport a resident alien for violation of a marijuana law years earlier. In *Galvan v. Press* (1954), the Court approved the deportation of Juan Galvan, a resident alien, for having been a member of the Communist Party, even though it was a legal party at the time that Galvan was a member.

RIGHTS TO EMPLOYMENT A number of Court rulings have affirmed the right of aliens residing legally in the United States to employment without discrimination by state or federal regulation. The Fourteenth Amendment to the Constitution, ratified in 1868, requires that all states give equal protection of the laws to all persons residing within their jurisdictions. In *Yick Wo v. Hopkins* (1886), the Court struck down a San Francisco city ordinance aimed at preventing Chinese nationals from operating laundries on the grounds that this was a violation of the Fourteenth Amendment.

Four decades later, in *Truax v. Raich* (1915), the Court ruled unconstitutional an Arkansas statute that limited the number of aliens that any employer could hire. Citing Yick Wo, the Court ruled that the language of the Fourteenth Amendment included noncitizens under its protection. The Court's decision observed that the right to work at common occupations was essential to the personal freedom that the amendment was intended to secure. Further, it observed that the power to control immigration is given by the Constitution to the federal government. If a state limits the opportunity for immigrants to earn a living, the state effectively limits immigration, which it does not have the authority to do.

The Court has permitted both state and federal governments to refuse employment to noncitizens in some circumstances. The job of police officer, for example, may be restricted to citizens only. In *Foley v. Connelie* (1978), the Court upheld a New York state law that allowed only citizens to become state troopers. Chief Justice Warren E. Burger, who wrote the decision in this case, explained that police officers are found throughout American society and exercise wide powers over those U.S. citizens who have contact with them. Similarly, in *Cabell v. Chavez-Salido* (1982), the Court upheld a California statute requiring probation officers and those in similar occupations to be U.S. citizens. The idea that governmental positions of authority and responsibility can be restricted on the basis of citizenship was also extended to teachers in *Ambach v. Norwick* (1979). In this case, the Court gave its support to a New York statute that prohibited giving permanent teacher certification to an alien unless the alien demonstrated an intention to become a U.S. citizen.

In general, the Court has ruled against barring noncitizens from civil service jobs, but it has left state and federal governments the right to exclude foreigners from civil service positions when there are compelling political reasons to do so. In *Sugarman v. Dowell* (1973), the Court struck down a New York law that allowed only citizens to get competitive civil service jobs because people holding high-level and elective positions, who were in the most sensitive and authoritative positions, were exempted. In *Hampton v. Mow Sun Wong* (1976), the Court ruled that a regulation of the federal Civil Service Commission that prohibited noncitizens from taking civil service jobs violated the Fourteenth Amendment guarantee of equal legal protection. However, the Court also indicated that the regulation would be permissible if it came from the president or Congress, rather than from a mere governmental agency.

The Court has distinguished between employment discrimination on the basis of ethnic or racial background and discrimination in employment on the basis of citizenship by private employers. Although discrimination against noncitizens by state or federal government is usually prohibited by the Fourteenth Amendment guarantee of equal protection, the employment policies of private employers are not laws and therefore are not covered by this guarantee. In private employment, employers are prohibited from discriminating on the basis of race, color, sex, religion, or national origin by Title VII of the Civil Rights Act of 1964. None of these prohibitions, however, keeps private employers from discriminating on the basis of citizenship. In *Espinoza v. Farah Manufacturing Co.* (1972), the Court ruled that Farah Manufacturing Company's decision to hire only U.S. citizens was not equivalent to discrimination on the basis of national origin because the company did employ large numbers of Americans of Mexican descent, the primary national origin of the noncitizens who were refused employment.

PUBLIC EDUCATION AND PUBLIC ASSISTANCE By definition, noncitizens who are in the United States illegally do not have the right to employment. However, the Court has issued rulings that have recognized the rights of both resident aliens and undocumented aliens to some of the other advantages of American society. One of the advantages of residence in the United States is access to the U.S. system of free public education. By the early twentieth century, free and compulsory public schools had been established in all areas of the United States. The right of children of noncitizen immigrants to attend these schools was widely accepted. Indeed, the "Americanization" of children from various ethnic backgrounds was seen by Americans in many areas with large immigrant populations as an important function of public education.

The right of children of illegal immigrants to education at the public expense was a much more controversial issue, particularly as popular concern over illegal immigration increased from the late 1960's onward. This issue came before the Court in the controversial case of *Plyler v. Doe* (1982). A section of the Texas Education Code allowed school districts in Texas to either prohibit undocumented alien children from attending public schools or to charge the families of these children tuition.

Those who opposed the Texas statute maintained that employers in the state deliberately attracted illegal immigrant labor and that keeping undocumented aliens out of the school system would help to maintain a permanently disadvantaged and undereducated class of workers. Those who supported it pointed out that undocumented aliens could not expect to enjoy the benefits of a society when they were in that society illegally. They also claimed that if the Court upheld the statute, states would be obligated to extend every public benefit to all illegal immigrants who managed to escape capture. In its 1982 decision, the Court for the first time explicitly stated that undocumented aliens did enjoy the equal protection of the law guaranteed by the Fourteenth Amendment and that the Texas statute was therefore unconstitutional. However, Justice William J. Brennan, Jr., who delivered the decision, also stated that some public benefits can be denied to adult illegal immigrants because adult aliens in the United States without proper documents are intentionally breaking the law.

Although the right of resident aliens to public education has been widely accepted, their right to public assistance has been controversial. The case *Graham v. Richardson* (1971) dealt with the right of aliens to receive welfare benefits. The petitioners in this case challenged two state statutes: an Arizona statute requiring individuals receiving disability benefits to be U.S. citizens or residents for a minimum of fifteen years and a Pennsylvania statute that denied general assistance benefits to noncitizens. The Court ruled that the states could not restrict to citizens the benefits of tax revenues to which aliens had also contributed because this would violate the equal protection clause of the Fourteenth Amendment. However, the Court also observed that the federal government had the power to set policies toward immigrants. This made it possible for Congress to restrict access of resident aliens to some welfare benefits in 1996.

RIGHTS OF SUSPECTED ILLEGAL ALIENS The U.S. Citizenship and Immigration Services (USCIS) is charged by Congress with regulating the movement of aliens into the United States. This means that USCIS officers have the power to detain, interrogate, and arrest those suspected of having entered the United States illegally. However, the Fourth Amendment guarantees to all those on U.S. soil—citizens or noncitizens—freedom from unreasonable searches and seizures. Because many Americans living near the Mexican border are of Mexican or Hispanic ancestry, moreover, the duty of the USCIS to find suspected illegal aliens raises the continual danger that Mexican or Hispanic Americans will be placed under suspicion without justification. In making rulings on issues in this area, the Court had to balance the duties of immigration officers with the Fourth Amendment rights of suspected illegal aliens.

One of the chief limitations on the detention of suspected illegal aliens resulted from the case of *Almeida-Sanchez v. United States* (1973). In this case, the Court ruled that immigration officials could not use roving patrols far from the border to stop vehicles without a warrant or probable cause. This meant that immigration officers had to be able to demonstrate that a search by a roving patrol took place either at the border or at the equivalent of a border, such as an airport.

The practice of detaining suspected illegal aliens because of appearance or the language they speak is a difficult matter because it can easily be seen as discrimination against members of minority groups in the United States. The District of Columbia circuit court, in *Cheung Wong v. Immigration and Naturalization Service* (1972), ruled that immigration officers were justified in stopping and interrogating two individuals who did not speak English and who were Chinese in appearance outside of a restaurant that was suspected of employing illegal immigrants. This issue came before the Court in *United States v. Brignoni-Ponce* (1975). The Court ruled that roving patrols could stop vehicles to question suspected illegal aliens, but they could not use appearance alone as a justification for stopping people. Race or apparent ancestry alone was not enough cause for an officer to detain an individual. In Brignoni-Ponce, though, the Court did allow officers to take ancestry into consideration along with other factors when deciding to investigate the legal status of a suspected alien.

NATURALIZATION AND DENATURALIZATION Resident aliens who are not U.S. citizens may become citizens through naturalization. The conditions under which an alien may become a citizen are determined by Congress,

Naturalization class in Chicago's Hull-House during the early twentieth century. (University of Illinois at Chicago, University Library, Jane Addams Memorial Collection)

and the power of Congress to set these conditions has been continually affirmed by the Supreme Court. The first Naturalization Act, passed in 1790, restricted citizenship through naturalization to "free white persons" of good character.

Before the Civil War (1861-1865), nonwhites born on U.S. soil were considered ineligible for citizenship. With the passage of the Fourteenth Amendment, nonwhites born in the United States were granted U.S. citizenship, but people who were not of European ancestry continued to be ineligible for naturalization. The Court upheld this racial restriction on naturalization in the case of *Ozawa v. United States* (1922). Takao Ozawa had immigrated to the United States as a child in 1894, graduated from Berkeley High School, and attended the University of California. When Ozawa applied for citizenship at the U.S. District Court for the Territory of Hawaii, the court ruled that he was qualified for citizenship in every way except one: He was not white. On appeal, the Supreme Court ruled that Ozawa was not entitled to naturalization as a U.S. citizen because he was not of European descent. Although the United States no longer has naturalization policies that intentionally discriminate on the basis of race, this is a result of legislation rather than of judicial rulings on discrimination in naturalization.

Naturalization laws continue to require that new citizens support the basic form of government found in the United States. Those who, during a ten-year period before application for naturalization, were members of anarchist, communist, or other organizations considered subversive may be barred from citizenship. The Court placed some limitations on these political restrictions in *Schneiderman v. United States* (1943).

Just as Congress determines the conditions under which individuals may be naturalized, it also historically determined the conditions under which they may be denaturalized, or stripped of their naturalized citizenship. Before the late 1950's, the Court usually did not question the right of Congress to take citizenship from the foreign born. However, in *Trop v. Dulles* (1958), Chief Justice Earl Warren recognized the seriousness of denaturalization when he observed that deprivation of citizenship could be seen as a violation of "the principles of civilized treatment." In *Schneider v. Rusk* (1964), the Court ruled that naturalized citizens could not lose their citizenship merely for living outside of the United States for extended periods of time. The greatest judicial limitation on denaturalization came in *Afroyim v. Rusk* (1967), in which a Polish-born citizen's citizenship was removed for voting in an Israeli election. The Court ruled that Congress has no constitutional power to remove citizenship without the voluntary renunciation of the individual concerned. After this case, denaturalization has been limited to cases in which the government can prove that a foreign-born person obtained citizenship illegally or fraudulently.

Carl L. Bankston III

FURTHER READING

Becker, Aliza. *Citizenship for Us: A Handbook on Naturalization and Citizenship.* Washington, D.C.: Catholic Legal Immigration Network, 2002. Practical guidebook for immigrants who wish to become American citizens.

Carliner, David, Lucas Guttentag, Arthur C. Helton, and Wade Henderson. *The Rights of Aliens and Refugees: The Basic ACLU Guide to Alien and Refugee Rights.* Carbondale: Southern Illinois University Press, 1990. Somewhat dated but still useful practical handbook on the rights of noncitizens put together by the American Civil Liberties Union.

Foner, Nancy, Rubén G. Rumbaut, and Steven J. Gold, eds. *Immigration Research for a New Century: Multidisciplinary Perspectives.* New York: Russell Sage Foundation, 2000. Collection of papers on immigration from a conference held at Columbia University in June, 1998. Among the many topics covered is naturalization.

Jacobson, David. *Rights Across Borders: Immigration and the Decline of Citizenship.* Baltimore: Johns Hopkins University Press, 1996. Sociologist's argument that the growth of immigrant populations in the United States and other countries has led to the granting of rights formerly reserved to citizens. Jacobson maintains that this has weakened the status of citizenship.

Kondo, Atsushi, ed. *Citizenship in a Global World: Comparing Citizenship Rights for Aliens.* New York: Palgrave, 2001. Collection of essays on citizenship and immigrants in ten different nations, including the United States and Canada.

LeMay, Michael C., and Elliott Robert Barkan, eds. *U.S. Immigration and Naturalization Laws and Issues: A Documentary History.* Westport, Conn.: Greenwood Press, 1999. Collection of essays on a variety of naturalization issues.

Neuman, Gerald L. *Strangers to the Constitution: Immigrants, Borders, and Fundamental Law.* Princeton, N.J.: Princeton University Press, 1996. Academic consideration of problems in applying U.S. constitutional law to noncitizens and discusses case law interpretations of immigrant rights.

SEE ALSO Citizenship; Immigration and Naturalization Service; Immigration law; Naturalization Act of 1790.

NATURALIZATION ACT OF 1790

THE LAW: Federal law defining rules for naturalization
DATE: March 26, 1790

IMMIGRATION ISSUES: Citizenship and naturalization; Government and politics; Laws and treaties

SIGNIFICANCE: This inaugural federal involvement in immigration—an area previously under control of individual states—established the first uniform rules for naturalization.

Naturalization is the legal process by which a state or country confers its nationality or its citizenship to a person after birth. In most cases, the primary beneficiaries of naturalization are immigrants.

After the American colonies gained their independence from Great Britain in 1787, each state adopted different rules for conferring U.S. citizenship upon its residents. President George Washington suggested that a uniform naturalization act at the federal level was needed.

Article I, section 8 of the U.S. Constitution empowers Congress to pass uniform laws for naturalization. Congress exercised this power, for the first time, when it passed "An act to establish an uniform Rule of Naturalization" on March 26, 1790. This act granted "all free white persons" with two years of residence the right of citizenship. In addition, the act stated that "the children of citizens of the U.S. that may be born beyond sea, or out of limits of the U.S., shall be considered as natural born citizens."

In effect, the act created two separate classes of people: free and white citizens, able to hold political office and entitled to the rights and privileges of citizenship, and nonwhite persons, ineligible for membership in the U.S. community. The act further reinforced the part of the Constitution that limits membership in Congress to citizens who meet stipulated residence requirements and the presidency to natural-born citizens. The Naturalization Act was repealed five years later.

Stephen Schwartz

FURTHER READING

Helewitz, Jeffrey A. *U.S. Immigration Law.* Dallas: Pearson Publications, 1998.
LeMay, Michael C., and Elliott Robert Barkan, eds. *U.S. Immigration and Naturalization Laws and Issues: A Documentary History.* Westport, Conn.: Greenwood Press, 1999.

SEE ALSO Alien and Sedition Acts; Cable Act; Chinese Exclusion Act; Immigration Act of 1917; Immigration Act of 1921; Immigration Act of 1924; Immigration Act of 1943; Immigration Act of 1990; Immigration and Nationality Act of 1952; Immigration and Nationality Act of 1965; Immigration and Naturalization Service; Immigration law; Immigration Reform and Control Act of 1986; Naturalization; Page law; War Brides Act.

NGUYEN V. IMMIGRATION AND NATURALIZATION SERVICE

THE CASE: U.S. Supreme Court ruling on the citizenship of a child of an unmarried U.S. parent who was born abroad

DATE: June 11, 2001

IMMIGRATION ISSUES: Asian immigrants; Citizenship and naturalization; Court cases

SIGNIFICANCE: In this ruling, the Supreme Court upheld a federal statute that established different citizenship rules for persons born abroad and out of wedlock depending on whether the father or mother was a U.S. citizen.

Tuan Anh Nguyen was born out of wedlock in Vietnam to a Vietnamese mother and Joseph Boulais, a U.S. citizen. From the age of six, Nguyen was raised by his father as a permanent U.S. resident. After Nguyen pled guilty to sexually assaulting a child at the age of twenty-two, an immigration judge ordered him deportable. Nguyen and Boulais appealed on the basis of citizenship claims to the Board of Immigration Appeals; however, they were unable to meet the citizenship requirements for one born abroad by a citizen father and a noncitizen mother. The appeals court for the Fifth Circuit found that the gender distinctions in the immigration laws were unconstitutional.

By a 5-4 margin, the Supreme Court, reversed the ruling of the lower court. In writing the opinion for the Court, Justice Anthony M. Kennedy applied the precedent of evaluating a gender-based classification with "intermediate scrutiny," meaning that the classification must serve important governmental objectives and that any discriminatory provisions must be substantially related to those objectives. Kennedy concluded that this particular gender-based distinction in immigration law was valid for two reasons: to ensure that a biological parent-child relationship exists and to ensure that the child and citizen parent have a demonstrated opportunity to develop a meaningful relationship consisting of "real, everyday ties."

Thomas Tandy Lewis

FURTHER READING

Jacobs, Nancy R. *Immigration: Looking for a New Home.* Detroit: Gale Group, 2000.

Legomsky, Stephen H. *Immigration and Refugee Law and Policy.* 3d ed. New York: Foundation Press, 2002. Legal textbook on immigration and refugee law.

LeMay, Michael C., and Elliott Robert Barkan, eds. *U.S. Immigration and Natu-

ralization Laws and Issues: A Documentary History. Westport, Conn.: Greenwood Press, 1999. History of U.S. immigration laws supported by extensive extracts from documents.

SEE ALSO   Amerasians; Vietnamese immigrants; War brides.

OPERATION WETBACK

THE EVENT: U.S. government program for the deportation of thousands of Mexican citizens
DATE: June 10-July 15, 1954
PLACE: California, Arizona, and Texas

IMMIGRATION ISSUES: Border control; Government and politics; Illegal immigration; Latino immigrants; Law enforcement; Mexican immigrants; Stereotypes

SIGNIFICANCE: Despite the investment of significant government resources, Operation Wetback had little long-range impact on the number of illegal immigrants living in the United States.

A fact of life for the nation of Mexico is the existence of a highly prosperous colossus to the north, the United States. While there has long been a tendency for Mexican workers to seek to enter the more prosperous United States to work, the government of Mexico took a number of steps during the 1940's and 1950's to provide good jobs to keep workers at home. These steps included the building of irrigation projects and factories. Most of these projects were located in northern Mexico and had the effect of drawing a large number of workers to the border area. Jobs were not available for all who came, and many chose to make the short trip across the border into the United States to find work. The average annual income of workers in the United States was more than ten times that of Mexican workers—a strong enticement for Mexican laborers to emigrate to the United States, legally or illegally, temporarily or on a permanent basis.

Mexican laborers who crossed the border into the United States during the early twentieth century most often found seasonal agricultural jobs. Starting about 1930, however, the Great Depression meant that many now-unemployed U.S. workers were willing to do back-breaking work in the fields for low pay. Accordingly, job opportunities for Mexicans evaporated, and those who did not leave voluntarily often were deported. Then, in 1941, war raised levels of employment in the United States, and as U.S. farmworkers departed to enter the military or to work in war factories, Mexican workers again began to enter the U.S. to do agricultural work. Most of the jobs they found were in California, Arizona, and Texas.

THE BRACERO PROGRAM   The U.S. and Mexican governments worked together to start a formal system called the bracero program. The program involved recruitment of Mexican laborers, the signing of contracts, and the temporary entry of Mexicans into the United States to do farmwork or other labor. The Mexican government favored the bracero program primarily because the use of contracts was expected to guarantee that Mexican citizens would be fairly treated and would receive certain minimum levels of pay and benefits. The U.S. government favored this formal system because it wanted to control the numbers of Mexicans coming into the United States and hoped the use of contracts would make it easier to ensure that the workers left when the seasonal work was completed. Labor unions in the United States supported the program because bracero workers could be recruited only after certification that no U.S. citizens were available to do the work.

The bracero program worked with some success from 1942 until its discontinuation in 1964. In some years, however, and in certain localities, the use of illegal, non-bracero workers from Mexico continued. Some U.S. employers found too much red tape in the process of securing bracero laborers, and

Mexicans crossing the Rio Grande into Texas in 1914 to escape the disorder of the Mexican Revolution. The tradition of Mexican immigrants wading across the river to enter the United States gave rise to the pejorative term "wetbacks" for undocumented Mexican immigrants. (Library of Congress)

they also noted that bracero wage levels were much higher than the wages that could be paid to illegal immigrants. Many Mexicans crossed the border illegally, because not nearly enough jobs were available through the bracero program. When the U.S. economy stumbled in 1953 and 1954, many U.S. citizens began to speak out against the presence of illegal aliens. They complained that illegal immigrants were a drain on U.S. charities and government programs. They also claimed that the immigrants took jobs at substandard wages that should go to U.S. citizens at higher wages.

When reporters first asked President Dwight D. Eisenhower and Attorney General Herbert Brownell if they intended to enforce vigorously the immigration laws, both men seemed uninterested in the issue. As popular agitation increased, however, the Eisenhower administration began to develop plans for Operation Wetback. The operation was designed to round up illegal aliens and deport them, while forcing large farming operations to use the limited and controlled bracero labor instead of uncontrolled and illegal alien labor. Operation Wetback was under the overall control of the Immigration and Naturalization Service (INS), directed by Joseph Swing, while day-to-day operations were supervised by an official of the U.S. Border Patrol, Harlon B. Carter.

OPERATION WETBACK BEGINS Operation Wetback took its name from a slang term first used in the southwestern United States to refer to Mexican immigrants who swam the Rio Grande or otherwise crossed into the U.S. illegally, seeking economic opportunities. The INS and its Border Patrol launched the operation in California on June 10, 1954, relying heavily on favorable press coverage to secure the support and cooperation of the general public. INS officials greatly exaggerated the number of agents they had in the field and the number of illegal aliens who had left or had been deported. Press coverage in California was generally quite favorable to Operation Wetback, praising the professional attitude of Border Patrol and INS agents. On the first day, more than a thousand persons were sent out of California on buses chartered by the INS. For several weeks, the number of daily deportations hovered around two thousand. The deportees were handed over to Mexican authorities at border towns like Nogales in Sonora, and the Mexican government sent them farther south by rail, hoping to prevent any quick reentry into the United States.

By July 15, the main phase of Operation Wetback in California was complete. On that day, Border Patrol agents began their work in Texas. There, they met stiff local opposition from powerful farm interests, who were quite content to hire illegal aliens and pay them only half the prevalent wage earned by U.S. or bracero workers. Agents met a hostile press as well, and in some cases had trouble securing a meal or lodging. Nevertheless, the operation resulted in the deportation by bus of tens of thousands of illegal workers from Texas. The INS conducted smaller phases of Operation Wetback in Arizona, Illinois, Missouri, Arkansas, Tennessee, and other states. Most of the illegals picked up nationwide were farmworkers, but some industrial workers were apprehended in cities from San Francisco to Chicago.

During the operation, some complaints were registered about the conduct of Border Patrol officers. The officers sometimes were characterized as harsh and hateful in their actions, and they were regularly accused of harassing U.S. citizens of Mexican ancestry. Some of these complaints seem to have been without foundation, particularly in Texas, where the powerful farm interests opposed the entire operation. On the other hand, there were a number of documented cases of U.S. citizens who had darker skin or Hispanic surnames being apprehended and deported to Mexico. Many of the aliens who were detained were kept in camps behind barbed wire pending their deportation. Some Mexicans and Mexican Americans spent several months hiding in terror, having quit their jobs to prevent their being apprehended at work. Deportees had to pay for their bus passage back to Mexico, to the dismay of human rights activists, who pointed out the unfairness of making someone pay for a trip he was being forced to take. The INS responded that the deportees should agree that paying for a bus trip back to Mexico was preferable to prosecution under the immigration laws and a possible jail sentence.

STEREOTYPES   Operation Wetback opened the door to stereotypes of Mexicans in the non-Hispanic community: Some press reports implied that the aliens were ignorant, disease-ridden union busters. As for the effectiveness of the operation in meeting its goals, nearly 100,000 illegal immigrants were returned to Mexico in the space of about three months. On the other hand, INS claims that more than one million illegal immigrants fled to Mexico on their own rather than face arrest were grossly exaggerated. Moreover, the boost to the bracero program given by Operation Wetback was only temporary; many employers returned to the use of illegal workers before the end of the 1950's. Operation Wetback, while effective in the short term, provided no long-term solutions to the needs of Mexican workers, U.S. employers, or those who clamored for a more restricted U.S. border.

Stephen Cresswell

FURTHER READING

García, Juan Ramon. *Operation Wetback: The Mass Deportation of Mexican Undocumented Workers in 1954.* Westport, Conn.: Greenwood Press, 1978. The only book on this subject, García's work thoroughly reviews the background, the deportation program, and the aftermath.

Gonzalez, Gilbert G. *Guest Workers or Colonized Labor? Mexican Labor Migration to the United States.* Boulder, Colo.: Paradigm, 2005. Reexamination of the history of Mexican immigration to the United States that looks at the subject in the context of American dominance over Mexico.

LeMay, Michael C., and Elliott Robert Barkan, eds. *U.S. Immigration and Naturalization Laws and Issues: A Documentary History.* Westport, Conn.: Greenwood Press, 1999. History of U.S. immigration laws supported by extensive extracts from documents.

Ngai, Mae M. *Impossible Subjects: Illegal Aliens and the Making of Modern America.* Princeton, N.J.: Princeton University Press, 2004. General history of the problem of illegal immigration in the United States that includes a chapter covering Operation Wetback and the bracero program.

Norquest, Carrol. *Rio Grande Wetbacks: Migrant Mexican Workers.* Albuquerque: University of New Mexico Press, 1971. Discusses Operation Wetback in the larger context of Mexico-United States immigration issues.

United States. Immigration and Naturalization Service. *Mexican Agricultural Laborers Admitted and Mexican Aliens Located in Illegal Status, Years Ended June 30, 1949-1967.* Washington, D.C.: Government Printing Office, 1968. Shows changes in numbers of bracero workers and apprehensions of illegal Mexican immigrants.

See also Border Patrol, U.S.; Bracero program; Deportation; Illegal aliens; Latinos; Latinos and employment; Mexican deportations during the Depression; Naturalization; Undocumented workers.

Ozawa v. United States

The Case: U.S. Supreme Court ruling on citizenship requirements
Date: November 13, 1922

Immigration issues: Asian immigrants; Citizenship and naturalization; Court cases; Japanese immigrants

Significance: In this case, the Supreme Court ruled that Japanese aliens did not qualify as "white" and therefore could not be naturalized as citizens.

During the early twentieth century, naturalization was under the effective control of local and state authorities. In California and other Pacific states, fears of the "yellow peril" or "silent invasion" of Asian immigrants were deeply entrenched and politically exploited. In such states, citizenship had been repeatedly denied to both Chinese and more recent Japanese settlers, although there were some rare exceptions. The prevailing belief among the nativist majority was that such settlers should be ineligible for U.S. citizenship.

Background Partly to test the Alien Land Law—a California law passed in 1913 that barred noncitizens from owning land in that state—Takao Ozawa sought U.S. citizenship in defiance of a 1906 law (U.S. Revised Statute, section 2169) that limited naturalization to "free white persons," "aliens of African nativity," and "persons of African descent." Although born in Japan, Ozawa had been educated in the United States. He was graduated from high school in Berkeley and for three years attended the University of California. He was aware that some issei (first-generation Japanese immigrants) had been naturalized, even in California. Specifically, Ozawa may have known of Iwao Yoshikawa, the first Japanese immigrant to be naturalized in California. Yoshikawa had arrived in San Francisco from Japan in 1887. A law clerk in his homeland, he had studied U.S. law in his adopted country and served as a court translator. In 1889 he began the naturalization process, which, presumably, was completed five years later, although there is no extant record of his naturalization. His case was publicized because it broached such issues as mandatory citizenship renunciation and the legality of dual citizenship.

Regardless of Ozawa's knowledge of Yoshikawa, on October 16, 1914, Ozawa applied for U.S. citizenship before the district court for the territory of Hawaii. He argued that he had resided in the United States and its territory of Hawaii for a total of twenty years, had adopted the culture and language of his host country, had reared his children as Americans in heart and mind, and was, by character and education, wholly qualified for naturalization.

The district court ruled against Ozawa on the grounds that his Japanese ethnicity denied him access to naturalization. Ozawa then took his case to the Ninth Circuit Court of Appeals, which passed it to the U.S. Supreme Court for instruction. In turn, the Supreme Court upheld the laws that in effect declared Ozawa ineligible for citizenship.

Rather than question the justice of the racial restrictions on naturalization, the opinion limited its focus to clarifying the meaning of the term "white persons" and distinguishing between "Caucasian" and "white person," determining that the latter, while a more inclusive term than the former, is not so inclusive as to include persons of Asian extraction. It concluded that

> a person of the Japanese race is not a free white person, within the meaning of U.S. Rev. Stat. § 2169 [the 1906 law], limiting the provisions of the title on naturalization to aliens being free white persons, and to aliens of African nativity, and to persons of African descent, and therefore such Japanese is not eligible to naturalization as a United States citizen.

In tracing the history of the naturalization laws, the Court attempted to demonstrate that all statutes preceding the 1906 act contested by Ozawa had the same intent: the selective admission to citizenship based on the interpretation of "white," not as a racial appellation but as a reflection of character. It argued that the words "free white persons" did not indicate persons of a particular race or origin, but rather that they describe "personalities" and "persons fit for citizenship and of the kind admitted to citizenship by the policy of the United States." According to that doctrine, any non-African alien, if desired by Congress, might be deemed "white." Thus, the Court reasoned, when the long-looked-for Martian immigrants reach this part of the earth, and in due course a man from Mars applies to be naturalized, he may be recognized as white within the meaning of the act of Congress, and admitted to citizenship, although he may not be a Caucasian.

Regardless of this race disclaimer, however, the Court, in reasoning through its arguments, distinguished between "whites" (all Europeans, for example) and "nonwhites" (such as the Chinese) on ethnic grounds pure and simple. The decision throughout sanctioned racial biases that assumed that an individual's character was in some way delimited by his or her racial heritage. For example, at one point it provided a formulaic approach to determining citizenship eligibility for persons of mixed blood, supporting the idea, widely observed, that in order to be construed as white, a person must be "of more than half white blood." Clearly, the decision upheld the seriously flawed assumption that character and racial heritage were inextricably interrelated.

NATIVIST SENTIMENT   The Supreme Court's ruling reflected the prevailing nativist bias against Asian immigrants, an attitude that was reflected in both law and policy through the first half of the twentieth century. In fact, no more formidable barriers to citizenship were erected than those facing the issei (first-generation Japanese), Chinese, and other Asian immigrants. In 1924, an isolationist Congress enacted an immigration act placing numerical restrictions on immigrants allowed into the United States based on national origin. One provision of the Immigration Act of 1924, also known as the Johnson-Reid Act, excluded immigrants ineligible for naturalization. Its obvious aim—to bar entry of Japanese aliens—quickly led to a deterioration in the diplomatic relations between Japan and the United States.

The plight of Japanese already in the United States also worsened in the anti-Asian climate. In separate rulings, the Supreme Court went so far as to revoke citizenship that had been granted to some issei. In 1925, it even denied that service in the armed forces made issei eligible for naturalization, overturning a policy that had previously been in effect. Not only were issei barred from naturalization; in many states, "alien land laws" prohibited them from owning land and even entering some professions.

That codified prejudice partly accounts for but does not justify the terrible treatment of Japanese Americans during World War II, when 112,000 of them, including 70,000 nisei (persons of Japanese descent born in the United States), were rounded up and incarcerated in detention centers that bore some grim similarities to the concentration camps of Europe. It was not until the passage of the Immigration and Nationality Act of 1952 that the long-standing racial barriers to naturalization finally came down.

John W. Fiero

FURTHER READING
Curran, Thomas J. *Xenophobia and Immigration, 1820-1930.* Boston: Twayne, 1975. Traces the origins of anti-immigrant movements in America, relating

the xenophobic tradition to the exclusionist laws and practices of the inclusive period.

Hosokawa, Bill. *Nisei: The Quiet Americans.* New York: William Morrow, 1969. Good general study of Japanese Americans and their struggle against legal and social discrimination. Some photographs; no bibliography or notes.

LeMay, Michael C., and Elliott Robert Barkan, eds. *U.S. Immigration and Naturalization Laws and Issues: A Documentary History.* Westport, Conn.: Greenwood Press, 1999. History of U.S. immigration laws supported by extensive extracts from documents.

O'Brien, David J., and Stephen Fugita. *The Japanese American Experience.* Bloomington: Indiana University Press, 1991. Scholarly study with focus on the legal and social problems confronting Japanese Americans before World War II and their rapid acculturation in its wake.

Segal, Uma Anand. *A Framework for Immigration: Asians in the United States.* New York: Columbia University Press, 2002. Survey of the history and economic and social conditions of Asian immigrants to the United States, both before and after the federal immigration reforms of 1965.

Takaki, Ronald T. *Strangers from a Different Shore: A History of Asian Americans.* Boston: Little, Brown, 1989. Excellent and sensitive overview of Asian American history, with extensive notes and photographs.

Wilson, Robert Arden, and Bill Hosokawa. *East to America: A History of the Japanese in the United States.* New York: William Morrow, 1980. General history of Japanese migration to North America. Appendices provide census statistics, text of an exclusionist law, and a letter to President Woodrow Wilson pleading the issei cause.

Yuji, Ichioka. "The Early Japanese Immigrant Quest for Citizenship: The Background of the 1922 Ozawa Case." *Amerasia* 4, no. 2 (1977): 12. Brief account of the reasons for Ozawa's legal action and his desire for citizenship.

SEE ALSO Citizenship; Immigration Act of 1921; Japanese immigrants; Naturalization; "Yellow peril" campaign.

PAGE LAW

THE LAW: Federal legislation designed to prevent Asian prostitutes from entering the United States

DATE: March 3, 1875

IMMIGRATION ISSUES: Asian immigrants; Chinese immigrants; Discrimination; Illegal immigration; Laws and treaties

SIGNIFICANCE: Designed to prohibit Chinese contract workers and prostitutes from entering the United States, the Page law was eventually used to exclude Asian women in general.

Chinese woman with her children and brother-in-law awaiting a streetcar in San Francisco around 1904. The sedate black outfit worn by the woman is typical of the dress worn by married Chinese women who wanted to distinguish themselves from prostitutes. (Library of Congress)

On February 10, 1875, California congressman Horace F. Page introduced federal legislation designed to prohibit the immigration of Asian female prostitutes into the United States. Officially titled "An Act Supplementary to the Acts in Relation to Immigration," the Page law evolved into a restriction against vast numbers of Chinese immigrants into the country regardless of whether they were prostitutes. Any person convicted of importing Chinese prostitutes was subject to a maximum prison term of five years and a fine of not more than five thousand dollars.

An amendment to the law prohibited individuals from engaging in the "coolie trade," or the importation of Chinese contract laborers. Punishment for this type of violation, however, was much less severe and was much more difficult to effect, given the large numbers of Asian male immigrants at the time. As a consequence of this division of penalties, the law was applied in a most gender-specific manner, effectively deterring the immigration of Asian females into the United States. Within seven years following the implementation of the law, the average number of Chinese female immigrants dropped to one-third of its previous level.

ENFORCEMENT AND IMPLEMENTATION An elaborate bureaucratic network established to carry out the Page law's gender-specific exclusions was a catalyst for the decline in Chinese immigration rates. American consulate officials supported by American, Chinese, and British commercial, political, and medical services made up the law's implementation structure. Through intelligence gathering, interrogation, and physical examinations of applicants, the consulate hierarchy ferreted out undesirable applicants for emigration and those suspected of engaging in illegal human trafficking.

This investigative activity evolved well beyond the original intent of the law's authors. Any characteristic or activity that could be linked, even in the most remote sense, to prostitution became grounds for denial to emigrate. Most applications to emigrate came from women from the lower economic strata of society; low economic status therefore became a reason for immigration exclusion. The procedure was a complicated one. Many roadblocks were placed in the way of prospective immigrants. Acquiring permission to emigrate took much time and effort. Passing stringent physical examinations performed by biased health care officials was often impossible. Navigating language barriers through official interviews aimed at evaluating personal character often produced an atmosphere of rigid interrogation, bringing subsequent denial of the right to emigrate. Such a complex system aimed at uncovering fraudulent immigrants placed a hardship upon those wishing to leave China.

Because Hong Kong was the main point of departure for Chinese emigrating to the United States, all required examinations were performed there with a hierarchy of American consulate officials determining immigrant eligibility. In a sense, the Page law actually expanded consulate authority beyond any previous level.

CORRUPTION CHARGES Such increased power of the consular general in implementing the law provided an opportunity for possible abuses of power. In 1878, the U.S. consul general in Hong Kong, John Mosby, accused his predecessors of corruption and bribery. According to Mosby, David Bailey and H. Sheldon Loring were guilty of embezzlement. Both men were accused of setting up such an intricate system to process immigration applications that bribery soon became the natural way to obtain the necessary permission to do so. Mosby went on to charge that Bailey had amassed thousands of dollars of extra income by regularly charging additional examination fees regardless of whether an exam was performed. Mosby also accused Bailey of falsifying test results and encouraging medical personnel to interrogate applicants in order to deny immigration permission to otherwise legal immigrants.

Most of the allegations of corruption surrounded the fact that monies allotted by the federal government for implementation of the Page law were far below the amount Bailey required to run his administration of it. Given this scenario, the U.S. government scrutinized Bailey's conduct. No indictments came from the official investigation, however, and Bailey, who had previously been promoted to vice consul general in Shanghai, remained in that position. Further examination of Bailey's tenure in Hong Kong has suggested that, if anything, he was an overly aggressive official who made emigration of Chinese women to the United States a priority issue of his tenure there rather than an opportunity for profit.

Bailey was replaced in Hong Kong by H. Sheldon Loring. Unlike his predecessor, Loring did not enforce the Page law with as much vigor, allowing a slight yet insignificant increase in the annual numbers of Chinese immigrants. Nevertheless, Loring did enforce the law in an efficient manner, publicly suggesting that any shipowner who engaged in the illegal transport of women would be dealt with to the fullest extent of the law. Even so, Loring was accused of sharing Bailey's enthusiasm for the unofficial expensive design of the immigration procedure. During Loring's tenure, questions about his character began to surface mostly on account of his past relationships with individuals who engaged in questionable business practices in Asia. By the time that Mosby replaced him, such questions had become more than a nuisance. The new U.S. consul to Hong Kong began to describe his predecessor as a dishonest taker of bribes. Once again, the official dynamics of such charges brought forth an official inquiry from Washington. Like the previous investigation of Bailey, however, this investigation produced no official indictment against Loring. The only blemish concerned an additional fee that Loring had instituted for the procuring of an official landing certificate. As there was precedent for such a fee, Loring, like his predecessor, was exonerated of all charges.

Having decided that his predecessors were indeed corrupt, yet unable to prove it, Mosby pursued enforcement of the Page law with relentless occupation. Keeping a posture that was above accusations of corruption, Mosby personally interviewed each applicant for emigration, oversaw the activities between the consulate and the health examiners, and eliminated the additional charges for the landing permits. In the end, the numbers of Chinese immigrants remained similar to those of Loring and below those of Bailey, with the numbers of Chinese female immigrants continuing to decline. Aside from being free from charges of corruption, Mosby's tenure in office was as authoritative as those of his predecessors.

Regardless of the personalities of the consulate officials in charge of implementing the Page law, the results were the same: The number of Chinese who emigrated to the United States decreased dramatically between the 1875 enactment of the law and the enactment of its successor, the Chinese Exclusion Act of 1882. Furthermore, the law's specific application to Chinese women ensured a large imbalance between numbers of male and female immigrants during the period under consideration. In the long run that imbalance negatively affected Asian American families who had settled in the United States.

The barriers that the Page law helped to erect against female Chinese immigrants made a strong nuclear family structure within the Asian American community an immigrant dream rather than a reality.

Thomas J. Edward Walker
Cynthia Gwynne Yaudes

FURTHER READING

Cheng, Lucie, and Edna Bonacich, eds. *Labor Immigration Under Capitalism.* Berkeley: University of California Press, 1984. Examines the development and intent of political movements among immigrants in the United States before World War II.

Foner, Philip, and Daniel Rosenberg, eds. *Racism, Dissent, and Asian Americans from 1850 to the Present.* Westport, Conn.: Greenwood Press, 1993. A documentary history that traces the political and social segregation of immigrants. Indicates the existence of more than one view among whites, African Americans, and others not of Asian descent on the position of Asians in the United States.

Gordon, Charles, and Harry Rosenfield. *Immigration Law and Procedure.* Albany, N.Y.: Banks Publishers, 1959. An excellent history of immigration and emigration law. Covers the period from the 1830's to the 1950's; sectional discussions of European, African, Chicano, and Asian immigrant experiences.

LeMay, Michael C., and Elliott Robert Barkan, eds. *U.S. Immigration and Naturalization Laws and Issues: A Documentary History.* Westport, Conn.: Greenwood Press, 1999. History of U.S. immigration laws supported by extensive extracts from documents.

Peffer, George Anthony. "Forbidden Families: Emigration Experience of Chinese Women Under the Page Law, 1875-1882." *Journal of American Ethnic History* 6 (Fall, 1986): 28-46. Solidly documented research article showing the relationship between the Page law and engendered immigration of Chinese people during the first seven years of its existence.

Tung, William L. *The Chinese in America, 1820-1973.* Dobbs Ferry, N.Y.: Oceana Publications, 1974. Provides chronological and bibliographical references on the changing status of Chinese people in American society. Includes good primary source materials.

SEE ALSO Asian American women; Chinese American Citizens Alliance; Chinese Exclusion Act; Chinese immigrants; Coolies; Discrimination; Mail-order brides; Picture brides; War brides; Women immigrants.

PALMER RAIDS

THE EVENT: Federal government roundup and deportation of suspected radicals
DATE: 1919-1920
PLACE: United States

IMMIGRATION ISSUES: African Americans; Civil rights and liberties; Government and politics; Law enforcement; Nativism and racism

SIGNIFICANCE: Fueled by extremist, anti-immigrant sentiments, the Palmer raids represented the most spectacular anti-civil liberties excesses of the Red Scare of 1919-1920.

In an attempt to rid the nation of political radicalism, the U.S. attorney general, A. Mitchell Palmer, ordered various police units of the federal government to raid the homes and headquarters of suspected radicals and aliens. The raids and the arrests that followed were directed against those, usually foreign-born, who were accused of radicalism. This offense covered everything from parliamentary socialism to Bolshevism, encompassing "radical feminism," anarchism, and labor militancy as well.

In the immediate postwar period, American resistance to anything foreign stemmed from rumors and formal pronouncements of a great radical foreign conspiracy aimed at overthrowing the American way of life. Many Americans, encouraged by political rhetoric and official pronouncements, were convinced that a communist revolution was imminent and that a reaffirmation of traditional American values, coupled with a good dose of law and order, was the only thing that would make America safe for Americans.

POLITICAL CONTEXT OF THE RAIDS   In several respects, Palmer's antiradical crusade continued the espionage and sedition prosecutions of the war years. The Overman Committee investigating German espionage during World War I, for example, simply switched to hunting communists and socialists after the war. The most spectacular excesses of the "Red Scare" ended by 1921, but the scare remained part of the political climate in the United States for many years to come. Antiradicalism, for example, played a significant role in the political agitation for immigrant restriction and antiforeign sentiments that followed the raids.

In 1919, the U.S. government and organizations purporting to defend "Americanism" responded to any activity that was perceived to be radical: strikes were busted (1919 steel and coal strikes, for example); newspapers called for government action against all radicalism, perceived or real; duly elected legislators were denied their seats in the New York State Assembly; and the National Security League, whose main weapon was "organized patriotism," successfully lobbied Congress to pass laws authorizing the deportation of aliens and other "irreconcilable radicals."

The American Legion, advocating the Americanization of United States society, declared that radicals were mostly from non-English-speaking groups. Individual state legislatures, among them those of Idaho and Oregon, came close to passing laws forbidding any publication not written in English. According to historian Frederick Allen,

> It was an era of lawless and disorderly defense of law and order, of unconstitutional defense of the U.S. Constitution, of suspicion and civil conflict—in a very literal sense, a reign of terror . . .

Public reaction to radicalism so affected Palmer that he ordered the Justice Department's Bureau of Investigation (the predecessor of the Federal Bureau of Investigation) to infiltrate and investigate all radical groups. Following the implementation of this program, the bureau's head, J. Edgar Hoover, reported back to Palmer that revolution was imminent. Palmer then organized a federal dragnet aimed at stepping up the raids and arrests. On January 2, 1920, federal agents arrested more than six thousand people, most without proper warrant, incarcerating them in jails and detention centers for weeks and even months without granting rights to legal counsel or bail. Of those arrested, 516 were eventually deported, including the feminist, anarchist, and militant labor organizer Emma Goldman and fellow anarchist and labor organizer Alexander Berkman.

AFRICAN AMERICAN VICTIMS The intolerance expressed in the Palmer raids took many forms. Some advocated book censorship and others inflicted agony on "hyphenated Americans," including African Americans, who were arguably the chief victims of the Palmer raids and their aftermath. As African Americans moved to the North, northern whites reacted in fear. Many of them perceived the influx of these visibly distinct Americans to be a threat to their social status.

The employment of African Americans threatened white workers with a status deprivation. In response, many whites struck out at the newcomers, rekindling racist fears of the past. For the emigrating African Americans, the move north signaled a refusal to accept a caste system in the South which had excluded so many of them from the general prosperity of the nation. Tension mounted as black aspirations clashed with racial norms. The racial conflict which followed immediately became linked to the antiradical mood of the time. White mainstream America feared social upset from any source, whether it was black Americans or radical immigrants.

THE KU KLUX KLAN The mood of society in 1919 was as conducive to racial tension as it was to the Red Scare. Fueled by a witch hunt to weed out Bolsheviks and other radicals from America's inner fabric, racial prejudice be-

A. Mitchell Palmer before he became U.S. attorney general. (Library of Congress)

came a natural extension of a patriotic call for complete Americanism. From Chicago to Tulsa, racial relations often became racial violence. It was in just such an atmosphere that the Ku Klux Klan experienced a rebirth.

Fighting for its own version of "one hundred percent Americanism," the Klan played upon the fears and hostility that existed between urban and rural America. Klan propaganda, advocating a concern that public morals were being weakened by the mixing of the races and by "Red-inspired" trade unionism, sought to rally traditional Americans to its banner. The Klan's chief organizer, Edward Y. Clarke, roused his constituents against a "Jewish-Banker-Bolshevik conspiracy" that the Klan saw leading an international movement to take control of America. This fit right in with Palmer's warning that a Bolshevik uprising would occur on May Day, 1920.

Racism was fused to anti-Bolshevism and all that it implied. Because Jews were perceived by many in rural Protestant America to be of foreign birth, the Klan's propaganda was received with patriotic fervor. Most rural Americans identified radicalism with foreigners. Jews, Roman Catholics, and immigrants fit into this xenophobic milieu. By 1921, Klan membership passed 100,000 and continued to grow.

The Americanism crusade fit in nicely with concerns of American business over the growth of trade unionism. Strikes, after all, were a threat to profits, and American businesspeople were in no mood to have profits reduced. Labor organizers, in turn, called for a reorganization of the industrial system to promote workers to a position on par with the power and prestige of industrial capitalists. In a countervailing move against trade unionism, the business community called upon patriotism to defeat any "Bolshevik-inspired" labor organizing activity. Trade unionism was labeled as anti-American, radical, and foreign by design. American business viewed the struggle of the worker for better wages as the beginning of armed revolution in America. Anything or anyone associated with workers' rights was therefore anti-American and should be treated as such. If this meant intolerance of constitutional guarantees, so be it.

LEGACY OF THE RAIDS   A search for a human rights perspective on the Palmer Raids revolves around three interrelated questions. First, what gave rise to the Red Scare which precipitated the raids? Second, why were the raids aimed for the most part at an alien component of the labor movement? Third, was the entire phenomenon an aberrant episode or an action which set the tone for the rest of the decade?

The Palmer raids became part of the "normalcy" of the Harding administration. Antiradicalism continued to play a role throughout the decade in the agitation for immigrant restriction and as a catalyst for the business community's countervailing response of trade unionism. Significant anti-immigration activity resulted in the passage of the Johnson-Reed Immigration Act of 1924, which ended three centuries of free European immigration. This law laid the groundwork for continued anti-alien activity as some native-born Americans lashed out against those who, by their mere presence, challenged traditional norms.

Union activity was confronted by the emergence of the antiunion "American Plan," pursued by business throughout the decade. This effort, launched by employers to resist labor unionization on every front, included the use of labor spies to infiltrate the labor movement, the manipulation of public opinion through antiradical and anti-alien propaganda, and the hiring of strikebreakers to counter organized labor's ultimate weapon. A major force behind the plan was the National Association of Manufacturers (NAM). Throughout the decade, NAM expended a very large amount of money and political influence to lobby against trade unionism. Palmer's replacement, James Daugherty, complemented this activity in the courts.

During Daugherty's tenure in office, he was influential in obtaining many federal injunctions against work stoppages, forcing striking workers back to work. The courts also made it possible for trade union activities to be classified as a restraint of trade and therefore to be made illegal. The prevailing mood of the nation greeted such determinations with enthusiasm. At the beginning of the decade, 20 percent of all nonagricultural workers belonged to labor unions. By the end of the 1920's, because of a combination of antiradicalism, employer pressure, and unfriendly government activity, this percentage was cut in half.

NATIVISM AND THE WOBBLIES Support for official antiradical activity also fanned the fires of nativism. The Palmer raids continued a wartime obsession for internal security. A postwar recession, high unemployment, and failures of international cooperation led to an overall atmosphere of an inability to confront emerging social pathologies. Antiradical and deportation remedies of the Departments of Justice and Immigration were part of the nativistic renewal of the period.

The Industrial Workers of the World (IWW, or Wobblies) played a key part in the postwar antiradical renewal. Communist influence within the group encouraged anti-Bolshevist passions to surface against it. Pursuit of the Wobblies had been going on since their organization in 1905. Their attempt to unite all workers into one big union, and their objection to and rejection of revered American values such as free enterprise and upward social mobility, painted an anti-American and therefore foreign picture of the organization.

Americans saw the Wobblies as a threat to the internal security of the nation and as a conduit of alien ideas, and the IWW became a feared organization. Whether it deserved this reputation was not the point. Federal policies toward the group took on an antiradical and antialien tone. By the time of America's entry into World War I, the immigration, espionage, and sedition laws had been broadened to allow arrest and deportation of IWW officials. Many were jailed for conspiracy because of their opposition to the war. The organization's leader, William Dudley (Big Bill) Haywood, fled from the United States to the Soviet Union, where he died and was buried in the Kremlin wall.

IWW paranoia, and the fervent nativism which it helped to spawn, was reaffirmed after the war. Wobblies, particularly in the Pacific Northwest, were rounded up in antiradical and antialien crusades. The use of troops in the raids and the denial of legal rights to those arrested and held became at once an official answer to a nation's security problem and an appeasement to an insecure public's extreme xenophobia. This "normalcy" continued throughout the decade.

Thomas J. Edward Walker

FURTHER READING

Briggs, Vernon M. *Immigration and American Unionism.* Ithaca, N.Y.: Cornell University Press, 2001. Scholarly survey of the dynamic interaction between unionism and immigration. Covers the entire sweep of U.S. national history, with an emphasis on the nineteenth century.

Cole, David. *Enemy Aliens: Double Standards and Constitutional Freedoms in the War on Terrorism.* New York: New Press, 2003. Study of the modern problem of protecting constitutional rights while combatting terrorism whose historical background touches on the Palmer raids.

Gentry, Curt. *J. Edgar Hoover: The Man and the Secrets.* New York: W. W. Norton, 1991. Critical biography of the long-time director of the Federal Bureau of Investigation that includes a chapter on the Palmer raids.

Higham, John. *Strangers in the Land.* 2d ed. New Brunswick, N.J.: Rutgers University Press, 1988. "Intellectual history" that encompasses and synthesizes political, economic, and social change by providing a summary of agitation for immigrant restriction and against immigration during the early twentieth century.

Kiel, R. Andrew. *J. Edgar Hoover: The Father of the Cold War.* Lanham, Md.: University Press of America, 2000. Extensive review of Hoover's career, including the era of the Palmer raids.

Preston, William, Jr. *Aliens and Dissenters.* Cambridge, Mass.: Harvard University Press, 1963. The significance of this study lies in its examination of the problems of aliens and dissenters. Deals with the period from 1890 to

1920, when the fear of foreigners and radicals increased in intensity. Concludes that such fears ultimately made aliens and radicals scapegoats for the country's ills.

Tuttle, William M., Jr. *Race Riot: Chicago in the Red Summer of 1919.* New York: Atheneum, 1982. History that attempts to explain the race riot and its causes in terms of individuals and groups. The analysis gets its foundation from a revealing overview of 1919's Red Summer and the Red Scare, detailing the racism and antiradicalism of that period.

Wexler, Alice. *Emma Goldman in Exile: From the Russian Revolution to the Spanish Civil War.* Boston: Beacon Press, 1989. Details the last twenty years of the life of American anarchist Emma Goldman, who was deported from the United States to Russia in 1919, at the height of the anticommunist movement. Presents the image of this radical feminist as "the most dangerous woman in America."

SEE ALSO Alien and Sedition Acts; Immigration Act of 1921; Immigration Act of 1924; Immigration law; Nativism; Naturalization; Sacco and Vanzetti trial.

PICTURE BRIDES

DEFINITION: Women who have arranged marriages with strangers—usually of the same nationality—in foreign lands that were facilitated by the prior exchange of photographs and letters

IMMIGRATION ISSUES: Families and marriage; Japanese immigrants; Women

SIGNIFICANCE: Picture bride marriages were especially common among Japanese immigrants to the United States and Hawaii before World War II.

Between 1907 and 1924, more than fourteen thousand women immigrated to Hawaii and the mainland United States from Japan and Korea. Many of these Asian immigrants were picture brides–women who were selected as wives on the basis of their photographs. Some of their weddings were conducted by proxy, with only the women and pictures of the grooms in attendance. When the women reached their destinations, photographs were used to match them with their husbands or husbands to be. Often, however, the parties involved did not match the photographs that had been exchanged.

The popularity of marrying picture brides among Japanese immigrants can be attributed to a combination of social, cultural, economic, and historical factors. It was first of all a logical extension of the tradition of arranged marriages. The lesser gender value placed upon daughters also encouraged their departure from their homeland into an alternative opportunity. In modern Japan, the exposure of women to education made them receptive toward the idea of travel, and the industrialization of the population paved the way for women to become laborers in America. More important, using family stability as a form of labor control, the plantations of Hawaii had long encouraged contracts between laborers and potential spouses.

The experiences of picture brides—especially their conflicts with their husbands as a result of differences in age, education level, family background, personal aspirations, and taste—are a constant source of inspiration for writers and artists, as in Cathy Song's poetry collection *Picture Bride* (1983) and Yoshiko Uchida's 1987 novel and director-writer Kayo Hatta's 1995 motion picture of the same title. Research indicates that picture brides could become accomplished in poetry and the arts, and hence serve as transmitters and creators of culture. Because picture brides often survived long after their husbands' deaths, they have come to be venerated as matriarchs and culture-bearers by younger generations.

Balance Chow

FURTHER READING

Hoobler, Dorothy, Thomas Hoobler, and George Takei. *The Japanese American Family Album*. New York: Oxford University Press, 1996.

Ichioka, Yuji. *The Issei: The World of the First Generation Japanese Immigrants, 1885-1924*. New York: Free Press, 1988.

Makabe, Tomoko. *Picture Brides: Japanese Women in Canada*. Translated by Kathleen Chisato Merken. Ontario: Multicultural History Society of Ontario, 1995.

Uchida, Yoshiko. *Picture Bride*. 1987. Seattle: University of Washington Press, 1997.

SEE ALSO Japanese immigrants; Mail-order brides; Page law; War brides; Women immigrants.

PLYLER V. DOE

THE CASE: U.S. Supreme Court ruling on the rights of noncitizens
DATE: June 15, 1982

IMMIGRATION ISSUES: Court cases; Illegal immigration

SIGNIFICANCE: This Supreme Court decision extended the equal protection clause of the Fourteenth Amendment to guarantee the right of noncitizens to public social services.

In May, 1975, the Texas legislature enacted a law that denied financial support for the public education of the children of undocumented aliens. The state's local school districts, accordingly, were allowed to exclude such children from public school enrollment. The children of noncitizen aliens who henceforth paid for their public school education still were permitted to enroll. Despite the statute, Texas public school districts continued enrolling the children of undocumented aliens until the 1977-1978 school year, when, amid a continuing economic recession and accompanying budget tightening, the law was enforced. An initial challenge to the 1975 law arose in the Tyler Independent School District in Smith County, located in northeastern Texas, but similar challenges in other school districts soon produced a class-action suit.

The problem that had inspired the state law was the massive influx—principally of Mexicans but also of persons from other Central American countries—into Texas, as well as into New Mexico, Arizona, and California. Some of these people entered the United States for seasonal agricultural jobs, while others, undocumented, remained. Most were poor and seeking economic opportunities unavailable to them in Mexico and Central America.

Figures released by the U.S. Immigration and Naturalization Service estimated that when the *Plyler* case arose, between two and three million undocumented aliens resided in Texas and other southwestern portions of the United States. Texas claimed that 5 percent of its population, three-quarters of a million people, were undocumented aliens, roughly twenty thousand of whose children were enrolled in Texas public schools. With recession adversely affecting employment, many of the state's taxpayers asked why they should bear the financial burdens of educating illegal aliens, as well as providing them with other benefits, such as food stamps and welfare payments.

The U.S. Supreme Court's 5-4 decision on *Plyler v. Doe* was delivered by Associate Justice William Joseph Brennan, Jr., a justice whom many observers considered a liberal but whose overall record was moderate. The *Plyler* majority ruling upheld a previous decision by the U.S. Fifth Circuit Court that had ruled for the defendants. Chief Justice Warren Burger vigorously dissented from the majority opinion, along with justices Byron White, William Rehnquist, and Sandra Day O'Connor.

On behalf of the Court's majority, Brennan declared that the 1975 Texas statute rationally served no substantial state interest and violated the equal protection clause of the Fourteenth Amendment. Ratified along with the Thirteenth and Fifteenth Amendments during the post-Civil War Reconstruction Era, the Fourteenth Amendment guaranteed "that no State shall . . . deny to any person within its jurisdiction the equal protection of the laws." Although the overriding concern of Reconstruction politicians, judges, and states ratifying the Fourteenth Amendment was to afford protection to newly emancipated African Americans, the equal protection clause increasingly had been interpreted to mean what it stated: guaranteeing equal protection of the laws to any person—precisely the line of reasoning taken by Brennan.

Brennan and the Court majority likewise disagreed with the Texas argument that undocumented aliens did not fall "within its jurisdiction," thus excluding them and their children from Fourteenth Amendment guarantees. Such an exclusion, Brennan declared, condemned innocents to a lifetime of hardship and the stigma of illiteracy.

IMPACT OF PLYLER The *Plyler* decision was novel in two important respects. It was the first decision to extend Fourteenth Amendment guarantees to each person, irrespective of that person's citizenship or immigration status. Second, the Court majority introduced a new criterion for determining the applicability of Fourteenth Amendment protections: the doctrine of heightened or intermediate scrutiny. The Court avoided applying its previous standard of strict scrutiny. It recognized that education was not a fundamental right and that undocumented aliens were not, as it had previously phrased it, a "suspect class," in the sense that they, like African Americans, historically had been victims of racial discrimination. Heightened scrutiny was warranted, Brennan and the majority agreed, because of education's special importance to other social benefits and because children of undocumented aliens were not responsible for their status.

Chief Justice Burger and the three other dissenting, generally conservative, justices, who were staunch advocates of judicial restraint, strongly criticized Brennan and the majority for what the dissenters considered to be arguing political opinions instead of adhering to sound jurisprudence. The dissenters seriously questioned heightened scrutiny as a judicial standard and found that the Texas statute substantially furthered the state's legitimate interests.

The *Plyler* decision represented a significant departure from the decision rendered by Chief Justice Roger B. Taney in *Scott v. Sandford* (1857), a decision that the Fourteenth Amendment was designed in part to nullify by political means. *Plyler*'s heightened standard of scrutiny, however, continued through the mid-1990's to be controversial and confusing, both within the Supreme Court and among legal observers. The issue arising when the equal protection clause was applied to cases not involving racial discrimination had been raised in *Buck v. Bell* (1927), when Justice Oliver Wendell Holmes denounced such decision making as "the usual last resort of constitutional arguments."

In *Plyler,* Brennan and the majority saw no chance to apply the Court's already accepted classification of strict scrutiny to equal protection cases, because *Plyler*'s defendants, the undocumented aliens, were not victims of institutionalized racial discrimination or of reverse discrimination. They were illegals as a consequence of their own conscious actions. Nevertheless, as legal scholars observed, in order to prevent hardship and stigmas from afflicting schoolchildren, who were not responsible for their parents' actions, the *Plyler* majority introduced an intermediate level of classification with their standard of heightened scrutiny. Such a standard raised questions about whether undocumented aliens and their families enjoyed rights to other government benefits, such as welfare assistance, medical care, and food stamps.

The difficulties confronted by Texas, by other Southwestern states, and by illegal aliens and their children were alleviated somewhat by a broad federal amnesty program launched in 1992.

Clifton K. Yearley

FURTHER READING

Aleinikoff, Thomas A., and David A. Martin. *Immigration: Process and Policy.* 2d ed. Saint Paul, Minn.: West, 1991. A careful review of modern U.S. immigration policies. Discusses the problems posed by illegal, undocumented aliens and the difficulties faced by government policy makers in coping with illegals.

Blasi, Vincent, ed. *The Burger Court.* New Haven, Conn.: Yale University Press, 1983. An authoritative yet readable analysis of the Chief Justiceship of Warren Burger, which did little to modify civil rights decisions of his predecessors. Also clarifies Brennan's attitudes and decisions.

Curtis, Michael Kent. *No State Shall Abridge.* Durham, N.C.: Duke University Press, 1986. A clear, scholarly exposition of the role played by the Fourteenth Amendment and the Bill of Rights in modern U.S. jurisprudence, including civil and criminal rights, racial and reverse discriminations, and interpretations of due process.

Hull, Elizabeth. *Without Justice for All.* Westport, Conn.: Greenwood Press, 1985. A precise study bearing on the problems raised in *Plyler,* the historical plight of resident and illegal aliens and their families, and the varying status of their constitutional rights.

Jacobs, Nancy R. *Immigration: Looking for a New Home.* Detroit: Gale Group, 2000. Broad discussion of modern federal government immigration policies that considers all sides of the debates about the rights of illegal aliens.

Mirande, Alfredo. *Gringo Justice.* Notre Dame, Ind.: University of Notre Dame Press, 1990. A spirited, dismaying critique of U.S. judicial and political treatment of Hispanic immigrants by both the states and the federal government. Provides excellent context for understanding important aspects of the *Plyler* case.

Nelson, William. *The Fourteenth Amendment.* Cambridge, Mass.: Harvard University Press, 1988. An authoritative analysis of the evolution of the Fourteenth Amendment from a set of political principles to a vital part of twentieth century judicial decision making. Good analyses of the Supreme Court's standards of scrutiny, including the intermediate or "heightened" scrutiny applied in *Plyler.*

SEE ALSO Asian American education; Florida illegal-immigrant suit; *Lau v. Nichols*; Mexican American Legal Defense and Education Fund; Naturalization; Proposition 187; Proposition 227.

POLISH IMMIGRANTS

IDENTIFICATION: Immigrants to North America from the eastern European nation of Poland and its neighbors

IMMIGRATION ISSUES: Demographics; European immigrants; Refugees

SIGNIFICANCE: Because of their large numbers and tendency to settle in culturally diverse areas, Polish Americans have figured prominently in interethnic relations. As they have moved through the assimilation process, Polish Americans have been both victimized by prejudice and accused of discriminating against other ethnic and racial groups.

Polish Americans are generally defined as those whose heritage was connected to the Polish language, culture, and Roman Catholicism. Polish Americans who arrived between 1608 and 1800 came for personal reasons, and those emigrating from 1800 to 1860 came to escape foreign control over their homeland. The third and largest wave, of 2.5 million immigrants between 1870 and 1924, sought to escape the economic hardships of their homeland. After World War II, a fourth wave of Poles came to the United States as displaced persons or political refugees fleeing the communist government.

INTERGROUP RELATIONS   The relatively small number of Poles arriving during the first two immigration periods meant that intergroup relations were rather limited. The settlers who arrived from 1608 to 1800 did not establish communities, and relations with others in the United States were almost exclusively on an individual basis. However, Polish Americans who served during the American Revolution were regarded positively, and the political refugees, who made up the bulk of the next wave, gained the respect of Americans for their dedication to independence, nationalism, and liberalism. The large group of Poles arriving during the 1870-1924 wave interacted as a group with established American society, with earlier immigrants, and with other eastern and southern European immigrants.

Because most Polish immigrants came to the United States to work as unskilled laborers in urban-industrial areas, established Americans viewed them as essential but not necessarily welcome additions. The vast differences in language and customs and the formation of distinct ethnic communities caused many people to question whether Poles could ever adapt to American society. Established Americans also mistrusted Poles because of their support of labor unions and their use of alcoholic beverages, which were contrary to Protestant ideals of individualism and sobriety.

Relations between Polish Americans and earlier immigrants were often strained. Poles resented the English, Welsh, Scottish, and Irish immigrants who constituted the skilled laborers and bosses in the mines, mills, and factories. The Poles reacted against Irish American control of the Roman Catholic hierarchy by forming their own ethnic national parishes. This desire for a separate Polish Catholic identity became so strong that a schism with Roman Catholicism occurred when the Reverend Francis Hodur founded the Polish National Church in 1904.

Although this group of Poles faced circumstances similar to those faced by other immigrants from southern and eastern Europe, relations between these groups were not always the best. Poles held stereotypical views of and harbored resentments against other Slavs, and many had come to the United States with a tradition of anti-Semitism. When Poles and Lithuanians shared churches, the result was less than harmonious, and splits were usually the result. Although direct confrontations with Italians were not common, each group often accepted the prevalent stereotypes about the other.

However, Polish American businesspeople often had solid working relationships with people of various ethnic backgrounds. Many young Polish immigrant women served as domestics in the homes of Euro-Americans or Jewish Americans and built a warm relationship with their employers. Despite the remnants of Old World anti-Semitism, Polish laborers and Jewish shopkeepers developed respectful and trusting business dealings. Poles cooperated with other immigrants from eastern and southern Europe to form labor unions. Their success in this venue played an important role in the establishment of unions as a powerful force in the United States.

Polish immigrant husking corn on a Connecticut farm in 1941. (Library of Congress)

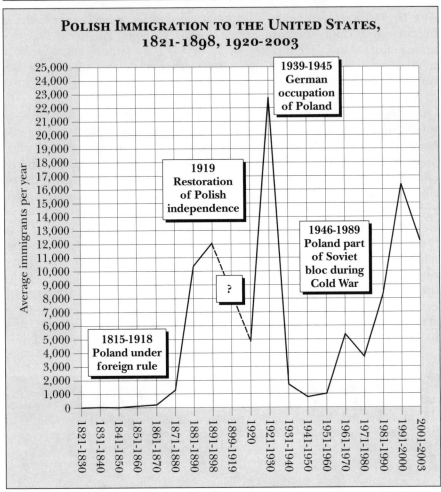

POLISH IMMIGRATION TO THE UNITED STATES, 1821-1898, 1920-2003

Source: U.S. Census Bureau. Data on specifically Polish immigration are not available for 1899-1919, when Poland was part of the Austro-Hungarian Empire.

ASSIMILATION AND INTERGROUP RELATIONS   By the 1920's, the passage of time and restrictive immigration laws hastened the assimilation process. Although Polish Americans were becoming more Americanized, new social structures were being established, altering intergroup relations. During the latter part of the twentieth century, Polish American intergroup relations involved the relations of the more elderly urban blue-collar workers, the white-collar professionals, and the new associations of refugees from Poland.

Many urban blue-collar workers came of age during the Great Depression and World War II. They endured a life of sacrifice and want but were able to gain social and economic mobility in the postwar boom years. However, by the 1970's, economic decline had hit the major employers of many Polish Americans, and an increasing number of African Americans and Hispanics had moved into traditionally Polish neighborhoods. Although most Polish Americans had adequate financial resources to sustain them into retirement, the combination of their weakened economic situation and the loss of their ethnic communities often resulted in resentment toward the newer residents. Although violent conflict was rare, tensions were high between urban Polish Americans and their new neighbors, the African Americans and Hispanics. Polish white-collar professionals, who often married non-Poles, tended to identify less with the ethnic group and more with the concerns of their socioeconomic class. At times, this caused them to become estranged from the older Polish Americans. The refugees from communism, relatively small in number, tended to affiliate with their socioeconomic and employment peers.

Despite the differences in class and status, Polish Americans still face a certain degree of discrimination. Stereotypes that depict Polish Americans as lacking intelligence have been especially hurtful. Polish American acceptance of such humor has, perhaps, contributed to this prejudice. Although Polish Americans increasingly identify with middle-class values, some of these traditional patterns of intergroup dynamics persist.

Paul J. Zbiek

FURTHER READING

Balch, Emily Greene. *Our Slavic Fellow Citizens.* New York: Charities Publication Committee, 1910. Reprint. New York: Arno Press, 1969. Classic early study of Slavic immigrants including Poles.

Bukowiczyk, John J. *Polish Americans and Their History: Community, Culture, and Politics.* Pittsburgh: University of Pittsburgh Press, 1996. Good general history of Polish immigrants in the United States.

Greene, Victor R. *A Singing Ambivalence: American Immigrants Between Old World and New, 1830-1930.* Kent, Ohio: Kent State University Press, 2004. Comparative study of the different challenges faced by members of eight major immigrant groups: the Irish, Germans, Scandinavians and Finns, eastern European Jews, Italians, Poles and Hungarians, Chinese, and Mexicans. Greene is also the author of *The Slavic Community on Strike: Immigrant Labor in Pennsylvania Anthracite* (Notre Dame, Ind.: University of Notre Dame Press, 1968.)

Lopata, Helena Z. *Polish Americans: Status Competition in an Ethnic Community.* Englewood Cliffs, N.J.: Prentice-Hall, 1976. Overview of the Polish American ethnic experience in one community.

Thomas, William I., and Florian Znaniecki. *The Polish Peasant in Europe and America.* Boston: Richard G. Badger, 1918. Reprint. Urbana: University of Illinois Press, 1996. Another classic study of Polish immigrants that examines the condition of Poles in both the Old World and the New World.

SEE ALSO Anglo-conformity; Eastern European Jewish immigrants; Euro-Americans; European immigrants, 1892-1943; German immigrants; Jewish immigrants; Russian immigrants.

PROPOSITION 187

THE LAW: California voter initiative to limit public services available to un-
documented immigrants
DATE: Voted on November 8, 1994
PLACE: California

IMMIGRATION ISSUES: Civil rights and liberties; Latino immigrants; Laws and
treaties; Mexican immigrants

SIGNIFICANCE: In this voter initiative, California residents expressed their resentment of the demands on state services made by the state's large undocumented worker population.

On November 8, 1994, approximately 60 percent of the voters of California
marked their ballots in favor of Proposition 187, the so-called Save Our State
or "SOS" initiative. Drafted by a conservative Orange County businessman,
the proposition was designed to end state-funded education and welfare benefits for illegal aliens. It also limited publicly funded medical assistance available to illegal aliens, who could be treated only in life-threatening emergen-
cies requiring immediate attention. Under provisions of the proposition,
teachers and physicians were required to report illegal aliens to the immigration authorities.

Hard pressed by an economic downturn and by a series of natural disasters
including earthquakes, fires, and floods, the state of California was home to
an estimated 1.6 million illegal aliens. Many of them held minimum-wage
jobs that most Americans were reluctant to fill. The estimated annual cost to
California for services related to illegal immigrants exceeded $3 billion. How
much of this was offset by various taxes paid by these workers was a subject of
debate.

Both supporters and opponents of Proposition 187 agreed that this legislation was unconstitutional, violating both the equal protection guarantees of
the U.S. Constitution and hundreds of antidiscrimination laws. The primary
motivation of those who supported the initiative was to get the matter of providing public services to illegal aliens into the courts. Their ultimate aim was
to overturn some legislation and to negate some of the related decisions
handed down by the U.S. Supreme Court.

Underlying the appearance of Proposition 187 on the ballot in 1994 was
the campaign of Governor Pete Wilson, who rode a wave of conservatism into
the state house in 1991. Wilson, a two-term U.S. senator with presidential am-
bitions for 1996, proposed legislation targeting illegal aliens. His programs
were popular among voters who faced diminished employment opportunities, increased taxes, and decreased public services. Illegal aliens were identified as a cause of these problems.

Wilson campaigned for the passage of Proposition 187 realizing that the national publicity such a campaign would generate could benefit him substantially among conservative voters, whose ranks were growing nationally. Despite its obvious defects, the proposition that six of every ten California voters approved enjoyed considerable popularity nationwide.

ECONOMIC EFFECTS Agriculture and mining had been mainstays of California's economy since the sprawling territory achieved statehood in 1850, becoming the thirty-first of the United States. Immigrants, legal and otherwise, helped to build the state and became a fundamental part of its economy. California had long been one of several significantly multiethnic states. Many people count this among California's greatest assets.

California's major industries, including defense and aerospace, began to feel severe economic pressures with the cessation of the Cold War during the late 1980's and early 1990's. Voters faced with uncertain economic futures resented having to pay taxes to help support those whose presence in their state and country was illegal. These undocumented immigrants contributed substantially to the state's economy, however, by taking jobs that their legally documented counterparts were often unwilling to take and by paying taxes for unemployment insurance and supplemental security income, benefits to which they did not have access.

Passage of Proposition 187 did not result in the disappearance of illegal immigrants from California. The conditions under which they remained there, however, were increasingly difficult. The full enactment of this initiative was blocked by the courts as test cases worked their way through the judicial system. Less than a week after the election, various groups had begun to test the law, and on November 14, 1994, a federal judge temporarily blocked enactment of the measure.

It has been argued that Proposition 187 not only violated the U.S. Constitution and various laws but also created unacceptable conflicts between state law and professional ethics and responsibilities. For example, physicians are professionally obligated to treat any patient who requires treatment. A law mandating that they report patients who seek their professional services to the government violates the standards by which the medical profession traditionally has been guided.

CONSEQUENCES The repercussions following the passage of Proposition 187 were enormous. The vote had implications far beyond the matter of what services should be available to illegal aliens and their dependents. It reflected a major shift in the thinking of many Americans about the kind of nation the United States is becoming and suggested an undercurrent of racism. The proposition expanded debates on immigration at the national level.

From the late 1960's to the early 1990's, Americans who had been unfairly disenfranchised became beneficiaries of legislation that accorded them the rights guaranteed by the Constitution. Those who had been discriminated against because of race, gender, religion, sexual preference, or physical disability were now protected. Such programs as affirmative action required preferential treatment for those falling into the above categories in terms of employment, education, and other opportunities in organizations that receive government funding. These programs were intended to reverse the effects of past discrimination.

In late July, 1995, the Board of Regents of the University of California voted to abolish affirmative action. They decided to end racial preferences in hiring and contracting by January, 1996, and end preferences in admissions to the nine campuses of the university system by January, 1997. Jack W. Peltason, president of the system, agreed to comply with the mandate, adding that the system sought to reflect California's ethnic diversity in the populations of its nine campuses. Chancellor Chang-lin Tien of the University of California, Berkeley, had never strongly supported affirmative action. He accepted the regents' recommendation that the universities in the system do everything they could to achieve diversity but without using preferences for admission based on race, gender, or ethnicity.

R. Baird Shuman

FURTHER READING

Bischoff, Henry. *Immigration Issues.* Westport, Conn.: Greenwood Press, 2002.

Jonas, Susanne, and Suzanne Dod Thomas, eds. *Immigration: A Civil Rights Issue for the Americas.* Wilmington, Del.: Scholarly Resources, 1999.

López, David, and Andrés Jiménez, eds. *Latinos and Public Policy in California: An Agenda for Opportunity.* Berkeley, Calif.: Berkeley Public Policy Press, 2003.

SEE ALSO   *Plyler v. Doe*; Proposition 227; Undocumented workers.

PROPOSITION 227

THE LAW: California voter initiative to abolish bilingual education in public schools
DATE: Voted on June 2, 1998
PLACE: California

IMMIGRATION ISSUES: Civil rights and liberties; Education; Language; Latino immigrants; Laws and treaties; Mexican immigrants

SIGNIFICANCE: After thirty years of experimentation with bilingual education in California's public schools, voters decided it did not work and voted overwhelmingly to end it in a ballot initiative.

California entrepreneur Ron Unz speaking at a press conference during his campaign in support of Proposition 227 in June, 1998. (AP/Wide World Photos)

Beginning the early education of schoolchildren in their own languages became a goal of California's bilingual education policy during the 1970's, when educators hoped that by giving children a strong educational start in their own languages, they would be better prepared to succeed after shifting over to English-language education. However, as time passed, that goal seemed impossible to achieve. California's schoolchildren speak an estimated 140 different languages in their homes. To teach each group of them in their own languages before teaching them in English was beyond the resources of California's massive education system.

In June, 1998, the issue of bilingualism was placed before the voters of California in a referendum. Their response was strong: "No Mas"—no more bilingual education in their public schools.

The liberal California of the 1960's appeared to have reprogrammed itself in latter years with regard to social issues. In 1994, for example, Californians voted against providing government benefits to undocumented immigrants. Next, they voted against affirmative action. Finally, in November, 1997, voter groups filed petitions for a movement called English for the Children—a ballot measure sponsored by Silicon Valley millionaire Ron Unz, whose mother was an immigrant from Russia. In 1994, the Republican Unz had unsuccessfully challenged Republican incumbent Pete Wilson in the primary election for governor.

California's bilingual education controversy was also developing around the same time that the board of the Oakland Unified School District made its widely ridiculed pronouncement that Ebonics—black English—should be regarded as a language separate from English. Ironically, just as African Americans were split on the Ebonics debate, California's Hispanic population was also splintered on the need for bilingual education.

THE UNZ INITIATIVE In 1987, just over 500,000 California children attended some type of bilingual classes. By 1997, the number had risen to nearly 1.4 million. According to a 1997 *U.S. News & World Report* story, California, with its burgeoning immigrant population, led the nation in proportion of its students who were not proficient in English, with a figure of 25 percent, compared with 6.7 percent of students nationally. By definition, these are students who cannot understand English well enough to keep up in school. Eighty-eight percent of California's public schools had at least one limited English proficient (LEP) student, and 71 percent had at least twenty LEP students. (In 1997 the acronym LEP was changed to EL, for English learners.)

Traditionally immigrants to the United States, speaking an assortment of languages, regard English as the language of upward mobility and want their children to learn it as quickly as possible. This attitude was still held by many immigrant families in California during the late 1990's, and some of them were among the opponents to bilingual education. The largest non-English speaking groups in California were Latinos, especially Mexican Americans, 84 percent of whom indicated in late 1997 that they would support the Unz bilingual education initiative, according to a *Los Angeles Times* poll. That figure compared impressively with the 80 percent of white voters who indicated that they would back the initiative.

The Unz measure was cochaired by Gloria Matta Tuchman, a Mexican American teacher who had used English immersion to teach students for about fifteen years. The measure also benefited from a strong endorsement from Jaime Escalante, the Bolivian immigrant who taught calculus to urban Latino youths and became California's most famous schoolteacher—thanks, in part, to the 1988 film *Stand and Deliver.*

The Unz initiative called for a one-year English immersion program, which many educators said wouldn't prepare students for academic work in English, although it would allow them to speak more easily to their friends on the playground. Initially many state Republicans avoided the bilingual education debate, fearing that the Democrats would label supporters "racists." They also recalled that while many Latinos had earlier begun by supporting Proposition 187, the ballot initiative to deny benefits to undocumented aliens, they later turned against it and also voted against the measure's Republican supporters during the 1996 elections.

Critics of the Unz measure argued that it ignored important research data that demonstrated successes in bilingual education programs. Supporters of the measure countered that bilingual education created an educational ghetto by isolating non-English speaking students and preventing them from becoming successful members of society. They also accused politicians and educators of profiting from bilingual education. For example, they noted that some bilingual teachers were paid up to five thousand dollars a year extra, while school districts were receiving hundreds of millions of extra dollars simply for placing students in bilingual classes.

Opposition to the referendum was led primarily by major African American organizations, Democrats, the ethnic news media, several Asian American groups, bilingual education teachers, Latino activists, and organizations such as the Mexican American Legal Defense and Education Fund, the California PTA, the California School Boards Association, the California Teachers Association, and the California Federation of Teachers. Several of these organizations publicly denounced the Unz measure and viewed it to be the third in a chain of anti-immigrant proposals that emerged during the mid-1990's.

In March, 1998, three months before the state measure actually passed, the California state board of education voted unanimously to discard its thirty-year-old bilingual education policy. Although California's basic bilingual education law had expired in 1987, state law still required native-language instruction when necessary to provide immigrant children with an equal chance for academic success.

CONSEQUENCES   In June, 1998, Californians voted, by a margin of 61 percent to 39 percent, for Proposition 227, which placed major restrictions on bilingual education, limiting parent choice on the education programs for their children. Proposition 227 mandated a one-size-fits-all approach to instruction of English learners. Afterward, Californians Together, a round table of education and civil rights groups and organizations, analyzed selected schools still providing bilingual instruction to substantial numbers of students and determined that their students could equal or exceed the performances of students in English-immersion classes.

Additional discussions and findings on California's and the nation's bilingual education future will likely come from education organizations and think tanks such as the National Clearinghouse for Bilingual Education located at George Washington University, and the National Association for Bilingual Education, also headquartered in the nation's capital.

Keith Orlando Hilton

FURTHER READING

Anderson, Jim, et al., eds. *Portraits of Literacy Across Families, Communities, and Schools: Intersections and Tensions.* Mahwah, N.J.: L. Erlbaum Associates, 2005.

Brittain, Carmina. *Transnational Messages: Experiences of Chinese and Mexican Immigrants in American Schools.* New York: LFB Scholarly Publications, 2002.

Hones, Donald F., and Cher Shou Cha. *Educating New Americans: Immigrants Lives and Learning.* Mahwah, N.J.: L. Erlbaum Associates, 1999.

Jonas, Susanne, and Suzanne Dod Thomas, eds. *Immigration: A Civil Rights Issue for the Americas.* Wilmington, Del.: Scholarly Resources, 1999.

Kenner, Charmian. *Becoming Biliterate: Young Children Learning Different Writing Systems.* Sterling, Va.: Trentham Books, 2004.

López, David, and Andrés Jiménez, eds. *Latinos and Public Policy in California: An Agenda for Opportunity.* Berkeley, Calif.: Berkeley Public Policy Press, 2003.

Osborn, Terry A., ed. *Language and Cultural Diversity in U.S. Schools: Democratic Principles in Action.* Westport, Conn.: Praeger, 2005.

Wiley, Terrence G. *Literacy and Language Diversity in the United States.* 2d ed. Washington, D.C.: Center for Applied Linguistics, 2005.

SEE ALSO Anglo-conformity; Asian American Legal Defense Fund; Bilingual Education Act of 1968; Cultural pluralism; English-only and official English movements; Generational acculturation; *Lau v. Nichols*; Proposition 187.

PUSH AND PULL FACTORS

DEFINITION: Conditions and forces that encourage people to migrate

IMMIGRATION ISSUES: Demographics; Labor; Sociological theories

SIGNIFICANCE: Because migration is costly and stressful, people generally migrate only when there are strong incentives to do so. For example, conditions where they live may become unusually bad, giving people a "push" to leave. On the other hand, conditions may appear unusually good somewhere else, and they feel a "pull" toward that location. Often a combination of "push" and "pull" factors motivates migration, but the "push" factor usually is necessary for migration to be seriously considered.

Traditionally, religious and political persecution have been powerful push factors. The New England Puritans and the Pennsylvania Quakers fled religious persecution by coming to North America. Persecution of Jews in czarist Russia in the nineteenth century also motivated thousands to flee farther west. Adolf Hitler and Joseph Stalin escalated such persecutions during the 1930's and 1940's, culminating in the torture and deaths of millions of Jews during the Holocaust and Soviet pogroms. During the 1990's, refugees fled from tyrannical regimes in Africa, the Balkans, and the Middle East. U.S. immigration policy has given favored status to people who can show they have been victims of such persecution.

The push may also arise from unfavorable economic circumstances. Potato famines during the 1840's led to a mass exodus from Ireland and the Scandi-

Many immigrants to North America endured great hardships in their transoceanic journeys. (Library of Congress)

navian countries, bringing many migrants to North America. Within the United States, the mechanization of cotton cultivation during the 1940's and 1950's greatly reduced the need for field hands in the South, causing thousands of African American families to move to the industrial North. The latter was a gradual process whereby the improvement in agricultural productivity reduced the number of people needed to produce food and fiber, leading to migrations from farms to towns and cities.

The strongest pull factors have been economic. People often move to locations where they expect to find good jobs and comfortable incomes. North America has exerted this kind of pull on the rest of the world since the mid-nineteenth century. Initially the great attraction was the vast abundance of fertile and relatively cheap land. By 1900, however, American manufacturing industries were also eager to employ relatively cheap and docile immigrant labor. Railroads, land speculators, and factory owners all sent recruiters to Europe to encourage immigrants.

The United States has continued to exert this kind of pull, partly because its labor market is relatively free from apprenticeship regulations and monopolistic labor union restrictions on who can be hired. The clearest evidence is the flood of migrants coming northward from Mexico, who in addition have been "pushed" by poor economic conditions and a lack of jobs in their mother country. A strong pull during the 1990's arose as American firms actively recruited people with computer skills, mostly from Asia. Immigration preferences are given to people with scarce job skills.

Finally, an important pull results from the desire to be reunited with family members. During the early 1990's, about half of all legal immigration into the United States involved spouses, children, or parents of U.S. citizens.

Paul B. Trescott

FURTHER READING

Akhtar, Salman. *Immigration and Identity: Turmoil, Treatment, and Transformation.* Northvale, N.J.: Jason Aronson, 1999.

Conley, Ellen Alexander. *The Chosen Shore: Stories of Immigrants.* Berkeley: University of California Press, 2004.

Jacobs, Nancy R. *Immigration: Looking for a New Home.* Detroit: Gale Group, 2000.

Zølner, Mette. *Re-imagining the Nation: Debates on Immigrants, Identities and Memories.* New York: P.I.E.-P. Lang, 2000.

SEE ALSO   History of U.S. immigration; Israeli immigrants; Justice and immigration; Twice migrants.

RACIAL AND ETHNIC DEMOGRAPHIC TRENDS

DEFINITION: Changing composition of populations

IMMIGRATION ISSUES: African Americans; Chinese immigrants; Demographics

SIGNIFICANCE: The demographic makeup of North America has changed greatly over the years, affecting the relations between and relative power and dominance of the various racial and ethnic groups that live in these nations of immigrants.

Contemporary drawing of a government census taker in 1870. (Library of Congress)

The United States, Canada, and Australia are the three most important "receiving" countries for immigrants worldwide. The United States and Canada, as a result of their immigration policies, have become two of the world's most ethnically diverse geographical areas. Two centuries ago, the population of these two nations was predominantly of white European heritage, but in the twenty-first century, nonwhites and people whose heritage is not European are expected to become an increasingly large part of their populations. Because the United States and Canada both possess a strong democratic ethos and high standard of living, they are likely to attract many more people, especially oppressed ethnic minorities.

UNITED STATES Since 1790, as required by the U.S. Constitution, a census has been conducted every ten years. The initial purpose of the census was to enable the U.S. government to determine an equitable apportionment of tax dollars and the number of representatives each area would send to Congress. During its early history, the census was executed by temporary workers in nonpermanent facilities. It was not until March, 1902, that the government created the Bureau of the Census with a full-time staff and permanent facilities.

A perennial issue for the bureau has been the underreporting of certain subpopulations, including the very young, the poor, immigrants, and nonwhites. The resulting lower numbers have often resulted in those populations having less government representation and fewer benefits. In the latter part of the twentieth century, the bureau made great efforts to correct these shortcomings by making questionnaires available in Spanish and developing methods for assessing the undocumented immigrant population.

REGIONAL BACKGROUNDS OF
U.S. IMMIGRANTS, 1820-1985
(PERCENT)

	1820-1860	1861-1899	1900-1920	1921-1960	1961-1970	1971-1980	1981-1985
Northern and western Europe	95	68	41	38	18	7	5
North America	3	7	6	19	12	4	2
Southern and eastern Europe	—	22	44	20	15	11	6
Asia	—	2	4	4	13	35	48
Latin America	—	—	4	18	39	40	35
Other	2	1	1	1	3	3	4

Source: L. F. Bouvier and R. W. Gardner, *Immigration to the U.S.* Washington, D.C.: Population Reference Bureau, 1986.

During its first hundred years, the United States had an open immigration policy. It was not until 1882 that Congress passed the Chinese Exclusion Act, which outlawed Chinese immigration for ten years. This anti-Chinese legislation followed thirty years of heavy Chinese immigration during which more than two hundred thousand Chinese came to the United States to escape overpopulation, poverty, and warfare in China.

The history of legal immigration to the United States between 1820 and 1985 exhibits dramatic changes in the regions of the world from which immigrants came. Most striking is the decline of European immigrants, largely whites, and the significant increase in immigrants from Latin America and Asia, mostly Hispanics and nonwhites. Experts have projected population changes that suggest that by 2080, the U.S. population will consist of 49.8 percent white non-Hispanics, 23.4 percent Hispanics, 14.7 percent African Americans, and 12 percent Asians and other persons.

CANADA Canada, founded by the British and French, had exclusionary laws that discouraged nonwhite, ethnic immigrants, but these laws were relaxed after World War II. The nation's present multicultural population reflects the new immigration policies: Of the almost 29 million people in Canada, as estimated in the 1996 census, about 40 percent are of British ancestry, 27 percent are of French, 20 percent are of other European, and 1.5 percent are of Indian and Inuit ancestry. The remaining population, 11.5 percent, consists of people of African, Asian, and Hispanic origins. Although the number of people with non-European ancestry in Canada's population is expected to increase in the next century, it is anticipated that people of European descent will continue to dominate its culture and seats of political power.

ANCIENT PEOPLES OF NORTH AMERICA   Recent archaeological research suggests that human beings, probably *Homo erectus*, were living in North America as far back as 135,000 years ago. At the time of the first European contact, about 12 million to 15 million Indians and 20,000 Inuit (Eskimos) were living in North America. According to the 1990 U.S. Census, about 2 million American Indians and around 81,000 Inuit lived in the United States. In Canada, in 1996, census takers reported fewer than 500,000 aboriginals, that is, people of either Indian or Inuit background. Mistreatment by whites and deadly epidemics account for the great reduction in the Indian population. Better living conditions (partly due to distance from early settlers) explain the increase in the Inuit population.

AFRICAN AMERICANS   The United States, with about 30 million African Americans, has the third-largest black population in the world (Brazil and Nigeria have larger populations); however, Canada has fewer than 1 million black people, mostly of West Indian descent. Contrary to popular belief, the first black people in North America were not slaves. In 1619, twenty black men became indentured servants to wealthy Virginian white men. However, most other Africans who landed in the United States came as slaves. From the beginning of the American slave trade in the seventeenth century to the Emancipation Proclamation in 1863, almost 90 percent of all African Americans in what is now the United States were slaves. The first U.S. Census in 1790 reported 757,000 African Americans. By 1800, they numbered 1 million. In the 1860 census, there were about 4,442,000 African Americans. The 1990 U.S. Census reported almost 30 million African Americans, or about 12.1 per-

REGIONAL BACKGROUNDS OF U.S. IMMIGRANTS DURING THE TWENTY-FIRST CENTURY

Region	2001	2002	2003
Europe	177,833	177,652	102,843
Asia (including Middle East)	337,566	326,871	236,039
Canada	30,203	27,299	16,555
Mexico	204,844	217,318	114,984
Caribbean	96,958	94,240	67,660
Central America	73,063	66,520	53,435
South America	68,279	73,400	54,155
Africa	50,209	56,135	45,640
Oceania	7,253	6,536	5,102
Not specified	18,110	17,664	9,414
Totals	1,064,318	1,063,635	705,827

Source: U.S. Census Bureau.

FOREIGN-BORN POPULATION IN THE UNITED STATES IN 2004 BY REGION OF BIRTH

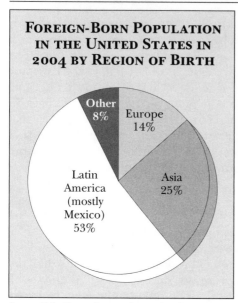

Other 8%

Europe 14%

Latin America (mostly Mexico) 53%

Asia 25%

Source: U.S. Census Bureau, Current Population Survey, 2004.

cent of the total U.S. population of almost 250 million. By 2080, it is projected that African Americans will reach around 14.7 percent of the U.S. population. Although African Americans made tremendous progress in the second half of the twentieth century, many serious problems still need to be addressed and solved.

HISPANICS Hispanics were among the earliest nonnative peoples to populate North America. In 1513, Juan Ponce de León discovered Florida, and in 1565, Spaniards settled St. Augustine in present-day Florida. They also colonized Mexico and parts of the American Southwest. As a result, Hispanics have largely been concentrated in the Southwestern states: Texas, New Mexico, Colorado, Arizona, and California. In the past one hundred years, large Hispanic populations have also developed in New York, New Jersey, Florida, and Illinois. In 1996, Hispanics numbered 28 million, or around 11 percent of the U.S. population. By 2080, this group is projected to constitute about 23.4 percent of the U.S. population and to be the largest ethnic group in the country.

ASIANS AND ARAB AMERICANS The first Asians to arrive in the United States were the Chinese. In 1849, there were only 54 Chinese in the whole nation. The 1990 U.S. Census estimated the Chinese American population at 1,645,000. The census counted 815,450 Japanese Americans, some 800,000 Korean Americans, about 815,000 East Indians, and 870,000 Arab Americans. More than two-thirds of the Arab Americans live in ten states and about one-third live in three metropolitan areas: Detroit, Michigan; New York City, and the Los Angeles area. Metropolitan Detroit has the largest Arab American community in the United States.

During the 1880's, Chinese and Japanese immigrants came to Canada to help construct the railroad and work on other industrial projects. They were soon followed by East Indians. From around 1900 until World War II, exclusionary laws kept most Asians from immigrating to Canada. However, after the war, Canada relaxed its immigration policies, and many Asians and other ethnic groups came to Canada.

THE FUTURE For the last five hundred years, the United States and Canada have been dominated by white European peoples and cultures. However, in the last fifty years, non-Europeans, nonwhites, Hispanics, and Asians have become the fastest-growing populations in these nations. Experts have predicted that by 2080 more than 50 percent of the U.S. population will be non-European and nonwhite and that the largest ethnic group will be Hispanic. In Canada, although the makeup of the population is changing, it is not likely that the U.S. population patterns will be duplicated. However, the proportion of British, French, and European people in the overall population is projected to fall. In the face of these trends, the power and influence of the dominant white group in the United States and Canada will probably diminish somewhat, and the two nations will continue to be pluralistic and democratic societies that attract refugees and immigrants.

R. M. Frumkin

FURTHER READING

Bean, Frank D., and Stephanie Bell-Rose, eds. *Immigration and Opportunity: Race, Ethnicity, and Employment in the United States.* New York: Russell Sage Foundation, 1999. Collection of essays on economic and labor issues relating to race and immigration in the United States, with particular attention to the competition for jobs between African Americans and immigrants.

Foner, Nancy, Rubén G. Rumbaut, and Steven J. Gold, eds. *Immigration Research for a New Century: Multidisciplinary Perspectives.* New York: Russell Sage Foundation, 2000. Collection of papers on immigration from a conference held at Columbia University in June, 1998. Among the many topics covered are race, government policy, sociological theories, naturalization, and undocumented workers.

Hughes, James W., and Joseph J. Seneca, eds. *America's Demographic Tapestry: Baseline for the New Millennium.* New Brunswick, N.J.: Rutgers University Press, 1999. Collection of articles on a variety of demographic topics.

Kertzer, David I., and Dominique Arel, eds. *Census and Identity: The Politics of Race, Ethnicity, and Language in National Census.* New York: Cambridge University Press, 2002. Articles on the Census Bureau's constantly evolving employment of racial and ethnic categories.

Nobles, Melissa. *Shades of Citizenship: Race and the Census in Modern Politics.* Stanford, Calif.: Stanford University Press, 2000. Study of the use made of census data in politics.

Perlmann, Joel, and Mary Waters, eds. *The New Race Question: How the Census Counts Multiracial Individuals.* New York: Russell Sage Foundation, 2002. Collection of critical essays on the U.S. Census's changing racial categories and the social and political effects of these changes.

Rodriguez, Clara E. *Changing Race: Latinos, the Census, and the History of Ethnicity.* New York: New York University Press, 2000. Examination of the use of racial and ethnic categories in the census with particular attention to Hispanics, who have been frequently reclassified.

Rumbaut, Rubén G., and Alejandro Portes, eds. *Ethnicities: Children of Immigrants in America.* Berkeley: University of California Press, 2001. Collection of papers on demographic and family issues relating to immigrants. Includes chapters on Mexicans, Cubans, Central Americans, Filipinos, Vietnamese, Haitians, and other West Indians.

Skerry, Peter. *Counting on the Census? Race, Group Identity, and the Evasion of Politics*. Washington, D.C.: Brookings Institution Press, 2000. Analytical study of the problems of accurately counting members of racial and ethnic groups in the U.S. Census.

Statistical Abstract of the United States, 2004-2005. 124th ed. Washington, D.C.: U.S. Census Bureau, 2005. Starting place for any research on demographics. Updated annually, this reference source is available on compact disc, and much of its information is freely available online on the U.S. Census Bureau's Web site.

SEE ALSO Censuses, U.S.; Demographics of immigration; Illegal aliens; Immigration "crisis."

REFUGEE FATIGUE

DEFINITION: Reluctance of host countries to extend or expand assistance, asylum, or resettlement to refugees

IMMIGRATION ISSUES: Refugees; Sociological theories

SIGNIFICANCE: Also known as "compassion" fatigue, refugee fatigue develops when the citizens of nations receiving large numbers of refugees begin feeling overburdened by the needs of the newcomers and fear being overrun by outsiders.

Refugees are typically victims of political persecution who are fleeing from their homelands in attempts to find asylum in other nations. Refugee, or compassion, fatigue is most likely to occur when the refugee population begins to become a significant burden on the host community's economic and social infrastructure, or at least when the perception develops that such burdens are growing. Refugees sometimes flee into areas where they can find support among ethnic kinspeople, as often happens in Africa. In Asia, however, the flight of Sino-Vietnamese refugees into the Philippines, Indonesia, Thailand, and Malaysia during the 1970's and 1980's excited substantial xenophobic responses that greatly accelerated perceptions of compassion fatigue in the region.

Such concerns may be allayed somewhat if other countries agree to provide opportunities to resettle in a third country and to finance the costs of temporary haven in the country of first asylum. However, donor country pop-

President Gerald Ford during his April, 1975, visit to California, where he greeted arriving refugees from Vietnam. (NARA/Gerald R. Ford Library)

ulations and governments often grow tired of accepting resettled refugees and financing large overseas programs. When both host nations and countries of resettlement experience refugee or compassion fatigue simultaneously, pressures grow to eliminate humanitarian aid programs and to repatriate refugees or asylum seekers to their original homelands. In some cases, racial or ethnic biases heighten popular resentment of such humanitarian programs; more often, economics is the central cause of compassion fatigue.

During the 1980's, owing to the civil wars in Central America, large numbers of asylum seekers joined the stream of illegal immigrants or undocumented immigrants from Mexico seeking work and safe haven in the United States. For many Americans, this influx led to fears of uncontrolled immigration and a hardening of attitudes toward those in distress.

Robert F. Gorman

FURTHER READING

Balgopal, Pallassana R., ed. *Social Work Practice with Immigrants and Refugees.* New York: Columbia University Press, 2000.

Bischoff, Henry. *Immigration Issues.* Westport, Conn.: Greenwood Press, 2002.

Cohen, Steve. *Deportation Is Freedom! The Orwellian World of Immigration Controls.* Philadelphia: Jessica Kingsley, 2005.

Legomsky, Stephen H. *Immigration and Refugee Law and Policy.* 3d ed. New York: Foundation Press, 2002.

Potocky-Tripodi, Miriam. *Best Practices for Social Work with Refugees and Immigrants.* New York: Columbia University Press, 2002.

Zolberg, Aristide R., and Peter M. Benda, eds. *Global Migrants, Global Refugees: Problems and Solutions.* New York: Berghahn Books, 2001.

SEE ALSO   Cuban refugee policy; Florida illegal-immigrant suit; Helsinki Watch report on U.S. refugee policy; Justice and immigration; Proposition 187; Proposition 227; Refugee Relief Act of 1953; Refugees and racial/ethnic relations.

REFUGEE RELIEF ACT OF 1953

THE LAW: Federal legislation that made it easier for political refugees to enter the United States
DATE: August 7, 1953

IMMIGRATION ISSUES: Laws and treaties; Refugees

SIGNIFICANCE: Enacted in the aftermath of World War II, which displaced millions of people from their homes in Europe, the Refugee Relief Act created a legal means for admitting displaced persons outside the national quota system, on an emergency basis.

The events of World War II and its immediate aftermath left millions of people displaced from their homelands. Included among those who had been made homeless by the destruction were Jewish survivors of the Nazi-perpetrated Holocaust and increasing numbers of political refugees who fled their homelands as communist governments took control in eastern Europe. In the United States, from the close of World War II well into the 1950's, a debate raged about how restrictive or generous U.S. immigration and asylum law should be in view of the nation's own interests and the larger humanitarian imperatives.

Since 1924, U.S. immigration law had been based on a quota system, which was viewed as highly discriminatory against various countries and peoples. Under the pressures of war, however, Congress had allowed temporary immigration to help labor-starved industry. With China as one of the main U.S. allies in the Pacific theater of World War II, Congress revoked the ban on Chinese immigration in 1943; in 1945, it approved the War Brides Act, which permitted the entry of the alien spouses and children of members of the U.S. armed forces. President Harry S. Truman approved the admission of about forty thousand wartime refugees after the war and urged Congress to adopt less restrictive legislation that would permit the resettlement of larger numbers of displaced persons (DPs).

Congress felt pressure to act, not only from the president but also from private charitable agencies that sought to liberalize admission policies in favor of DPs in Europe and elsewhere. Two Jewish aid agencies, the American Council on Judaism (ACJ) and the American Jewish Committee (AJC), joined forces with numerous Christian and other non-Jewish agencies to form the Citizens' Committee on Displaced Persons. This new group was headed by Earl G. Harrison and included on its board of directors many prominent U.S. citizens, among them Eleanor Roosevelt. The committee heavily lobbied the predominantly restrictionist Congress and supported legislation calling for the admission of 400,000 DPs.

A long and rancorous debate followed, which produced a substantially watered-down bill known as the Displaced Persons Act of 1948. This act permitted 202,000 admission slots for DPs in Europe who feared to return to communist-held countries. While retaining the immigration quotas of previous years, the act allowed countries to borrow against future years' quotas to accommodate DPs with immediate needs. It only permitted entry of people displaced prior to April 21, 1947, in the Allied occupied zones of Germany and Austria who were registered with the International Refugee Organization (IRO) and who were not communists. It required that the DPs be guaranteed employment by U.S. charitable agencies or other sponsors, and it gave preference to DPs with professional skills. While criticizing its discriminatory features, Truman signed the legislation, which also established the Displaced Persons Commission.

Efforts by the Citizens' Committee on Displaced Persons and others to liberalize the Displaced Persons Act continued, as events in Europe and the deepening of the Cold War led to a climate more supportive of DP resettlement. Although delayed by Senator Patrick A. McCarran of Nevada, amendments eventually passed by Congress expanded the numbers of admission slots to 341,000 and relaxed the cutoff dates for eligibility and entry into the United States. When the Displaced Persons Act expired on December 31, 1951, President Truman relied on the regular immigration quotas and on the U.S. Escapee Program, established under the authority of the 1951 Mutual Security Act, to provide asylum in the United States to political refugees from communism. Truman also established a Commission on Immigration and Naturalization, which held hearings that demonstrated considerable support for liberalized admission of refugees from communism.

Even as the 1952 Immigration and Nationality Act, sponsored by Senator McCarran (and therefore often called the McCarran-Walter Act), reemphasized the restrictive quota system for regular immigration, consensus was building to place emergency refugee admissions outside the regular immigration quota system. The Refugee Relief Act of 1953, also sometimes referred to as the Church bill because of the strong support it received from religious refugee assistance agencies, was the result of this ongoing debate about how to restructure U.S. immigration and refugee policy.

The Refugee Relief Act of 1953 made 209,000 special immigrant visas available to refugees and other special categories of persons. These were not tied in any way to the regular immigration quotas for countries under the 1952

Immigration and Nationality Act. This was seen as a major reform by private humanitarian organizations. In the years that followed, the 1953 act enabled the emergency entry of refugees from communism. President Dwight D. Eisenhower, for example, invoked the act just before it was to expire, to provide emergency resettlement opportunities for Hungarian refugees in the waning months of 1956. Eisenhower also took advantage of his parole power, as acknowledged during the 1952 Immigration and Nationality Act and earlier immigration legislation, to provide asylum opportunities for Hungarian refugees. The United States eventually accepted more than thirty-two thousand Hungarians. Thus, through the provisions of the Refugee Relief Act of 1953, subsequent ad hoc emergency refugee legislation, and the Immigration and Nationality Act of 1952, the U.S. government coped with refugee admissions until 1980, when Congress passed the more comprehensive and progressive Migration and Refugee Act.

The Refugee Relief Act of 1953 was one brief but essential mechanism by which the U.S. government sought to fulfill humanitarian and political objectives relating to refugees. It represented an improvement on the Displaced Persons Act, although that much-maligned piece of legislation eventually led to the resettlement of about four hundred thousand persons to the United States, by far the single largest number of European refugees resettled by any country in the immediate postwar era. The Refugee Relief Act of 1953 also represented a bridge to later legislation, such as the Migration and Refugee Act of 1980, by treating emergency refugee admission outside the context of regular immigration quotas. It also represented the mistaken belief during the early 1950's that refugee situations were temporary and amendable to ad hoc solutions.

During the early 1950's, the United States and other Western nations established the groundwork for more stable legal and institutional mechanisms for dealing with refugee situations. The United States supported the creation of the United Nations Relief and Rehabilitation Administration in 1943 and the IRO in 1947 to cope with the needs of displaced persons and refugees in postwar Europe. Both were viewed as temporary agencies, as were the United Nations High Commission for Refugees (UNHCR) and the Intergovernmental Committee for European Migration (ICEM), which began operations in 1952. In time, however, these bodies developed into permanent features of the international humanitarian landscape with the support of later U.S. administrations.

The building of both legal and institutional mechanisms for coping with humanitarian problems was often highly controversial, heavily steeped in political motivation, and shortsighted. As measured in the huge numbers of persons assisted and protected over the years, however, the efforts are viewed by many as precious if difficult ones, of which the Displaced Persons Act of 1948 and the Refugee Relief Act of 1953 were imperfect but necessary components.

Robert F. Gorman

FURTHER READING

Carlin, James L. *The Refugee Connection: A Lifetime of Running a Lifeline.* New York: Macmillan, 1989. Fascinating autobiographical account of the development of post-World War II displaced persons and refugee policy.

Legomsky, Stephen H. *Immigration and Refugee Law and Policy.* 3d ed. New York: Foundation Press, 2002. Legal textbook on immigration and refugee law.

LeMay, Michael C., and Elliott Robert Barkan, eds. *U.S. Immigration and Naturalization Laws and Issues: A Documentary History.* Westport, Conn.: Greenwood Press, 1999. History of U.S. immigration laws supported by extensive extracts from documents.

Loescher, Gil, and John A. Scanlan. *Calculated Kindness: Refugees and America's Half-Open Door, 1945 to Present.* New York: Free Press, 1986. The first two chapters of this comprehensive analysis of U.S. immigration and refugee policy address the Displaced Persons and Refugee Relief Acts.

Nichols, J. Bruce. *The Uneasy Alliance: Religion, Refugee Work, and U.S. Foreign Policy.* Oxford, England: Oxford University Press, 1989. A detailed account of the relations between private voluntary organizations and the U.S. government in the fields of humanitarian aid, immigration, and refugee policy. See especially chapter 5.

Sanders, Ronald. *Shores of Refuge: A Hundred Years of Jewish Immigration.* New York: Schocken Books, 1988. This detailed historical account briefly examines the impact of U.S. refugee acts on Jewish immigration.

Shanks, Cheryl. *Immigration and the Politics of American Sovereignty, 1890-1990.* Ann Arbor: University of Michigan Press, 2001. Scholarly study of changing federal immigration laws from the late nineteenth through the late twentieth centuries, with particular attention to changing quota systems and exclusionary policies.

Zucker, Norman L., and Naomi Flink Zucker. *The Guarded Gate: The Reality of American Refugee Policy.* New York: Harcourt Brace Jovanovich, 1987. Focuses mainly on refugee and asylum policy after the passage of the 1980 Migration and Refugee Act, but situates this discussion against developments after World War II.

SEE ALSO Immigration Act of 1943; Immigration and Nationality Act of 1952; Refugee fatigue; Refugees and racial/ethnic relations.

REFUGEES AND RACIAL/ETHNIC RELATIONS

IMMIGRATION ISSUES: Nativism and racism; Refugees

SIGNIFICANCE: The controversies attending large refugee flows into the United States have been both a product of and a determinant of U.S. refugee policy. Fears of increased cultural and racial heterogeneity and the perceived international political interests of the United States have affected public policy and practice in this area.

Refugees are viewed by some factions within the white majority population in the United States as being relatively nonaffluent and unwilling to assimilate to American culture. Furthermore, these factions and some well-established minority groups have expressed resentment over the success of the "ethnic enclave" strategy that has created significant local political power and prosperity for more recently arrived groups. In addition, some refugee groups have expressed anger at the perceived discriminatory application of refugee legislation. The result has been an exacerbation of tensions across racial and ethnic lines.

HISTORY OF U.S. REFUGEE POLICY   In 1951, the United Nations held the Convention Relating to the Status of Refugees, which established the still-accepted definition of a refugee and prohibited "refoulement," that is, forcible repatriation. The United States was instrumental in establishing that to be a refugee, a person must be fleeing personal governmental persecution, not economic deprivation. This definition served U.S. Cold War interests by embarrassing new communist regimes that were generating large refugee populations. However, the United States did not sign the convention, preferring to handle asylum issues through domestic legislation.

Throughout the 1950's, the United States avoided making commitments to refugees that were of little political value to the nation. The ideological focus of U.S. refugee policy that developed throughout the 1950's and 1960's is illustrated by the fact that from the mid-1950's through 1979, only 0.3 percent of refugee admissions were to people from noncommunist countries.

"POLITICAL" VS. "ECONOMIC" REFUGEES   U.S. legislation still extends asylum to "political refugees," but those fleeing bad economies are termed "economic migrants" and are deported if they immigrate illegally. Awareness is growing that governmental oppression, economic malaise, and widespread social problems often go hand in hand, making it increasingly difficult to disentangle the reasons that people leave their homelands. Many displaced people are fleeing reigns of terror perpetuated by their governments, ethnic conflicts, civil wars, and systematic and severe economic deprivation, but these people are not technically eligible for asylum. Although it seems clear that unprecedented numbers of forcibly displaced people are inadequately protected, the official recognition of a broader definition of "refugee" is unlikely because of the undeniable economic and perceived social and cultural costs of growing populations of people who have received asylum.

The U.S. government has become increasingly concerned about the dramatically increasing numbers of asylum seekers, especially those who enter the country illegally, outside of established refugee-processing channels. The government's position is understandable, as is that of the illegal entrants. For example, from 1980 to the early 1990's, hundreds of thousands of Salvadorans fled in the face of death squads that had murdered their relatives and associates, and a similar situation existed in Guatemala. Yet, during this period,

Homeless Italian earthquake refugees on their way to America during the early twentieth century. (Library of Congress)

only fifty-four Salvadorans and no Guatemalans were accepted for resettlement in the United States, in spite of the fact that Central American refugee camps could assist only a small fraction of these people. Many of those remaining entered the United States illegally.

CHARGES OF POLITICAL AND RACIAL BIAS   U.S. refugee policy was openly directed by Cold War considerations until 1980. Although there was some criticism of the U.S. refusal to extend asylum to those fleeing the regimes of U.S.-supported authoritarian leaders—the shah of Iran (Muhammad Reza Pahlavi), François "Papa Doc" Duvalier in Haiti, General Augusto Pinochet in Chile, and President Ferdinand Marcos of the Philippines—the flow of refugees was controlled, and a possible domestic political backlash avoided.

The 1980 Refugee Act removed the requirement that refugees be fleeing communist regimes. That year, 800,000 immigrants and refugees entered the United States legally, a number that surpassed the combined total for the rest of the world. Growing sentiment for more restrictive policies emerged. The administration of President Ronald Reagan responded by reducing refugee admissions by two-thirds and heavily favoring those from communist countries, in spite of the new law. The Mariel boatlift (1980) brought 115,000 Cubans to the United States in five months, and the policy of forcibly returning Haitians, Salvadorans, and Guatemalans to brutal governments while admitting less physically threatened refugees from communist countries was soundly criticized in some quarters.

The differential treatment accorded asylum seekers from Haiti and Cuba has generated charges of racial bias. As tens of thousands of desperate Haitians were deported or detained at sea and returned before reaching the United States, the U.S. government welcomed hundreds of thousands of Cubans fleeing Fidel Castro's regime. The Congressional Black Caucus set up a task force to study the issue and, after failing to change the U.S. policy, joined prominent church leaders and the Voluntary Agencies Responsible for Refugees in stating publicly that racism was behind the differential treatment of Haitians and other asylum seekers because of a reluctance on the part of the United States to admit large numbers of black refugees. Even as this controversy raged, the government announced that all Vietnamese and Laotians who reached safe haven would be considered refugees, while those fleeing Haiti were subjected to case-by-case screening and deportation.

President George Bush continued Reagan's policies. After the fall of the government of Jean-Bertrand Aristide in Haiti created an upsurge of "boat people," the Bush administration successfully petitioned the Supreme Court to lift a ban on forced repatriation and intercepted and returned tens of thousands of Haitians. The administration of President Bill Clinton continued this practice and then forced the reinstatement of the Aristide government in an effort to stem the flow of refugees.

Jack Carter

FURTHER READING

Briggs, Vernon M., Jr., and Stephen Moore. *Still an Open Door? U.S. Immigration Policy and the American Economy.* Washington, D.C.: American University Press, 1994. Discusses the effect of growing restrictionist sentiment on refugee policy in the United States.

Edmonston, Barry, and Jeffrey S. Passel, eds. *Immigration and Ethnicity: The Integration of America's Newest Arrivals.* Washington, D.C.: Urban Institute Press, 1994. Examination of assimilation issues and controversies.

Foner, Nancy, Rubén G. Rumbaut, and Steven J. Gold, eds. *Immigration Research for a New Century: Multidisciplinary Perspectives.* New York: Russell Sage Foundation, 2000. Collection of papers on immigration from a conference held at Columbia University in June, 1998. Among the many topics covered are race, government policy, sociological theories, naturalization, and undocumented workers.

Gabaccia, Donna R. *Immigration and American Diversity: A Social and Cultural History.* Malden, Mass.: Blackwell, 2002. Survey of American immigration history, from the mid-eighteenth century to the early twenty-first century, with an emphasis on cultural and social trends, with attention to ethnic conflicts, nativism, and racialist theories.

Legomsky, Stephen H. *Immigration and Refugee Law and Policy.* 3d ed. New York: Foundation Press, 2002. Legal textbook on immigration and refugee law.

Loescher, Gil, ed. *Refugees and the Asylum Dilemma in the West.* University Park: Pennsylvania State University Press, 1992. Set of essays addressing refugee-related problems and policies in Western nations, including the United States and Canada.

Loescher, Gil, and Robert Scanlan. *Calculated Kindness: Refugees and America's Half-Open Door, 1945 to Present.* New York: Free Press, 1986. Study of U.S. refugee policy from World War II through the mid-1980's.

Reitz, Jeffrey G., eds. *Host Societies and the Reception of Immigrants.* La Jolla, Calif.: Center for Comparative Immigration Studies, University of California, San Diego, 2003. Collection of articles on interactions between immigrants and other members of their new societies in countries around the world, including the United States and Canada. Emphasis is on large urban societies. Includes chapters on African Americans and immigrants in New York City.

Stepick, Alex, et al. *This Land Is Our Land: Immigrants and Power in Miami.* Berkeley: University of California Press, 2003. Study of competition and conflict among Miami's largest ethnic groups—Cubans, Haitians, and African Americans.

SEE ALSO Cuban immigrants; Cuban immigrants and African Americans; Cuban refugee policy; Melting pot; Refugee fatigue; Refugee Relief Act of 1953; Vietnamese immigrants.

RUSSIAN IMMIGRANTS

IDENTIFICATION: Immigrants to North America from Russia

IMMIGRATION ISSUES: Demographics; European immigrants; Jewish immigrants

SIGNIFICANCE: Russian Americans have blended well with mainstream American society, many having peasant or industrial backgrounds similar to those of other European immigrants, while others were refugees from the Russian upper class or Jews who did not consider themselves Russian. Some immigrants were, however, suspected of promoting communism or being members of the Russian mafia.

Throughout the late nineteenth and twentieth centuries, large numbers of Russians immigrated in successive waves to the United States and Canada. Many were members of the Russian Orthodox Church, and Orthodoxy remains one of the visible hallmarks of Russian immigrant communities. Its rituals and teachings are followed in Russian communities in Alaska, Los Angeles, and Brooklyn's Brighton Beach. Nevertheless, Russian Jews were, and are, numerically the largest group of immigrants, particularly to the United States. However, because Russia was not very accepting of Jews, many of these immigrants were more likely to identify themselves as Jews rather than Russians upon entering the United States and Canada. In addition, because

Siberians preparing to emigrate to the United States in 1910. (Library of Congress)

SOVIET AND RUSSIAN IMMIGRATION TO THE UNITED STATES, 1821-2003

Russian Revolution of 1905-1906

Russian Revolution of 1917

1918-1921 Civil war

1921 Creation of Soviet Union

1939-1945 World War II

1946-1989 Cold War

1991 Collapse of Soviet Union

Source: U.S. Census Bureau.

many came from western Russia, the so-called Pale of Settlement to which Russian Jews were restricted, which was once part of Poland-Lithuania, they might equally well have considered themselves Polish or Lithuanian Jews.

The first Russians to reach the shores of North America came as traders, adventurers, and explorers. These hardy fur traders and missionaries settled the Alaskan wilderness when that territory belonged to Russia. The first Russians settled on Kodiak Island, Alaska, in 1784, and converted many local people to the Russian Orthodox religion, which many still practiced during the early twenty-first century. However, with the sale of Alaska to the United States in 1867, many of these first settlers returned to Russia.

THE FIRST WAVE A huge influx of immigrants from czarist Russia reached North America between 1881 and 1914. Almost half of these were Jews fleeing pogroms and other forms of persecution following the 1881 assassination of Czar Alexander III, for which the Jews were blamed. During this period, Jews were allowed to live only in the Pale of Settlement in western Russia, lands taken from Poland during the partitions of Poland a hundred years earlier.

623

A Russian Jew in New York City during the early twentieth century. (Library of Congress)

Most of these Jews lived in *shtetls*, and many were impoverished. Only about sixty-five thousand ethnic Russians left Russia during this period, most for economic reasons. Others, from the Carpathian area of the Ukraine and the eastern reaches of the Austro-Hungarian Empire, did self-identify as Russians and were adherents of the Orthodox or the Uniate religion.

THE SECOND WAVE   The second wave of immigration occurred as a result of events in Russia that made it impossible for many persons, particularly members of the upper classes, to remain there. These events were the Bolshevik Revolution of October 1917 and the ensuing Russian Civil War. More than two million people fled the new communist nation, many to the Balkans, western Europe, and Manchuria. Of these, approximately thirty thousand came to the United States. Among them were former White Russian soldiers (as opposed to the Red Communist armies), aristocrats, clergy, artists, and intellectuals. United in their hatred of the Bolsheviks, many intended to stay only until the Bolsheviks were ousted. Ironically, anticommunist movements in the United States often singled out these extremely anticommunist Russians for oppressive treatment, suspecting that a communist lurked behind every fur hat.

THE THIRD WAVE   A small wave of Russian immigration resulted from the massive dislocations of World War II. Germany had at various times occupied much of the Soviet Union, captured many Russians, and made them work in forced labor camps. After the war, many of these people were forcibly returned to the Soviet Union, where they were often accused of collaboration with the enemy. Others, fearing similar oppression, chose to remain in displaced-person camps in Germany and Austria until they were allowed to immigrate to North America. This brought approximately twenty thousand Russians to the shores of North America.

THE FOURTH WAVE   In contrast to earlier emigrations from Russia and the Soviet Union, these immigrants left Russia near the end of the twentieth century without hindrance on the part of the government in power. The impetus for this emigration was in large part agreements between the United States and the Soviet Union allowing Jews to leave Russia, nominally for Israel, but often in fact for the United States. Following their lead, a number of other Russians emigrated as well. This migration caused some social disturbances in the United States because a number of Russian mafia members who were among the newcomers caused major problems for newly arrived immigrants and the population at large.

Gloria Fulton

FURTHER READING

Conley, Ellen Alexander. *The Chosen Shore: Stories of Immigrants.* Berkeley: University of California Press, 2004. Collection of firsthand accounts of modern immigrants from many nations, including Russia.

Hardwick, Susan Wiley. *Russian Refuge: Religion, Migration, and Settlement on the North American Pacific Rim.* Chicago: University of Chicago Press, 1993. Exploration of religious reasons behind Russian immigration to the United States.

Magocsi, Paul R. *The Russian Americans.* New York: Chelsea House, 1987. Traces the immigration and settlement of Russians in North America, focusing on historical and economic issues, the people who might be considered Russian Americans, and the extent to which these peoples have become assimilated in North American society.

Meltzer, Milton. *Bound for America: The Story of the European Immigrants.* New York: Benchmark Books, 2001. Broad history of European immigration to the United States written for young readers.

Shasha, Dennis Elliott, and Marina Shron. *Red Blues: Voices from the Last Wave of Russian Immigrants.* New York: Holmes & Meier, 2002. Study of post-Cold War Russian immigration to the United States.

Wertsman, Vladimir, ed. *The Russians in America: A Chronology and Fact Book.* Dobbs Ferry, N.Y.: Oceana Publications, 1977. Now dated but still useful reference book on Russians in the United States.

SEE ALSO   Eastern European Jewish immigrants; European immigrant literature; Garment industry; Mail-order brides; Polish immigrants; Soviet Jewish immigrants.

625

SACCO AND VANZETTI TRIAL

THE EVENT: Robbery and murder trial of two Italian immigrants
DATE: 1920-1921
PLACE: Dedham, Massachusetts

IMMIGRATION ISSUES: European immigrants; Nativism and racism

SIGNIFICANCE: One of the most famous U.S. trials of the twentieth century, the robbery and murder case against Nicola Sacco and Bartolomeo Vanzetti, generated worldwide protests, strikes, and riots as it focused the international spotlight on the small town of Dedham, Massachusetts. The trial was a celebrated example of anti-immigrant feeling during a period of heightened nativism.

The two events, which may or may not have been connected, that culminated in the arrest of Sacco and Vanzetti began on December 24, 1919, payday for the L. Q. White Shoe Company of Bridgewater, Massachusetts. A truck carrying approximately thirty-three thousand dollars in company payroll was unsuccessfully attacked. Pinkerton Agency detectives investigated the incident, and during eyewitness interviews they determined that one of the suspects appeared to be foreign-born, with a dark complexion and mustache, and that he fled in a large vehicle, probably a Hudson. The identified license plate had been stolen a few days earlier in Needham, Massachusetts, as had a Buick touring car. Thus, despite witnesses to the contrary, the detectives concluded that the Buick likely had been used in the robbery. No suspects were arrested, although tips emerged connecting the getaway car to a group of Italian anarchists.

On April 15, 1920, in nearby South Braintree, the payroll for the Slater and Morrill Shoe Factory was being escorted, on foot, from the office to the factory by two security guards, Frederick Parmenter and Alessandro Berardelli. En route, the guards were attacked, robbed, and murdered by two men who escaped in a waiting vehicle. At the inquest, twenty-three eyewitnesses testified that the assailants appeared to be Italian, but few claimed they could positively identify the men.

Recalling the tip about Italian anarchists storing a car in Bridgewater, police chief Michael E. Stewart traced the lead to Feruccio Coacci, an Italian scheduled for deportation. Coacci revealed that the car belonged to his housemate, Mike Boda, a known anarchist, and that it was currently being repaired in a garage in West Bridgewater. A police guard was planted outside the garage to wait for Boda.

Meanwhile, as a result of the prevalent U.S. attitude toward radicals and in the wake of a national roundup and arrest of aliens, Italians Nicola Sacco and Bartolomeo Vanzetti had decided it would be wise to destroy their anarchist literature. The abundance of material required transportation, and they arranged to borrow Boda's vehicle. Although the trap was laid for Boda, Sacco and Vanzetti were arrested as they attempted to claim the car. Neither man had a police record, but both were armed.

Because the men were not informed of the reason for their arrest, they assumed they were being held as anarchists. Although they were read their rights, the language barrier may have obstructed their complete understanding. They were fingerprinted, their weapons confiscated but not tagged, and they were questioned for seven days without being charged. There was no lineup; the two were paraded in front of witnesses who were asked if they were the men involved in the holdup. On May 12, 1920, Vanzetti was charged with attempted murder and robbery at Bridgewater.

THE TRIALS Vanzetti's trial began on June 22, 1920, in Plymouth, Massachusetts, with Judge Webster Thayer presiding. The initial interviews by the Pinkerton detectives were not admitted, and all witnesses for the defense were of Italian origin. After only five hours of deliberation, the jury found Vanzetti guilty of assault with intent to rob and murder. Six weeks later, he was sentenced to twelve to fifteen years for intent to rob. The attempted murder charge was dropped after it was discovered that one of the jurors had brought his own shell casings for comparison.

In September, 1920, Sacco and Vanzetti were charged with the murder of Alessandro Berardelli and Frederick Parmenter during the South Braintree robbery. Each pleaded not guilty. A committee for their defense raised enough money to hire the radical California attorney Fred Moore, who cited the case as an establishment attempt to victimize the working man.

In 1976, the Community Church of Boston began honoring the memory of Sacco and Vanzetti by presenting the annual Sacco-Vanzetti Memorial Award for Contributions to Social Justice to outstanding social activists. (The Community Church of Boston)

The new trial began on May 31, 1921, in Dedham, Massachusetts, once again under Judge Thayer, who, as the presiding judge in Vanzetti's first trial, should have been disqualified. On June 4, the all-male jury was sworn in, and on June 6, Sacco and Vanzetti were marched, handcuffed, into the courtroom. Throughout the trial, the prosecution presented a bounty of circumstantial evidence: less-than-convincing "eyewitness" testimony; a cap from the scene, alleged to be Vanzetti's, that was too small; expert testimony qualified with "I am inclined to believe"; no positive identification on the getaway car; ballistic evidence that was technical and confusing; and the accusation of "consciousness of guilt," based on the false statements of the two when they thought they were being held for anarchy. Judge Thayer charged the jury to be "true soldiers" who would display the "highest and noblest type of true American citizenship," and he referred to the defendants as "slackers." On July 14, once again after a five-hour deliberation, the jury returned a verdict of guilty of first-degree murder. The standard penalty in Massachusetts at the time was death by electrocution.

AFTERMATH AND EXECUTIONS   Sacco and Vanzetti remained incarcerated for six years while motions were filed in their behalf. The presiding judge heard all appeals, and each was weighed and denied by Judge Thayer. One motion stated Judge Thayer himself had demonstrated out-of-court prejudice against the two. Despite the growing doubt about the guilt of the men, Thayer remained adamant, and his animosity grew toward Moore. On November 8, the defense committee forced Moore to resign and hired William G. Thompson.

While the legal avenues encountered roadblocks, Sacco was slipped a note from another prisoner, Celestino Madeiros, who confessed to the crime. From the note, Thompson traced a link to the Morelli brothers, an Italian gang in Providence. This group had attacked the shoe factory in the past, and one member of the gang bore a resemblance to Sacco. Based on the new evidence, Thompson filed a motion for retrial, which was denied, and in April of 1927, Sacco and Vanzetti were sentenced to die the week of July 10. Due to the public outcry, the date was moved to August 10, and Vanzetti wrote a plea for clemency to Massachusetts governor Alvan T. Fuller. In the letter, he asked not for pardon but for a complete review of the case.

On June 1, the governor appointed a committee to review the case, but after examining their findings, he denied a new trial. On August 10, Sacco and Vanzetti were readied for execution. Thirty-six minutes before the time set for the execution, the governor issued a postponement, awaiting results of a Supreme Court appeal. On August 19, the U.S. Supreme Court refused to hear the case, citing no authority.

In Europe and South America, mobs rioted and marched on U.S. embassies. In France, Italy, and the United States, workers struck in protest. Five hundred extra policemen, armed with machine guns and tear gas, barricaded the crowd of thousands outside the jail. Just after midnight, on August 23, 1927, Sacco and Vanzetti were executed.

Public interest in the case lived on, however, as many people continued to work to clear Sacco and Vanzetti's names. On August 23, 1977, Massachusetts governor Michael Dukakis proclaimed the date Sacco and Vanzetti Day, thus officially removing any stigma from their names.

Joyce Duncan

FURTHER READING

Dickinson, Alice. *The Sacco-Vanzetti Case.* New York: Franklin Watts, 1972. An abbreviated overview of the case, including chronology and photos.

Ehrmann, Herbert. *The Case That Will Not Die: Commonwealth vs. Sacco and Vanzetti.* Boston: Little, Brown, 1969. Liberally illustrated account by the case's assistant defense attorney from 1926 to 1927.

Frankfurter, Marion Denman, and Gardner Jackson, eds. *The Letters of Sacco and Vanzetti.* New York: Octagon Books, 1971. Correspondence by both men written from prison, including Vanzetti's letter to the governor.

Joughin, G. L., and E. M. Morgan. *The Legacy of Sacco and Vanzetti.* New York: Harcourt, Brace, 1948. Early but masterful analysis of the case.

Russell, Francis. *Tragedy in Dedham.* New York: McGraw-Hill, 1962. Illustrated chronological recitation of events, including a discussion of public temperament.

Weeks, Robert, ed. *Commonwealth vs. Sacco and Vanzetti.* Englewood Cliffs, N.J.: Prentice-Hall, 1958. Provides insights from court records and other primary-source documents on the trial of the reputed anarchists.

SEE ALSO   Euro-Americans; Italian immigrants; Nativism.

SANTERÍA

IDENTIFICATION: Afro-Cuban religion

IMMIGRATION ISSUES: African Americans; Cuban immigrants; Latino immigrants; Religion; Slavery; West Indian immigrants

SIGNIFICANCE: Santería is a cultural retention with origins in the African diaspora to the New World. Its existence is an example of the survival of elements of African cultures, despite the destructive forces of involuntary migration and slavery.

The basic tenets, rituals, practices, and associated institutional mechanisms of Santería derive from the Yoruba priests and priestesses of the *orishas,* who were slaves at the close of the eighteenth and during the early decades of the nineteenth centuries. Santería, "the way of the saints," is an admixture of Yoruba and other African practices with Roman Catholic traditions developed as a functional adaptation by many Cubans.

The Cuban immigrants who entered the United States after Fidel Castro's successful revolution in their homeland brought these religious practices with them. These rituals enjoy special significance as part of the new immigrants' coping repertoire, enabling them to adjust better to acculturation in the United States. The practices of Santería are part of the larger spiritualistic belief system of other black West Indians (Jamaicans, Trinidadians, Haitians, Puerto Ricans, and Guyanese) who immigrated to the United States. As these immigrants begin to live in urban spatial proximity and strive to maintain and regain their African cultural heritage, they and native African Americans have adopted Santería. In cities such as Miami and New York, there are many spiritual adherents.

Aubrey W. Bonnett

FURTHER READING
Boswell, Thomas D., and James R. Curtis. *The Cuban American Experience.* Totowa, N.J.: Rowman & Allanheld, 1983.
Vickerman, Milton. *Crosscurrents: West Indian Immigrants and Race.* New York: Oxford University Press, 1999.

SEE ALSO Cuban immigrants; Cuban immigrants and African Americans; Haitian immigrants; West Indian immigrants.

SCANDINAVIAN IMMIGRANTS

IDENTIFICATION: Immigrants to North America from Western Europe's Scandinavian peninsula, which contains Sweden and Norway

IMMIGRATION ISSUES: Demographics; European immigrants

SIGNIFICANCE: Scandinavians were the earliest known European immigrants to North America, and modern Scandinavian Americans still have strong links to their cultural heritages.

The earliest European immigrants to the Western Hemisphere are believed to have been Vikings of Scandinavian origin. In 986 C.E., a Norse expedition headed by Bjarni Herjolfsson sighted land thought to have been on the east coast of Canada. It was followed some dozen years later by Leif Eriksson, who made landing. Norse expeditions attempted to colonize Vinland (Newfound-

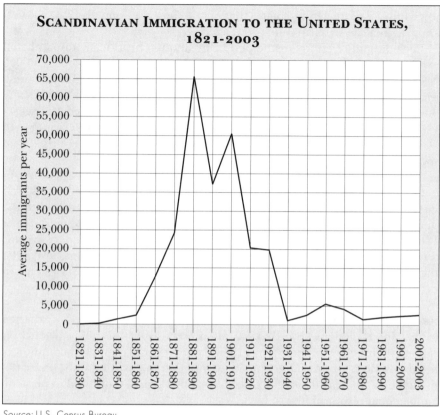

SCANDINAVIAN IMMIGRATION TO THE UNITED STATES, 1821-2003

Source: U.S. Census Bureau.

land) in 1003-1006 and 1007-1008 but ultimately failed because of infighting and conflicts with the native communities. These and subsequent expeditions did not result in permanent settlements on the North American continent.

The first documented Scandinavian settlements in North America were Swedish and included a community along the Delaware River in 1638. John Hanson, the first president of the Continental Congress, claimed to be a fourth-generation descendant of immigrants who traced their family ties to Swedish royalty. Early Swedish enclaves founded in Delaware (Maryland), Massachusetts, New Jersey, and Pennsylvania still maintain their cultural affiliations.

THE NINETEENTH CENTURY   In nineteenth century Scandinavia, social and economic conditions were stifling: Primogeniture ensured that only first sons could inherit their families' estates, land foreclosures abounded, and the nobility controlled much of the property and paid few taxes. Cleng Peerson (originally Kleng Peterson Hesthammer), a dissenter persecuted by the Lutheran State Church of Norway, left for the United States in 1821. He became so enamored of the United States that he purchased a sloop, the *Restauration*, and began a career as an immigrant agent.

Peerson and other agents helped bring about a historically unparalleled exodus of citizens from both Sweden and Norway. Approximately 750,000 Norwegians emigrated to North America between 1849 and 1914; the Swedish exodus during this same period totaled approximately 1.2 million, nearly one-fourth of Sweden's population. By 1890, about four hundred Minnesota towns sported Swedish names, and Norwegian-speaking travelers in North Dakota could find more people who spoke their native language than who spoke English.

Seafarers historically, Norwegians founded communities on both coasts, in places such as Massachusetts and the Pacific Northwest. Many also followed Peerson to Texas to bask in the milder climate. Others were attracted to the open lands of the upper Midwest, particularly after the Homestead Act of 1862 allotted 160 acres of newly opened land to anyone who could "prove up" a claim. Some enterprising couples positioned their bedrooms, and even their conjugal beds, exactly on the property line between two allotments in order to qualify for both allotments, or 320 acres.

RELIGIOUS INFLUENCES   Both Swedish and Norwegian immigrants carried with them a religious faith that saturated every aspect of their existence. It shaped their behavior, the cycle of their daily lives, and even their community identities. Both groups came from heavily Lutheran environments, where the mandate of "the Word alone, grace alone, faith alone" translated to immediate personal responsibility to God.

Lutheranism, however, was not always a uniting influence for Scandinavians. Subdivisions within the church, called synods, reflected ethnic affiliations. The Swedish Lutherans supported the Augustana synod, and Norwegian Lutheranism included at least six synods. Some of the Norwegian Lutherans were followers of Hans Neilsen Hauge, a reformer who experienced a call to preach the gospel to Norway while working on his farm. His American followers were pious and hardworking, separating themselves from those whom they regarded as frivolous. Haugeans, for example, abstained from dancing, believing that it facilitated contact between the sexes that was fraught with temptation and spiritual peril.

Swedish Covenant, Methodist, Baptist, Mormon, and a few Roman Catholic denominations also attracted both Swedish and Norwegian immigrants, and each group took their differences seriously. Haugeans, especially, abhorred anything resembling Roman Catholicism, while Catholics regarded Lutherans as spiritual heretics deprived of ritual. Interfaith marriages, when they did occur, alienated entire families; moving to different ethnic or religious communities could result in social isolation. In many instances, an unmarried pregnant woman was not allowed to marry the father of her child if he was not of her religion.

The Swedish and Norwegian pioneers' work ethic was also rooted in their religious orientation. Both groups frowned on complainers; both subscribed to biblical passages reminding the faithful that labor was an opportunity bestowed by God. Sunday Sabbath, however, was observed with diligence—any activity resembling work, even use of scissors or knitting needle, was avoided, and a farmer who worked in his fields on a Sunday invited general disapproval. Sundays were devoted to worship and visiting with neighbors.

INTERGROUP RELATIONS Despite the many traits and attitudes they shared, Norwegians and Swedes preserved distance from each other, both socially and theologically. Norwegians tended to view Swedes as somewhat undisciplined, and Swedes typically regarded Norwegians as cold and dour. A cemetery might well have separate sections for each ethnicity; the family of one Norwegian woman, for example, was disappointed that she had to be buried in the Swedish section of a cemetery because she had married a Swedish man.

The Scandinavians' relationships with other immigrant groups were usually civil and often amicable. As long as ethnic boundaries coincided with those of cities and schools, mutual respect prevailed. Sometimes, however, school athletic rivalries became metaphors for national differences, as exemplified by the rivalry between two small towns in southern Minnesota, one predominantly Polish Catholic and the other, Norwegian Lutheran. Rivalries

Poster for a popular late 1890's stage play that built its humor on exaggerated stereotypes of Scandinavian immigrants by depicting its title character as a big, simple-minded, and good-natured oaf. The image at the right shows Yonson about to be victimized by hustlers after his arrival in New York. During the 1960's, the name "Yon Yonson" was again popularized, this time in a musical ditty that begins, "My name is Yon Yonson/ I come from Wisconsin. . . . " (Library of Congress)

persisted for years, often to the point that character traits were assumed, by each side, to correlate with place of residence. The two small schools did not consolidate until the latter part of the twentieth century.

The ethnic and national boundaries began to blur in the twentieth century. Within the Lutheran Church, ethnic and synodical mergers began to bring Swedes, Norwegians, Danes, Germans, and Finns together in worship. Automotive mobility brought together groups of people who had never been face to face before. Religious intermarriages were no longer exotic, much less reprehensible.

However, there was one group with whom the Scandinavian Americans did not get along: the Native Americans. The Native Americans in the areas where Scandinavian Americans settled saw no particular advantage in the mainstream society's intruding into theirs. The Scandinavian immigrants, like other settlers, viewed American Indians' lifestyle as anachronistic and in need of "civilizing." They defined civilization in terms of religious conversion, manifested by "whitening" of dress and behavior.

A church worker involved in relations between Indian tribes and Scandinavian Americans noted that Norwegians, particularly, were in cultural opposition to the Native Americans. Norwegians were insular, while Native Americans were committed to their communities. Norwegians avoided dependence on others, while to the Native Americans, giving honored both the giver and the recipient. Many of these differences contributed to the cultural separation that persisted into the twenty-first century between Scandinavian Americans and American Indians, particularly in towns bordering Indian reservations.

Although Scandinavian Americans initially sought to immerse themselves totally in the mainstream culture, they gradually took steps to preserve their culture. The colleges they built preserved their ethnic and doctrinal definitions, until, following the path of the ethnic small towns, they, too, became more inclusive. Swedish and Norwegian Americans also established museums and hosted festivals and found them to be not only personally but also economically bountiful. Ethnicity, once a stigma, was now a distinction.

Brenda E. Reinertsen Caranicas

FURTHER READING

Greene, Victor R. *A Singing Ambivalence: American Immigrants Between Old World and New, 1830-1930.* Kent, Ohio: Kent State University Press, 2004.

Meltzer, Milton. *Bound for America: The Story of the European Immigrants.* New York: Benchmark Books, 2001.

SEE ALSO European immigrant literature; European immigrants, 1790-1892; German and Irish immigration of the 1840's; German immigrants; Literature.

SCOTCH-IRISH IMMIGRANTS

IDENTIFICATION: Immigrants to North America from Ireland who were of Protestant Scots descent

IMMIGRATION ISSUES: European immigrants; Irish immigrants

SIGNIFICANCE: The Scotch-Irish immigrants who came to North America and settled on the western frontier in the eighteenth century initially thought of themselves simply as Irish; however, as American nativist sentiments turned against the predominantly Roman Catholic Irish who began immigrating in large numbers during the early nineteenth century, they started calling themselves "Scotch-Irish" to dissociate themselves from the newcomers.

Now more commonly known as "Scots-Irish," the Scotch-Irish originated largely from Ulster, the northern counties of Ireland. Their immigration to North America began around 1695 and continued through the early nineteenth century, the largest wave arriving between 1717 and 1775. These consisted of native Ulster Protestants and Scots who had settled Ulster. Mostly Presbyterian, they brought to the New World a strong Calvinist tradition. Some may originally have been Roman Catholic but adopted Protestantism after arrival, in response to social prohibitions on Catholicism. Desires for land and religious freedom were the primary motives for immigration. Edged out by English settlers for arable land in the low country, the Scotch-Irish traveled the wagon roads that led to the western areas of Virginia and the Carolinas.

The Scotch-Irish developed a reputation for being rugged, devout, and fiercely independent, leaving a stamp on the regions they pioneered. Past experiences created a deep suspicion of authority among the Scotch-Irish. A majority of Scotch-Irish Americans supported the American Revolution and later backed the Confederacy in the Civil War.

Although early Scotch-Irish settlers referred to themselves simply as "Irish," the term "Scotch-Irish" came into use in the nineteenth century, as Protestant Irish disdained identification with a newer group of immigrant Catholic Irish, a visible immigrant community by the late nineteenth century. As such, the Scotch-Irish may be properly classified as a subculture.

Gene Redding Wynne, Jr.

FURTHER READING

Coffey, Michael, ed. *The Irish in America.* New York: Disney Enterprises, 1997.

Fallows, Marjorie. *Irish Americans: Identity and Assimilation.* Englewood Cliffs, N.J.: Prentice-Hall, 1979.

Griffin, William D. *A Portrait of the Irish in America.* New York: Charles Scribner's Sons, 1981.

McCaffrey, Lawrence J. *The Irish Diaspora in America.* Washington, D.C.: Catholic University of America Press, 1984.

Paulson, Timothy J. *Irish Immigrants.* New York: Facts On File, 2005.

SEE ALSO Anti-Irish Riots of 1844; Celtic Irish; European immigrants, 1790-1892; German and Irish immigration of the 1840's; Immigration and Nationality Act of 1965; Irish immigrants; Irish immigrants and African Americans; Irish immigrants and discrimination; Irish stereotypes.

SEPHARDIC JEWS

IDENTIFICATION: Jews who follow the liturgy and customs developed by Jews in medieval Spain and Portugal as well as Babylonian Jewish traditions

IMMIGRATION ISSUES: European immigrants; Jewish immigrants; Religion

SIGNIFICANCE: An upper class consisting mostly of intellectuals and members of the business elite, Sephardic Jews were the first Jewish immigrants to North America.

Sephardic Jews (derived from *sepharad*, a place of exile) have a proud multicultural heritage that combines Islamic and Christian influences. Members have published biblical commentaries, literature, and works on science, philosophy, and legal issues. Persecuted by Roman Catholics during the Inquisition, they were forced to become Christian or face expulsion from the Iberian Peninsula. Most of them left Spain in 1492 and Portugal in 1497 and settled in Holland, Brazil (Recife), Martinique, and various islands in the West Indies, where they prospered as a merchant class.

Sephardic Jews were the first Jewish immigrants to arrive in the North American colonies. Some historians believe that Sephardic Jews accompanied Columbus on his voyage to America in 1492. Other historical records indicate that in 1634, the Portuguese Jew Mathias de Sousa arrived in Maryland and established the first American Jewish settlement. Shortly after, another Sephardim, Jacob Barsimson, arrived in the colonies on a Dutch West India Company boat. During the mid-seventeenth century, some Sephardic Jews settled in Rhode Island and Virginia.

In 1654, twenty-three Jewish refugees from Brazil arrived in New Amsterdam. These refugees were not welcomed by the governor, Peter Stuyvesant, whom some historians describe as a bigot and anti-Semitic. The policy of tolerance for Jews, followed in the Dutch American colonists' native land, was applied in the colonies, and the Jews were allowed to remain, but some historians claim that this deference toward the Jews was primarily sparked by the colonists' fear of losing economic benefits in New Amsterdam. The Sephardic Jews in New Amsterdam were not allowed to build a temple or practice their religious beliefs in public; however in 1682, they rented a house for prayer meetings, and in 1730, the first synagogue, Shearith Israel, was built in New Amsterdam.

Gradually, Sephardic Jews succeeded in becoming participants in the political process. They became a dominant force; however, in the first part of the nineteenth century they seemed to lose connection with their Jewish ancestry. Prominent, wealthy Sephardic families moved in the same social circles as Christian families such as the Rockefellers. Intermarriage with Christians led to a weakening of Jewish faith and culture among the Sephardic Jews, who remained prominent society members and set standards of morality, education, and social life. Competition arose between Sephardic and Ashkenazic Jews, who often attended Sephardic synagogues and followed Sephardic ritual. Language was another barrier; the Sephardi spoke Ladino (medieval Castilian with an admixture of Hebrew), while the Ashkenazi spoke Yiddish (German, with an admixture of eastern European languages and Hebrew). Nineteenth century American Jews opted to assimilate into the Anglo-Saxon culture, thereby creating their own brand of Judaism. Sephardic Jews were soon outnumbered by Ashkenazi immigrants who began to dominate American Jewish culture.

Maria A. Pacino

FURTHER READING

Marcus, Jacob R. *The Colonial American Jew, 1492-1776.* 3 vols. Detroit, Mich.: Wayne State University Press, 1970.

Pool, David de Sola, and Tamara de Sola Pool. *An Old Faith in the New World: Portrait of Shearith Israel, 1654-1954.* New York: Columbia University Press, 1955.

SEE ALSO American Jewish Committee; Ashkenazic and German Jewish immigrants; Eastern European Jewish immigrants; Israeli immigrants; Jewish immigrants; Jewish settlement of New York; Jews and Arab Americans; Soviet Jewish immigrants; Twice migrants.

SEPTEMBER 11 TERRORIST ATTACKS

THE EVENT: Terrorist hijackings of commercial jetliners that were used to kill several thousand people in attacks on New York City and Washington, D.C.
DATE: September 11, 2001
PLACE: New York, New York; Washington, D.C.; rural Pennsylvania

THE EVENTS OF SEPTEMBER 11, 2001

At 8:45 A.M. on September, 11, 2001, an airliner flying out of Boston crashed into the north tower of New York City's World Trade Center, ripping a hole in several upper floors and starting a fire so intense that people on higher floors could not evacuate the building. At first, the crash was believed to be an accident. However, when a second airliner struck the Trade Center's south tower eighteen minutes later, it was clear that neither crash had been accidental. Fearing that a large-scale terrorist attack was underway, government agencies shut down local airports, bridges, and tunnels. Less than one hour after the first crash, the Federal Aviation Administration ordered—for the first time in history—a stop to all flight operations throughout the United States. Only moments later, a third airliner crashed into the Pentagon Building outside Washington, D.C.

Meanwhile, the intense fires in the Trade Center towers—fed by the airliners' jet fuel—so weakened the buildings that they could no longer support their upper floors. At 10:05 A.M., the entire south tower collapsed; twenty-three minutes later, the north tower collapsed. Between those events, a fourth airliner crashed in a field outside Pittsburgh, Pennsylvania.

As was later determined, all four airliners had been hijacked by operatives of a shadowy Middle Eastern organization known as al-Qaeda that was determined to kill as many Americans and do as much damage to the United States as possible. By any measure, the scheme was a great success. The cost of the physical damage of the attacks could be measured in billions of dollars. Although the extent of human fatalities was not as great as was initially feared, about three thousand people lost their lives—a number greater than all the American fatalities during the Japanese attack on Pearl Harbor on December 7, 1941. In addition, the sense of security from outside threats that Americans had long enjoyed was shattered. The impact of the terrorist attacks on American attitudes toward immigrants would be significant.

IMMIGRATION ISSUES: Border control; Civil rights and liberties; Discrimination; Government and politics; Middle Eastern immigrants

SIGNIFICANCE: Often simply called "Nine-Eleven," the terrorist attacks on the United States of September 11, 2001, hardened attitudes of the American public toward immigrants—especially those from the Middle East—and led to a tightening of border controls.

At the end the end of the twentieth century and the beginning of the twenty-first century, more foreign-born people were entering the United States than at any previous time in the nation's history. From 1990 through 2001, nearly 12 million people entered the country as legal permanent immigrants. Approximately 3 million came in as temporary nonimmigrants, and well over 1 million arrived as refugees and political asylum seekers. The population of illegal, or undocumented, immigrants living in the United States grew from about 5 million people in 1996 to about 7 million in 2000, according to estimates of the Immigration and Naturalization Service (INS). Many of the undocumented immigrants had been admitted as temporary nonimmigrants and did leave after their visas expired.

While most immigrants and visitors to the United States were job-seekers or tourists, a tiny minority were radical opponents of American policies. On September 11, 2001, Islamic radicals living in the United States hijacked four commercial airliners. They flew two of the planes into the twin towers of New York City's World Trade Center, destroying the buildings and killing thousands of people. A third plane hit the Pentagon, the headquarters of the U.S. military outside Washington, D.C., and a fourth crashed in rural Pennsylvania after a struggle between passengers and hijackers. Of the nineteen hijackers, fifteen were from Saudi Arabia, two from the United Arab Emirates, one from Lebanon, and one from Egypt. All nineteen had entered the United States legally, on visas granted by the Immigration and Naturalization Service. The events of September 11, 2001, intensified concerns that American borders had become too open.

HOMELAND SECURITY AND THE END OF THE INS On September 20, only nine days after the terrorist attacks, President George W. Bush reacted to the attacks by establishing the Office of Homeland Security, headed by former Pennsylvania governor Tom Ridge. In January, 2002, this cabinet-level office became the Department of Homeland Security. The new department was in-

The towers of the World Trade Center shortly after both buildings were struck by jet airliners.
(www.bigfoto.com)

Nuns studying the pictures posted in New York City of persons missing after the destruction of the World Trade Center towers. (Library of Congress)

tended to centralize efforts against terrorism, and the functions of nearly two dozen already existing agencies were to be brought under the department's control.

The INS was one of the agencies placed under Homeland Security. Originally created in 1933 from the merger of the Bureau of Immigration and the Bureau of Naturalization, the INS moved from the Department of Labor to the Department of Justice in 1940, reflecting a heightened concern over immigration as a security issue during the years before the United States entered World War II. Security questions once again encouraged change in 2001 and 2002, as many people asked how the nineteen foreign-born perpetrators of the September 11 attacks had been allowed to enter the United States. Concerns that the INS was too lax on security grew more intense after March, 2002, when news sources reported that not long before the terrorist attacks, the INS had approved changes in visa statuses, from tourist to student, for Mohammed Atta and Marwan al-Shehhi—two of the hijackers who died piloting planes into the World Trade Center. A year later, on March 1, 2003, the functions and offices of the INS were transferred to U.S. Citizenship and Immigration Services (USCIS), a bureau of the Department of Homeland Security.

CHANGE IN IMMIGRATION POLICY   Almost immediately after September 11, the federal government began passing new laws to tighten control over immigration. The most important of these laws was Public Law 107-56, whose full title was "Uniting and Strengthening America by Providing Appropriate Tools Required to Intercept and Obstruct Terrorism Act of 2001," the USA PATRIOT Act, or, more simply, the Patriot Act. It was passed by Congress on October 26, 2001. The act provided new reasons for denying immigrants entry into the United States, gave a broader definition to the concept of terrorist activity, and increased the number of justifications for deporting visitors and immigrants. Perhaps most controversially, the Patriot Act gave new powers to the U.S. attorney general, including the power to detain any persons the attorney general reasonably suspects of being connected to terrorist activity.

In November, 2001, Congress passed the Border Security Act, authorizing more funds for immigration and customs staff, providing for the sharing of information on deportation cases among federal agencies, tracking foreign students, and tightening oversight in other ways. The Department of Justice also issued a variety of new directives and regulations in the months following September 11, including interviews with recently arrived Middle Eastern men and provisions for detaining terrorist suspects. Supporters of the new legal approaches argued that these steps were necessary to combat terrorism. Critics countered that they constituted an assault on civil liberties. Many observers also saw the parts of the crack down on terrorism as especially oppressive to Middle Eastern and Muslim immigrants in the United States.

CONSEQUENCES OF CHANGING POLICIES   Changing immigration policies had little apparent impact on overall levels of legal permanent migration into the United States. In 2002, the federal government granted legal immigrant status to 1,063,732 people, approximately the same number as in the previous year and more than had been accepted as immigrants in any year since 1991. The number of immigrants dropped to 705,827 in 2003, but even that figure was still a larger number of legal immigrants than in either 1998 or 1999. Permanent immigration remained fairly stable because the Citizenship and Immigration Services bureau was processing people who had applied in earlier years and because much of the immigration into the United States was based on the re-unification of family members.

Despite a general overall stability in immigration figures, immigration from a number of countries with large Islamic populations began an apparent drop. Overall immigration from nations in North Africa and Asia with large or predominantly Islamic populations dropped from a historic high of nearly 80,000 people in 2001 to under 73,000 in 2002 and to under 52,000 in 2003. The numbers of temporary visitors from Islamic countries dropped even more noticeably. Visitors from the predominantly Islamic nations of North Africa and Asia decreased from 1,135,452 in 2001 to 808,322 in 2002 and 745,613 in 2003. Declines in visitors from Saudi Arabia, the United Arab Emirates, and Egypt were among the most marked. Whereas 66,721 Saudi Arabians had entered the United States in 2001, only 16,154 came in 2003. Those arriving from the United Arab Emirates decreased from 17,247 in 2001 to 5,368 in 2003. The numbers of Egyptian visitors went down by almost half: from 61,826 to 31,430 in 2003.

The new federal policies affected enforcement of laws directed at undocumented immigrants from Islamic countries much more than they affected legal immigration levels. The total number of deportable noncitizens, from all parts of the world, who were located by American officials actually decreased steadily from 2000 through 2003. However, numbers of people from Islamic nations in North Africa and Asia who were classified as subject to deportation and were located by American officials jumped dramatically from 2,613 in 2001 to 4,902 in 2002 and then to 15,026 in 2003.

Carl L. Bankston III

FURTHER READING

Barnett, R. *Restoring the Lost Constitution: The Presumption of Liberty.* Princeton, N.J: Princeton University Press, 2004. Broad essay on the erosion of civil liberties in the United States after the terrorist attacks of September 11, 2001.

Brzezinski, Matthew. *Fortress America: On the Frontline of Homeland Security—An Inside Look at the Coming Surveillance State.* New York: Bantam Books, 2004. Offering both hypothetical and real stories about the war on terror since September 11, 2001, this book takes a critical look at the Department of Homeland Security, the sacrificing of civil liberties, and damage done to international alliances.

Cole, David. *Enemy Aliens: Double Standards and Constitutional Freedoms in the War on Terrorism.* New York: New Press/W. W. Norton, 2003. Critical analysis of the erosion of civil liberties in the United States since September 11, 2001, with attention to the impact of federal policies on immigrants and visiting aliens.

Daniels, Roger. *Guarding the Golden Door: American Immigration Policy and Immigrants Since 1882.* New York: Hill & Wang, 2004. Comprehensive history of American immigration policy, from the beginnings of a major wave of European immigration in the late nineteenth century to the years following the September 11 terrorist attacks.

Elaasar, Aladdin. *Silent Victims: The Plight of Arab and Muslim Americans in Post 9/11 America.* Bloomington, Ind.: Author House, 2004. Study of the increased pressures on Arab and other Muslim immigrants to the United States after the 2001 terrorist attacks.

Goldberg, Daniel, Victor Goldberg, and Robert Greenwald. *It's a Free Country: Personal Freedom in America After September 11.* New York: Nation Books, 2003. Forty-one articles and cartoons emphasizing civil liberties issues arising from antiterrorism efforts.

Leone, Richard C., and Greg Anrig, Jr. *The War on Our Freedoms: Civil Liberties in an Age of Terrorism.* New York: BBS PublicAffairs, 2003. Three experts on civil liberties warn of the consequences of the war on terrorism to American freedoms, while documenting how each generation of Americans has witnessed struggles between order and liberty.

Steger, Manfred B. *Judging Nonviolence: The Dispute Between Realists and Idealists.* New York: Routledge, 2003. Balanced treatment of the arguments for and against nonviolence, written in the aftermath of the September 11, 2001, terrorist attacks on the United States, with discussions of major social political movements that employed nonviolence.

White, Jonathan R. *Defending the Homeland: Domestic Intelligence Law Enforcement and Security.* Stamford, Conn.: Wadsworth, 2003. Survey of law enforcement in the United States discussing how the criminal justice system has changed since September 11, 2001.

SEE ALSO Arab American stereotypes; Arab immigrants; Border Patrol, U.S.; Coast Guard, U.S.; Deportation; Illegal aliens; Immigration and Naturalization Service; Muslims.

SETTLEMENT HOUSE MOVEMENT

THE EVENT: Rise of charitable settlement houses in major urban centers
DATE: 1890's-early twentieth century

IMMIGRATION ISSUES: Families and marriage; Women

SIGNIFICANCE: The settlement house movement provided social services and cultural programs to immigrant and poor urban women and their families and professional opportunities to college-educated women who desired to work on behalf of social reform.

The settlement house movement began among Christian Socialists and university-affiliated reformers in England and spread to major cities in North America during the 1890's. The houses, which were established primarily in the urban centers of the Midwest and Northeast, multiplied from six in 1891 to more than four hundred in 1910. They became principal agencies of social reform during the Progressive era.

PHILOSOPHY AND IDEALS A reaction to growing urbanization, immigration, and changes in labor patterns, settlement houses emphasized social action to improve impoverished living conditions and exploitative labor practices. Influenced by the Social Gospel movement, they emphasized character building and an organic vision of society based on cultural mediation and mutual reciprocity between native-born citizens and immigrants and between the middle class and the poor. They simultaneously advocated social assimilation to middle-class norms and cultural pluralism or diversity. These positions often came into conflict. The original settlement houses were also experiments in collective living. Located in poor ethnic neighborhoods, they attracted resident workers who were mainly young, idealistic, college-educated men and women from well-to-do households.

PROGRAMS AND SERVICES Early programs focused on providing services for children, including day care nurseries for the children of working mothers, kindergartens, boys' and girls' clubs, recreation programs, nature outings, playgrounds, and gymnasiums. Citizenship classes, emphasizing literacy and the English language, were held for adults, as well as practical training

Cooking class in Chicago's Hull-House. (University of Illinois at Chicago, University Library, Jane Addams Memorial Collection)

courses in home economics, dressmaking, cooking, sanitation, and nutrition. Medical and nursing services were provided by some houses, most notably by the extensive visiting nurse service of the Henry Street Settlement House in New York. Family counseling and job referral bureaus were offered to working women. Exhibitions, art history, and the performing arts, including music and drama, also played an important part in settlement house programming. Resident workers and teachers such as Ellen Gates Starr of Hull-House believed in the uplifting value of fine art appreciation.

Efforts were made to attract Italian, Greek, and East European women to the houses by appealing to nationalist loyalties, including the planning of ethnic festivals, receptions, and celebrations of folk dancing and crafts. At Hull-House, a labor museum was established in which immigrant women demonstrated the history of textile arts. The museum program sought to bridge cultural gaps that had developed between first-generation immigrants, who were highly skilled in handicrafts and traditional manufactures, and their children, who were more familiar with factory work and mechanization, many having lost respect for older ways.

INSTITUTIONALIZATION AND REFORM　Many of the programs that existed on a trial basis in the settlement houses were adopted by public school systems, park and urban planning agencies, and the developing juvenile justice system and social work institutions. In addition to providing services and stimulating appreciation of diverse cultural heritages, settlement workers were also in the forefront of the formation of social policy. They gathered data to educate the population at large as to the needs of the urban poor, and they lobbied for municipal reform and state and federal legislation that addressed the issues of housing, labor, women's rights, and prostitution. Many of the reforms that they advocated became central tenets of the Progressive Party platform during Theodore Roosevelt's presidential bid in 1912.

ETHNICITY AND RACE　While settlement workers saw themselves as advocates for the lower classes, their application of middle-class values was sometimes at odds with immigrant women's perspectives. Conflicts existed, for example, over economic issues involved in child labor. While settlement workers sought to abolish the practice, many immigrant families relied on the income that children earned. Settlement workers also stressed white slavery aspects of prostitution, portraying the prostitute as a victim and emphasizing the sexual double standard and the curbing of male behavior while avoiding the idea of sex work as a chosen occupation.

Few immigrant women ascended to positions of leadership in the protective leagues that emerged from the houses or in the resident work itself. While most settlements were run by native-born whites on behalf of white ethnic immigrants, some offered separate branches for black residents, and a few, such as the Phillis Wheatley Settlement in Minneapolis, were founded specifically as residence facilities for African Americans.

WOMEN'S OPPORTUNITIES AND THE LEGACY OF REFORM   Although settlement houses served both men and women, women such as Lillian Wald of the Henry Street Settlement House and Jane Addams of Hull-House were among the earliest founders of houses and the most prominent leaders of the movement. The settlement houses in general provided outlets of usefulness for educated women, aid to working women with families, and models of effective female leadership, networking, and authority.

Many women who initially were involved in settlement work went on to positions of influence in organizations, unions, and government agencies, broadening the impact of the settlement houses on the wider sphere of reform. Florence Kelley went from settlement experience to founding the National Consumers' League in 1899, which worked to improve labor conditions for women and children. Julia Lathrop and Grace Abbott both became directors of the Children's Bureau. Alice Hamilton became a leading expert on industrial medicine and a professor at Harvard Medical School. The National Women's Trade Union League (NWTUL), a labor organization, and the National Association for the Advancement of Colored People (NAACP), a civil rights group, were formed with support from settlement workers.

Alice Gannett of the Henry Street Settlement House led the lobbying efforts that resulted in the passage of the Mothers' Aid Law of 1913, which provided pensions to needy mothers of dependent children, and Sophonisba Breckinridge and Edith Abbott were leaders in the new field of social work. Both Addams and Wald became central figures in the war-era pacifist movement, with Addams chair of the Women's Peace Party and head of the Women's International League for Peace and Freedom (WILPF), and Wald president of the American Union Against Militarism.

The settlement house movement bridged the gap between older Victorian concepts of charity and philanthropy and modern social work. Over time, the unique nature of the houses was eclipsed by the professionalization of social services, which changed the cooperative volunteer staffing of the settlements to salaried and specialized positions. Post-World War I conservatism and changes in fund-raising methods also diminished the operations of the houses.

Barbara Bair

FURTHER READING

Addams, Jane. *Twenty Years at Hull House.* Edited by Victoria Bissell Brown. Boston: Bedford/St. Martin's, 1999. Scholarly edition, with additional autobiographical materials, of a book that Addams first published in 1911. Provides detailed account of the establishment, operation, and philosophy of Hull-House.

Bryan, Mary Linn McCree, and Allen Davis. *One Hundred Years at Hull-House.* Bloomington: Indiana University Press, 1990. Compendium of primary sources about Hull-House, including numerous photographs.

Carson, Mina. *Settlement Folk: Social Thought and the American Settlement Movement, 1885-1930.* Chicago: University of Chicago Press, 1990. An extensively documented examination of the contribution of U.S. settlement-house workers to the development of social welfare. Provides a historical and ideological context for the work of Hull-House.

Davis, Allen. *Spearheads for Reform: The Social Settlements and the Progressive Movement, 1890-1914.* New York: Oxford University Press, 1967. An overview of the origin, guiding principles, activities, and accomplishments of American social settlements during their early years.

Deegan, Mary Jo. *Race, Hull-House, and the University of Chicago: A New Conscience Against Ancient Evils.* Westport, Conn.: Praeger, 2002. Study of Hull-House, from 1892 to 1960, in the context of racial and ethnic issues.

Glowacki, Peggy, and Julia Hendry. *Hull-House.* Charleston, S.C.: Arcadia, 2004. Study of Hull-House, from 1892 to 1960, in the context of racial and ethnic issues.

Levine, Daniel. *Jane Addams and the Liberal Tradition.* Westport, Conn.: Greenwood Press, 1980. A useful discussion of the background, context, daily operations, institutional growth, and community influence of Hull-House.

Shpak Lissak, Rivka. *Pluralism and Progressives: Hull House and the New Immigrants, 1890-1919.* Chicago: University of Chicago Press, 1989. Scholarly study of settlement houses that focuses on the services they provided to new immigrants.

SEE ALSO Hull-House; Machine politics; Women immigrants.

SIKH IMMIGRANTS

IDENTIFICATION: Immigrants to North America from a religious community whose origins are in South Asia's Punjab region

IMMIGRATION ISSUES: Asian immigrants; Demographics; Religion

SIGNIFICANCE: The numbers of Sikhs in the United States have never been large, but after the relaxation of restrictions on immigration from Asia during the 1960's, highly educated and affluent Sikhs settled in every major American city.

The founder of Sikhism, Guru Nanak Dev (1469-1539), advocated peace, a casteless society, the oneness of God, and the unifying of Hindus and Muslims. Vicious persecution contributed to this peaceful community being transformed into the *Khalsa*, a soldier-saint brotherhood who believed it was right to draw the sword for a just cause.

Sikh American holding a flag during New York City's Sikh Day. (Frances M. Roberts)

The Sikhs' tenth and last Guru, Gobind Singh (1666-1708), instituted the 5Ks, a term used for the symbols Sikhs wear, uncut hair under a turban being the most noticeable. Throughout their history, Sikhs have been respected for their martial valor, innovativeness, adaptability to diverse situations, and migratory tradition. Sikh communities are found throughout the world.

The initial influx, from 1904 to 1923, consisted primarily of Sikhs who originated in rural Punjab and had agricultural backgrounds but were residing in Canada. They migrated south to escape being targets of violence. Some obtained employment in the lumber trade around Bellingham and Everett, Washington. In 1907, about one thousand Sikhs were expelled from the Pacific Northwest because local laborers believed they were depressing wages. The Sikhs and other Indians moved south to work on the farms in the Sacramento, San Joaquin, and Imperial Valleys in the summer and labored in the California cities of Yuba City, Stockton, and El Centro in the winter. Their numbers probably never exceeded six thousand. Contemporary newspaper articles talked about the "Hindoo invasion" and "turbaned tide."

In 1918, the "Hindoo" conspiracy trials brought adverse publicity to the Sikh and Indian community of California. In 1913, the Ghadr (revolutionary) Party was formed and headquartered in San Francisco with the aim of gaining India's independence from Great Britain. The defendants in the Hindoo case, active members of the Ghadr Party, were charged with violating U.S. neutrality laws. Much of the evidence and impetus to prosecute came from British agents.

In 1923, immigration from India to the United States was effectively halted; legislation prevented South Asians from owning land, becoming citizens, or bringing spouses to the United States. As a result, some Sikhs married Mexican women. The Ghadr Party remained active, but at a reduced level. During the 1930's, many Sikhs returned to India, and the population decreased to less than fifteen hundred. In 1946, the Luce-Celler Bill was passed, giving people of Asian Indian descent the right to become American citizens and creating an immigration quota for India.

In 1965, immigration legislation ended the national origins quotas. Immigration to the United States was based on the candidate's ability to meet a set of qualifications. In India, a cadre of highly educated doctors, engineers, and scientists was ready to take advantage of the new laws. The Sikhs who immigrated under the relaxed laws are residentially dispersed in affluent suburbs. They gather in their local *gurdwaras*, or Sikh places of worship, which are part of the landscape of every major city in North America.

Arthur W. Helweg

FURTHER READING

Chi, Tsung. *East Asian Americans and Political Participation: A Reference Handbook.* Santa Barbara, Calif.: ABC-Clio, 2005.

Helweg, Arthur W., and Usha M. Helweg. *An Immigrant Success Story: East Indians in the United States.* Philadelphia: University of Pennsylvania Press, 1990.

La Brack, Bruce. *The Sikhs of Northern California, 1904-1974.* New York: AMS Press, 1988.

Motwani, Jagat K. *America and India in a "Give and Take" Relationship: Sociopsychology of Asian Indian Immigrants.* New York: Center for Asian, African and Caribbean Studies, 2003.

Singh, Jaswinder, and Kalyani Gopal. *Americanization of New Immigrants: People Who Come to America and What They Need to Know.* Lanham, Md.: University Press of America, 2002.

SEE ALSO Asian Indian immigrants; Asian Indian immigrants and family customs; Twice migrants.

SOUTHEAST ASIAN IMMIGRANTS

IDENTIFICATION: Immigrants to North America from the Southeast Asian nations of Cambodia, Laos, Thailand, and Vietnam

IMMIGRATION ISSUES: Asian immigrants; Demographics; Families and marriage; Refugees

SIGNIFICANCE: There are substantial Southeast Asian populations throughout North America, each with distinctive family customs.

Since 1975 large numbers of Southeast Asians from Laos, Cambodia, Thailand, and Vietnam have settled throughout the United States and southern Canada. Most of those from Laos, Cambodia, and Vietnam arrived in North

America as refugees after socialist governments came to power in those countries at the end of the Vietnam War. The Hmong, a minority group from the mountains of Laos, were among these refugees. The Thais arrived in North America as immigrants, not refugees, with the largest numbers entering as students or as spouses of U.S. or Canadian citizens. However, much of the Thai settlement is also a consequence of American involvement in the war in Southeast Asia from 1965 to 1975, because Thailand borders Cambodia and Laos and the war established many links between America and Thailand.

California holds the largest concentrations of Southeast Asians in North America. Of the 149,014 Laotians in the 1990 U.S. Census, 58,058, or 39 percent, lived in California. Similarly, California was home to 32,064, or 35 percent, of the 91,275 U.S. Thais; 68,190, or 46 percent, of the 147,411 U.S. Cambodians; 46,892, or 52 percent, of the 90,082 U.S. Hmong; and 280,223, or 46 percent, of the 614,547 U.S. Vietnamese. Canada has a relatively small Thai population, found chiefly in Toronto, but by the late 1980's it was home to more than 100,000 Southeast Asians from the other groups. About three-quarters of Canadian Southeast Asians are Vietnamese, and they are primarily concentrated in Ontario Province, particularly in Toronto.

SIZE AND YOUTH OF FAMILIES   The Southeast Asians come from countries in which large families are customary and, as a consequence, their families tend to be much larger than those of other Americans. In the United States, for example, U.S. Census data show that the average American family had only 3.16 people per family. The average Canadian family was slightly larger. The average Cambodian family, by contrast, had 5.03 people, the average Laotian family 5.01, the average Vietnamese family 4.36, and the average Hmong family 6.58. Only the Thais, with an average family size of 3.48 people were close to other Americans. This is probably a reflection of the fact that so many Thais came to the United States as students or were married to non-Asian Americans.

Partly as a result of large family size, Southeast Asians tend to be younger than other Americans. In 1990 about one-fourth of all Americans were younger than eighteen. That same year nearly half of all Cambodian Americans and Laotian Americans were younger than eighteen. More than one-third of Vietnamese Americans and nearly two-thirds of Hmong Americans were younger than eighteen. Only the Thais were similar to other Americans. The extreme youth of the refugee groups means that passing on traditional family customs and relations is an especially large task for Laotian, Cambodian, Hmong, and Vietnamese parents.

FAMILY RELATIONS   Husbands are regarded as the heads of families among all Southeast Asian groups, but women often wield much power, especially over matters having to do with the household. Children in traditional Southeast Asian families are expected to show a great deal of respect for elders. Older brothers and sisters are expected to take responsibility for younger siblings, and younger children are expected to defer to their older siblings. The psychologist Nathan Caplan has argued that highly cooperative family relations may be one of the reasons why Southeast Asian children often do well in American schools, since brothers and sisters frequently help one another in doing schoolwork.

Since women are regarded as the core of the family and the central carriers of tradition in all Southeast Asian cultures, parents tend to place higher expectations and restrictions on daughters than on sons. This sometimes causes resentment on the part of American-born daughters and may lead to friction within families. Both sons and daughters sometimes come into conflict with parents when the children attempt to live out American values of individual independence.

MARRIAGE AND WEDDING CUSTOMS   The wedding customs of Thais, Laotians, and Cambodians are quite similar. In common traditional Thai and Laotian weddings, bridegrooms visit brides' houses on the evening before the wedding. Buddhist monks bless elaborate begging bowls filled with water. Then a long strand of cotton thread is tied around couples' and monks' wrists and looped around the blessed water. This ceremony is intended to unite the souls (known in both Lao and Thai as *kwan*) of the betrothed.

The next morning, monks, friends, and relatives sprinkle couples with the consecrated water. Later in the day, brides and bridegrooms sit together, dressed in traditional clothing, in front of a feast and wedding gifts in the presence of their families and guests. The monks recite prayers for couples' happiness and well-being.

In Cambodian weddings the ceremony usually begins in the morning at the brides' homes, where Buddhist monks chant blessings. Locks of hair are cut from the heads of the betrothed. Cotton threads soaked in holy water are tied around the wrists of brides and bridegrooms. A circle of married couples then passes around a candle in order to bless the marriages. Such weddings are followed by a large feast, which may be held in a private home or in a restaurant, depending on the convenience and means of the families.

Among the Hmong, marriages are traditionally arranged by go-betweens, who negotiate a price to be paid to the brides' families. Marriages are made public by a two-day feast. In Laos, if families could not agree on a bride-price or if prospective husbands were unacceptable to brides' families, suitors would often elope with the young women or kidnap them. Because the Hmong in America who have tried in some instances to follow this practice have been charged with kidnapping and rape, this custom has become very rare.

Wedding customs of Vietnamese Americans are quite different from those of other Southeast Asians, because the Vietnamese have been much more influenced by Chinese civilization than other Southeast Asians and many Vietnamese are Roman Catholics. Although Roman Catholic and Buddhist Vietnamese maintain many social ties with one another, marriages of people of different religious faiths are fairly rare. Roman Catholic and Buddhist Vietnamese in North America often live in separate communities. Although wedding customs differ among Vietnamese of different religions, wedding feasts following marriage ceremonies are a central tradition for all.

FAMILY HOLIDAY CELEBRATIONS   Holiday celebrations are important to Southeast Asian American families, because they provide opportunities for elders to pass on traditions and customs to younger people. Among all groups, New Year's celebrations are the most widely held and most important. The Laotian, Cambodian, and Thai New Year is usually held in mid-April. Thais and Laotians in America frequently dress in traditional clothes and hold cultural exhibitions during New Year's events, and they enjoy the custom of throwing water on each other. The Cambodians hold parties and dances and sometimes play a customary game in which young men and women throw a rolled-up scarf back and forth. At the Hmong New Year's Festival, held at the time of the new moon in December, young men and women play a similar courting game, tossing a ball back and forth. The Vietnamese New Year, held in January or February, is a lively three-day celebration with a variety of family and community rituals.

Carl L. Bankston III

FURTHER READING

Barr, Linda. *Long Road to Freedom: Journey of the Hmong.* Bloomington, Minn.: Red Brick Learning, 2004.

Caplan, Nathan, John K. Whitmore, and Marcella H. Choy. *The Boat People and Achievement in America: A Study of Family Life, and Cultural Values.* Ann Arbor: University of Michigan Press, 1989.

Cargill, Mary Terrell, and Jade Quang Huynh, eds. *Voices of Vietnamese Boat People: Nineteen Narratives of Escape and Survival.* Jefferson, N.C.: McFarland, 2000.

Chan, Sucheng. *Survivors: Cambodian Refugees in the United States.* Urbana: University of Illinois Press, 2004.

_____, ed. *Hmong Means Free: Life in Laos and America.* Philadelphia: Temple University Press, 1994.

Conley, Ellen Alexander. *The Chosen Shore: Stories of Immigrants.* Berkeley: University of California Press, 2004.

Mote, Sue Murphy. *Hmong and American: Stories of Transition to a Strange Land.* Jefferson, N.C.: McFarland, 2004.

Ng, Franklin, ed. *Asian American Encyclopedia.* 6 vols. New York: Marshall Cavendish, 1995.

Proudfoot, Robert. *Even the Birds Don't Sound the Same Here: The Laotian Refugees' Search for Heart in American Culture.* New York: Peter Lang, 1990.

Segal, Uma Anand. *A Framework for Immigration: Asians in the United States.* New York: Columbia University Press, 2002.

Tenhula, John. *Voices from Southeast Asia: The Refugee Experience in the United States.* New York: Holmes & Meier, 1991.

Zhou, Min, and Carl L. Bankston III. *Growing Up American: The Adaptation of Vietnamese Children to American Society.* New York: Russell Sage Foundation, 1998.

See also Asian American education; Asian American literature; Asian American stereotypes; Asian American women; Farmworkers' union; Filipino immigrants; Hmong immigrants; Model minorities; *Nguyen v. Immigration and Naturalization Service*; Refugees and racial/ethnic relations; Vietnamese immigrants.

Soviet Jewish immigrants

IDENTIFICATION: Jewish immigrants to North America who emigrated from the Soviet Union before its breakup during the early 1990's

IMMIGRATION ISSUES: Demographics; European immigrants; Jewish immigrants; Refugees

SIGNIFICANCE: After suffering through a long history of oppression under the Russian czars and Soviet rulers, Jews living in the Soviet Union pressed for the right to emigrate. Many who were allowed to leave came to the United States, where they found it difficult to assimilate with other Jews.

When the Bolsheviks assumed power in Russia in 1917, they promised to end the periodic pogroms (massacres) and frequent discrimination that Russian Jews had experienced under the czars. However, the Soviet government soon engaged in widespread, though perhaps less overt, forms of discrimination and persecution against the country's Jewish population. In addition, because the Soviet Union's official communist ideology included a commitment to atheism, Jews, along with other religious groups, were essentially barred from practicing their religion. Houses of worship were closed or destroyed, and religious leaders were imprisoned.

During the era of détente during the 1970's, the Soviet government permitted a significant increase in Jewish emigration. This was partly caused by the passage in the U.S. Congress of the Jackson-Vanik amendment, which tied American-Soviet trade to an increase in the Soviet Union's Jewish emigration permits. Although many Soviet Jews emigrated to Israel, a large portion of these emigrants eventually settled in the United States. Jewish American groups had lobbied the federal government both to pressure the Soviet government to release Jews and to permit more Soviet Jews to settle in the United States.

Although the immigration campaign was highly successful, Soviet Jewish immigrants did not always integrate with the American Jewish community as well as had been hoped. The immigrants were frequently more secular, having grown up in an officially atheistic state. They also tended to be poor and eager to make use of resources made available by American Jewish groups. Politically, many Soviet Jewish immigrants were more conservative than the mainstream American Jewish groups. Also, many of the immigrants did not speak English. A number of American Jewish leaders expressed disappointment about their inability to incorporate and assimilate the new immigrants.

A second wave of Soviet Jewish emigration took place during the late 1980's and early 1990's, when Soviet leader Mikhail Gorbachev liberalized his country's emigration laws. The collapse of the Soviet Union in 1991 in particular created a renewed impetus for Soviet Jews (and others) to leave their country. Many Soviet Jews were attracted to the United States by concerted campaigns by Jewish American groups. The number of Jewish immigrants from the former Soviet Union increased from about 200 in 1986 to a peak of 185,000 in 1990. A total of more than 700,000 Soviet Jews immigrated to the United States between 1987 and 1997.

Many refugees from the Soviet Union who could not obtain Soviet passports, traveled under League of Nations passports such as this one, which was issued shortly after Joseph Stalin took power in the Soviet Union. (Library of Congress)

The fact that many Soviet Jewish immigrants do not look, speak, or behave like mainstream American Jews has underscored an important principle of racial and ethnic relations. Frequently, cultural and societal differences—rather than purely racial, ethnic, or religious differences—have led to friction between groups. Similarly, the mere sharing of ethnic or racial backgrounds does not ensure intergroup harmony.

Steve D. Boilard

FURTHER READING

Altshuler, Stuart. *The Exodus of the Soviet Jews.* Lanham, Md.: Rowman & Littlefield, 2005.

Shasha, Dennis Elliott, and Marina Shron. *Red Blues: Voices from the Last Wave of Russian Immigrants.* New York: Holmes & Meier, 2002.

Wertsman, Vladimir, ed. *The Russians in America: A Chronology and Fact Book.* Dobbs Ferry, N.Y.: Oceana Publications, 1977.

SEE ALSO American Jewish Committee; Ashkenazic and German Jewish immigrants; Eastern European Jewish immigrants; Israeli immigrants; Jewish immigrants; Jewish settlement of New York; Jews and Arab Americans; Justice and immigration; Mail-order brides; Russian immigrants; Sephardic Jews.

TAIWANESE IMMIGRANTS

IDENTIFICATION: Immigrants to North America from the East Asian island nation of Taiwan, which is also known as Nationalist China

IMMIGRATION ISSUES: Asian immigrants; Demographics

SIGNIFICANCE: Because of Taiwan's special relationship with mainland China, the large number of Taiwanese immigrants in the United States have played an important role in relations among Taiwan, China, and the United States.

The Immigration and Nationality Act of 1965 brought a surge of Asian immigration to the United States. From 1965 to 1980, many Taiwanese who came to the United States as graduate students decided to remain as immigrants because the economic opportunities were better in America than in Taiwan. Many of these immigrants settled in ethnic communities such as Flushing and Queens in New York and Monterey Park in California. The Taiwanese immigrants felt comfortable in these communities because within them they could speak their native language and interact with other Taiwanese immigrants.

In 1981, when Congress set a yearly quota of twenty thousand Taiwanese immigrants, the characteristics of those arriving changed. The new immigrants typically had not studied in the United States and were less likely to speak English. The concentration of non-English-speaking immigrants in certain areas such as Monterey Park caused a backlash, spawning efforts to have English declared the official language in states such as California during the mid- and late-1980's.

By the end of the twentieth century, more than 250,000 Taiwanese Americans lived in the United States. Of this group, 20 percent were born in the United States and 40 percent were naturalized citizens. The median age of this group was about thirty-five, and with a college graduation rate of 60 percent, a member of this group was much more likely to have completed higher education than was the average American. Eight percent of this group held doctoral degrees, and 48 percent were employed in managerial or profes-

Chiang Kai-shek (1887-1975) established the Republic of China on the island of Taiwan in 1949, after Mao Zedong's Communist Party took control of the mainland and created the People's Republic of China. Taiwan had a close relationship with the United States through the Cold War, until the 1970's, when the United States recognized the People's Republic. The question of Taiwan's independence from China remained unresolved into the twenty-first century. (Library of Congress)

sional positions. Taiwanese Americans tended to be very prosperous, with average incomes higher than the national median; 71 percent of them owned their own homes.

Throughout the history of Taiwanese immigration, organizations devoted to the social, economic, and political welfare of Taiwanese Americans have existed across the United States. Part of their social and cultural purpose has been to maintain Taiwanese cultural traditions among the immigrants and their descendants and to familiarize other Americans with those traditions. Therefore, many Taiwanese American organizations have introduced their communities to such cultural practices as eating moon cakes to celebrate the autumn festival, celebrating the Lunar New Year, and preparing rice dumplings for the Dragonboat Festival.

Taiwanese American organizations have also attempted to exert political influence in both the United States and Taiwan. In the United States, they have attempted to affect U.S. foreign policy toward China and Taiwan. They have organized demonstrations to protest overseas incidents that have affected Taiwan and have lobbied members of Congress to support Taiwan's efforts to remain free of China. Through political activities designed to affect their homeland, Taiwanese Americans have helped to create a more democratic Taiwan by helping to elect prodemocracy members to the Kuomintang (parliament) and by supporting the prodemocracy candidate during the 1996 presidential elections.

Annita Marie Ward

FURTHER READING

Chee, Maria W. L. *Taiwanese American Transnational Families: Women and Kin Work*. New York: Routledge, 2005.

Chen, Hsiang-Shui. *Chinatown No More: Taiwan Immigrants in Contemporary New York*. Ithaca, N.Y.: Cornell University Press, 1992.

Ng, Franklin, ed. *Asian American Encyclopedia*. 6 vols. New York: Marshall Cavendish, 1995.

Pyong Gap Min. *Asian Americans.* Thousand Oaks, Calif.: Sage Publications, 1995.

Zinzius, Birgit. *Chinese America: Stereotype and Reality—History, Present, and Future of the Chinese Americans.* New York: P. Lang, 2004.

SEE ALSO Amerasians; Asian American education; Chinatowns; Chinese American Citizens Alliance; Chinese Exclusion Act; Chinese exclusion cases; Chinese immigrants; Chinese immigrants and California's gold rush; Chinese immigrants and family customs; Chinese Six Companies; Coolies; Immigration Act of 1943.

THAI GARMENT WORKER ENSLAVEMENT

THE EVENT: Southern California garment factory that employed seventy-two Thai immigrants in slavelike conditions until raided by Immigration and Naturalization Service officers

DATE: August 2, 1995

PLACE: El Monte, California

IMMIGRATION ISSUES: Asian immigrants; Labor; Slavery

SIGNIFICANCE: This highly publicized incident helped to call attention to how the largely hidden problem of slavery in the modern world reaches even into industrialized democracies such as the United States.

Before dawn on August 2, 1995, U.S. Immigration and Naturalization Service (INS) officials staged a raid on a garment factory in El Monte, California. The factory, surrounded by barbed wire, held seventy-two workers from Thailand, some of whom had lived and worked in the factory for years. When the workers first arrived in the United States, their employers took them from the airport directly to the factory. Each night, the workers, who sewed clothing that was sold under major brand names, were locked up and guarded. They worked from 7:00 A.M. to midnight every day, for $1.60 per hour, with no extra pay for working more than forty hours a week. Most of this pay was withheld by their employers as repayment for transportation costs to the United States. Factory owners often held children of the workers hostage to force the adults to keep working. The employers also threatened to beat workers who tried to escape.

CAPTIVES Neighbors thought that the high walls and barbed wire surrounding the El Monte factory had been put in place to keep criminals out,

657

not to keep workers in. Immigration officers had been suspicious for a long time, however, and in 1992, the INS had sought a warrant to search the building. On that first occasion, federal prosecutors refused to grant the warrant, saying that the evidence of wrongdoing was not sufficient.

By the time INS officers gained legal permission to stage their raid on the factory, some of the workers had been imprisoned for as long as seven years. The operation began during the late 1980's when the Manasurangkun brothers from Thailand, Wirachai, Phanasak, and Surachai, together with their mother, Suni, joined with three other Thai people to recruit poor women in their native land. By bringing these women to the United States, the Manasurangkuns and their partners could get inexpensive labor to sew clothing for name-brand manufacturers. Over time, the treatment of the workers grew increasingly harsh, and the Manasurangkuns hired guards to keep them from escaping. According to Rojana Cheunchujit, a worker who spoke English and came to serve as a spokesperson for the others, the Thai women had to work sixteen hours a day and sleep on a dirty floor with cockroaches and mice. Two women who tried to escape were beaten and sent back to Thailand.

CONSEQUENCES The case of the Thai workers in El Monte helped call attention to the plight of garment workers in the United States. Since the 1960's, the sewing of clothing has moved away from large factories and toward small producers who supply large retail stores with a variety of clothes designed to appeal to consumers with varied tastes. These large retail stores are relatively few in number and control much of the American market. To make profits, clothing manufacturers have had to keep their costs down because the retail stores want to supply customers with inexpensive clothes. The clothing manufacturers compete with each other to make garments as cheaply as possible, and the manufacturers therefore try to find the cheapest workers they can. Because immigrants, especially those in the country illegally, will work for lower wages than other people in the United States, by the 1990's, a majority of garment workers were immigrant women.

The slavelike conditions found at the El Monte factory are rare in the United States. Nevertheless, many garment workers labor in difficult and often illegal circumstances. For example, a 1994 investigation by California labor officials looked into the operations of sixty-nine randomly selected manufacturers. All but two of these manufacturers were found to be breaking federal or state laws or both. Half of them were violating minimum wage laws, 68 percent were violating laws regarding overtime, and 93 percent were violating health and safety regulations.

The publicity created by the raid at El Monte led to an investigation of the clothing industry by the U.S. Labor Department within two weeks after the incident. The Labor Department warned more than a dozen of the largest U.S. retail merchants that they may have received goods made by the Thai workers. Labor Secretary Robert B. Reich called a meeting with the retailers to discuss ways to avoid selling goods made by enslaved workers.

Within two weeks of the raid, the California Labor Department demanded business records from sixteen garment makers believed to have had connections with the El Monte factory. California labor commissioner Virginia Bradshaw found that many of the manufacturers who did business with the El Monte factory were themselves engaging in illegal activities, and the California Labor Department fined several of them $35,000 each for failing to register their operations with the state.

In late September, 1999, the California State Assembly passed Assembly Bill 633, a law designed to crack down on clothing sweatshops, businesses employing workers to make clothes under unfair and illegal conditions. Cheunchujit testified before the assembly when it was considering the law.

The workers also sued the companies that hired the El Monte factory to make clothes. In July, 1999, their attorneys agreed with these companies that the workers would be paid $1.2 million for back wages and damages. Under the agreement, the workers would receive $10,000 to $80,000 each, depending on how many years they had been forced to work in the factory. The Manasurangkuns pleaded guilty to charges of smuggling the workers into the United States and keeping them in slavelike conditions. The four family members and three other Thai people who worked with them were sentenced to prison terms.

Carl L. Bankston III

FURTHER READING

Bales, Kevin. *New Slavery: A Reference Handbook.* Santa Barbara, Calif.: ABC-Clio, 2001.

Bush, M. L. *Servitude in Modern Times.* Cambridge, England: Polity Press, 2000.

Miers, Suzanne. *Slavery in the Twentieth Century: The Evolution of a Global Problem.* Lanham, Md.: Rowman & Littlefield, 2003.

SEE ALSO   Asian Pacific American Labor Alliance; *Clotilde* slave ship; Eastern European Jewish immigrants; Garment industry; Southeast Asian immigrants; Triangle Shirtwaist Company fire; Women immigrants.

TIBETAN IMMIGRANTS

IDENTIFICATION: Immigrants to North America from the Tibetan region of China

IMMIGRATION ISSUES: Asian immigrants; Demographics

SIGNIFICANCE: Though nominally Chinese citizens, Tibetans are members of a distinct ethnic group whose homeland was once autonomous from China. A small number of Tibetan refugees live in the United States.

In May, 1951, one year after Chinese troops had occupied Tibet, the governments of Tibet and China agreed that China's government would have control of Tibet and that the Dalai Lama would be the political leader of Tibet while the Panchen Lama would be the spiritual leader. In 1959, after an uprising in Tibet, the Dalai Lama and about 100,000 of his followers left Tibet to live in India. The Panchen Lama remained in China, but in 1964, he was removed from power by the Chinese government. The next year, Tibet was made an autonomous region of China, and, by 1966, the Chinese government had control of Tibetan newspapers, radio, and television. The Chinese refused to accept the Panchen Lama's successor, chosen by the Dalai Lama and the Tibetan priesthood, and substituted their own candidate for the position.

During the 1990's, a small number of the Dalai Lama's followers moved to the United States, and by 1999, Tibetans were living in thirty-four states. These Tibetans brought the situation in their homeland to the attention of Americans in the hope that the United States would use its political influence to get the Chinese to recognize the autonomy of Tibet and the authority of the Dalai Lama and the members of the Lama priesthood.

Throughout the United States, various groups such as the Students for a Free Tibet worked to make Americans aware of Tibetan culture and of its problems, presenting statistics on the numbers of Tibetans believed to have been killed by the Chinese and the number of monasteries that were reputedly destroyed. These Tibetans claimed that China had denied them freedom of religion by not allowing Tibetans to choose their own successor to the Panchen Lama or even to hang pictures of the Dalai Lama. As evidence of human rights violations, they related an incident involving Ngavong Choephel, who, in July, 1995, after going to Tibet as a Fulbright scholar to make a film on Tibetan arts, was arrested by the Chinese, charged with being a U.S. spy, and sentenced to eighteen years in prison. These groups noted that self-determination, a universal right named in the United Nations Declaration of Human Rights, was not available to Tibetans.

In 1997, the American Episcopal Church passed a resolution urging talks between China and the Dalai Lama. July 6, the birthday of the Dalai Lama, was recognized as World Tibet Day with an interfaith call for freedom of worship for Tibetans. Festivals were held across the United States; popular rock groups such as Pearl Jam participated in a concert in Washington, D.C., in support of negotiations for a free Tibet. President Bill Clinton and Vice President Al Gore met with the Dalai Lama, and in 1997, Clinton announced the creation of a post for Tibetan Affairs in the State Department. The Tibetan campaign to raise American awareness had become so successful that many Americans plastered "Free Tibet" stickers on their automobile bumpers in support of the cause.

Two pro-Tibetan movies were released by Hollywood in 1997, *Seven Years in Tibet*, starring Brad Pitt, and *Kundun*, a biography of the Dalai Lama, directed by Martin Scorsese. *Kundun* was released even though the Chinese government threatened economic reprisals against the Disney Company, which was responsible for the film. Both movies heightened Americans' sympathies toward Tibet. During the opening week of *Seven Years in Tibet*, the International Campaign for Tibet handed out 150,000 action kits, explaining how moviegoers could help free Tibet.

Annita Marie Ward

FURTHER READING

Bernstorff, Dagmar, and Hubertus von Welck, eds. *Exile as Challenge: The Tibetan Diaspora.* Rev. Eng. ed. Hyderabad, India: Orient Longman, 2003.

Ng, Franklin, ed. *Asian American Encyclopedia.* 6 vols. New York: Marshall Cavendish, 1995.

Powers, John. *History as Propaganda: Tibetan Exiles Versus the People's Republic of China.* New York: Oxford University Press, 2004.

Pyong Gap Min. *Asian Americans.* Thousand Oaks, Calif.: Sage Publications, 1995.

SEE ALSO Asian American stereotypes; Chinese immigrants; Immigration and Nationality Act of 1952; Twice migrants.

TRIANGLE SHIRTWAIST COMPANY FIRE

THE EVENT: Lethal fire in a garment sweatshop employing mostly immigrant labor
DATE: March 25, 1911
PLACE: New York, New York

IMMIGRATION ISSUE: Labor

SIGNIFICANCE: This tragic accident that killed 146 people, most of them immigrant women, led to tougher laws in New York State to protect women and spurred union organizing among women.

On March 25, 1911, a deadly fire broke out in the building that housed the Triangle Shirtwaist Company, located in the Greenwich Village district of New York City. The entire structure was soon consumed by flames. The firm was a notorious sweatshop where a predominantly female force of immigrant workers turned out cheap clothing in wretched, unsanitary, and unsafe conditions. Such establishments were common in the garment district of New

York at the beginning of the twentieth century, a time when poor women had to take work where they could find it. As the fire spread from the discarded rags where it had started, the trapped workers sought to escape by jumping out of windows to the pavement; they fell ten stories to their deaths. Others died inside from the effects of the smoke. Those who sought to flee found that exit doors did not open or that faulty fire escapes blocked their route. The death toll reached 146, most of them women. Dramatic pictures filled the New York newspapers the next day, depicting the horrors of the scene. The fire became one of the worst fatal accidents in the history of American industrialism.

Protests about the unsafe conditions followed. A rally was organized by the National Women's Trade Union League (NWTUL) and drew eighty thousand marchers. An outraged public became even more incensed when a jury acquitted the building's owners of wrongdoing. The popular outcry against sweatshops accelerated the campaign of the NWTUL and the International Ladies' Garment Workers' Union (ILGWU) to reform the system in New York City that kept many women in economic serfdom to the clothing trade. The ILGWU, led by Rose Schneiderman and other female activists, joined with middle-class reformers in demands for a state investigating commission to probe the causes of the blaze and to recommend laws to prevent future fires in the garment district.

Several days after the Triangle Shirtwaist Company disaster, a procession was held to commemorate the victims of the fire. (Library of Congress)

The New York State Factory Investigating Commission made its report in 1914 and advocated sweeping changes in health and safety regulations. At first, the New York legislature resisted an effort to implement the commission's findings, but leading Democrats, including state senator Robert F. Wagner and future governor Alfred E. Smith, pressed for and secured passage of tougher laws against sweatshops. The Triangle Shirtwaist Company fire became a landmark episode in the effort to improve working conditions for all American women and to safeguard them against the devastating effects of industrial accidents. It represented a turning point in the struggle for decent treatment of women in the workplace during the era of progressive reform from 1900 to 1920 in the United States.

Lewis L. Gould

FURTHER READING

Crute, Sheree. "The Insurance Scandal Behind the Triangle Shirtwaist Fire." *Ms.* 11 (April, 1983): 81-83. Discusses the profits made from the fire by the factory owners. Includes an interview with Pauline Newman, a labor union activist who began working at the Triangle Shirtwaist Company when she was ten years of age.

Ley, Sandra. *Fashion for Everyone: The Story of Ready-to-Wear, 1870's-1970's.* New York: Charles Scribner's Sons, 1975. A history of the women's clothing industry in the United States, discussing designers, fashions of the times, labor struggles, and methods of clothing production and distribution.

Mitelman, Bonnie. "Rose Schneiderman and the Triangle Fire." *American History Illustrated* 16, no. 4 (July, 1981): 38-47. A profusely illustrated account of the fire. Includes the text of a speech given days after the disaster by labor union activist Rose Schneiderman, whose impassioned call for action stirred many to demand reform legislation.

Naden, Corinne. *The Triangle Shirtwaist Fire, March 25, 1911.* New York: Franklin Watts, 1971. A brief, simple summary of the fire, its causes, and its aftermath, with detailed maps of each floor of the Triangle Shirtwaist Company on the day of the fire. Written for young readers, with numerous illustrations.

Stein, Leon. *The Triangle Fire.* 1962. Reprint. New York: Carroll & Graf, 1985. The definitive work on the subject, written on the fiftieth anniversary of the fire. A detailed account drawn from court transcripts, official reports, newspaper articles, and interviews with survivors, which meticulously reconstructs the event through the eyes of the participants.

SEE ALSO Garment industry; Thai garment worker enslavement; Women immigrants.

TWICE MIGRANTS

DEFINITION: People who emigrate to other countries more than once

IMMIGRATION ISSUE: Sociological theories

SIGNIFICANCE: Multiple migration is not a new phenomenon; however, it has become more common among migrant workers from developing nations.

Migration is the physical movement of people within a social system. Sociologists have studied the subject through the examination of emigration and immigration—what pushes people to leave their homeland (emigrate) and what pulls people to enter a new culture and country (immigrate). In the latter part of the twentieth century, more complex approaches to migration have emerged as a result of the growing diasporic population of workers. For example, international demands for labor and the shift of capital across national boundaries have increased the rate of multiple migration.

Scholar Parminder Bhachu examined a group of Asians of Sikh origin who first migrated to East Africa and then to the United Kingdom. In Africa, this group formed settled communities and shared past experiences as Asians of Sikh origin; they also, however, developed a strong East African identity, which was later reproduced in the United Kingdom. Thus, this Asian group created ties in more than one nation or culture through multiple migration. An increasing number of people migrate not just once or twice but even three times to various countries.

Mary Yu Danico

FURTHER READING

Bhachu, Parminder. *Twice Migrants: East African Sikh Settlers in Britain.* New York: Tavistock, 1985.

Reitz, Jeffrey G., ed. *Host Societies and the Reception of Immigrants.* La Jolla, Calif.: Center for Comparative Immigration Studies, University of California, San Diego, 2003.

SEE ALSO Deportation; History of U.S. immigration; *Immigration and Naturalization Service v. Chadha*; Israeli immigrants; Japanese Peruvians; Justice and immigration; Push and pull factors; Sephardic Jews; Sikh immigrants; Tibetan immigrants.

UNDOCUMENTED WORKERS

DEFINITION: Immigrants who enter the United States illegally—without proper visas, passports, or other types of legal documentation, to obtain employment

IMMIGRATION ISSUES: Border control; Economics; Illegal immigration; Latino immigrants; Law enforcement; Mexican immigrants

SIGNIFICANCE: The term undocumented workers commonly applied to Mexican and Central American workers in the United States. Undocumented workers have formed the largest immigrant workforce since World War II.

Historically, undocumented workers were referred to as "wetbacks," a reference to the notion that Mexican immigrants illegally cross the U.S.-Mexico border by swimming the Rio Grande (known on the Mexican side of the border as the Río Bravo), which runs along part of the Texas border. Although some illegal immigrants wade across the river, in reality few, if any, swim across, since the river is seldom deep enough to necessitate swimming. Not only was the term "wetback" an inaccurate descriptor for most individuals who entered the country illegally; it soon came to have derogatory and dis-

Undocumented Mexican farmworkers waiting to be sent back to Mexico at Calexico in 1972, during a period when an estimated 300,000 Mexicans were entering the United States illegally every year in search of employment. (NARA)

criminatory connotations when it was applied to all Mexicans and even to native-born U.S. citizens of Mexican or any other Latin American descent who were living in the United States.

The term "undocumented worker" is less politically charged than "wetback" or "illegal alien" and is a much more accurate and neutral descriptor of the individuals who come to the United States in search of work without legal papers.

Celestino Fernández

FURTHER READING

Ahmed, Syed Refaat. *Forlorn Migrants: An International Legal Regime for Undocumented Migrant Workers.* Dhaka, Bangladesh: University Press, 2000. International perspectives on undocumented workers by an Asian scholar.

Bischoff, Henry. *Immigration Issues.* Westport, Conn.: Greenwood Press, 2002. Collection of balanced discussions about the most important and most controversial issues relating to immigration, including the regulation of undocumented workers.

Foner, Nancy, Rubén G. Rumbaut, and Steven J. Gold, eds. *Immigration Research for a New Century: Multidisciplinary Perspectives.* New York: Russell Sage Foundation, 2000. Collection of papers on immigration from a conference held at Columbia University in June, 1998. Among the many topics covered are government policy and undocumented workers.

Jacobs, Nancy R. *Immigration: Looking for a New Home.* Detroit: Gale Group, 2000. Broad discussion of modern federal government immigration policies that considers all sides of the debates about the rights of illegal aliens.

Ngai, Mae M. *Impossible Subjects: Illegal Aliens and the Making of Modern America.* Princeton, N.J.: Princeton University Press, 2004. Scholarly study of social and legal issues relating to illegal aliens in the United States during the twenty-first century.

Staeger, Rob. *Deported Aliens.* Philadelphia: Mason Crest, 2004. Up-to-date analysis of the treatment of undocumented immigrants in the United States since the 1960's, with particular attention to issues relating to deportation.

Yoshida, Chisato, and Alan D. Woodland. *The Economics of Illegal Immigration.* New York: Palgrave Macmillan, 2005. Analysis of the economic impact of illegal immigration in the United States.

SEE ALSO Florida illegal-immigrant suit; Haitian immigrants; History of U.S. immigration; Illegal aliens; Immigration Reform and Control Act of 1986; Mexican American Legal Defense and Education Fund; Naturalization; *Plyler v. Doe*; Proposition 187; Proposition 227; Refugee fatigue; September 11 terrorist attacks.

UNIVERSAL NEGRO IMPROVEMENT ASSOCIATION

IDENTIFICATION: Early black nationalist organization
DATE: Founded in 1916
PLACE: New York, New York

IMMIGRATION ISSUES: African Americans; Civil rights and liberties

SIGNIFICANCE: Founded by a Jamaican immigrant, the Universal Negro Improvement Association was an organization dedicated to supporting African American racial pride and did much to advance the growth of black nationalism during the 1920's.

In March, 1916, a young black Jamaican, Marcus Mosiah Garvey, arrived in New York City. He had come to the United States in the hope of securing financial help for the Universal Negro Improvement Association (UNIA), which he had founded in Jamaica two years earlier. After delivering his first public speech in Harlem in May, Garvey began a long speaking tour that took him through thirty-eight states. In May, 1917, he returned to Harlem and—with the help of his secretary and future wife, Amy Ashwood—organized the first American chapter of the UNIA. Though hardly noticed at the time, the establishment of this organization was a significant first step in the growth of black nationalism in the United States. Within a few years, the UNIA would claim millions of members and hundreds of branches throughout the United States, the Caribbean region, and Africa, and Garvey would be one of the most famous black people in the world.

THE BEGINNINGS OF THE UNIA   Garvey was born in St. Ann's Bay, Jamaica, in 1887. He claimed to be of pure African descent. His father was a descendant of the maroons, or Jamaican slaves, who successfully revolted against their British masters in 1739. During his early years, Garvey gradually became aware that his color was considered by some in his society to be a badge of inferiority. Jamaica, unlike the United States, placed the mulatto in a higher caste as a buffer against the unlettered black masses. This reality caused a sense of racial isolation and yet pride to grow in the young black man. By his twentieth birthday, Garvey had started a program to change the lives of black Jamaicans. While working as a foreman in a printing shop in 1907, he joined a labor strike as a leader. The strike, quickly broken by the shop owners, caused Garvey to lose faith in reform through labor unions. In 1910, he started publishing a newspaper, *Garvey's Watchman*, and helped form a political organization, the National Club. These efforts, which were not particularly fruitful, gave impetus to Garvey's visit to Central America where he was able to observe the wretched conditions of black people in Costa Rica and Panama.

Garvey's travels led him to London, the center of the British Empire. There the young man met Dusé Mohamed Ali, an Egyptian scholar, who increased the young Jamaican's knowledge and awareness of Africa. During his stay in England, Garvey also became acquainted with the plight of African Americans through reading Booker T. Washington's *Up from Slavery* (1901). Washington's autobiography raised questions in Garvey's mind:

> I asked, where is the black man's Government? Where is his King and his Kingdom? Where is his President, his country and his ambassador, his army, his navy, his men of big affairs? I could not find them, and then I declared, I will help to make them.

Returning to Jamaica in 1914, Garvey created a self-help organization for black people to which he gave the imposing title, the Universal Negro Improvement and Conservation Association and African Communities League. This new organization, renamed the Universal Negro Improvement Association, based its philosophy on the need to unite "all people of Negro or African parentage." The goals of the UNIA were to increase racial pride, to aid black people throughout the world, and "to establish a central nation for the race." Garvey, elected the first president of the UNIA, realized that black people would have to achieve these goals without assistance from white people. This self-help concept, similar to the philosophy (but not the practice) of Booker T. Washington, led Garvey to propose a black trade school in Kingston, Jamaica, similar to Washington's Tuskegee Institute. The idea did not attract wide support, and Garvey was temporarily frustrated.

In 1915, Garvey decided to come to the United States in order to seek aid for his Jamaica-based organization. Although he had corresponded with Washington, the black leader had died before Garvey arrived in the United States in 1916. Garvey went directly to Harlem, which during the early twentieth century was becoming a center of black culture.

The lives of African Americans were rapidly changing in the first two decades of the twentieth century. Metropolitan areas in the North were experiencing mass migrations of African Americans from the South. In New York City, for example, the black population increased from 91,709 in 1910 to 152,467 in 1920. African Americans were attracted by the promise of jobs and by the possibility of escaping the rigid system of segregation in the South.

African Americans found, however, that they could not escape racism simply by moving. Northern whites also believed in the racial inferiority of African Americans and opposed black competitors for their jobs. The new immigrants, like their foreign-born counterparts, were crowded into the northern ghettos without proper housing or the possibility of escape. Racial violence broke out in several northern cities. The North proved not to be a utopia for African Americans.

These harsh realities aided Garvey in establishing the UNIA in New York. The population of Harlem was not attracted to the accommodationist philosophy of Washington or the middle-class goals of the National Association for the Advancement of Colored People. Indeed, urban African Americans were wary of all prophets, even Garvey; but the young Jamaican was able to obtain support from the Jamaican immigrants in Harlem, who felt isolated, and he established a branch of the UNIA there in 1917. At first, the organization encountered difficulties. Local politicians tried to gain control of it, and Garvey had to fight to save its autonomy. The original branch of the UNIA was dissolved, and a charter was obtained from the state of New York which prevented other groups from using the organization's name. By 1918, under Garvey's exciting leadership, the New York chapter of the UNIA boasted 3,500 members. By 1919, Garvey optimistically claimed 2 million members for his organization throughout the world and 200,000 subscribers for his weekly newspaper, *The Negro World*.

Marcus Garvey, the founder of the Universal Negro Improvement Association, was deported from the United States in 1927 and eventually returned to his Jamaican homeland, where he died in relative obscurity. (Library of Congress)

THE BLACK STAR LINE AND THE COLLAPSE OF THE UNIA In an effort to promote the economic welfare of African Americans under the auspices of the UNIA, Garvey established in 1919 two joint stock companies—the Black Star Line, an international commercial shipping company, and the Negro Factories Corporation, which was to "build and operate factories . . . to manufacture every marketable commodity." Stock in these companies was sold only to black investors. The Black Star Line was to establish commerce with Africa and transport willing emigrants "back to Africa." Although both companies were financial failures, they gave many black people a feeling of dignity. As a result of his promotional efforts in behalf of the Black Star Line, the federal government, prodded by rival black leaders, had Garvey indicted for fraudulent use of the mails in 1922. He was tried, found guilty, and sent to prison in 1923. Although his second wife, Amy Jacques-Garvey, worked to hold the UNIA together, it declined rapidly. In 1927, Garvey was released from prison and deported as an undesirable alien. He returned to Jamaica and then went to London and Paris and tried to resurrect the UNIA, but with little success. He died in poverty in London in 1940. Although a bad businessman, Garvey was a master propagandist and popular leader who made a major contribution to race consciousness among African Americans.

John C. Gardner
updated by R. Kent Rasmussen

FURTHER READING

Cronon, E. David. *Black Moses: The Story of Marcus Garvey and the Universal Negro Improvement Association.* Madison: University of Wisconsin Press, 1955. Often reprinted, this biography remains the best introduction to Garvey's life.

Garvey, Marcus. *Philosophy and Opinions of Marcus Garvey.* Edited by Amy Jacques-Garvey, with new introduction by Robert A. Hill. New York: Atheneum, 1992. Classic collection of Garvey's speeches and writings assembled by his wife.

Hill, Robert A., ed. *The Marcus Garvey and Universal Negro Improvement Association Papers.* 10 vols. Berkeley: University of California Press, 1983-2006. The most extensive collection of original documents by and about Garvey and his movement.

Hill, Robert A., and Barbara Bair, eds. *Marcus Garvey: Life and Lessons.* Berkeley: University of California Press, 1987. Collection of Garvey's most didactic writings, including autobiographical material that he wrote in 1930. A long appendix includes biographies of figures important in his life.

Lewis, Rupert, and Maureen Warner-Lewis, eds. *Garvey: Africa, Europe, the Americas.* Kingston, Jamaica: Institute of Social and Economic Research, University of the West Indies, 1986. Collection of original research papers on international aspects of Garveyism.

SEE ALSO African immigrants; Afro-Caribbean immigrants; Jamaican immigrants; Literature; West Indian immigrants.

VIETNAMESE IMMIGRANTS

IDENTIFCATION: Immigrants to North America from the Southeast Asian nation of Vietnam

IMMIGRATION ISSUES: Asian immigrants; Demographics; Families and marriage; Refugees

SIGNIFICANCE: Large numbers of Vietnamese refugees fled to North America after the Vietnam War, disrupting their lives and forcing them to adapt to mainstream American culture.

In order to understand Vietnamese American family customs, it is important to examine briefly the historical background of Vietnamese immigration to North America. Technically, the Vietnamese were not immigrants at all, but refugees. Refugees are people who leave their native land and are afraid to return because of persecution and the threat of death. The Vietnamese sought safety in North America, a direct result of U.S. involvement in the war between North and South Vietnam.

BACKGROUND When the United States ended its military involvement in Vietnam in 1974, it left behind many Vietnamese citizens who had been connected to the United States in some way. During the period immediately preceding the fall of Saigon on April 30, 1975, about 100,000 Vietnamese were evacuated. Many of this "first wave" were people who feared that

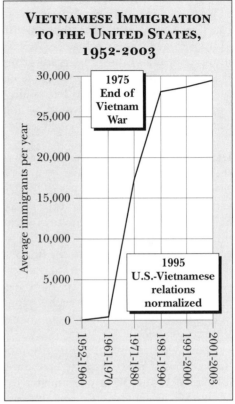

VIETNAMESE IMMIGRATION TO THE UNITED STATES, 1952-2003

1975 End of Vietnam War

1995 U.S.-Vietnamese relations normalized

Average immigrants per year

30,000
25,000
20,000
15,000
10,000
5,000
0

1952-1960
1961-1970
1971-1980
1981-1990
1991-2000
2001-2003

Source: U.S. Census Bureau.

their involvement with the Americans would lead to persecution or death under North Vietnamese communist rule. Most of this first group of refugees were educated urban-dwellers, about half of whom were Roman Catholic.

Within two years after the fall of Saigon, the second wave of Vietnamese began leaving Vietnam. Many left by boat in order to escape ethnic and religious persecution as well as deprivation. Of this group, many were ethnic Chinese. Others were Montagnards who had allied themselves with American intelligence during the Vietnam War. Other minority groups fleeing Vietnam included the Cham and the Khmer, as well as the Hmong from nearby Cambodia. The second wave of refugees was generally less educated than earlier immigrants, and they were often from the countryside.

A final group of refugees were the Amerasians, the children of American military personnel and (usually) Vietnamese women. The Amerasians, called *bui doi* (dust of life), were subjected to harassment and discrimination in Vietnam under communist rule. While many were killed, many other Amerasian children lived homeless in the streets. Eventually, some 68,000 settled in the United States under a special program for Amerasians.

To speak of Vietnamese Americans as a homogeneous group is clearly an error. The refugees brought with them different customs, biases, and prejudices. Moreover, while their refugee status allowed them to enter North America more easily than other immigrant groups, it was also a source of trauma and pain. Many expected the move to be temporary and that they would soon return to Vietnam. Many had left family members behind, thinking that they would return or that they would be able to send for their families after they were settled.

DEMOGRAPHICS   When the Vietnamese refugees came to the United States, they were settled by voluntary agencies who found sponsors for each family to help with the transition to life in the United States. As a result, the Vietnamese people were deliberately scattered throughout the country, the reasoning being that they would assimilate more quickly if they were on their own in the midst of mainstream American culture. What the well-intentioned voluntary agencies failed to consider is the importance of family in Vietnamese culture. Since most refugees had left their extended families behind, they needed to establish communities where other Vietnamese could take the place of the larger family. Therefore, once the refugees were initially settled in the United States, many moved a second time to be nearer to family members and other Vietnamese people.

Many Vietnamese subsequently moved to California. The 1990 census showed that 45 percent of the Vietnamese American population lived in California, where the city of Westminster, in Southern California, has become the center of Vietnamese culture and economics in the United States. By 1998, the population of Vietnamese Americans had reached one million. Between 2000 and 2003, new immigrants from Vietnam entered the United States at a rate of more than 28,000 persons a year.

During the 1990's, Westminster alone had some 1,500 Vietnamese businesses. Texas has about 11 percent of the Vietnamese American population, followed by Washington with 4.8 percent, Virginia with 3.5 percent, and Louisiana with 2.9 percent. Florida and Pennsylvania also have significant Vietnamese American populations.

Most Vietnamese Americans live in established Vietnamese communities in urban areas. They represent 8 percent of the total Asian American population and numbered around 593,213 in 1990. Of these, 31 percent arrived before 1980, 49 percent arrived between 1980 and 1990, and 20 percent are native born. In 1990 most Vietnamese Americans lived in family units headed by a father and a mother, although about 16 percent lived in female-headed households.

CULTURAL IDENTITY   For the Vietnamese, family is the most important foundation of their society. The trauma and disruption caused by war and flight forced the refugees into situations in which their cultural norms shifted. In response to the fact that many Vietnamese were deprived of their families, "adopted" kin groups grew up in Vietnamese communities, and family members moved to be closer to other family members arriving in North America.

When the Vietnamese refugees arrived in North America, they quickly looked for work in order to survive and as a matter of self-respect. Among immigrant groups, Vietnamese Americans have a high employment rate. Nevertheless, many found themselves in jobs of lower socioeconomic status than the ones they left behind in Vietnam. In addition, Vietnamese women often found work more easily than did their husbands, largely because they looked for lower-status jobs. Nevertheless, the Vietnamese American self-perception is that they are hard-working, tenacious survivors; most adapted to their changed circumstances fairly quickly.

RELIGION, HOLIDAYS, AND CEREMONIES   One way that Vietnamese Americans maintain their cultural identity is through the observance of their religions. Many of the early refugees were Roman Catholics, and Vietnamese Americans have demonstrated leadership in the Roman Catholic Church. The majority of Vietnamese are Buddhists, and Buddhism affects the way most Vietnamese Americans view life. For the Buddhist, all life is suffering and the end to suffering comes only with the suppression of desire, which can be accomplished by following the Eightfold Path, which includes right speech, right action, right intention, right views, right livelihood, self-discipline, self-mastery, and contemplation. Confucianism is also a strong tradition among Vietnamese Americans. This philosophy has at its core the attention to social and familial order. A hierarchical system, Confucianism teaches the importance of filial piety.

There are a number of other smaller religious sects among the Vietnamese, including Taoism, Cao Dai, and Hoa Hao, which also exert influence on the Vietnamese American community. In each case, however, the buildings housing the various religious institutions often serve as meeting places and community centers for Vietnamese Americans.

Vietnamese Americans also preserve their cultural identity through the observance of Vietnamese holidays and traditions. By far the most important festival for Vietnamese Americans is Tet Nguyen Den, the Lunar New Year. It usually falls on three days at the end of January and the beginning of February. Tet is a family holiday, and all members of the family express appreciation and respect for one another. During Tet people give each other gifts, wear their best clothing, prepare special foods, and honor their ancestors. For Vietnamese Americans, this holiday is the cultural, social, and spiritual high point of the year.

THE FAMILY AND CULTURAL CHANGE   As family structure is the underpinning of Vietnamese culture, each person thinks of himself in relation to the other members of his nuclear and extended family. The father is traditionally the head of the family, while the mother must ensure harmony within the family unit. Children are valued and considered treasures. They are responsi-

Vietnamese-Chinese grocery store in New York City's Lower Manhattan. (Smithsonian Institution)

ble for taking care of their parents in old age. Much of this structure arrived intact with the refugees. Yet, because so many refugees left members of their families behind and because so many men found that their wives must work in order to help support their families, family structure and identity shifted as Vietnamese Americans grew into the American mainstream culture.

Children and adolescents have been placed under pressure by the tension between traditional and North American culture. Since they often learn English more quickly than their parents, young people find themselves having to translate and solve problems for their parents, leading to a role reversal that would not be typical in Vietnamese society. In addition, young people are subjected to the same pressures that other young North Americans face: drugs, alcohol, and gangs. Although much has been made of gangs among Vietnamese American youths, most scholars think that this has been exaggerated. In spite of the difficulties encountered by young Vietnamese, it seems clear that most young people still value education as do their families. As a group, Vietnamese Americans excel in school and continue their education past high school.

Vietnamese Americans continue to work toward stability within the mainstream culture. Many Vietnamese incorporate American ways without disregarding Vietnamese ways. In spite of the difficulties that Vietnamese Americans have experienced in their new home, the family remains the source of support and stability for their culture.

Diane Andrews Henningfeld

FURTHER READING

Bass, Thomas. *Vietnamerica: The War Comes Home.* New York: Soho Press, 1996. Important account of the lives of Vietnamese refugees who came to the United States after the Vietnam War ended.

Caplan, Nathan, Marcella H. Choy, and John K. Whitmore. *Children of the Boat People: A Study of Educational Success.* Ann Arbor: University of Michigan Press, 1991. Widely cited study about the second generation of Vietnamese Americans.

Cargill, Mary Terrell, and Jade Quang Huynh, eds. *Voices of Vietnamese Boat People: Nineteen Narratives of Escape and Survival.* Jefferson, N.C.: McFarland, 2000. Firsthand narratives of Vietnamese immigrants who fled their homeland at the conclusion of the Vietnam War.

Conley, Ellen Alexander. *The Chosen Shore: Stories of Immigrants.* Berkeley: University of California Press, 2004. Collection of firsthand accounts of modern immigrants from many nations, including two from Vietnam.

Du Phuoc Long, Patrick, with Laura Ricard. *The Dream Shattered: Vietnamese Gangs in America.* Boston: Northeastern University Press, 1996. Account of young Vietnamese Americans involved in crime.

Nguyen, Qui Duc. *Where the Ashes Are: The Odyssey of a Vietnamese Family.* Reading, Mass.: Addison-Wesley, 1994. Study of the experience of one Vietnamese family that immigrated to the United States.

Rumbaut, Rubén G., and Alejandro Portes, eds. *Ethnicities: Children of Immigrants in America.* Berkeley: University of California Press, 2001. Collection of papers on demographic and family issues relating to immigrants; includes a chapter on Vietnamese immigrants.

Rutledge, Paul James. *The Vietnamese Experience in America.* Bloomington: Indiana University Press, 1992. Perhaps the best general study of Vietnamese American resettlement.

Vu, Nguy, ed. *Risking Death to Find Freedom: Thirty Escape Stories by Vietnamese Boat People.* Westminster, Calif.: VAALA & NV Press, 2005. Firsthand accounts of Vietnamese refugees who fled their homeland after the Vietnam War.

Yarborough, Trin. *Surviving Twice: Amerasian Children of the Vietnam War.*

Dulles, Va.: Potomac Books, 2005. Study of the often difficult adjustments that Vietnamese immigrants have had to make in the United States.

Zhou, Min, and Carl L. Bankston III. *Straddling Two Social Worlds: The Experience of Vietnamese Refugee Children in the United States.* New York: ERIC Clearinghouse on Urban Education, Institute for Urban and Minority Education, Teachers College, Columbia University, 2000. Sociological study of Vietnamese immigrant chidren in the United States.

SEE ALSO Amerasians; Asian American stereotypes; Asian American women; Hmong immigrants; *Nguyen v. Immigration and Naturalization Service*; Refugee fatigue; Southeast Asian immigrants; War brides.

VISAS

DEFINITION: Endorsements made on passports of people entering countries other than their own to indicate that the passports have been examined and that their bearers may proceed into the countries

IMMIGRATION ISSUES: Border control; Labor; Law enforcement

SIGNIFICANCE: Visas issued by U.S. consular officers are usually required of noncitizens as a condition of entry into the United States.

United States immigration law provides a double buffer restricting noncitizen admission to the United States. With few exceptions, noncitizens must obtain visas issued by consular officers, State Department officials working in the noncitizens' countries. Without a visa, most noncitizens are summarily excluded from the United States by the U.S. Citizenship and Immigration Services, a branch of the Department of Homeland Security. Even if noncitizens have visas, the INS can still deny them entry based on the INS's assessment of their eligibility to enter the United States. A visa is a travel document allowing noncitizens to travel to the United States and present themselves for admission. Although usually necessary for entry, it does not guarantee entry.

State Department consular officers issue two basic types of visas: immigrant visas, for those persons coming to the United States to become permanent resident aliens, and nonimmigrant visas, for those who plan to come to the United States temporarily for pleasure, work, or study. Most immigrant visas are distributed to persons who have family ties to persons in the United States and to persons who possess job skills needed by U.S. employers. Out of approximately 675,000 immigrant slots each year, 55,000 are issued by a lottery weighted in favor of individuals from countries with low levels of immigration to the United States.

FAMILY IMMIGRANT VISAS   United States immigration policy favors noncitizens with certain family ties to persons in the United States. Children, spouses, and parents of U.S. citizens are called "immediate relatives" and receive the highest priority under the Immigration and Nationality Act of 1952, better known as the McCarran-Walter Act. To be considered a "child" for immigration purposes, a person must be under twenty-one years of age and unmarried. Unless they have undesirable traits, such as a criminal background, immediate relatives can obtain immigrant visas. The United States grants an unlimited number of immediate relative visas every year.

Other noncitizens seeking immigrant visas based on family ties are subject to an annual numerical quota, fluctuating between 226,000 and 480,000 annually. These visas are split into four categories for processing and numerical purposes: unmarried sons and daughters (grown unmarried children) of U.S. citizens; spouses, children, and unmarried sons and daughters of permanent resident aliens; married sons and daughters of U.S. citizens; and siblings of U.S. citizens. Because of the quotas placed on these categories of immigrants, backlogs develop. For example, there is about a ten-year wait to bring a sibling to the United States from Costa Rica.

EMPLOYMENT IMMIGRANT VISAS   United States immigration policy also favors industrious aliens who possess skills desired by or in short supply in the U.S. labor market. This policy conflicts with another policy, which seeks to protect the United States labor market. This tension is resolved in two ways: first, by placing numerical limits (approximately 140,000) on the number of these visas issued annually and, second, by imposing job offer and labor market tests on employment immigration, allowing noncitizens to receive an employment-based immigrant visa only if they have an offer of employment in the United States. Immigrants can meet this second condition only if there are no qualified U.S. workers able and willing to work in the jobs sought by immigrants, if employers pay prevailing wages, and if the hiring of aliens does not otherwise adversely affect the U.S. labor market.

If it is in the national interest, the attorney general's office may waive the job offer and labor market requirements for aliens who are members of professions for which an advanced degree is required or for aliens of exceptional ability. The job offer and labor market requirements are inapplicable to aliens with extraordinary abilities, as documented by sustained national or international acclaim, and to outstanding professors and researchers. The labor market test is also not applicable to certain multinational managers and executives engaged in intracompany transfers.

NONIMMIGRANT BUSINESS AND EMPLOYMENT VISAS   Many people seek to come to the United States temporarily to perform some type of work for an infinite variety of reasons. Some come for business meetings and others to market their goods. Still others come to perform warranty work or to start new businesses. Some noncitizens come to the United States temporarily as

U.S. Visa Categories

Family-based immigrant visas (all immigrant visa categories except the immediate relative category are subject to numerical restrictions)
Visas for immediate relatives: spouses, children, and parents of U.S. citizens

- First preference: unmarried sons and daughters of U.S. citizens

- Second preference: spouses and the unmarried sons and daughters (including children) of permanent resident aliens

- Third preference: married sons and daughters of U.S. citizens

- Fourth preference: brothers and sisters of U.S. citizens

Employment-based immigrant visas

- First preference: "priority workers," which includes aliens of extraordinary ability, outstanding professors and researchers, and certain multinational executives and managers

- Second preference: aliens who are members of the professions holding advanced degrees and aliens of exceptional ability

- Third preference: skilled workers, professionals, and other workers

- Fourth preference: diverse group of "special immigrants," including certain religious ministers, retired U.S. employees, and former U.S. military personnel

- Fifth preference: aliens who come to the United States to create employment opportunities by investing and engaging in a new commercial enterprise

Visas for diversity immigrants (aliens who win a lottery weighted in favor of aliens from countries and regions that have a low immigrant stream to the United States)

Nonimmigrant visas (nonimmigrant visas are designated by the letter of the alphabet preceding the description; for example, an F Visa is a study visa)

- A. Ambassadors, public ministers, other foreign government officials, their spouses, children, and servants

- B. Temporary visitors for business or pleasure

- C. Aliens in transit

- D. Alien crew members

- E. Treaty traders, treaty investors, and their spouses and children

- F. Students attending an academic institution, and their spouses and children

- G. Representatives of foreign governments to international organizations, officers and employees of international organizations, and the spouses, children, and servants of such persons

(continued)

- H. Temporary workers, including registered nurses, workers in "speciality occupations," agricultural workers, other workers, and the spouses, children, and servants of such persons

- I. Foreign media representatives, and their spouses and children

- J. Exchange visitors, including those participating in academic exchanges, and their spouses and children

- K. Fiancés of U.S. citizens

- L. Certain intracompany transferees, and their spouses and children

- M. Vocational students, and their spouses and children

- N. Officials of the North Atlantic Treaty Organization (NATO), and their spouses and children

- O. Aliens of extraordinary ability in certain fields, their spouses and children, and certain assistants

- P. Certain artists and entertainers, and their spouses and children

- Q. Aliens participating in certain international cultural exchanges

- R. Religious workers, and their spouses and children

- S. Certain aliens who, according to the attorney general or the secretary of state, possess critical reliable information concerning criminal or terrorist organizations and the spouses, unmarried sons and daughters (including children), and parents of such persons

part of an intracompany transfer and others to enter the U.S. labor market for a temporary period of time, often in the hope of becoming permanent residents in the future.

U.S. law categorizes the variety of justifications for coming to the United States for business or employment purposes by offering different types of visas for different situations. For example, the B visa allows noncitizens to come to the United States for business meetings. The H visa, for temporary workers, raises the same concerns about protecting the U.S. labor market as employment-based immigrant visas. The tension is resolved in a similar fashion by imposing annual quotas on the number of H visas and by requiring a labor market test. In some situations, these quotas can be circumvented if aliens qualify for an L visa as company managers, executives, or employees who have specialized knowledge and come to the United States in an intracompany transfer. These quotas may also be circumvented if persons qualify for an E visa as the employees of treaty traders or treaty investors—persons who, pursuant to treaties between their countries and the United States, come to the United States to engage in substantial trade with their home countries or to develop and direct enterprises in which they have made a substantial investment.

Several million foreigners come to the United States as tourists every year on B visas. Additionally, several hundred thousand persons come to the United States to study or participate in cultural exchanges. Many of these people travel on F, J, or M visas. Foreign students at U.S. academic institutions have most likely traveled to the United States on F visas, which normally allow students to stay in the United States for the duration of their studies. J visas are used by students in special circumstances, such as when the U.S. government or a foreign government pays for students' education or when students come to the United States to acquire skills that are specifically needed in their native countries. In such instances, J visa holders may not apply for permanent residence in the United States until they have returned to their home countries for two years. M visas are used by vocational students and are more restrictive because of the higher incidence of immigration fraud and abuse among vocational students.

VISA PROCESSING For most immigrant categories, visa processing begins with a visa petition filed with the INS by a petitioning employer or family member in the United States. The alien seeking an immigration benefit is considered the beneficiary of the petition. Once the INS has done its background work, the file is sent to a visa consular officer overseas for processing. Depending on the category, some nonimmigrant visas begin with petitions to the INS and others in the visa consular office.

Even if persons seeking a visa fit into one of the INS's immigrant or nonimmigrant categories, visa consular officers deny them visas if it is determined that the persons are inadmissible. Aliens can be held inadmissible on certain health-related grounds, because of prior abuse of U.S. immigration laws, because of certain criminal activity, on national security grounds, and because they may become an economic burden. Additionally, if visa consular officials doubt that nonimmigrants will leave the United States at the appointed time, such aliens can be denied visas.

To ensure that visa applicants qualify for admission to the United States, a personal interview with the visa consular office is often required. There is no judicial review of a denial of a visa application.

Michael A. Scaperlanda

FURTHER READING

Beshara, Edward C., et al. *Emigrating to the U.S.A.: A Complete Guide to Immigration, Temporary Visas, and Employment.* New York: Hippocrene Books, 1994. Comprehensive reference on practical immigration issues designed for immigrants.

Hing, Bill Ong. *Immigration and the Law: A Dictionary.* Santa Barbara, Calif.: ABC-Clio, 1999. Useful handbook of terms used in immigration law.

Kurzban, Ira. *Kurzban's Immigration Law Sourcebook: A Comprehensive Outline and Reference Tool.* 8th ed. Washington, D.C.: American Immigration Law Foundation, 2002. Comprehensive overview of U.S. immigration law and visas. Frequently updated.

Legomsky, Stephen H. *Immigration and Refugee Law and Policy.* 3d ed. New York: Foundation Press, 2002. Legal textbook on immigration and refugee law.

LeMay, Michael C., and Elliott Robert Barkan, eds. *U.S. Immigration and Naturalization Laws and Issues: A Documentary History.* Westport, Conn.: Greenwood Press, 1999. History of U.S. immigration laws supported by extensive extracts from documents.

Lynch, James P., and Rita J. Simon. *Immigration the World Over: Statutes, Policies, and Practices.* Lanham, Md.: Rowman & Littlefield, 2002. International perspectives on immigration, with particular attention to the immigration policies of the United States, Canada, Australia, Great Britain, France, Germany, and Japan.

SEE ALSO Demographics of immigration; Green cards; Immigration Act of 1990; *Immigration and Naturalization Service v. Chadha*; Immigration "crisis"; Immigration law; September 11 terrorist attacks; Undocumented workers; War brides.

WAR BRIDES

DEFINITION: Foreign spouses of American service personnel serving abroad during wartime

IMMIGRATION ISSUES: Asian immigrants; Chinese immigrants; Citizenship and naturalization; Demographics; European immigrants; Families and marriage; Women

SIGNIFICANCE: Despite war-related problems, foreign brides, fiancés, and children of servicemen entered the United States in large numbers between 1943 and 1975 and raised new isses relating to U.S. immigration policies.

War brides were non-American immigrants who were married or engaged to American servicemen stationed or assigned in a foreign country during, or as a result of World War II, the Korean War, or the Vietnam War. Estimates of the number of war brides from World War II vary widely from 115,000 to one million, depending on whether children and other dependents are included, on the chosen time period, and on who is included as a war bride. World War II war brides came from almost sixty nations. The first and largest single group was British. Others came later from Japan, the Philippines, Korea, Thailand, Vietnam, and China.

WAR BRIDES AND IMMIGRATION LAW   The military at first discouraged overseas marriages and engagements because it was feared that they would not last and that they would divert servicemen's attention from the task at hand: fulfilling their military duties and responsibilities. Evidence from World War I suggested otherwise, as 6,400 of the 8,000 marriages between foreign women and American servicemen were permanent. Eventually, the military had to accept the inevitable. Secretly at first, and then by U.S. congressional legislation, war brides and fiancés were transported to the United States during and immediately following World War II, from 1943 to 1952.

Although war brides were at first subject to the same naturalization process as other immigrants, they were exempt from quota limits. Most who came during World War II were wives and families of husbands who had been wounded or released from enemy prisoner of war camps. After the war, laws were passed with the intent of providing more orderly means for war brides to enter the United States. Asian war brides faced special problems because of the Oriental Exclusion Act of 1924. However, race and gender were removed as a bar to immigration to the United States after passage of the McCarran-Walter Act of 1952. The number of Asian war brides increased dramatically from 1952 to the end of the Vietnam War in 1975.

BRITISH WAR BRIDES   The first and largest contingent of war brides, fiancés, and children, approximately seventy thousand persons from Great Britain,

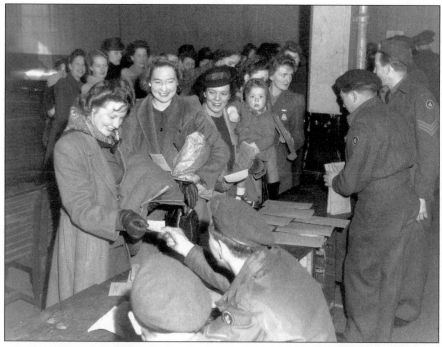

World War II English war brides arrive in North America by ship. (Pier 21 Society)

entered the United States during the mid-1940's. During wartime they were secretly transported on ships carrying wounded servicemen, former prisoners of war, and enemy prisoners. After the war ended, considerable resentment was directed toward the transportation of war brides to the United States, because they occupied space that could have been filled by returning servicemen. At first, most military brides were ineligible for army transport, because only officers and noncommissioned officers in the top three enlisted ranks were allowed to use military transportation. The alternative for those in the lower four ranks was expensive commercial transportation until 1944, when they too became eligible for transportation at the army's expense.

The foreign wives of military husbands did not automatically receive U.S. citizenship. Rather, war brides were eligible for visas only and had to meet the same naturalization requirements as other immigrants. War brides were advantaged by not being included in immigration quotas established for their native countries. Children were admitted without restriction as long as fathers had been over twenty-one years of age when the children were born and had lived in the United States for more than ten years.

Responding to pleas and pressures, Congress approved Public Law 271, the War Brides Act of December 28, 1945, the single most important piece of legislation pertaining to World War II war brides. The visa requirement was waived. If husbands of war brides were serving in the armed forces or had been honorably discharged, their wives and minor children could become U.S. citizens provided they had applied for citizenship during the three-year life of the act and had passed a medical examination. As had been the case earlier, war brides were nonquota immigrants.

One problem remained; Public Law 271 was directed at war brides and children only. It did not apply to alien fiancés or, indeed, fiancés of American servicewomen. Congress responded again by passing Public Law 471, the Fiancés Act, on June 29, 1946. Foreign women and men engaged to present or former members of the armed forces whose status was identical to those included in Public Law 271 could obtain passport visas allowing them to enter the United States as temporary visitors for three months. If their marriages occurred during those three months, Public Law 271 applied. Otherwise, fiancés, with some exceptions, were compelled to leave the United States or be deported. In fact, the U.S. attorney general now possessed the power to require prospective American spouses to provide a bond, usually five hundred dollars, to cover all possible deportation expenses. Public Law 471 was in effect for eighteen months, until December 28, 1947.

Plans were made to provide thirty ships to transport sixty thousand British war brides, grooms, and children by the end of June, 1946. An additional sixteen thousand came from Australia and New Zealand. The first official contingent of 452 war brides (thirty of whom were pregnant), 173 children, and one war groom left England on January 26, 1946. The youngest bride was sixteen years old and had an eighteen-month-old daughter, while the oldest was forty years old and had a seventeen-year-old daughter from a previous marriage. Their American spouses had been wounded, were hospitalized in the United States, or had been deployed there.

Of the seventy thousand World War II British war brides who entered the United States, most came from lower-middle-class backgrounds. Most also had completed their education at age fourteen. Their average age was twenty-four. British war brides were less likely than those from other nations to settle in a single ethnic community, in large part because of the absence of a language barrier. They were well received. Yet, many retained a strong bond with their homeland and were never completely assimilated into American society.

BRIDES FROM GERMANY AND AUSTRIA War brides came in much smaller numbers from other European nations, including from World War II enemy countries Germany and Austria. American servicemen were warned against marrying German women. Order Number 1067, issued in April, 1945, by the Allied Chiefs of Staff, made it clear that Germany was occupied as a defeated nation, not for liberation. Fraternization with German officials and the German population was strongly discouraged. Yet, Order 1067 was seldom enforced and almost universally ignored. German women who kept company with Americans were often referred to as "Ami whores" by other Germans. The term was applied both to German prostitutes and to German women employed by Americans. The tension created by opponents of fraternization was reduced when American military personnel who had participated in liberating the Nazi prisoner of war camps or who had fought against the Germans were sent home and replaced by troops who had not experienced wartime conditions.

Restrictions on fraternization were lifted in Austria in August, 1945, and in Germany the following October. A year later the ban on American servicemen's marrying Austrian and German women was lifted. By the end of December, 1946, 2,500 soldiers had applied to marry German women. Marriages, however, could not take place until American soldiers were within thirty days of completing their overseas tours of duty.

ASIAN WAR BRIDES Initially, all Asians—whether nominal allies, such as the Chinese, or enemies—were subject to prewar immigration laws and quotas. During World War II Congress passed Public Law 199, the Magnuson Act of 1943, which repealed the 1882 Chinese Exclusion Act but set a quota of only 105 Chinese immigrants annually. Eventually, Chinese wives of American citizens were given nonquota status through an act passed on August 9, 1946. Most of the six thousand Chinese war brides married Chinese American soldiers.

The most significant legislation assisting all Asian war brides, the McCarran-Walter Act, was passed by Congress on June 27, 1952. It repealed the Oriental Exclusion Act of 1924 by eliminating both race and gender as a barrier to immigration. From 1947 to 1975 more than 165,000 Asian war brides entered the

United States. Most were Japanese (66,000) and Filipino (52,000), although 28,000 Koreans, 11,000 Thais, and 8,000 Vietnamese were also admitted.

Asian war brides experienced prejudice and discrimination from both native-born Americans and from their fellow Asians, including women who lived in the United States. As one Korean author expressed it, they were "caught in the shadows between the Korean and American communities" and would never be able to become members of Korean American society. Because of the difficulty in learning the English language, Asian war brides relied heavily on their American husbands. Isolation and the depression it provoked was the most common concern expressed by Asian war brides. Living on military bases magnified their loneliness. Yet, most chose to remain in the United States rather than return to their native countries.

John Quinn Imholte

FURTHER READING

Gimbel, John. *The American Occupation of Germany: Politics and the Military.* Stanford, Calif.: Stanford University Press, 1968.

Hibbert, Joyce. *The War Brides.* Toronto, Canada: PMA Books, 1978.

Moore, John Hammond. *Over-Sexed, Over-Paid, and Over Here: Americans in Australia, 1941-45.* St. Lucia, Queensland: University of Queensland Press, 1981.

Shukert, Elfrieda Berthiaume, and Barbara Smith Scibetta. *War Brides of World War II.* Novato, Calif.: Presidio Press, 1988.

Virden, Jenel. *Goodbye Piccadilly: British War Brides in America.* Urbana: University of Illinois Press, 1996.

SEE ALSO Filipino immigrants and family customs; Japanese immigrants; Korean immigrants and family customs; Mail-order brides; Page law; Picture brides; Russian immigrants; War Brides Act; Women immigrants.

WAR BRIDES ACT

THE LAW: Federal law easing restrictions on immigration of war brides
DATE: December 28, 1945

IMMIGRATION ISSUES: Asian immigrants; Citizenship and naturalization; European immigrants; Families and marriage; Laws and treaties; Women

SIGNIFICANCE: The War Brides Act relaxed immigration regulations to allow foreign-born spouses and children of U.S. military personnel to settle in the United States more easily.

Between 1939 and 1946, more than sixteen million U.S. servicemen, primarily single and between eighteen and thirty years of age, were deployed to war theaters in foreign lands. Although the U.S. government discouraged servicemen from marrying at all—believing the single soldier, without distractions, would be of more value to the war effort—one million marriages to foreign nationals occurred during and shortly after the war. Aware of the potential for these liaisons, the U.S. War Department had issued a regulation requiring personnel on duty in any foreign country or possession of the United States to notify their commanding officer of any intention to marry at least two months in advance.

PASSAGE OF THE ACT   Before passage of the act, federal immigration law demanded strict adherence, and the waiting period was waived rarely for war brides, with a possible exception for the pregnancy of the bride-to-be. Usually, permission to marry was granted; however, certain couples, for example U.S.-German, U.S.-Japanese, and those of different races, either encountered longer waiting periods or were denied permission completely.

Many of those couples who had been granted permission and had married were separated for two to three years. In October, 1945, the Married Women's Association picketed for transport to allow their families to reunite. Evidently, the three thousand members' voices were heard; on December 28, 1945, the Seventy-ninth Congress passed an act to expedite the admission to the United States of alien spouses and alien minor children of U.S. citizens who had served in or were honorably discharged from the armed forces during World War II. These spouses had to meet the criteria for admission under the current immigration laws, including thorough medical examinations, and their applications had to be filed within three years of the date of the act.

THE WAR BRIDE SHIPS   Following passage of the War Brides Act, thirty vessels, primarily hospital ships and army troopships, were selected to transport the women, children, and a few men—who were dubbed "male war brides"—to the United States. Even the steamships *Queen Elizabeth* and the *Queen Mary* were recruited for the task, because of their large passenger capacities. Transportation requests were prioritized by the military as follows: dependents of personnel above the fourth enlisted grade, dependents of personnel already placed on orders to the United States, wives of prisoners of war, wives of men wounded in action, and wives of men hospitalized in the United States. At the bottom of the priority pool were fiancés and spouses in interracial marriages.

Before debarking, each spouse (usually a woman) had to present her passport and visa, her sworn affidavit from her husband that he could and would support her upon arrival, two copies of her birth certificate, two copies of any police record she might have, any military discharge papers she might have, and a railroad ticket to her destination from New York. The families who saw them off knew they might never see their children and grandchildren again.

The American Red Cross was officially requested by the War Department to function as a clearinghouse for the brides, and many Red Cross volunteers served as "trainers" for the women in how to become American wives. Since many war brides did not speak English, the Red Cross also offered classes to aid in practical communication skills.

On January 26, 1946, the first war bride ship, the SS *Argentina*, left Southampton, England, with 452 brides, 173 children, and 1 groom on board. Lauded as the "Pilgrim Mothers" voyage or the "Diaper Run," the voyage was highly publicized. Many of the brides, upon arriving in the United States on February 4, were greeted by the U.S. press.

In Germany and Japan, permission to marry had not easily been attained and often was not granted at all. The ban on marriage to Germans was lifted on December 11, 1946, with twenty-five hundred applications submitted by the end of the year; in Japan, the ban lingered much longer.

During the first months of occupation during the war, approximately one-half million U.S. soldiers had been stationed in or near Yokohama. Many young women, fearing for their lives, hid from these "barbarians," but since the U.S. military was often the only source of employment, the women were forced to venture out. The country was in a cultural flux, resulting from economic deprivation, matriarchal predominance and female enfranchisement, and Emperor Hirohito's renouncement of divinity. As the U.S. soldiers and Japanese women worked together, romantic relationships often developed, and because official permission to marry could not be obtained, many such couples were wed in secret in traditional Japanese ceremonies.

Although as many as 100,000 Japanese brides were deserted, others sought immigration to the United States. However, one proviso of the War Brides Act was that émigrés could not be excluded under any other provision of immigration law. The Oriental Exclusion Act of 1924 was still in place, and although Public Law 199 had overridden the act to allow Chinese immigration, the Japanese were still excluded. Many were not allowed admission to the United States until July, 1947, when President Harry S. Truman signed the Soldier Brides Act, a thirty-day reprieve on race inadmissibility.

THE BRIDES IN AMERICA In many cases, life for the war brides in the United States was not what they had expected. Many were treated poorly by isolationists who placed personal blame on all foreigners for U.S. involvement in the war, and many had to tolerate the scorn of former sweethearts who had been jilted because of them. Because of the influx of soldiers returning to the civilian population, available housing and jobs were limited. Often the brides found themselves in the middle of a family-run farm, with some as sharecroppers. Frequently, when adjustment to civilian life was difficult for the former military man, he would rejoin his outfit, leaving the bride behind with his family—strangers who were sometimes hostile to the foreigner in their midst. Many of the marriages made in haste soured just as quickly through homesickness, promises unkept, or abuse. War brides who were unhappy or abused often stayed in their marriages, however, from fear of losing their children or of being deported.

Marriage did not confer automatic citizenship on foreign brides. They were required to pass exams to be naturalized, and many were still incapable of communicating in any but their native tongues. Public assistance was unavailable for these women.

Within one year of the mass exodus from Europe and Asia, one out of three of the war marriages had ended in divorce, and it was predicted that by 1950, the statistics would be two out of three. This prediction proved incorrect, however. Many war brides not only preserved their marriages but also became valuable members of their new communities and contributors to American culture. In April, 1985, several hundred of these women, men, and children journeyed to Long Beach, California, for a reunion, appropriately held aboard the dry-docked *Queen Mary*.

Joyce Duncan

FURTHER READING

Hibbert, Joyce. *The War Brides*. Toronto: PMA Books, 1978. Discussion of the mobilization and acclimation of war brides.

Kubat, Daniel, et al. *The Politics of Migration Policies*. New York: Center for Migration Studies, 1979. Discusses immigration laws and the political control behind them.

LeMay, Michael C., and Elliott Robert Barkan, eds. *U.S. Immigration and Naturalization Laws and Issues: A Documentary History*. Westport, Conn.: Greenwood Press, 1999. History of U.S. immigration laws supported by extensive extracts from documents.

Shanks, Cheryl. *Immigration and the Politics of American Sovereignty, 1890-1990*. Ann Arbor: University of Michigan Press, 2001. Scholarly study of changing federal immigration laws from the late nineteenth through the late twentieth centuries, with particular attention to changing quota systems and exclusionary policies.

Shukert, Elfrieda Berthiaume, and Barbara Smith Scibetta. *War Brides of World War II*. Novato, Calif.: Presidio Press, 1988. Perhaps the definitive work on the subject of war brides; includes many interviews with brides.

SEE ALSO Filipino immigrants and family customs; Immigration Act of 1943; Immigration and Nationality Act of 1952; Japanese immigrants; Korean immigrants and family customs; Mail-order brides; Page law; Picture brides; Russian immigrants; War brides; Women immigrants.

WEST INDIAN IMMIGRANTS

IDENTIFICATION: Immigrants to North America from the West Indian islands of the Caribbean Sea

IMMIGRATION ISSUES: African Americans; Demographics; West Indian immigrants

SIGNIFICANCE: The success of black West Indian Americans has drawn the attention of sociologists and other scholars and created some conflict with other African Americans.

Black West Indian immigrants and their descendants, a small group among the African American population, have achieved considerable economic, educational, and political success in the United States relative to native African Americans. Notable conservatives such as economist Thomas Sowell of Stanford's Hoover Institution and author Dinesh D'Souza contend that this group's relative success in part demonstrates the error in attributing the economic and social plight of some African Americans exclusively to racism. The group's exceptionalism has also been noted by sociologists such as Stephen Steinberg in *The Ethnic Myth: Race, Ethnicity, and Class in America* (1981) and Reynolds Farley and Walter Allen in *The Color Line and the Quality of Life in America* (1989).

The portrayal of exceptionalism is only part of this group's profile. Structural shifts in the U.S. economy mean that segments of this community will face severe sociopsychological adjustments to migration, coupled with constricted assimilation to American society. Pressures against full assimilation are greater for lower-class West Indians. Typically, middle- and upper-class professionals alternate between a more inclusive West Indian American or particularistic African American identity, and the lower/working class chooses a more ethnically focused, West Indian identity.

West Indian Americans are immigrants from the former British West Indian Islands, Belize, and Guyana and their U.S.-born descendants. Most of the West Indian immigrants arrived in the United States during the late nineteenth and early twentieth centuries. In 1924, restrictive immigration legislation effectively halted immigration from the islands. Most of the immigrants settled in the Northeast, creating urban ethnic communities in Miami, Florida; Boston, Massachusetts; Newark, New Jersey; Hartford, Connecticut; and New York City; they settled in Brooklyn and formed ethnic enclaves in East Flatbush, Flatbush, Crown Heights, Canarsie, and Midwood districts.

WEST INDIAN EXCEPTIONALISM   Generally, West Indian immigrants have been perceived as models of achievement for their frugality, emphasis on education, and ownership of homes and small businesses. Economist Sowell ar-

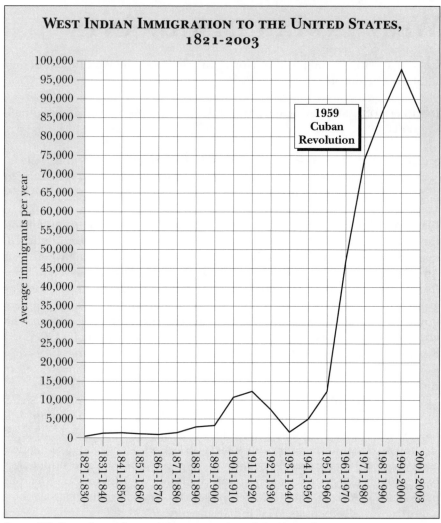

WEST INDIAN IMMIGRATION TO THE UNITED STATES, 1821-2003

Average immigrants per year

1959 Cuban Revolution

Source: U.S. Census Bureau. Data includes immigrants from all Caribbean isles.

gued that the group's successes, including those of famous members such as General Colin Powell, derived from a distinctive cultural capital source and an aggressive migrant ideology, legacies of their native lands. Home ownership and economic entrepreneurship were financed partly by using a cultural source of capital, an association called *susu* (known in West Africa as *esusu*), that first reached the West Indian societies during the era of slavery. A *susu* facilitates savings, small-scale capital formation, and micro lending. These traditional associations have been incorporated into mainstream financial organizations such as credit unions and mortgage and commercial banks as they adapt to serve the needs of West Indian Americans.

Demographer Albert Murphy, in a report for Medgar Evers College's Caribbean Research Center in New York, found that in 1990, 29.1 percent of West Indian Americans had a bachelor's degree or higher degree, compared with the U.S. average of 20.3 percent. In addition, their median household income in 1989 was $28,000, compared with $19,750 for African Americans overall and $31,435 for whites.

POLITICAL AND SOCIAL INCORPORATION Early immigrants such as Pan-Africanists Edward Blyden and Marcus Garvey and poet activist Claude McKay were among the first West Indian Americans to become well-known and well-respected figures. Other famous West Indian Americans include Congresswoman Shirley Chisholm; Franklin Thomas, the head of the Ford Foundation; federal judge Constance Baker Motley; Nobel laureate Derek Walcott; and actor Sidney Poitier. Activist Stokely Carmichael, Deputy U.S. Attorney General Eric Holder, and Earl Graves, businessman and publisher of *Black Enterprise*, have also made impressive efforts on behalf of African Americans.

From the 1930's to the 1960's, West Indian American politicians were elected with the help of the African American vote; many of the West Indians, believing their stay in the United States to be temporary, did not become citizens and were ineligible to vote. During the 1970's, this trend changed, and two congressional districts in New York with heavy concentrations of West Indians became represented by African Americans. However, West Indian Americans, becoming increasingly dissatisfied with African American representation, have been fielding their own candidates in state and local elections in New York, Connecticut, and New Jersey. These efforts have been aided by the fact that since 1993, when legislation less favorable to the immigrant population was passed, West Indian Americans have been acquiring U.S. citizenship in greater numbers. This trend in resurgent ethnic political awareness suggests that West Indian Americans may succeed in electing a member of their group to office.

DIFFERENTIAL ASSIMILATION At the beginning of the twentieth century, West Indian Americans and African Americans held negative stereotypes of each other and rarely interacted socially. During the 1930's, 1940's, and 1950's, the

Born on the island of St. Lucia in 1930, Derek Walcott won the Nobel Prize for Literature in 1992. (Virginia Schendler)

children of some West Indian immigrants downplayed their ethnicity and attempted to integrate into the African American community, but both groups' images of each other changed slowly. Powell, in his autobiography, *My American Journey* (1995), recalls his African American father-in-law's reaction when he proposed marriage to his daughter Alma: "All my life I've tried to stay away from those damn West Indians and now my daughter's going to marry one!"

The late 1960's, with its emphasis on racial solidarity and group identity, eroded much of the conflict between African Americans and West Indian Americans and supplanted it with black nationalist sentiments and identity. At the turn of the twenty-first century, many West Indian Americans were caught in an identity crisis, unsure of whether they should be West Indians with a strong ethnic orientation, African Americans with a focus on their racial identity, or "West Indian Americans" with a more hybrid identity. Class pressures play influential roles in this identity dilemma. Lower- and working-class West Indian Americans have strong affiliations with their ethnicity and its cultural symbols, using the ethnic community as a "structural shield" in their coping repertoire. However, a growing segment of West Indian American professionals regard themselves as West Indian Americans because this identity unites the more desirable choices by eliminating obstacles to their ultimate assimilation as Americans. In addition, this community is not monolithic, and class divisions segment the group as well as influence its responses to racism and other societal challenges.

Aubrey W. Bonnett

FURTHER READING

Bean, Frank D., and Stephanie Bell-Rose, eds. *Immigration and Opportunity: Race, Ethnicity, and Employment in the United States.* New York: Russell Sage Foundation, 1999. Collection of essays on economic and labor issues relating to race and immigration in the United States, with particular attention to the competition for jobs between African Americans and immigrants.

Conley, Ellen Alexander. *The Chosen Shore: Stories of Immigrants.* Berkeley: University of California Press, 2004. Collection of firsthand accounts of modern immigrants from many nations, including the Caribbean island of Barbados.

Heron, Melonie P. *The Occupational Attainment of Caribbean Immigrants in the United States, Canada, and England.* New York: LFB Scholarly Publications, 2001. Useful study of the employment of Afro-Caribbean immigrants.

Parrillo, Vincent. *Strangers to These Shores.* 5th ed. Boston: Allyn & Bacon, 1997. General treatment of race and ethnic relations with sections on both Jamaicans and Rastafarians.

Rumbaut, Rubén G., and Alejandro Portes, eds. *Ethnicities: Children of Immigrants in America.* Berkeley: University of California Press, 2001. Collection of papers on demographic and family issues relating to immigrants that includes chapters on West Indians.

Vickerman, Milton. *Crosscurrents: West Indian Immigrants and Race.* New York: Oxford University Press, 1999. Study of the West Indian immigrant experience that contains interviews with Jamaicans in New York City who tell of contending forces of racism and equal treatment in the United States.

Waters, Mary C. *Black Identities: West Indian Immigrant Dreams and American Realities.* Cambridge, Mass.: Harvard University Press, 1999. Examines the Jamaican immigrant experience in the United States.

Watkins-Owens, Irma. *Blood Relations: Caribbean Immigrants and the Harlem Community, 1900-1930.* Bloomington: Indiana University Press, 1996. Study of West Indians in New York City's predominantly African American community.

Zphir, Flore. *Trends in Ethnic Identification Among Second-Generation Haitian Immigrants in New York City.* Westport, Conn.: Bergin & Garvey, 2001. Close study of Haitian immigrants in New York City.

SEE ALSO Afro-Caribbean immigrants; Cuban immigrants; Dominican immigrants; Haitian boat people; Haitian immigrants; Jamaican immigrants; Latinos.

WHITE ETHNICS

DEFINITION: Immigrants to North America from eastern and southern European nations

IMMIGRATION ISSUES: European immigrants

SIGNIFICANCE: Immigrants from southern and eastern European nations and their descendants are often regarded as "ethnics" because they tend to retain their ethnic identities.

White ethnics, or eastern and southern European Americans, have immigrated from or are the descendants of immigrants from countries such as Italy, Poland, Russia, Czechoslovakia, Hungary, Yugoslavia, and Austria. Southern Europeans began coming to the United States in large numbers between 1800 and 1920. Many of the immigrants were peasants and unskilled laborers. These immigrants settled in the cities and were often employed in entry-level jobs in plants and factories. Many southern Europeans and their descendants remained in this labor sector well into the twentieth century.

Immigrants from southern Europe faced prejudice upon their arrival to the United States. Protestantism was the dominant religion in the United States, and many people feared that the increase in Roman Catholic immigrants from southern Europe would negatively affect the Protestant mores of the country. Immigration from this area was sharply reduced with the passage of the National Origins Act in 1924 but increased again in 1965 when restrictive immigration policy ended with the passage of the Immigration and Nationality Act of 1965.

Many southern European Americans live in New England, the Mid-Atlantic States, and the Midwest. Indicators of status such as educational attainment, occupational level, and income show that southern Europeans as a group have reached parity with the Anglo-Protestant population and generally have surpassed non-European groups. In general, southern European Americans are highly assimilated, and their ethnicity is displayed primarily in symbolic ways.

Amy J. Orr

FURTHER READING

Benmayor, Rina, and Andor Skotnes, eds. *Migration and Identity.* New Brunswick, N.J.: Transaction, 2005.

Burgan, Michael. *Italian Immigrants.* New York: Facts On File, 2005.

Greene, Victor R. *A Singing Ambivalence: American Immigrants Between Old World and New, 1830-1930.* Kent, Ohio: Kent State University Press, 2004.

SEE ALSO Ashkenazic and German Jewish immigrants; Eastern European Jewish immigrants; Ethnic enclaves; European immigrant literature; European immigrants, 1790-1892; European immigrants, 1892-1943; German immigrants; Gypsy immigrants; Irish immigrants; Irish immigrants and discrimination; Jewish immigrants; Nativism; Polish immigrants; Russian immigrants; Soviet Jewish immigrants.

WOMEN IMMIGRANTS

IMMIGRATION ISSUES: Demographics; Families and marriage; Refugees; Women

SIGNIFICANCE: Immigrant women have often had to contend with exploitative work situations and greater-than-aveerage risks of physical abuse, including domestic violence.

Since the seventeenth century, women have journeyed alone or as members of families to North America. Coming first from England, Africa, Ireland, northern and western Europe, in the nineteenth century they immigrated from southern and eastern Europe and from China and Japan. The major source of immigration shifted in the twentieth century from Europe to Latin America and Asia.

Poster issued by the Young Women's Christian Association (YWCA) in 1919 to call attention to the contributions of women immigrants. (Library of Congress)

HISTORY In early colonial America, women arrived from England as wives or were imported as purchased wives. Many came as indentured servants who were bought and sold like slaves; they endured physical and sexual abuse. Some were transported as convicts. Female slaves were brought from Africa. Throughout the eighteenth century, although female immigrants experienced extreme job discrimination, they worked in a variety of trades.

Between 1820 and 1880, many women settled in the rural Midwest, where life on the prairies was lonely and harsh. In urban areas, the most commonly available work for young single women was domestic service, although as the century progressed they began to find employment in factories. Married women often preferred to undertake piecework at home or to take in boarders. Compared to men, there was a high proportion of destitute immigrant women. In towns and cities, women joined the developing union movement and began to speak out against intolerable working conditions. Their first strike was organized in 1825, when the United Tailoresses of New York demanded higher wages. By 1859, of the six million workers in the United

States, half a million were women. They labored as domestic servants (33,000), teachers (55,000), and factory workers (181,000), half of whom were employed in textile mills. Leonora Barry, an Irish immigrant, commented on the largest problem for female workers:

> Through long years of endurance they have acquired, as a sort of second nature, the habit of submission and acceptance without question of any terms offered them.

From 1880 to 1920, arrivals from Europe substantially increased. For women, positions as domestic servants continued to be most easily secured. In 1900, when white-collar jobs became available to women, Irish women worked in Canada and the United States as office workers, shop clerks, or teachers. Chinese and Japanese women immigrated to Hawaii, the continental United States, and Canada. As the number of Asian immigrants on the Pacific Coast increased, an exclusionary movement developed. The 1882 Chinese Exclusion Act abruptly curtailed Chinese immigration; it would not be repealed until 1943. The 1907 Gentlemen's Agreement strictly limited Japanese immigration. It did not exclude family members of residents, however, and therefore many Japanese women immigrated to the United States as "picture brides." In 1917, the ban on Chinese immigrants was extended to all Asian countries.

Japanese women arriving at the Angel Island immigrant reception center in San Francisco Bay during the 1920's. Under the federal Cable Act of 1922, female immigrants could no longer automatically assume the U.S. citizenship of their American husbands. (Smithsonian Institution)

The Early Twentieth Century In the twentieth century, many female immigrants continued to live under grim circumstances. Entering the labor force at an unprecedented rate, they faced discrimination and grueling conditions. Urban domestic service was managed by a network of unregulated and exploitative city agencies. Rents were frequently inflated. The Chicago Immigrant Protective League was founded in 1907 to help foreign-born arrivals find work, housing, and education. In New York City, new immigrants found work in sweatshops, in which conditions ranged from unhealthy to dangerous. In the winter of 1909, some women organized and voted to strike. As a result, membership increased in the International Ladies' Garment Workers' Unions. Demands were won in more than three hundred shops, and some women succeeded in becoming union officials. Yet, improved factory conditions were not sufficient to prevent a number of fires, including one in 1911 at the Triangle Shirtwaist Company that killed 146 people, mostly women. That same year, social scientist Francis Kellor described immigrants as "the poorest protected of all humanity in this country . . . even worse than children."

Immigration during the first decade of the twentieth century exceeded by thirty-five million the total of any previous decade. Nativistic sentiment prompted Congress to enact new restrictions on immigration, including a literacy test (1917), a quota system (1921, 1924, and 1927), and the extension of deportation criteria. The Great Depression provoked further exclusion, so that total immigration for the decade of the 1930's was lower than at any previous point since the 1820's.

Post-World War II During World War II (1939-1945), issei (first-generation Japanese immigrants) were interned with their families in camps by the U.S. government. Following the war, the War Brides Act (1945) allowed Chinese, Japanese, and European women to enter the United States as wives of servicemen. Similarly, during the 1960's and 1970's, such marriages were common throughout Southeast Asia. In 1962, the Migration and Refugee Assistance Act was passed to help Cubans resettle in the United States. By 1965, the major source of immigration had shifted from Europe to Latin America and Asia. The Immigration Act of 1965, which amended the Immigration and Naturalization Act of 1952 abandoned national origins quotas and introduced preference categories.

After 1976, no country could send more than 20,000 people in any one year to the United States; the rule resulted in a higher proportion of blue-collar immigration. The 1980 Refugee Act was introduced to deal with the refugees from Indochina who were admitted following the end of hostilities in Vietnam in 1975. During the 1970's, a "mail-order bride" industry developed that enabled women from the Philippines, Thailand, and eastern Europe to immigrate to the United States.

In 1991, procedural guidelines for immigration screening were developed by the United Nations High Commission for Refugees. Canada developed gender-sensitive rules to make it easier for women to pass through the screening process. In 1992, in order to manage the immigration of refugees more strictly, Canada introduced new restrictive laws.

During the 1990's, women were as likely as men to immigrate to the United States. Developing nations, such as Mexico and the Philippines, became the primary source of immigration. In 1993, Mexico provided the largest number of immigrants, including numerous undocumented women. As more American women sought employment out of the home, Central American women, migrating in order to gain economic and social security, filled the need for domestic help in cities. In 1993, *The Chicago Review* addressed the exploitation of immigrant women: "To earn their living they perform the most varied jobs, many of them menial and sub-human."

Concern surfaced regarding immigrant beneficiaries of two welfare programs in the United States: Aid to Families with Dependent Children (AFDC) and Supplemental Security Income (SSI). In 1993, 6.0 percent of the immigrant population were on public assistance, compared with 3.4 percent of all citizens. Twenty-nine percent of all legal immigrants were living below the poverty line. Since 70 percent of all Americans living below the poverty line were female, it is probable that a high percentage of them were immigrant women.

When women depart from their own cultures, they may lose their customary support systems. They have often left patriarchal and hierarchical traditions. In the United States, they enter a more egalitarian world with a more open sexuality. Gender and family roles can be thrown into disequilibrium. Domestic violence against immigrant women has increased, and there has been a higher incidence of depression and substance abuse among these women. Often eager to take advantage of opportunities, immigrant women are more willing than men to accept any job that is offered, even working in garment sweatshops. Women from different immigrant groups face many of the same issues, but how they cope with these issues varies from one culture to another.

Susan E. Hamilton

FURTHER READING

Afzal-Khan, Fawzia, ed. *Shattering the Stereotypes: Muslim Women Speak Out.* New York: Olive Branch Press, 2005.

Agosin, Marjorie. *Uncertain Travelers: Conversations with Jewish Women Immigrants to America.* Edited by Mary G. Berg. Hanover, N.H.: University Press of New England, 1999.

Neidle, Cecyle S. *America's Immigrant Women.* Boston: Twayne, 1975.

Peffer, George Anthony. *If They Don't Bring Their Women Here: Chinese Female Immigration Before Exclusion.* Urbana: University of Illinois Press, 1999.

Strum, Philippa, and Danielle Tarantolo, eds. *Women Immigrants in the United States: Proceedings of a Conference Sponsored by the Woodrow Wilson International*

Center for Scholars and the Migration Policy Institute, September 9, 2002. Washington, D.C.: Woodrow Wilson International Center for Scholars, 2003.

SEE ALSO Amerasians; Asian American women; Cable Act; Garment industry; Hull-House; Indentured servitude; Mail-order brides; Page law; Picture brides; Settlement house movement; Thai garment worker enslavement; Triangle Shirtwaist Company fire; War brides.

WONG KIM ARK CASE

THE CASE: U.S. Supreme Court decision on legal status of children of immigrants who are born in the United States
DATE: March 28, 1898

IMMIGRATION ISSUES: Asian immigrants; Chinese immigrants; Citizenship and naturalization; Court cases

SIGNIFICANCE: In this ruling the Supreme Court held that children born in the United States, even to temporary sojourners, are subject to U.S. jurisdiction, regardless of their race or nationality.

After the Civil War, the Constitution of the United States was amended to deal with the end of slavery and the legal status of the freed slaves. Under existing law, notably the 1857 Dred Scott case (*Dred Scott v. Sandford*), even free African Americans could not become citizens. The Thirteenth Amendment ended slavery. The Fourteenth Amendment, which was drafted to confer citizenship on the newly freed slaves and to protect their rights from infringement by state governments, begins:

> All persons born or naturalized in the United States and subject to the jurisdiction thereof, are citizens of the United States and of the State wherein they reside.

The Fourteenth Amendment ended neither racial prejudice nor various racially based legal discriminations. In 1882, 1884, and 1894, Congress passed a series of laws known as the Chinese Exclusion Acts. These statutes were designed to keep persons of Chinese ancestry out of the United States. They were particularly aimed at the importation of Chinese laborers and at the "coolie" system—a form of indentured labor. The acceptance of low wages by imported Chinese immigrants angered many Americans.

Wong Kim Ark was born in San Francisco in 1873. His parents were Chinese subjects permanently domiciled in the United States. In modern terminology, they would have been called "resident aliens." They had been in business in San Francisco and were neither employees nor diplomatic agents of the government of China. In 1890 they returned to China after many years in the United States. Wong Kim Ark also went to China in 1890, but he returned to the United States the same year and was readmitted to the country on the grounds that he was a U.S. citizen. In 1894 he again went to China for a temporary visit but was denied readmission to the United States on his return in August, 1895.

The government's position was that under the Chinese Exclusion Acts, a Chinese person born to alien parents who had not renounced his previous nationality was not "born or naturalized in the United States" within the meaning of the citizenship clause of the Fourteenth Amendment. If the government's position was correct, Wong Kim Ark was not a citizen of the United States and was not entitled to readmission to the country. Wong brought a *habeas corpus* action against the government in the U.S. District Court for the Northern District of California. That court's judgment in favor of Wong was appealed to the U.S. Supreme Court by the government.

Justice Horace Gray wrote the Supreme Court's opinion for a 6-2 majority. Gray's argument begins with the assumption that the citizenship clause of the Fourteenth Amendment has to be read in the context of preexisting law. The Court's opinion begins with a long review of citizenship practices and legal customs. The U.S. tradition had been to distinguish between "natural-born" and naturalized citizens. This distinction came from English common law. In England, for hundreds of years prior to the American Revolution, all persons born within the king's realms except the children of diplomats and alien enemies were said to have been born under the king's protection and were natural-born subjects. This rule was applied or extended equally to the children of alien parents. Moreover, the same rule was in force in all the English colonies in North America prior to the revolution, and was continued (except with regard to slaves) under the jurisdiction of the United States when it became independent. The first American law concerning naturalization was passed in the First Congress. It, and its successor acts, passed in 1802, assumed the citizenship of all free persons born within the borders of the United States. It was not until the passage of the Chinese Exclusion Acts that any U.S. law had sought to alter the rule regarding natural-born citizens.

On the European continent, however, the law of citizenship was different. Most other European countries had adopted the citizenship rules of ancient Roman law. Under the Roman civil law, a child takes the nationality of his or her parents. Indeed, when *United States v. Wong Kim Ark* reached the Supreme Court, the government argued that the European practice had become the true rule of international law as it was recognized by the great majority of the countries of the world.

This was the historical and legal context for the Fourteenth Amendment's language "All persons born or naturalized in the United States. . . ." According to Justice Gray, the purpose of the Fourteenth Amendment was to extend the rule providing citizenship for natural-born persons to the freed slaves and their children. The amendment did not establish a congressional power to alter the constitutional grant of citizenship. Gray's opinion reviews many of the Court's prior opinions upholding the principle. The Chinese Exclusion Acts, passed after the passage of the Fourteenth Amendment, could not affect the amendment's meaning, according to the majority, and therefore did not affect the established rule of natural-born citizenship.

The grant of constitutional power to Congress to "establish a uniform rule of naturalization" did not validate the Chinese Exclusion Acts. Wong, as a natural-born citizen, had no need of being naturalized. The Court held that "Every person born in the United States and subject to the jurisdiction thereof, becomes at once a citizen of the United States, and needs no naturalization." Moreover, the majority held that Congress' power of naturalization is "a power to confer citizenship, not to take it away." In other words, Congress had the power to establish uniform rules for naturalization but could not alter the plain-language and common-law meaning of the Fourteenth Amendment's citizenship clause.

The dissenting justices saw the case differently. Chief Justice Melville Fuller wrote an extensive dissent in which Justice John Marshall Harlan joined. In their view, the common-law rule sprang from the feudal relationship between the British crown and children born within the realm. American law was not bound to follow the common-law rule because there were differences between "citizens" and "subjects." In a republic such as the United States, citizenship was a status created by and conferred by the civil law. Because nothing in U.S. law had explicitly endorsed the common-law principle of citizenship, the Fourteenth Amendment did not have to be read so as to include it. Fuller argued that Congress is free to pass statutes that define and interpret the citizenship clause of the Fourteenth Amendment. In the dissenters' view, then, the Chinese Exclusion Acts could constitutionally limit the reach of the phrase "born or naturalized in the United States and subject to the jurisdiction thereof." Under this interpretation, Wong Kim Ark would not have been a citizen and his exclusion would have been constitutional. The Court's decision in this case was important because it stripped the government of the power to deny the citizenship of persons born in the United States of alien parents.

Robert Jacobs

FURTHER READING

Chan, Sucheng, ed. *Entry Denied: Exclusion and the Chinese Community in America, 1882-1943.* Philadelphia: Temple University Press, 1991. Good discussion of the effects and technical aspects of the Chinese Exclusion Acts.

Lee, Erika. *At America's Gates: Chinese Immigration During the Exclusion Era, 1882-1943.* Chapel Hill: University of North Carolina Press, 2003. Study of immigration from China to the United States from the time of the Chinese

Exclusion Act to the loosening of American immigration laws during the 1960's, with an afterward on U.S. immigration policies after the terrorist attacks of September 11, 2001.

LeMay, Michael C., and Elliott Robert Barkan, eds. *U.S. Immigration and Naturalization Laws and Issues: A Documentary History.* Westport, Conn.: Greenwood Press, 1999. History of U.S. immigration laws supported by extensive extracts from documents.

McKenzie, Roderick Duncan. *Oriental Exclusion: The Effect of American Immigration Laws, Regulations, and Judicial Decisions upon the Chinese and Japanese on the American Pacific Coast, 1885-1940.* New York: J. S. Ozer, 1971. Discusses the human aspect of the Chinese exclusion laws.

SEE ALSO Asian American stereotypes; Burlingame Treaty; Chinatowns; Chinese American Citizens Alliance; Chinese Exclusion Act; Chinese exclusion cases; Chinese immigrants; Chinese immigrants and California's gold rush; Chinese immigrants and family customs; Chinese Six Companies; Coolies; Immigration Act of 1943; Migration; Page law; "Yellow peril" campaign.

XENOPHOBIA

DEFINITION: Irrational or exaggerated fear of foreigners

IMMIGRATION ISSUES: Discrimination; Nativism and racism; Religion

SIGNIFICANCE: Xenophobia and nativism gave birth to the eugenics movement and influenced theories about which human characteristics are desirable or undesirable, and these unscientific theories have been cited as justifications for restricting immigration from some parts of the world.

Members of premodern (traditional) societies often exhibit distrust and fear of any persons not immediately known to them. Social scientists call this unreasoning and seemingly instinctual fear of strangers "xenophobia." Xenophobia manifests itself in modern societies among members of subcultures, religious sects, ethnic groups, and political movements. Because people of similar beliefs and cultural backgrounds often tend to associate largely with one another, they develop little understanding of people with different beliefs and cultural backgrounds. As a result, in a pluralistic society such as the United States, xenophobia develops between Jews and Christians, between African Americans and European Americans, and between the members of many other groups that have limited interaction with people with backgrounds different from theirs.

Often xenophobia leads directly to ethnocentrism, a conviction that one's own group and its culture are superior to all other groups and their cultures. Xenophobia and ethnocentrism form essential elements of "nativism." Sociologists include nativist movements as part of a larger category called "revitalization movements." Revitalization movements usually occur within societies or groups that have suffered stress and whose cultures have suffered disorganization. Such movements aim to better the lives of their members, often at the expense of the members of other groups. Modern examples include the African American separatist movement in the United States, the Nazi movement in Germany during the period between the world wars, the Branch Davidian religious sect of the late twentieth century, the Indian Ghost Dance movement in the western United States during the last quarter of the nineteenth century, and many others. Several nativist movements, fueled by xenophobia, have actively advocated the use of eugenics to revitalize their own culture by eliminating foreign traits from their memberships.

EUGENICS Eugenics is a branch of science that deals with the improvement of the hereditary qualities of human beings through controlled or selective breeding. Eugenicists argue that many undesirable human characteristics (for example, inherited diseases such as hemophilia and Down syndrome) can be eliminated through careful genetic screening of couples planning to marry. Moderate eugenicists advocate the creation of a central data bank of genetic records for entire populations. A person contemplating marriage would be able to investigate the genetic endowment of his or her chosen partner to ascertain whether that person had a genetic weakness.

More radical eugenicists argue that governments should take a direct hand in racial improvement by passing laws forbidding genetically flawed individuals from reproducing. Others hold that genetically flawed individuals should be medically sterilized. Eugenicists justify their positions on economic and scientific grounds: They maintain that the human race cannot spare scarce resources to tend to those born with genetic handicaps and that people must somehow compensate for the retrogressive evolutionary effects of modern technology.

According to many eugenicists, the cost of keeping genetic defectives alive through the use of modern medical technology will eventually bankrupt world society. These eugenicists also believe that if genetically unsound men and women are allowed to breed uncontrollably, all of humanity will eventually inherit their debilitating characteristics. Before the rise of modern industrial society and the development of medical science, genetically defective individuals rarely lived long enough to reproduce, which controlled their negative influences on the human gene pool. Today, society not only expends increasingly scarce medical care on these people but also allows them to perpetuate and to spread their genes. The only way to reverse this retrogressive evolution, say the eugenicists, is to control or prevent the reproduction of that part of the world's population that carries dysfunctional genes.

The debate concerning eugenics has taken on a greater urgency with the recent strides that have been made in genetic engineering, particularly cloning. This new technology may make possible not only the medical elimination of genetic defects but also the "engineering" of desirable characteristics. It is apparently possible that genetic engineers may in a few decades be able to increase the intelligence of future generations (or decrease it). They may also be able to ensure that progeny will be tall (or short) or fair complected (or dark), to determine their hair color, and even to determine their sex. For some people, these possibilities presage a brilliant future. For others, they conjure up frightening images of an Orwellian nightmare. In either case, ethical questions are profound and complex.

CONSEQUENCES   The instances in which governments or societies have implemented eugenics principles have not inspired confidence that eugenics goals will ever be achieved. They have not only failed to eliminate undesirable characteristics in the populations on which they were tested but also, in virtually every instance, have resulted in abuses that are indefensible in any moral court. Those who have controlled eugenics programs have been influenced in the passage and implementation of eugenic laws by xenophobia, nativism, and outright racism, rather than by sound scientific principles.

The leading spokesperson for the eugenics movement in the United States for many years was Charles B. Davenport. Davenport taught zoology and biology at Harvard University and the University of Chicago during the late nineteenth and early twentieth centuries. Like many scientists of his era, Davenport assumed that each "race" had its own characteristics. Davenport led a grassroots nativist movement in the United States that eventually succeeded in passing eugenics laws at both the national and state levels. The Immigration Act passed by large majorities in both houses of the U.S. Congress in 1924 governed who could immigrate to the United States from abroad. Its language made immigration from northern Europe relatively easy, while residents of Africa and Asia found themselves virtually excluded. As several of its supporters (including future president Calvin Coolidge) acknowledged, the Immigration Act was designed to prevent the decline of the "Nordic" race by limiting the influx of members of "inferior" races.

Scientists in Germany, especially anthropologists and psychiatrists, began advocating eugenics legislation before the beginning of the twentieth century. Eugenics seemed to offer scientific validation for the racial theories of Adolf Hitler and other Nazi leaders (theories based not on scientific evidence but on xenophobia and nativism).

Shortly after the outbreak of World War II, German doctors and directors of medical institutions—apparently authorized by Hitler—began the so-called euthanasia program. In mental institutions, hospitals, and institutions for the chronically ill, doctors began to kill (by neglect, by lethal injection, and by poisonous gas) those persons judged to be "useless eaters." Although it was supposedly terminated after 1941, the program resulted in the deaths

German dictator Adolf Hitler (holding hat) and Italian dictator Benito Mussolini inspecting troops during Hitler's visit to Italy. Hitler and Mussolini both came to power on the strength of their fascist principles, which were strongly xenophobic. (Library of Congress)

of many thousands of people. Some of the personnel involved in the euthanasia program formed the nucleus of the units that carried out the legalized murder of enormous numbers of people in Nazi concentration camps in Poland from 1942 to 1945. Most of the victims were members of races deemed "inferior" by Nazi ideologists: Jews, Gypsies, and Slavs. It is little wonder that many people are fearful of the policies advocated by contemporary eugenicists.

Beginning during the 1930's, the affinity between Nazi racial theories and eugenics caused most biological and medical scientists around the world to renounce eugenics policies and experiments. The information about the concentration camps that became known at the many war crimes trials held after 1945 seemed to have dealt a death blow to eugenicist dreams of a perfected human race. By the mid-1950's, eugenics societies around the world were seemingly bereft of members and influence. Nevertheless, an increasing number of physicians began to recognize the many possible benefits of continued genetic research.

By the 1970's, genetic researchers had shown conclusively that some ethnic and racial groups were especially susceptible to certain genetic disorders. African Americans are particularly prone to the single-gene disorder called sickle-cell anemia, Ashkenazic Jews to Tay-Sachs disease, and Americans whose ancestors came from the Mediterranean area to Cooley's anemia. The new eugenics/genetics societies in the United States led a movement that resulted in the National Genetic Diseases Act of 1976, which funded research into the detection and treatment of genetic disorders. A number of states extended their postnatal screening programs to include many single-gene disorders. Doctors developed a medical procedure known as amniocentesis, which allowed them to identify genetic and chromosomal disorders during the early stages of pregnancy. If an unborn fetus was identified as genetically flawed, parents could elect abortion.

During the 1970's, eugenicists also turned their attention to the population explosion. They found increasing cause for alarm because most of the human population increase was occurring in the Third World (Africa, Asia, and Latin America) and among the bottom socioeconomic strata of industrialized nations. Fearing for the quality of the human gene pool, many eugenics groups began to advocate and finance "family planning" programs in the Third World and among domestic socially disadvantaged populations. These new programs clearly indicate that the nativism and xenophobia that influenced earlier generations of eugenicists are still operative.

Paul Madden

FURTHER READING

Curran, Thomas J. *Xenophobia and Immigration, 1820-1930*. Boston: Twayne, 1975. Traces the origins of anti-immigrant movements in America, relating the xenophobic tradition to the exclusionist laws and practices of the inclusive period.

Davenport, Charles Benedict. *Heredity in Relation to Eugenics*. New York: Holt, 1911. Despite its age, this study is still valuable in understanding the arguments of early eugenicists.

Gabaccia, Donna R. *Immigration and American Diversity: A Social and Cultural History*. Malden, Mass.: Blackwell, 2002. Survey of American immigration history from the mid-eighteenth century to the early twenty-first century. Provides an emphasis on cultural and social trends, with attention to ethnic conflicts, nativism, and racialist theories.

Graham, Loren R. *Between Science and Values*. New York: Columbia University Press, 1981. Thoughtful and provocative exploration of the moral and ethical issues raised by genetic engineering; Graham is critical of the old eugenics and of the xenophobia and ethnocentrism upon which it was based.

Higham, John. *Strangers in the Land: Patterns of American Nativism, 1860-1925*. New York: Atheneum, 1963. Study showing how nativism was given a measure of scientific legitimacy by the eugenics movement.

Kevles, Daniel J. *In the Name of Eugenics: Genetics and the Uses of Human Heredity*. New York: Alfred A. Knopf, 1985. Study clearly demonstrating the influence of nativism, xenophobia, and outright racism on the leading eugenicists.

Muller-Hill, Benno. *Murderous Science: Elimination by Scientific Selection of Jews, Gypsies, and Others—Germany, 1933-1945*. Translated by George R. Fraser.

Oxford, England: Oxford University Press, 1988. Establishes the relationship between the eugenics movement in Germany and both the euthanasia program and the mass murder in concentration camps.

SEE ALSO   Alien and Sedition Acts; Assimilation theories; Cuban refugee policy; Cultural pluralism; English-only and official English movements; History of U.S. immigration; Immigration Act of 1921; Japanese segregation in California schools; Mongrelization; Nativism; Palmer raids; Sacco and Vanzetti trial.

"YELLOW PERIL" CAMPAIGN

THE EVENT: Anti-Asian immigration nativist campaign
DATE: 1890's-early twentieth century
PLACE: West Coast

IMMIGRATION ISSUES: Asian immigrants; Chinese immigrants; Discrimination; Japanese immigrants; Nativism and racism

SIGNIFICANCE: The *San Francisco Bulletin*'s "yellow peril" campaign against Japanese immigrants strengthened anti-Asian feeling in the United States and strained relations between the U.S. and Japanese governments.

In 1890, only about two thousand Japanese people were living in North America. They worked mainly as laborers and farmhands in California and the Pacific Northwest. Despite their minuscule numbers, the use of Japanese to break a labor strike in the coal mines in British Columbia began what was to become a widespread anti-Japanese campaign.

Typical of the political rhetoric that was to become prevalent was a campaign slogan used in 1887 by Dr. O'Donnell of San Francisco: "Japs must go." Although the slogan had little effect on O'Donnell's failed political campaign, it was a sign of things to come.

In 1889, the editor of the *San Francisco Bulletin* began a series of editorials attacking Japanese immigrants and making a case that they were dangerous to white American workers and to American culture. On May 4, 1892, he wrote:

> It is now some three years ago that the *Bulletin* first called attention to the influx of Japanese into this state, and stated that in time their immigration threatened to rival that of the Chinese, with dire disaster to laboring interests in California.

The *San Francisco Bulletin*'s yellow peril campaign helped strengthen the growing anti-Japanese fervor in California. The campaign was not only against

This turn-of-the-twentieth-century toy gun bears the message, "Chinese must go." When its trigger is pulled, the figure in the hat kicks the Chinese figure. (Asian American Studies Library, University of California at Berkeley)

Japanese laborers, who they claimed threatened "real" American workers, but also against their perceived threat to American culture. Met with hostility, prejudice, and discrimination, Japanese in many urban areas settled into ethnic enclaves known as Little Tokyos, where they could feel safe and comfortable among fellow compatriots and secure employment.

EFFECTS On June 14, 1893, the San Francisco Board of Education passed a resolution requiring all Japanese students to attend the already segregated Chinese school instead of the regular public schools. Because of Japanese protests, the resolution was rescinded; however, it marked the beginning of legal discrimination against the Japanese in California. In 1894, a treaty between the United States and Japan allowed citizens open immigration, but both governments were given powers to limit excessive immigration. In 1900, because of American protests, Japan began a voluntary program to limit Japanese emigration to the United States.

The Alaska gold rush of 1897-1899 attracted a great number of white laborers, and when the Northern Pacific and Great Northern Railroads worked to build a connecting line from Tacoma and Seattle to the East, extra laborers were needed. The companies turned to Japanese immigrants as workers.

Some of these laborers came from Japan and Hawaii. The rapid influx of Japanese laborers created further anti-Asian sentiments and hostility. With the 1882 Chinese Exclusion Act up for renewal in 1902, the anti-Japanese sentiment occurred in the overall context of a growing anti-Asian movement, especially among labor unions and various political groups.

In April of 1900, the San Francisco Building Trades Council passed a resolution to support the renewal of the Chinese Exclusion Act and to add the Japanese to this act to "secure this Coast against any further Japanese immigration, and thus forever settle the mooted Mongolian labor problem." The county Republican Party lobbied extensively to get the national Republican Party to adopt a Japanese exclusion plank in their national platform. San Francisco mayor James Phelan and California governor Henry Gage joined the calls for Japanese to be included in the renewal of the Exclusion Act. However, when the exclusion law was extended in 1902, Japanese people were not included.

After the 1905 defeat of Russia by Japan in the Russo-Japanese War, a growing fear of Japanese power led to further agitation and political tactics to limit Japanese immigration and influence in America. Whereas Chinese people were hated and despised by various politicians, labor leaders, and some regular citizens, Japanese people were feared. In 1905, the *San Francisco Chronicle* launched another anti-Japanese campaign, emphasizing the dangers of future immigration. Later, the San Francisco Labor Council, at the urging of A. E. Ross and with the support of San Francisco mayor Eugene Schmitz, launched boycotts against Japanese merchants and white merchants who employed Japanese workers. Later that year, sixty-seven labor organizations formed the Asiatic Exclusion League (originally called the Japanese and Korean Exclusion League), and the American Federation of Labor passed a resolution that the provisions of the Chinese Exclusion Act be extended to include Japanese and Koreans.

This turn-of-the-twentieth-century advertisement for rat poison carried a double message: It used the negative stereotype of a Chinese "coolie" eating rats to make its point about the effectiveness of the product, while pointing a finger at the Chinese figure next to the words, "They must go!" (Asian American Studies Library, University of California at Berkeley)

In 1906, anti-Asian sentiments continued to grow. San Francisco was struck by a major earthquake in April, and civil unrest increased. Japanese persons and businesses were attacked and looted. On October 11, 1906, the San Francisco School Board ordered that all Japanese, Korean, and Chinese students attend a segregated "Oriental school." (This regulation was later changed to include only older students and those with limited English proficiency.) Japan protested that the school board's action violated the U.S.-Japan treaty of 1894, bringing the San Francisco situation into international focus.

THE GENTLEMEN'S AGREEMENT   To assuage Japan, President Theodore Roosevelt arranged with the school board to rescind its order in exchange for federal action to limit immigration from Japan. In the ensuing U.S.-Japan "Gentlemen's Agreement," Japan promised not to issue passports to laborers planning to settle in the United States and recognized U.S. rights to refuse Japanese immigrants entry into the United States. In an executive order issued on March 14, 1907, Roosevelt implemented an amendment to the Immigration Act of 1907, which allowed the United States to bar entry of any immigrant whose passport was not issued for direct entry into the United States and whose immigration was judged to threaten domestic labor conditions.

Subsequent California legislation, the Heney-Webb bill or Alien Land Law of 1913, attempted to limit Asian interests within the state by prohibiting Asians from owning property. Although anti-Japanese sentiments lessened during World War I after Japan joined the Allies in the war against Germany, almost immediately following the war these sentiments resurfaced. The 1917 and 1924 Immigration Acts barred Asian laborers from the United States. In California, a campaign to pass the 1920 Alien Land Law attracted the support of the American Legion and the Native Sons and Daughters of the Golden West.

In an effort to avoid widespread prejudice and discrimination, the Japanese American Citizens League (JACL), founded in 1930 and consisting of second-generation Japanese Americans (nisei), sought to follow a path of economic success through individual efforts, the cultivation of friendship and understanding between themselves and other Americans, and assimilation into American culture. During the 1930's and 1940's, nisei were urged by JACL leaders to prove their worth as patriotic Americans by contributing to the economic and social welfare of the United States and to the social life of the nation by living with other citizens in a common community. Their efforts would find a new obstacle in 1941, however, when President Franklin D. Roosevelt issued Executive Order 9066 allowing internment of Japanese Americans in segregated camps.

Gregory A. Levitt

FURTHER READING

Gabaccia, Donna R. *Immigration and American Diversity: A Social and Cultural History.* Malden, Mass.: Blackwell, 2002. Survey of American immigration history from the mid-eighteenth century to the early twenty-first century. Provides an emphasis on cultural and social trends, with attention to ethnic conflicts, nativism, and racialist theories.

Ichihashi, Yamato. *The American Immigration Collection: Japanese in the United States.* 1932. Reprint. New York: Arno Press, 1969. Thorough description of Japanese immigration into the United States with an excellent chapter on anti-Japanese agitation.

Lee, Erika. *At America's Gates: Chinese Immigration During the Exclusion Era, 1882-1943.* Chapel Hill: University of North Carolina Press, 2003. Study of immigration from China to the United States from the time of the Chinese Exclusion Act to the loosening of American immigration laws during the 1960's, with an afterward on U.S. immigration policies after the terrorist attacks of September 11, 2001.

McWilliams, Carey. *Prejudice: Japanese-Americans, Symbol of Racial Intolerance.* Boston: Little, Brown, 1944. A dated but excellent account of anti-Japanese American prejudice and discrimination up to World War II.

Takaki, Ronald. *Strangers from a Different Shore: A History of Asian Americans.* Boston: Little, Brown, 1989. An excellent overview of the broader picture of Asian immigration and settlement in the United States.

Wilson, Robert A., and Bill Hosokawa. *East to America: A History of the Japanese in the United States.* New York: William Morrow, 1980. An excellent account of Japanese immigration and settlement in the United States.

SEE ALSO Asian American stereotypes; Burlingame Treaty; Chinatowns; Chinese American Citizens Alliance; Chinese Exclusion Act; Chinese exclusion cases; Chinese immigrants; Chinese immigrants and California's gold rush; Chinese immigrants and family customs; Chinese Six Companies; Coolies; Immigration Act of 1943; Migration; Page law; Wong Kim Ark case.

ZADVYDAS V. DAVIS

THE CASE: U.S. Supreme Court ruling on detention and deportation of aliens
DATE: June 28, 2001

IMMIGRATION ISSUES: Civil rights and liberties; Court cases

SIGNIFICANCE: In a decision that would have an immediate impact on thousands of people, the Supreme Court ruled that the government may not detain deportable aliens indefinitely simply because no other country is willing to accept them.

Kestutis Zadvydas, a person of Lithuanian ancestry, was born in a displaced persons camp in Germany and entered the United States as a child. After he built a long criminal record, the Immigration and Naturalization Service (INS) ordered him to be deported to his country of citizenship. However, both Lithuania and Germany rejected his citizenship claims and refused to accept him. After being detained by the U.S. government for more than five years, Zadvydas claimed that the due process clause of the Fifth Amendment prohibited the INS from indefinitely detaining him without condemnation in a criminal trial. The INS justified the detention by reference to an interpretation of a 1996 federal statute. A federal appeals court refused to exercise judicial review over the immigration policies of the legislative and executive branches.

By a 5-4 margin, the Supreme Court repudiated the idea of allowing the INS unlimited discretion for detaining Zadvydas and others in similar circumstances. Writing for the majority, Justice Stephen G. Breyer emphasized that the due process clause of the Fifth Amendment put "important constitutional limitations" on legislative and executive policies toward all persons who had entered the country, even if they were in the country illegally. After a "reasonable" period of six months, if deportation appeared unlikely in the foreseeable future, he wrote that the INS had the burden of showing an adequate reason for keeping the person in custody. He observed that preventive detention would be appropriate when there was sufficient evidence that a person was dangerous to society.

Thomas Tandy Lewis

FURTHER READING

Bischoff, Henry. *Immigration Issues.* Westport, Conn.: Greenwood Press, 2002.

Blake, Nicholas J., and Raza Husain. *Immigration, Asylum and Human Rights.* New York: Oxford University Press, 2003.

Legomsky, Stephen H. *Immigration and Refugee Law and Policy.* 3d ed. New York: Foundation Press, 2002.

LeMay, Michael C., and Elliott Robert Barkan, eds. *U.S. Immigration and Naturalization Laws and Issues: A Documentary History.* Westport, Conn.: Greenwood Press, 1999.

SEE ALSO Chinese detentions in New York; Deportation; Haitian immigrants; Helsinki Watch report on U.S. refugee policy; Immigration and Naturalization Service; Naturalization; September 11 terrorist attacks.

APPENDICES

BIBLIOGRAPHY

General Studies

Barkan, Elliott R. *And Still They Come: Immigrants and American Society, 1920 to the 1990's.* Wheeling, Ill.: Harlan Davidson, 1996. Looks at the changing composition of the immigrant population during the twentieth century and considers the impact of immigrants on American society.

Bodnar, John. *The Transplanted: A History of Immigrants in Urban America.* Bloomington: Indiana University Press, 1985. A look at how immigrants adjusted to American society that considers the situations immigrants faced in their homelands and how they drew on their homeland traditions in adjusting to life in the new country. Looks primarily at European immigrants but also Chinese, Japanese, and Mexicans.

Daniels, Roger. *Coming to America: A History of Immigration and Ethnicity in American Life.* 2d ed. New York: HarperCollins, 2002. An excellent general treatment of immigration history. Looks at the motives and experiences of immigrants from 1500 to the end of the twentieth century and considers major issues relating to immigration.

Glazer, Nathan, and Daniel Patrick Moynihan. *Beyond the Melting Pot: The Negroes, Puerto Ricans, Jews, Italians, and Irish of New York City.* 2d ed. Cambridge, Mass.: MIT Press, 1970. A classic study of the identifications and inter-group relations of American ethnic and immigrant groups.

Kennedy, John F. *A Nation of Immigrants.* Norwalk, Conn.: Easton Press, 1991. A new edition of President Kennedy's classic 1958 book calling for an end to discrimination in immigration laws. Kennedy's championing of the change in immigration laws helped to lead to the historic 1965 shift in immigration policy.

Takaki, Ronald. *A Different Mirror: A History of Multicultural America.* Boston: Little, Brown, 1993. A history of the United States from the perspective of its ethnic groups. Tends to emphasize non-white, non-European groups and their experiences with racism.

Post-1965 Immigrants

Hamamoto, Darrell Y., and Rodolfo D. Torres, eds. *New American Destinies: A Reader in Contemporary Asian and Latino Immigration.* New York: Routledge, 1997. Essays cover U.S. immigration history, labor force participation among immigrants, new theoretical frameworks for studying immigration, various lived experiences among these immigrant populations, and community-building.

Millman, Joel. The *Other Americans: How Immigrants Renew Our Country, Our Economy, and Our Values.* New York: Penguin Books, 1997. The author, a journalist, takes an anecdotal approach to recounting the lives of contemporary American immigrants. He argues that immigrants are re-building the American economy and reclaiming lost neighborhoods.

Portes, Alejandro, and Rubén G. Rumbaut. *Immigrant America: A Portrait.* Berkeley: University of California Press, 1996. A description of the nature and variety of immigrant settlement in the United States in the late twentieth century. Offers an optimistic view of the role of immigrants in American life.

Reimers, David M. *Still the Golden Door: The Third World Comes to America.* 2d ed. New York: Columbia University Press, 1992. An excellent history of late twentieth century immigration to the U.S. This second edition includes a detailed discussion of the 1990 Immigration Act, an evenhanded examination of issues connected to undocumented or illegal immigration, and consideration of the new immigrants arriving from areas in and around the former Soviet Union in the early 1990's.

Rosenzweig, Mark R., and Guillermina Jasso. *The New Chosen People: Immigrants in the United States.* New York: Russell Sage Foundation, 1990. Slightly dated now, but a good introduction to the post-1965 immigrants and the issues facing them.

Ueda, Reed. *Postwar Immigrant America: A Social History.* Boston: Bedford Books of St. Martin's Press, 1994. Begins by looking at the legacy of the restrictive immigration policy of the United States, then describes the transformation of American immigration policy to a worldwide one in 1952 and 1965. Provides a good section on the changing face of immigration as a result of post-1965 immigration policy. Considers America as a world melting pot. In the last chapter, the author is somewhat critical of the rise of ethnic identity politics.

Immigration Policy, Law, and Theoretical Issues

Borjas, George. *Heaven's Door: Immigration Policy and the American Economy.* Princeton, N.J.: Princeton University Press, 1999. An examination of the economic effects of immigration. Borjas finds that immigrants contribute to the American economy, but that the large numbers of low-skilled workers tend to intensify economic inequality in the United States and harm lower-paid native born workers.

Daniels, Roger. *Guarding the Golden Door: American Immigration Policy and Immigrants Since 1882.* New York: Hill & Wang, 2004. A detailed history of American immigration policy since the late nineteenth century.

Hing, Bill Ong. *Defining America Through Immigration Policy.* Philadelphia: Temple University Press, 2004. A broad survey of federal immigration policies and their impact on the social structure of the United States.

Hirschman, Charles, Philip Kasinitz, and Josh DeWind, eds. *The Handbook of International Migration: The American Experience.* New York: Russell Sage Foundation, 1999. A comprehensive compilation of research and thinking on American immigration. The authors of the various chapters look at theories of international migration and at how immigrant groups change in the United States. They consider the social, economic, and political consequences of immigration.

Assimilation and Adaptation of Immigrants

Gordon, Milton M. *Assimilation in American Life.* New York: Oxford University Press, 1966. The classic work on immigrant adaptation, written before the great wave of immigration following the 1965 change in immigration law. Gordon argues that immigrant groups tend to follow stages of assimilation, beginning with acculturation and ending with marital assimilation.

Light, Ivan, and Parminder Bhachu, eds. *Immigration and Entrepreneurship: Culture, Capital, and Ethnic Networks.* New Brunswick, N.J.: Transaction Publishers, 1993. A study of how culture and ethnic networks together can channel immigrants into small business ownership.

Portes, Alejandro, ed. *The New Second Generation.* New York: Russell Sage Foundation, 1996. A selection of topical essays that examine the main challenges facing the children of immigrants.

Rumbaut, Rubén, and Alejandro Portes, eds. *Ethnicities: Children of Immigrants in America.* Berkeley: University of California Press, 2001. The authors of the chapters in this book look at the patterns of adaptation of children of specific immigrant groups in the United States in the late twentieth and early twenty-first century. The research collected here is based on the Children of Immigrants Longitudinal Study.

Suárez-Orozco, Carola, and Marcelo M. Suárez-Orozco. *Children of Immigration.* Cambridge, Mass.: Harvard University Press, 2002. Written by the co-directors of the Harvard Immigration Project, the book examines how immigrant children and children of immigrants are faring in the United States. It gives particular attention to their special needs as students and to how American schools are addressing these special needs.

The Debate over Modern Immigration

Beck, Roy. *The Case Against Immigration: The Moral, Economic, Social, and Environmental Reasons for Reducing U.S. Immigration Back to Traditional Levels.* New York: W. W. Norton, 1996. Beck is an environmental and population control activist who makes a case for drastically reducing immigration in this book.

Briggs, Vernon M. *Mass Immigration and the National Interest.* Armonk, N.Y.: M. E. Sharpe, 1992. The author, an economist, argues that nineteenth and early twentieth century immigration aided the U.S. economy but the post-1965 immigration does not.

Brimelow, Peter. *Alien Nation: Common Sense About America's Immigration Disaster.* New York: Random House, 1996. A controversial argument for drastically cutting back immigration that maintains the large numbers of immigrants arriving from non-European societies cannot be easily assimilated into American culture.

Camarota, Steven. *Importing Poverty: Immigration's Impact on the Size and Growth of the Poor Population in the United States.* Washington, D.C.: Center for Immigration Studies, 1999. Looks at the composition of the poor population in 1979, 1989, and 1997 in order to suggest how immigration affected the growth of the poor population in the United States.

Heer, David. *Immigration in America's Future: Social Science Findings and the Policy Debate*. Boulder, Colo.: Westview Press, 1996. An evenhanded presentation of social scientific research on the impact of immigration on American life. The author presents and interprets data on trends in immigration and asks readers to decide the policy implications for themselves.

Perea, Juan, ed. *Immigrants Out! The New Nativism and the Anti-Immigrant Impulse in the United States*. New York: New York University Press, 1997. A collection of essays that attack laws, policies, and popular movements seen as anti-immigrant. The essays have the common thread of suggesting that all efforts to limit immigration are reflections of a latent nativism.

Reimers, David M. *Unwelcome Strangers: American Identity and the Turn Against Immigration*. New York: Columbia University Press, 1998. Traces the history of American attitudes toward immigration. The author questions the major arguments against immigration, while suggesting that there are also difficulties with simply assuming that the United States can continually absorb large numbers of immigrants.

Nativism in American History

Bennett, David H. *The Party of Fear: From Nativist Movements to the New Far Right in American History*. 2d ed. New York: Vintage Books, 1995. A comprehensive history of anti-immigrant movements in American history that argues those opposed to immigrants have been dedicated to protecting the nation against what they saw as alien ideas and people. He maintains that after 1919, fear of aliens shifted from fear of the foreigners themselves to fear of foreign ideologies, particularly communism.

Billington, Ray Allen. *The Protestant Crusade, 1800-1860: A Study of the Origins of American Nativism*. New York: Macmillan, 1938. A classic study of nativism that helped bring the topic into the mainstream of historical work. As the title indicates, Billington places a great deal of emphasis on anti-Catholicism in American nativism.

Higham, John. *Strangers in the Land: Patterns of American Nativism, 1860-1925*. New Brunswick, N.J.: Rutgers University Press, 1992. A study of the interconnected forces of nationalism and ethnic prejudice in American life during the great wave of migration at the turn of the nineteenth and twentieth centuries.

Migration, Gender, and Family Issues

Abel, Emily K., and Marjorie Pearson, eds. *Across Cultures: The Spectrum of Women's Lives*. New York: Gordon and Breach, 1989. Gender issues across cultures are addressed in this anthology. In terms of migration, Carole H. Browner and Dixie L. King discuss "Cross-Cultural Perspectives on Women and Immigration."

DiQuinzio, Patrice, and Iris Marion Young, eds. *Feminist Ethics and Social Policy*. Bloomington: Indiana University Press, 1997. Chapters address social policy from a feminist perspective. Immigration law is of particular importance in Uma Narayan's chapter, "'Male-Order' Brides: Immigrant Women, Domestic Violence, and Immigration Law."

Ehrenreich, Barbara, and Arlie Russell Hochschild, eds. *Global Woman: Nannies, Maids, and Sex Workers in the New Economy.* New York: Metropolitan Books, 2003. While some chapters address migration patterns from the "global south" or developing countries to the developed locale of the U.S., migration flows throughout the world are addressed throughout the book. In particular, the gendered dynamics of migration are well-illustrated by all of the contributions. Further, an analysis of transnational flows of love and support offer a unique perspective on the "emotional labor" of women migrant workers.

Gabaccia, Donna R., ed. *Seeking Common Ground: Multidisciplinary Studies of Immigrant Women in the United States.* Westport, Conn.: Praeger, 1992. This anthology provides analyses of U.S. immigration and women immigrants from a feminist perspective.

Hondagneu-Sotelo, Pierrette, ed. *Gender and U.S. Immigration: Contemporary Trends.* Berkeley: University of California Press, 2003. The editor points out that gender is an important aspect of migration and shapes migration patterns, but that gender has received relatively little attention in migration studies. Hondagneu-Sotelo brings together some of the best work in this area.

Huang, Fung-Yea. *Asian and Hispanic Immigrant Women in the Work Force: Implications of the United States Immigration Policies Since 1965.* New York: Garland, 1997. Using data from the Current Population Survey, Huang highlights the similarities and differences between two immigrant groups of women, Asian and Hispanic, and the differences between women who entered the U.S. with husbands versus those who entered independently.

Kelson, Gregory A., and Debra L. DeLaet, eds. *Gender and Immigration.* London: Macmillan Press, 1998. Beginning with an analysis of the invisibility of women in international migration scholarship, contributions to this anthology address issues ranging from immigration policy and gender relations to gender, marriage patterns, and sexuality among immigrants.

Luibhéld, Eithne, and Lionel Cantú, eds. *Queer Migrations: Sexuality, U.S. Citizenship, and Border Crossings.* Minneapolis: University of Minnesota Press, 2005. This book provides a novel perspective on migration as the editors bring together research on sexual orientation and U.S. immigration.

Immigrants and Literature

Fine, David M. *The City, the Immigrant, and American Fiction, 1880-1920.* Metuchen, N.J.: Scarecrow Press, 1977. This book is one of the best studies of American immigrant fiction in the late nineteenth and early twentieth centuries. It places this writing in the context of American immigration history.

Mendoza, Louis G., and Subramanian Shankar, eds. *Crossing Into America: The New Literature of Immigration.* New York: New Press, 2003. A collection of literature, diary entries, and letters that map the "great second wave" of American immigration. Young, new writers along with authors such as Jamaica Kincaid, Maxine Hong Kingston, and Richard Rodriguez discuss the many varied experiences of new immigrants to America.

Muller, Gilbert H. *New Strangers in Paradise: The Immigrant Experience and Contemporary American Fiction.* Lexington: University Press of Kentucky, 1999. Explores the immigrant experiences and emerging identities of Holocaust survivors, Chicanos, Latinos from the Caribbean, African-Caribbean immigrants, and Asian Americans through their contemporary fiction.

African Americans and New African Immigrants

Berlin, Ira. *Generations of Captivity: A History of African American Slaves.* Cambridge, Mass.: Belknap Press of Harvard University Press, 2003. Looks at the history of slaves in America, beginning with the first involuntary immigrant generations, which Berlin calls the Charter Generations. Emphasizes regional variations in the character of slavery.

_____. *Many Thousands Gone: The First Two Centuries of Slavery in North America.* Cambridge, Mass.: Belknap Press of Harvard University Press, 1998. Probably the most authoritative work on black slavery in North America.

Conniff, Michael L., and Thomas J. Davis. *Africans in the Americas: A History of the Black Diaspora.* New York: St. Martin's Press, 1994. Takes a comparative approach to the history of involuntary African immigrants and their descendants in the Caribbean, Brazil, Spanish America, and North America.

Curtin, Philip D. *The Atlantic Slave Trade: A Census.* Madison: University of Wisconsin Press, 1969. A classic and fundamental source of information on numbers of slaves, mortality rates, and living conditions during the slave trade.

Kasinitz, Philip. *Caribbean New York: Black Immigrants and the Politics of Race.* Ithaca, N.Y.: Cornell University Press, 1992. The author, a prominent sociologist specializing in immigration, compares the experiences of pre-1965 West Indian immigrants to those who came after 1965 and argues that the status and power of Caribbean immigrants decreased as African Americans became more politically involved in the years after the Civil Rights movement.

Asian Americans

Chang, Iris. *The Chinese in America: A Narrative History.* New York: Viking, 2003. A well-written history of Chinese Americans that looks forward to their possible future definitions of racial identity.

Fadiman, Anne. *The Spirit Catches You and You Fall Down.* New York: Farrar, Straus and Giroux, 1997. A case study of a Hmong child in the United States who suffered a seizure. The book gives insight into the traditional shamanistic beliefs of Hmong refugees in the U.S. and how these contrast with American views of health and the world.

Freeman, James A. *Hearts of Sorrow: Vietnamese American Lives.* Stanford, Calif.:

Stanford University Press, 1989. The story of fourteen Vietnamese refugees and their struggles to adapt to life in the United States.

Min, Pyong Gap, ed. *Asian Americans: Contemporary Trends and Issues.* 2d ed. Thousand Oaks, Calif.: Pine Forge Press, 2005. A broad overview of the Asian American experience that provides chapters on issues relevant to Asian Americans and descriptions of individual Asian ethnic groups. Also includes eight photo essays. This is an essential work for anyone interested in contemporary Asian Americans.

Spickard, Paul R. *Japanese Americans: The Formation and Transformations of an Ethnic Group* New York: Twayne, 1996. Tells the history of Japanese Americans, beginning with those who arrived between 1890 and 1910 and continuing on to new Japanese immigrants arriving in the late twentieth century.

Zhou, Min, and Carl L. Bankston III. *Growing Up American: How Vietnamese Children Adapt to Life in the United States.* New York: Russell Sage Foundation, 1998. Combines a general discussion of Vietnamese American refugees with a case study of Vietnamese children in a particular community.

European Groups

Bailyn, Bernard. *From Protestant Peasants to Jewish Intellectuals: The Germans in the Peopling of America.* Oxford, England: Berg, 1988. A history of the different waves of immigration of one of the largest ethnic groups in America.

Mangione, Jerre, and Ben Morreale. *La Storia: Five Centuries of the Italian American Experience.* New York: Harper Perennial, 1993. Although it deals with Italian Americans throughout American history, the central part of this book concerns the mass immigration of Italians between 1880 and 1924.

Miller, Kerby A., and Patricia Mulholland Miller. *Journey of Hope: The Story of Irish Immigration to America.* New York: Chronicle Books, 2001. A history of Irish Americans that presents their time in America as a triumphant success story.

Thomas, William I., and Florian Znaniecki. *The Polish Peasant in Europe and America: A Classic Work in Immigration History.* Edited by Eli Zaretsky. Urbana: University of Illinois Press, 1996. A new, abridged edition of a 1927 sociological study. The book is very important in the social scientific study of immigration, as well as a good introduction to Polish American settlement.

Latinos

Davis, Mike. *Magical Urbanism: Latinos Reinvent the US Big City.* New York: Verso, 2000. Looks at how Latinos, as the fastest growing and perhaps largest segment in American society, are transforming American urban life.

Galarza, Ernesto. *Merchants of Labor: The Mexican Bracero Story.* Santa Barbara, Calif.: McNally and Loftin, West, 1978. A history of the Bracero program that describes the treatment of Mexican laborers and the impact of the program.

Massey, Douglas S., Rafael Alarcon, Jorge Durand, and Humberto González. *Return to Aztlan: The Social Process of International Migration from Western Mexico.* Berkeley: University of California Press, 1990. Combines historical, anthropological, and survey data to study migration to the United States from four communities in Mexico.

Portes, Alejandro, and Robert L. Bach. *Latin Journey: Cuban and Mexican Immigrants in the United States.* Berkeley: University of California Press, 1985. A key work on Latin American immigration, contrasting two important but very distinctive groups.

Sanchez, George J. *Becoming Mexican American: Ethnicity, Culture, and Identity in Chicano Los Angeles, 1900-1945.* New York: Oxford University Press, 1993. Looks at how Mexicans, coming to Los Angeles as temporary sojourners, gradually became permanent residents and at the institutions and social networks created by them.

Suro, Roberto. *Strangers Among Us: How Latino Immigration Is Transforming America.* New York: Alfred A. Knopf, 1998. Looks at the essential issues connected to Latino migration to the United States. The author takes stands on issues, arguing, for example, that legal Latino immigrants need to take a position against illegal immigration.

Danielle Antoinette Hidalgo
Carl L. Bankston III

TIME LINE OF U.S. IMMIGRATION HISTORY

All legislative acts mentioned below are federal laws unless otherwise noted. Subjects of essays in the main text are printed in SMALL CAPS on their first mentions. For additional historical statistics, see the articles on "Census, U.S.," "Demographics of immigration," and "Racial and demographic trends," as well as the articles on individual immigrant groups.

c. 15,000 B.C.E	Ancestors of Native Americans begin crossing the Bering Strait into North America.
1003-1008	Norse explorers make tentative attempts to establish settlements in North America.
1492	Christopher Columbus's first voyage to the New World opens the Western Hemisphere to immigration from the Old World.
1565	Spanish found St. Augustine in Florida—the earliest permanent European settlement in North America.
1607	(April) English settlers arrive in Chesapeake Bay and found JAMESTOWN COLONY.
1619	First African slaves arriving in Virginia represent the first AFRICAN IMMIGRANTS to North America.
1620	(November) Earliest Pilgrims land at Plymouth.
1624	Thirty French Belgian families, sponsored by the Dutch West India Company, found New Amsterdam on the tip of Manhattan Island.
1626	First African slaves arrive in the Dutch lands of the northeast.
1629-1640	Puritan Great Migration to New England takes place.
1634	SEPHARDIC JEWS found the first recorded settlement of JEWISH IMMIGRANTS in North America in Maryland.
1638	First recorded settlement of SCANDINAVIAN IMMIGRANTS is founded along the Delaware River.
1654	Jewish immigrants begin arriving in New Amsterdam from Brazil.
1664	Dutch cede control of the colony of New Netherlands to England.
1680's	GERMAN IMMIGRANTS who are beginning to arrive in Pennsylvania become known as the "Pennsylvania Dutch" as their settlement continues into the eighteenth century.
1681	William Penn receives proprietorship of Pennsylvania from King Charles II of England.
1695	SCOTCH-IRISH IMMIGRANTS begin arriving in North America.

1784	Russians begin settling in Alaska.
1790	NATURALIZATION ACT OF 1790, the first federal law addressing naturalization issues, stipulates that any "free white person" may obtain U.S. CITIZENSHIP after two years of residency.
1790	Federal government conducts the first national census.
1790	Revenue Marine, the forerunner of the U.S. COAST GUARD, is established.
1798	Naturalization law is revised to require fourteen years of residence before becoming a citizen.
1798	Passage of the ALIEN AND SEDITION ACTS gives the U.S. president the authority to deport all foreigners who are regarded as dangerous.
1799	(February) FEDERAL RIOT OF 1799 in Philadelphia is the first mass public reaction to the Alien and Sedition Acts.
1800	Led by the Federalist Party, the U.S. Congress passes the Alien Acts. These include the Nationalization Act, which lengthens the residency requirement for citizenship and makes citizenship more difficult for immigrants to acquire; the Alien Act, which gives President John Adams the authority to deport any non-citizen thought to be dangerous; and the Alien Enemies Act, which permits the capture and imprisonment of enemy aliens in time of war.
1802	Congress reduces the residency requirement for becoming a citizen to five years.
1808	Congress bans the importation of slaves. It continues to be legal to hold native-born slaves and some slaves continue to be smuggled into the United States from Africa and the Caribbean.
1819	U.S. begins to collect data on immigrants by requiring ship's captains and others bringing in immigrants to keep records and submit manifests.
1834	Inventor Samuel F. B. Morse's anti-Roman Catholic tract, *Foreign Conspiracy Against the Liberties of the United States* calls for the formation of the Anti-Popery Union to resist the influence of Catholic immigrants.
1844	(May-July) ANTI-IRISH RIOTS in Philadelphia express anti-immigrant sentiments of NATIVISM.
1845	Ireland experiences a potato crop failure, beginning the Great Irish Famine, which prompts almost 500,000 people to migrate from Ireland to North America between 1845 and 1850.
1848	(February) Treaty of Guadalupe Hidalgo ends the Mexican War; Mexico cedes its northern territories to the United States, and about 100,000 Mexicans suddenly become citizens of the United States.

1849	CALIFORNIA GOLD RUSH begins and attracts a wave of CHINESE IMMIGRANTS to the United States. Some of these immigrants settle in San Francisco, where they build the first American CHINATOWN.
1854	Chinese district associations in the United States join together to form the CHINESE SIX COMPANIES, which becomes the primary organization representing Chinese residents.
1854	Anti-immigrant Native American Party, also known as the "Know-Nothing Party" wins every statewide office and a majority of seats in the state legislature in Massachusetts elections.
1857	William Marcy Tweed becomes a leader of New York City's Tammany Hall and uses his influence in MACHINE POLITICS to assist arriving immigrants while soliciting their political support.
1859	*CLOTILDE* SLAVE SHIP is the last American ship to deliver involuntary AFRICAN IMMIGRANTS to the United States.
1861-1865	U.S. Civil War disrupts immigration from Europe.
1866	KU KLUX KLAN is founded in Tennessee.
1868	In order to encourage Chinese immigrants to settle on the West Coast, the United States persuades the Chinese government to ratify the BURLINGAME TREATY, which allows people to leave China for America.
1869	Transcontinental railroad is completed. This releases immigrant workers, many of them Chinese, into the job market, especially in California.
1870	Naturalization Act of 1870 extends naturalization rights to people of African descent, but excludes other non-whites.
1875	(March) Congress passes the PAGE LAW to prevent Asian prostitutes from entering the United States.
1880	ITALIAN IMMIGRANTS begin entering the country in large numbers.
1882	CHINESE EXCLUSION ACT bans the entry of Chinese laborers into the United States for ten years.
1884-1893	Constitutionality of the Chinese Exclusion Act is tested in the CHINESE EXCLUSION CASES.
1885	(December) U.S. Supreme Court approves taxing immigrants in the so-called HEAD MONEY CASES.
1888	American Protective Association is founded to combat the growing influence of Roman Catholic immigrants.
1889	Jane Addams establishes HULL-HOUSE in Chicago, helping to begin the SETTLEMENT HOUSE MOVEMENT.
1890's	Anti-Asian "YELLOW PERIL" CAMPAIGN develops on the West Coast.
1891	(March) Bureau of Immigration—the forerunner of the IMMIGRATION AND NATURALIZATION SERVICE—is established, and Congress sets health qualifications for new immigrants.

1892	Geary Act extends the Chinese Exclusion Act for an additional ten years and requires Chinese in the United States to obtain a certificate of residence.
1892	First newspaper for ARAB IMMIGRANTS is started in New York City.
1892	Quarantine station for immigrants opens on the northwest side of Angel Island in San Francisco Bay.
1892	(January) Ellis Island, the largest and most famous immigrant station in the United States, opens. During the turn of the century wave of immigration, from 1892 to 1924, three-quarters of all the immigrants arriving in the United States arrive through Ellis Island.
1895	CHINESE AMERICAN CITIZENS ALLIANCE is formed in San Francisco.
1898	(March) In the WONG KIM ARK CASE, the Supreme Court rules that children born in the United States are U.S. citizens, regardless of the status of their parents.
1903-1905	Approximately 7,200 KOREAN IMMIGRANTS arrive in Hawaii to work on sugar plantations.
1904	Congress extends the Chinese Exclusion Act indefinitely.
1904	First wave of SIKH IMMIGRANTS arrives in North America.
1906	AMERICAN JEWISH COMMITTEE is formed as an advocacy group for Jewish immigrants.
1906	Hawaii Sugar Planters Association hires attorney A. F. Judd to travel to the Philippines to recruit field workers and make arrangements for bringing the workers to Hawaii. By 1930, three quarters of the agricultural workers in Hawaii are Filipinos.
1906	Upton Sinclair's novel *The Jungle* exposes harsh living conditions of immigrants working in Chicago.
1906	(October) JAPANESE SEGREGATION IN CALIFORNIA SCHOOLS begins when the San Francisco school board orders the segregation of Japanese pupils.
1907	Immigration Act of 1907 increases the head tax on new immigrants from two to four dollars and, in a provision aimed at JAPANESE IMMIGRANTS, gives the president of the United States the authority to deny admission to any immigrants he believes have a negative influence on labor conditions.
1907	(March) United States and Japan reach the GENTLEMAN'S AGREEMENT, under which the United States allows Japanese residents to attend San Francisco public schools, and Japan agrees to end the emigration of Japanese laborers to the United States.
1908	Israel Zangwill's play *The Melting Pot* introduces the term "MELTING POT" to the English language.

1910	Immigration station begins operating at China Cove on Angel Island in San Francisco Bay. The Angel Island facility will operate until 1940, handling 100,000 immigrants granted entry into the United States, most of them from Asia. These include 60,000 Chinese immigrants.
1910	Mexican Revolution begins. Political and economic chaos in Mexico over the following ten years cause an estimated quarter of a million Mexicans to resettle across the border in the United States.
1911	California legislators introduce twenty-seven bills for ALIEN LAND LAWS designed to prevent Japanese immigrants from owning land in the state.
1911	(March) TRIANGLE SHIRTWAIST COMPANY FIRE kills 146 GARMENT WORKERS—mostly WOMEN IMMIGRANTS—in New York City.
1916	Naturalist Madison Grant advances the idea of "MONGRELIZATION" in *The Passing of the Great Race*, which classified national and ethnic groups as "races."
1916	Marcus Garvey founds the UNIVERSAL NEGRO IMPROVEMENT ASSOCIATION in New York City.
1917	(April) United States enters World War I, and President Woodrow Wilson establishes regulations on enemy aliens, restricting the movements and rights of people from the countries with which the United States is at war. Federal agents intern 6,300 people under these regulations.
1917	(May) IMMIGRATION ACT OF 1917 bars the entry of immigrants who cannot read or write in English or in their own languages, as well as immigrants from Asia.
1917	(October) Russian Revolution begins period of increasing Russian emigration.
1919-1920	Under the direction of U.S. attorney general A. Mitchell Palmer, federal agents round up and deport foreign radicals with state and local police assistance in a series of purges known as the PALMER RAIDS.
1920-1921	SACCO AND VANZETTI TRIAL reveals depth of American prejudice against Italian immigrants.
1921	(May) IMMIGRATION ACT OF 1921 creates the first national origins quota law. This limits immigrants from any particular country to 3 percent of the number of people from that country in the United States in 1910. The act also places a ceiling of 350,000 immigrants per year.
1922	(September) CABLE ACT restricts the citizenship rights of immigrants.
1922	(November) In OZAWA V. UNITED STATES, the U.S. Supreme Court rules that Japanese aliens are not "white" and cannot be naturalized as citizens.

1924	(May) IMMIGRATION ACT OF 1924, also known as the National Origins Act, tightens the national origins quotas by limiting immigration from any country to 2 percent of the number of people from that country living in the United States in 1890. The annual ceiling on immigrants is lowered to 165,000. The act also creates the U.S. BORDER PATROL.
1927	Marcus Garvey is declared an undesirable alien and is deported.
1929	Congress makes annual immigration quotas by national origin permanent and sets the annual ceiling on immigrants at roughly 150,000. The restrictions of the 1920's bias immigration heavily in favor of northern and western Europe, which receives 83 percent of the visas to enter the United States as immigrants. Southern and eastern Europe receive 15 percent of the visas and only 2 percent of the visas go to the rest of the world.
1929	LEAGUE OF UNITED LATIN AMERICAN CITIZENS is founded as an advocacy organization for LATINOS.
1930	(August) JAPANESE AMERICAN CITIZENS LEAGUE is founded.
1931	Federal government begins MEXICAN DEPORTATIONS to conserve jobs for American citizens.
1934	(March) Tydings-McDuffie Act places the Philippines on track toward independence from the United States, reclassifies Filipinos from American nationals to aliens, and restricts the admission of FILIPINO IMMIGRANTS to the United States to only fifty persons per year. After World War II, the Philippines becomes independent, the quota for Filipino immigrants is raised to one hundred per year, and Filipinos become eligible to naturalize as U.S. citizens.
1937	Sociologist Marcus Lee Hansen publishes *The Problem of the Third Generation Immigrants*, which introduces the concept of the HANSEN EFFECT.
1939	SS *Louis*, carrying more than 900 German Jewish refugees, is met off the coast of Florida by a Coast Guard patrol boat sent to prevent refugees from swimming ashore.
1939	John Steinbeck's novel *The Grapes of Wrath* chronicles the internal migrations of Americans fleeing the Oklahoma Dust Bowl.
1940	In response to war in Europe and Asia, the Alien Registration Act requires the registration and fingerprinting of all non-citizens in the United States. About 5 million non-citizens register.
1941	(December) Japan's attack on the Pearl Harbor naval base near Honolulu, Hawaii, brings the United States into World War II.
1942	Wartime labor needs lead the United States to establish the BRACERO PROGRAM, which brings Mexican laborers, primarily in agriculture, to the United States. The program continues through 1964 and helps to establish a pattern of labor migration from Mexico.

1942	(February) JAPANESE AMERICAN INTERNMENT begins when President Franklin D. Roosevelt signs an executive order requiring all persons of Japanese ancestry living west of the Rocky Mountains on the mainland United States to be sent to remote camps for the duration of World War II. Later, JAPANESE PERUVIANS were deported from Peru to the United States, where they were immediately interned in the Japanese American camps.
1943	(December) IMMIGRATION ACT OF 1943 repeals Asian exclusion laws.
1945-1990	More than 5 million AFRO-CARIBBEAN IMMIGRANTS—including Cubans and Haitians—enter the United States.
1945	(May) End of World War II in Europe leaves many people homeless
1945	(December) WAR BRIDES Act enables wives and children of U.S. servicemen to enter the country on a non-quota basis.
1948	In response to urging by President Harry S. Truman, Congress passes the Displaced Persons Act of 1948 to deal with the problem of refugees and displaced people in Europe following the war. Truman is criticized for excluding more than 90 percent of displaced Jews. The act is revised in 1950 and most of the discrimination against Jewish refugees is removed.
1950-1953	United States fights in the Korean War.
1951	United Nations holds Convention Relating to the Status of Refugees.
1952	(June) IMMIGRATION AND NATIONALITY ACT OF 1952, also known as the McCarran-Walter Act, becomes the basis of U.S. immigration policy. It establishes a four-category preference system, makes it easier for Asians to immigrate, and makes it tougher for communists to enter the United States. The act retains the national origins quota system.
1953	(August) President Harry S. Truman's appeal to Congress to help escapees from the communist countries of Eastern Europe leads to the passage of the REFUGEE RELIEF ACT OF 1953, which allows 200,000 more visas than are authorized under national immigration quotas.
1954	Ellis Island closes. From 1892 through 1953, the Ellis Island immigration facility has processed more than 12 million immigrants.
1954	(June-July) U.S. government deports thousands of Mexican laborers in OPERATION WETBACK.
1956	President Dwight D. Eisenhower authorizes the admission of 38,000 Hungarian refugees who have fled Hungary after a failed anticommunist uprising.

1957	Congress passes the Refugee-Escapee Act, which defines refugees as those escaping from communist or communist-dominated countries.
1958	Future president John F. Kennedy publishes *A Nation of Immigrants*, calling attention to the contributions made by immigrants.
1959	Fidel Castro leads revolutionary forces to power in Cuba.
1959	Tibetan uprising against the Chinese government prompts 100,000 Tibetans to go to India.
1959-1962	First CUBAN IMMIGRANTS to flee Castro's new government arrive in the United States and settle primarily in the LITTLE HAVANA area of Miami.
1960	U.S. government creates the Cuban Refugee Program to handle the processing and resettlement of Cuban refugees.
1963	Miami-Dade County, with its growing population of Cubans and other Hispanics, becomes the location of the first bilingual education program in U.S. public schools.
1964	Milton Gordon publishes *Assimilation in American Life*, a major study of the assimilation of immigrants into American society.
1965-1973	Chartered planes known as "Freedom Flights" bring more than 260,000 Cuban refugees to the United States. Fidel Castro orders the flights ended on April 6, 1973.
1965	Thanks to relaxation of immigration restrictions, JAMAICAN IMMIGRANTS begin arriving in larger numbers than ever before.
1965	President Lyndon Johnson makes the long-closed and decaying immigrant station at Ellis Island part of the Statue of Liberty National Monument. Planning begins for the restoration of Ellis Island.
1965	(October) IMMIGRATION AND NATIONALITY ACT OF 1965, also known as the Hart-Cellar Act, expands the preference system adopted by the 1952 Immigration and Nationality Act. The new law repeals the national origins quota system and makes family reunification the primary basis of immigration law. The act also establishes a ceiling of 170,000 on immigration from the Eastern Hemisphere and 120,000 from the Western Hemisphere.
1966	(January) The term "MODEL MINORITY" first appears in a *New York Times Magazine* article by sociologist William Petersen.
1968	BILINGUAL EDUCATION ACT, which is passed as Title 7 of the Elementary and Secondary Education Act, provides funds for special programs for speakers of minority languages.
1968	MEXICAN AMERICAN LEGAL DEFENSE AND EDUCATION FUND is formed in San Antonio, Texas, to promote Latino rights.

1972-1980	Around 50,000 HAITIAN BOAT PEOPLE flee from the dictatorship of Jean-Claude Duvalier, arriving illegally on the coast of Florida in hastily constructed, overcrowded boats. In response, the U.S. government begins the practice of interdiction, stopping the Haitian boats at sea and returning most of their passengers to Haiti.
1974	ASIAN AMERICAN LEGAL DEFENSE FUND is formed to defend and promote the legal rights of Asian Americans.
1974	(January) In LAU v. NICHOLS the U.S. Supreme Court rules that public schools must provide bilingual education to limited-English-speaking students.
1975	(April) After fall of Saigon government, U.S. president Gerald Ford authorizes the admission of 130,400 refugees from Vietnam, Laos, and Cambodia. Most of those in this first wave of refugees are VIETNAMESE IMMIGRANTS and the numbers of SOUTHEAST ASIAN IMMIGRANTS increase.
1976	First HMONG IMMIGRANTS begin arriving in the United States.
1977	U.S. attorney general Griffin Bell uses his parole authority to allow thousands of people from Cambodia, Laos, and Vietnam to resettle in the United States. President Jimmy Carter signs legislation permitting these refugees to become permanent residents.
1978	Federal government adopts a new worldwide ceiling of 290,000 immigrants per year, replacing the Eastern and Western ceilings established in 1965.
1979	Islamic revolution in Iran leads to large increase in the numbers of IRANIAN IMMIGRANTS to the United States and other nations.
1980-1990	Civil wars rage in El Salvador, Nicaragua, and Guatemala. An estimated one million political and economic refugees from these countries flee north to the United States, settling mostly in California and on the East Coast.
1980's	Liberalization of emigration laws under Mikhail Gorbachev leads to an increase in the numbers of SOVIET JEWISH IMMIGRANTS to the United States.
1980	In response to the large numbers of immigrants that have begun to arrive from Southeast Asia and other locations, Congress passes the Refugee Act. This places refugees in a category separate from other immigrants, and it provides a definition of refugees as people fleeing their countries because of persecution on grounds of race, religion, nationality, or political opinion. The president is given authority to establish the number of refugees to be allowed into the United States. The ceiling on regular immigrants is lowered from 290,000 per year to 270,000 per year.
1980	(April-September) Fidel Castro opens the port of Mariel to Cubans who want to leave the country. More than 115,000 people take advantage of the MARIEL BOATLIFT to cross to Key West, Florida.

1981	Congress sets an annual quota of 20,000 TAIWANESE IMMIGRANTS.
1982	(June) In PLYLER V. DOE, the U.S. Supreme Court extends the Fourteenth Amendment's equal protection clause to give noncitizens the right to public social services.
1983	(June) IMMIGRATION AND NATURALIZATION SERVICE V. CHADHA, a U.S. Supreme Court ruling on deportation has wide-ranging political ramifications.
1984	(December) United States and Cuba agree that Cuba will take back nearly 3,000 criminals and mental patients who have arrived with the Mariel boatlift and the United States would issue visas to political prisoners and others who wished to leave Cuba.
1986	Concerns over illegal immigration into the United States lead Congress to pass the IMMIGRATION REFORM AND CONTROL ACT OF 1986. This raises the annual ceiling on legal immigration from the 270,000 established six years earlier to 540,000. To decrease the jobs drawing ILLEGAL ALIENS into the country, the act introduces stiff penalties for employers of those in the country illegally. The act also offers amnesty to illegal aliens who can prove that they have resided in the United States since January 1, 1982.
1988	Congress passes the Civil Liberties Act, which authorizes each internee of a wartime relocation camp for Japanese Americans to receive $20,000 and an apology from the United States. About 60,000 Japanese Americans apply for and receive these reparations.
1989	(June) HELSINKI WATCH REPORT ON U.S. REFUGEE POLICY criticizes American treatment of refugees.
1990's	TIBETAN IMMIGRANTS begin arriving in the United States.
1990	(September) National Immigration Museum opens at Ellis Island.
1990	(November) IMMIGRATION ACT OF 1990 raises the worldwide ceiling on immigration to 700,000 for 1992 through 1994, with the ceiling to go down to 675,000. The act revises the 1952 Immigration Act so that immigrants can no longer be excluded because of political beliefs or affiliations.
1992	President George Bush issues Executive Order 12807, directing the Coast Guard to interdict undocumented aliens at sea and to return them to their places of origin.
1992	(May) ASIAN PACIFIC AMERICAN LABOR ALLIANCE is formed to promote the interests of Asian and Pacific islander immigrants.
1993	(June) CHINESE DETENTIONS IN NEW YORK, as federal authorities take into custody 276 illegal immigrants.

1994	North American Free Trade Agreement (NAFTA) is established among the United States, Canada, and Mexico. The act is intended primarily to reduce barriers to trade, but it also requires the three countries to ease restrictions on the movement of business executives and professionals. This promotes professional migration from Canada to the United States, in particular.
1994	(April) In the FLORIDA ILLEGAL-IMMIGRANT SUIT, the state of Florida demands restitution from the federal government for its own expenditures on illegal immigrants.
1994	(June) The Congressional Commission on Immigration Reform, also known as the Jordan Commission, calls for limiting legal immigration to 500,000 per year, with 100,000 slots to be granted to immigrants with needed job skills, and the report calls for strict controls on the hiring of illegal immigrants where necessary.
1994	(August) Responding to the large numbers of Cubans attempting to leave their country after Fidel Castro declares that he is not opposed to people leaving, the U.S. changes its CUBAN REFUGEE POLICY when President Bill Clinton declares that Cuban refugees will no long be allowed automatic entry to the United States.
1994	(November) California voters approve PROPOSITION 187, a voter initiative designed to limit public services available to undocumented immigrants.
1995	THAI GARMENT WORKER ENSLAVEMENT scandal is revealed when captive immigrant garment workers are freed in Southern California.
1996	Congress votes to increase the numbers of Border Patrol agents from 5,000 to 10,000 over the following five years and it orders the construction of fences along the U.S.-Mexico border.
1996	Welfare Reform Act denies public assistance services to resident aliens for a period of time.
1996	(March) Immigration and Naturalization Service creates a self-petitioning process for immigrants who are battered spouses and battered children of U.S. citizens and legal permanent residents. If approved, the petitions enable immigrants to remain in the United States after separating from abusive spouses.
1998	Population of MUSLIMS in the United States reaches about 6 million persons.
1998	(June) California voters approve PROPOSITION 227, a voter initiative designed to end bilingual education in public schools.
1999	(November) Elián GONZÁLEZ RESCUE off the southern coast of Florida touches off a diplomatic conflict between the United States and Cuba.
2001	In ZADVYDAS V. DAVIS the Supreme Court rules that the government may not detain deportable aliens indefinitely simply because no other country accepts them.

2001   (June) In NGUYEN V. IMMIGRATION AND NATURALIZATION SERVICE the U.S. Supreme Court rules on the citizenship of children born abroad and out of wedlock who have only one American parent.

2001   (September) In SEPTEMBER 11 TERRORIST ATTACKS, nineteen Islamic radicals hijack four American airlines; they fly two planes into the towers of New York's World Trade Center, destroying the buildings and killing thousands of people. A third plane hits part of the Pentagon, and a fourth crashes in Pennsylvania after a struggle between passengers and hijackers. Nine days later, U.S. president George W. Bush reacts to the events of September 11 by creating the Office of Homeland Security. The following January this is upgraded to the Department of HOMELAND SECURITY.

2001   (October) Congress passes Public Law 107-56, known as the USA Patriot Act. The act includes new reasons for denying entry into the United States, gives a broader definition to the concept of terrorist activity, and increases the causes for deporting visitors and immigrants.

2001   (November) Congress passes the Border Security Act, authorizing more funds for immigration and customs staff, providing for the sharing of information on deportation cases among federal agencies, tracking foreign students, and tightening oversight in other ways.

2003   (March) Functions and offices of the Immigration and Naturalization Service are transferred to U.S. Citizenship and Immigration Services (UCIS), a bureau of the Department of Homeland Security. Actor Arnold Schwarzenegger—an immigrant from Austria—is elected governor of California.

2004   Approximately 9 million illegal aliens are believed to be living in the United States.

2005   With a budget of more than $40 billion, the Department of Homeland Security has such responsibilities as protecting national targets, coordinating domestic intelligence and preparedness, and monitoring the flow of immigration.

Carl L. Bankston III
Danielle Antoinette Hidalgo

INDEXES

CATEGORY INDEX

AFRICAN AMERICANS

African immigrants, 3
Afro-Caribbean immigrants, 11
Clotilde slave ship, 168
Cuban immigrants and African
    Americans, 180
Discrimination, 201
Haitian boat people, 297
Haitian immigrants, 300
Irish immigrants and African
    Americans, 400
Jamaican immigrants, 415
Korean immigrants and African
    Americans, 469
Ku Klux Klan, 477
Literature, 507
Palmer raids, 584
Racial and ethnic demographic
    trends, 606
Santería, 629

Universal Negro Improvement
    Association, 667
West Indian immigrants, 689

ASIAN IMMIGRANTS

Alien land laws, 19
Amerasians, 22
Asian American education, 52
Asian American Legal Defense
    Fund, 56
Asian American literature, 57
Asian American stereotypes, 60
Asian American women, 63
Asian Indian immigrants, 67
Asian Indian immigrants and family
    customs, 72
Asian Pacific American Labor
    Alliance, 76
Chinatowns, 130

Index of Court Cases

Index of Laws and Treaties

Proposition 227 (California), 28, 85, 502, 532, 600-604

Refugee Act of 1980, 179, 191, 311-313, 463, 620, 697
Refugee Relief Act of 1953, 355, 361, 548, 614-617

Scott Act of 1888, 143, 145, 157
Sedition Act of 1798, 257-258
Sixth Amendment, 294
Soldier Brides Act of 1947, 687

Thirteenth Amendment, 166, 201, 205, 699
Tydings-McDuffie Act of 1934, 728

Virginia Charter of 1606, 165
Voting Rights Act of 1965, 401
Voting Rights Act of 1975, 501

War Brides Act of 1945, 355, 435, 614, 683, 685-688, 697
War Measures Act of 1942 (Canada), 435

INDEX OF PERSONAGES

SUBJECT INDEX

AAJF. *See* American Arab and Jewish Friends

AALDF. *See* Asian American Legal Defense Fund

AAUG. *See* Association of Arab American University Graduates

Abbott, Edith, 646

Abourezk, James, 44

Abraham, Spencer, 44, 47

Acadia, 508

Accent discrimination, 1-3

ACCESS. *See* Arab Community Center for Economic and Social Services

Acculturation, 221, 530; of Arabs, 48; and assimilation, 80; of Cubans, 630; of Dominicans, 209, 211; and ethnic enclaves, 273; generational, 273-276

Achick, Tong K., 154

ACJ. *See* American Council on Judaism

Act to Protect Free White Labor Against Competition from Chinese Coolie Labor of 1862 (California), 61

Adamic, Louis, 229

Adams, John, 16-17

ADC. *See* American-Arab Anti-Discrimination Committee

Addams, Jane, 332-334, 646

AFDC. *See* Aid to Families with Dependent Children

Affirmative action, 121, 123, 206, 600-601; and immigrants, 9; and Latinos, 181; white resentment of, 552

AFL. *See* American Federation of Labor

African Americans; and Cuban immigrants, 180-184; and Irish immigrants, 400-401; and Korean immigrants, 469-472; stereotypes, 691

African immigrants, 3-11

Afro-Caribbean immigrants, 6, 9, 11-15, 181; and Santería, 629-630

Afroyim v. Rusk, 568

Agricultural Labor Relations Act, 251

Agricultural Workers Organizing Committee, 251-252

Agriculture, 243, 384, 605; and British immigrants, 107; European, 241, 281, 316, 410, 445; and European immigrants, 235, 281; and Filipino immigrants, 260; and Irish immigrants, 403; and Jamaican immigrants, 417; and Japanese immigrants, 19, 433, 439, 517; and Mexican immigrants, 99, 101, 103-107, 191, 251-257, 572-573; and World War II, 103-107

Aid to Families with Dependent Children, 698

AJC. *See* American Jewish Committee

Alabama; *Clotilde* slave ship, 168-171; and Ku Klux Klan, 479-480

Alaska; Filipino immigrants, 280; gold rush, 708; Native Americans, 123-124; Russian immigrants, 622-623; and U.S. Census, 123-124

Alianza Federal de Mercedes, La, 128

Alien Act of 1798, 257-258, 319

Alien and Sedition Acts of 1798, 15-18, 257-258

Alien Enemies Act of 1798, 257-258

Alien Land Law of 1913 (California), 19, 204, 433, 441, 576, 710; repeal of, 435

Alien Land Law of 1920 (California), 21, 710

Alien land laws, 19-22, 578; in California, 204, 433, 435, 441, 576, 710

Alien Registration Act of 1940, 728

Alien Registration Receipt (green) Cards, 293-295

Almeida-Sanchez v. United States, 566

ALRA. *See* Agricultural Labor Relations Act

Amalgamated Clothing Workers, 271

Ambach v. Norwick, 564

Brazil, 50; African slaves, 484; black
    population, 609; Jewish settlers, 443,
    450-451, 636
Breckinridge, Sophonisba, 646
Brennan, William Joseph, Jr., 566,
    591-592
Breslin, Jimmy, 233
Breyer, Stephen G., 712
Brimelow, Peter, 375
British immigrants, 190, 194, 316; in
    Canada, 608; demographics, 192; as
    dominant group, 107-109; first
    settlements, 316, 419-423; Gypsies,
    295; indentured servants, 388;
    Protestants, 235-236; and quotas,
    191; war brides, 681-683
Brown v. Board of Education, 206, 499
Brownell, Herbert, 574
Bryan, William Jennings, 20
Buck, Pearl S., 22, 23
Buck v. Bell, 592
Buddhism, 67; and Koreans, 468, 473,
    476; and Southeast Asians, 651; and
    Vietnamese, 673
Buffalo Hump, 286
Burger, Warren E., 372, 501, 564,
    591-592
Burlingame, Anson, 111
Burlingame Treaty, 109-113, 141-142
Burma, 324
Bush, George, 85, 298-299, 302, 436;
    and Haiti, 620
Bush, George W.; and Homeland
    Security Department, 328, 639; and
    Mexico, 335

Cabell v. Chavez-Salido, 564
Cable, John L., 113-115
Cable Act of 1922, 113-115, 425
Cabot, John, 409
CACA. *See* Chinese American Citizens
    Alliance
Cadwalader, George, 31
Cahan, Abraham, 228
California; Agricultural Labor
    Relations Act of 1975 (California),
    251, 254; alien land laws, 19-21;
    Angel Island, 432, 434, 546, 696;
    Arab immigrants, 34; Asian

Americans, 64; Asian immigrants,
    69; and Border Patrol, 97;
    Chinatowns, 131-132; Chinese
    immigrants, 136, 155; Delano Grape
    Strike, 128, 253, 255; Filipino
    immigrants, 259-261, 264; gold rush,
    115-119, 146, 151-156, 160; Hmong
    immigrants, 324; illegal aliens, 335;
    Jamaican immigrants, 417; Japanese
    immigrants, 277, 425, 431, 438-443,
    709; Korean immigrants, 467, 544;
    and Ku Klux Klan, 480; Latinos, 128,
    505, 591, 610; Little Saigon, 54;
    Little Tokyos, 516; Mexican
    immigrants, 536; natural disasters,
    598; Operation Wetback, 572-576;
    Proposition 187, 268, 461, 598-600,
    602; Proposition 227, 28, 85, 502,
    532, 600-604; segregation in, 278,
    708; Sikh immigrants, 648;
    Southeast Asian immigrants, 650;
    Taiwanese immigrants, 655; Thai
    garment workers, 657-659;
    undocumented immigrants,
    598-600; Vietnamese immigrants,
    672. *See also* Los Angeles; San
    Francisco
California, University of, 63, 600
Callaghan, Morley, 510
Cambodia, 23-24, 526, 671
Cambodian immigrants, 53, 62, 64,
    649-650
Canada; Arab immigrants, 33, 36; Asian
    immigrants, 63-64, 67-68;
    bilingualism, 89; borders, 97;
    Chinatowns, 193; Chinese
    immigrants, 155; Filipino
    immigrants, 259, 264; and Japan,
    193; Japanese immigrants, 62;
    Japanese internment, 57, 517;
    Korean immigrants, 474; Little
    Tokyos, 517; Muslim immigrants,
    557; Sikh immigrants, 648;
    Southeast Asian immigrants, 650;
    and U.S. Border Patrol, 96, 98-99
Canadian immigrants in the United
    States, 192
Capra, Frank, 414
Caputo, Philip, 233

immigrants, 536; police brutality in, 183

DeVoto, Bernard, 233

Dillingham, William Paul, 344, 346

Dillingham Commission, 244, 349, 543

DiMaggio, Joe, 413

DiPrima, Diane, 233

Disasters, 310, 327-328; in California, 598; and Homeland Security Department, 329

Discrimination, 201-207, 412, 551-552, 564-565; and accents, 1-3; and acculturation, 275; vs. Afro-Caribbeans, 13-14; alien land laws, 19-22; vs. Arab Americans, 36, 40, 42-44, 454; vs. Asian Americans, 56, 65, 77, 319, 321-322; vs. Chinese, 61, 132, 136, 140-147, 154, 156, 158, 161; and civil rights laws, 499; vs. Cuban immigrants, 526-527; vs. Dominican immigrants, 210; and ethnic enclaves, 219-222, 708; vs. European immigrants, 561; vs. Filipino immigrants, 263; vs. Haitians, 302; vs. Hawaiians, 306; and immigration law, 261, 344, 364, 386, 568, 614, 618; vs. Iranians, 394; vs. Irish immigrants, 231, 235, 400, 402-403; vs. Japanese immigrants, 424, 431, 438-443; vs. Jews, 445-446; vs. Latinos, 492, 504-505; in literature, 57; vs. Mexican immigrants, 104, 126-127, 532-537, 666; vs. Polish Americans, 597; vs. war brides, 685; vs. women immigrants, 695, 697

Disney Company, 661

Displaced persons, 359, 594, 614-617

Displaced Persons Act of 1948, 355, 615-616; expiration of, 615

Displaced Persons Commission, 615

Doak, William N., 535-536

Domestic Preparedness, Office of, 329

Dominican immigrants, 207-211, 247, 375, 494; families, 496; holidays, 498; and Puerto Ricans, 210; and Puerto Rico, 486

Dominican Republic, 13, 484, 486

Donato, Pietro di, 233

Donleavy, J. P., 233

Douay Bible, 30

Douglas, William O., 501

Dps. *See* Displaced persons

Dred Scott v. Sandford, 699

Drug traffic; and Coast Guard, U.S., 172

D'Souza, Dinesh, 689

Duane, William, 17, 258

Dukakis, Michael, 629

Duke, David, 480

Dunne, Peter Finley, 231

Dust Bowl, 253

Dutch immigrants, 107, 225, 235, 318, 544

Dutch West India Company, 443, 450-452, 636

Duvalier, François, 298, 301, 620

Duvalier, Jean-Claude, 298, 301

Eastern European Jewish immigrants. *See* Jewish immigrants, Eastern European

Eaton, Edith Maud (Sui Sin Far), 57

Eaton, Winifred (Onoto Watanna), 57

Ebonics, 602

EBPSUSA. *See* El Bireh Palestine Society of the USA

Ecuador, 91

Education, 247, 460-461, 565-566; and Amerasians, 25; and Arab Americans, 35, 43-45; and Asian Americans, 52-55, 64-65, 69-70, 74, 77, 549-554; and assimilation, 82, 275; and Chinese, 158-159; and cultural pluralism, 189; and discrimination, 206; and Hmongs, 53-54, 62, 325; and illegal aliens, 590-593; and immigration policy, 191, 194; and Jamaicans, 417-418; and Japanese, 278, 438-443, 708; and Koreans, 468, 474; and Laotians, 54; and Latinos, 491, 494, 506; and "model minorities," 550, 552-553; and Pacific islanders, 305, 307; and Roman Catholic Church, 238; and Scandinavians, 238; and Taiwanese, 655; teachers, 238; and Vietnamese, 675; and West Indians, 689. *See also* Bilingual education

362-366, 373, 378, 499, 547; amendment of, 384; and Korean immigrants, 474; and Taiwanese, 655

Immigration and Naturalization Service, 97, 312-313, 334-338, 366-371, 506, 574; and Florida illegal-immigrant suit, 267-269; and green cards, 293; and Homeland Security Department, 640; Operation Wetback, 572-576; reorganization of, 335; and Thai garment workers, 657-659

Immigration and Naturalization Service v. Chadha, 371-372

Immigration Commission, United States, 344, 349

Immigration "crisis," 372-376

Immigration history, 316-323

Immigration law, 376-383; and deportation, 195-200, 377-378, 380-382; and discrimination, 344, 364, 386, 568, 614, 618; and terrorist attacks, 641

Immigration quotas. *See* Quotas

Immigration Reform and Control Act of 1986, 62, 191, 336, 378, 383-387, 463, 532, 547; and au pairs, 84; and employment, 492; revision of, 357

Immigration Restriction League, 344, 350

Indentured servitude, 387-390; and African immigrants, 483, 609; and Asian immigrants, 67; and British immigrants, 317; and Chinese immigrants, 133, 139, 699; and English immigrants, 107; and slavery, 4; and women, 695

Indian Civil Rights Act of 1968, 203

Indian Self-Determination and Education Assistance Act, 203

Indiana, 101

Indians. *See* Asian Indian immigrants; Native Americans

Indians, American. *See* Native Americans

Indigenous superordination, 391-392

Indonesia, 612

Industrial Workers of the World, 587-588

INS. *See* Immigration and Naturalization Service

Institute for Palestine Studies, 45

Intergovernmental Committee for European Migration, 616

Internal Security Act of 1951, 359

International Ladies' Garment Workers' Union, 271, 662, 697

International Red Cross. *See* Red Cross

International Refugee Organization, 615-616

IPS. *See* Institute for Palestine Studies

Iran, 620

Iranian immigrants, 392-395

IRCA. *See* Immigration Reform and Control Act of 1986

Irish immigrants, 119-120, 236, 281-284, 318, 395-400, 543; and African Americans, 400-401; and alcohol, 236; demographics, 225-226, 235; and discrimination, 402; employment of, 238; and Federal riot of 1799, 257-258; and immigration law, 340; and nativism, 29-33, 559; persecution of, 320; and Philadelphia riots, 29-33; and Poles, 594; prejudice against, 320; and Roman Catholic Church, 29-33, 402, 559; Scotch-Irish, 107, 120, 235, 402, 635-636; and slavery, 237, 400; stereotypes, 282, 399, 403-405, 545; women, 696

Irish riot. *See* Federal riot of 1799

IRO. *See* International Refugee Organization

Irving, Washington, 509

Israel; and American Jewish Committee, 26; and American Jews, 448, 455-457; and Arab Americans, 41-42, 46-47, 455-457; and Falasha Jews, 540; and Israeli Americans, 405-409; and Russian Jews, 625, 653

Israeli immigrants, 405-409; stereotypes, 407. *See also* Jewish immigrants

Italian immigrants, 409-415; businesses, 514-516; demographics,